Vijay Mukhi's

The 'C' Odyssey

UNIX – The Open-Boundless C

Vijay Mukhi's

The 'C' Odyssey

UNIX – The Open-Boundless C

Meeta Gandhi
Tilak Shetty
Rajiv Shah

BPB PUBLICATIONS
B-14, CONNAUGHT PLACE, NEW DELHI-110001

FIRST EDITION–1992

Distributors:

BPB BOOK CENTRE
376, Old Lajpat Rai Market, Delhi–110006

BUSINESS PROMOTION BUREAU
8/1, Ritchie Street, Mount Road, Madras–600002

BUSINESS PROMOTION BUREAU
4-3-268-C, Giriraj Lane, Bank Street, Hyderabad–500195

COMPUTER BOOK CENTRE
12, Shrungar Complex, M. G. Road, Bangalore–560001

Published by Manish Jain for B.P.B Publication
B-14, Connaught Place,
New Delhi-110 001
Printed by him at Pressworks

For

Pradeep Mukhi And Shivanand Shetty

Without whose steadfast faith
we would have dropped anchor
long ago

Also in the team are...

Technical Editors: Rahul C. Thakkar
Ramnath Sharma

DOS - The Charted Waters:

Hemin Shah, Ajay Patel, Venkatesh Nakhate, Pinak Marfatia, Rajesh Shedde

Advanced DOS - The Uncharted Waters:

Apurva Shah, Manish Gokani, Homi Bharda

UNIX - The Open Boundless C:

Project Coordinator: Deepak Ahuja
Ashok Menon, Manoj Punwani, Atul Shah, Hemin Shah, Rajesh Gabha, Homi Bharda

Networks And RDBMS - New Worlds To Conquer:

Lancy Quadros, Jitendra Singh, G. V. Baadker, Ashok Menon, Rati Ganesh
Technical Support: Wockhardt

C++ And Graphics - The Future Of C:

Hemin Shah, Ajay Patel, Pinak Marfatia, Venkatesh Nakhate, Rajesh Shedde

Windows - The Brave New World:

Manish Gokani

OS/2 - Into Infinite Worlds:

Rajesh Menon, Deepak Ahuja

Editor: Meenakshi Chellam

Foreword

If you took a leisurely walk down the choked arteries that line computer paths, there's one horn you'll hear blaring incessantly. C. Loud and sonorous, the booms have dominoed into echoes that have transcended space and time boundaries.

In this absolutely crammed world, where men who know C are the men who matter, there are four C connoisseurs that I rate as the best there ever were. My mom, my dad, my dear aunt and my sister-in-law. All of whose knowledge of computers rests languidly at the fact that it is what their youngest born tinkers around with, teaches and writes books about. It is from these denizens of C that I drew the inspiration to imbibe the true spirit of C.

For C is not merely a programming tool, a super-efficient road roller that smoothens all the bumps that ever arose. Rather, it is a philosophy and a way of life. Like a benevolent parent, it allows a long rope within a loosely woven web of rules and principles, encouraging bouts of exploration on one's own.

C is an attitude.

It is this feeling that I wanted to share most with others. The excitement of having glanced beneath diaphanous veils and seen what lay there. It was a revelation that opened even more gates for me. Most books that I have read so far - and I have as unreasonable a passion for collecting books on C as philatelists have for stamps, have been "how to" books on C. They left me incomplete though, because they had not captured the soul behind those nuts and bolts.

Hence, this book.

Here was an honest language, humble and straightforward, that admitted its weakness without a qualm - it could not do everything. And that perhaps was the secret of its strength. It was nurtured by people whose goal was not to please ruling committees, but to design an apparatus that catalyzed efficiency. Like the proverbial knives for slicing butter, C was the finely honed one which could cut your hand while cutting through the butter neatly. It is this ability to produce clean and unjagged slabs, and the macho drops of blood, that has brought the world to heel. Today, evolution theorists would go one step further from Darwin and admit that survival of the C-fit is what propagation of species is all about.

C had to be separated from its relegated place in the herd and its character unveiled.

Hence this book.

And the best way I could treat something so honest would be with total honesty. It was quite some time ago that I admitted, rather ruefully, that I wasn't the greatest writer around. And this was one book that I wasn't going to sacrifice at the altar of my ego. So I garnered a team of professional writers to work with my team of professional computerists and baked this mammoth pie.

As we embarked on a task we knew would be awesome, there were more realities we woke up to along the way. The philosophy which could very well have sat comfortably in 20 pages grew into seven volumes, aggregating roughly 3500 pages.

We've tried to move away from the serious and unbending tone that most texts on all things technical take. And we're not sorry for having fun. Fun, it has been all the way. But that's what C is all about. How to mix business with pleasure. We've littered the search with blasphemously unserious comments, lightened the most complicated and poker faced concepts with a few laughs. And our happy faces could brighten a dark and moonless night.

What was most appropriate was the colorful group of people we were. Like the band of Clipper players, who breathed music but were famous for the Clipper 5.0 and P.J Plauger, who cut his teeth on science fiction and dirtied his fingers in software, we were a varied bunch of people. We had psychology students, archaeology graduates, commerce collegians, engineers, hoteliers and bankers, all scrubbing joyously at unraveling the mystery of C.

And I think our versatile personality has seeped through in our Odyssey.

You can join this seven sea Odyssey from anywhere - the beginning, the end or the middle. Each one is an individual trip by itself, unserialized and distinct. But you'd definitely be a better C-farer if you found your feet in the first, the C-Primer. Once you've imbibed the philosophy that I've been harping about, perhaps the rest of the volumes - C under UNIX, C under OS/2 and PM, C under Windows, C with Networks and RDBMS' ... will appear in a slightly different light? That's what I divined.

My teaching background shouts through a loudspeaker out of this Odyssey. I like to teach, although I've tried to refrain from preaching. We've resisted the temptation of writing "textbook" programs sandpapered with error checks, we've restrained ourselves from writing small code fragments that you have to fit together like a jigsaw puzzle. Our aim has not been to fish for you so you could eat fish today, but rather it has been to teach you to fish so that you can eat fish for the rest of your life.

We've worked towards a certain crescendo that rises steadily as we move on. From simple two line programs that do or do not work to programs spreading over reams that definitely do work. We have about 1800 programs, some original, some borrowed. We've siphoned from Dr. Dobbs and other treasure houses of programs, sometimes word for word. We've not attempted to change a single comma at times, because we didn't know how to. They were the best we could have laid our hands on and we grabbed them with both hands. And we'd be happiest if you grabbed a few of ours too. That's again the spirit of C. No dark secrets and no locked doors.

I must also warn you of the errors that may have slipped into some corner of our 3500 page tryst. We looked very hard but sometimes the sandman just couldn't wait and exhaustion and sometimes the sandman just couldn't wait and exhaustion and sleep drove the pins into our eyes. Before we embarked on book writing, we never could understand how prestigious books could harbor errors, silly errors that were carelessly allowed to reside. Now we know. Only too well.

But nobody, not even Microsoft, IBM and God are perfect.

Our aim was to motivate you to don your starched thinking caps. And stoke the fire in your belly and the light in your eye. The flame that burns within a true C programmer is like a beacon that kindles the darkest skies. So, this book.

And there's also the quiet large-heartedness of C that I wanted to drag out of the closet. C opens the coffers that lie under powder-coated steel plates hammered together to make the computer, lays it bare and gives you the freedom to meander, to carry the wealth in the direction you choose. Like my parents. They opened the doors wide for me, armed me with priceless heirlooms and set me free ... to buy the hundreds of C books that fortify my library shelves.

There's still the debt I owe my mom, dad, my aunt and my dear sister-in-law, Vaidehi Mukhi for teaching me C. The rest of the people who made this a success

Hence this book.

Vijay Mukhi's

Table of Contents

Introduction

C and UNIX. That's the way the world seems to be moving. You know these two and your mobility is assured. And as more and more college students graduate after having worked on UNIX based machines, rest assured that the decision to learn C & UNIX will pay off.

And that's exactly what we have tried to do. Give you a comprehensive view of how C & UNIX interact so beautifully - like a made for each other couple. Right from the basics of multi-tasking to the use of Inter-Process-Communication's we have covered the whole gamut of C-UNIX operations.

Chapter 1, UNIX : The Multi-tasking Operating System - Starts with multi-tasking. The ability to run programs simultaneously. Background processes, child parent relationships. Process Identifiers, forking processes, process synchronization, sharing data between processes using files, buffering, the 'exec' family of functions and the environment block all have been done in great depth with lots of code to illustrate the concepts.

Chapter 2, UNIX : The Multi-User Operating System - From multi-tasking the logical progression would be UNIX as a multi- user system. And that's where we have taken you. Into the world of simultaneous users crying for a time-slice of UNIX's attention. But before we have gone into the code we have taken up UNIX's booting-up process and shared with you all certain aspects that we experimented with and discoveries we made as a result. User ID, Group ID, logged in users, the concept of time, another way of implementing a background process, the way UNIX looks at disks and devices, file permissions, data security, links and everything else that goes to make UNIX such an efficient multi- user environment.

Chapter 3, On Files - All about handling files on a multi- user, multi-tasking UNIX. File locking, record locking and all other modes to maintain data security and ensure that no discrepancies take place when two users are working simultaneously on the same file.

Chapter 4, Communicating Across Processes - IPC's. This is probably the most important not to mention exciting topic in the entire volume. All the implementations that allow processes to communicate with each other have been taken up in great detail. Signals, Pipes, Named Pipes, Message Queues, Semaphores and Shared Memory. Right from the absolute starting stage to complex programs that enable multiple users to talk to each other we have covered the entire gamut of communication possibilities.

Chapter 5, The Leftovers - The miscellaneous functions that found no real place in any of the other chapters but are important nonetheless have been clubbed together here. A must if you want use UNIX more efficiently.

Chapter 6, On Curses - The single line interface of UNIX has always been a bother which is why we would have a full screen to interact with. There is a function library called CURSES which uses what is known as the Extended Terminal Interface to give you full screen control and a host of functions that can give your application a pretty face.

While some of what we have covered in UNIX may be hard going, there is definitely a pot of gold at the end of the rainbow. After all, the world seems to be crying out for UNIX programmers.

UNIX : The Multi-tasking Operating System

UNIX at last. But where do we start. We could take history first, but then again, so does every other book. It is common knowledge that UNIX is a creation of Ken Thompson and Dennis Ritchie. The latter also devised C, the language a major part of UNIX is now written in.

Alternatively, we could talk about the fact that UNIX is multi-tasking and multi-user, and the only hardware-independent Operating System around. The last, of course, thanks to the fact that it is written in C. But who does not know all this? After all UNIX is probably the most talked about OS in the computer industry, the popularity of DOS notwithstanding.

But while DOS has remained 'standardized', more due to the fact that no competitor has appeared on the scene, a standard for UNIX is yet a dream. And with each passing conference that fails, a never to be realized one. So we have SCO UNIX and AT&T on one side and the OSF version on the other. And a lot of people swear by one or the other.

What is it about UNIX that is different? Surely not the mere fact that it was written out of pure necessity, by a group unhappy with the turn the MULTICS computing environment had taken. Or that it came into being in spite of the AT&T management repeatedly turning down Ken Thompson's request for a time-sharing machine like the DEC-10 on which he intended to build his own OS.

UNIX's very inception seems to have sowed the seeds of the idiosyncrasies that are more the rule than the exception. Like the naming of various utilities, BIFF or AWK for example. First housed in the PDP/7, the smallest and most unused machine in the Bell labs, UNIX went on to be promoted to the PDP/11. And as people in AT&T came to know about it, its popularity grew. But a marketable proposition, no way, infact far from it.

What seems to have really got UNIX going was a paper published on it in a computer journal, 'Communications'. That started the stampede. From then on there was no looking back as more and more people began to get interested. Another equally important reason for its popularity was that the source code was available along with the OS. The source code was small and easily modifiable. This made it an instant hit with programmers.

Individuals from different corners of the world started using it. Writing utilities around the KERNEL, or modifying the KERNEL itself. They ported it to hardware as diverse as DEC and the VAX. And as these voices increased in number they began to be heard around the computer world.

But to think of UNIX as a mere OS would be a gross understatement. It is much more, a complete philosophy signifying that small and simple is beautiful. The entire OS is geared around this idea, giving us the ability to write small programs that do one task and connect them to others. The result is a synergy, a workbench of tools that are more than the sum of their parts.

But over and above this, it is also an evolutionary process, moving constantly towards infinity. Reflecting not just an attitude but a path to the future. A future that is not stagnant but continuously growing.

And as if to underline this sense of a process the word process itself has been used to signify a program that runs under UNIX.

But before we come to creating processes we need to explore one very basic question? The answer to it will greatly direct our attitude to C under UNIX and that after all is what this book is all about.

Is C under DOS the same as C under UNIX ?

We spent more than three hours trying to decide on this. There were as many people on either side of the fence. And none willing to budge.

However, most of us were agreed that in the end C remained a single entity no matter what the OS under which it was run. Why ? The basic structure of C, its power, its data types, its control structures, its syntax all remain the same no matter which OS it runs under. So where's the difference ?

To prove a point to the non-believers we wrote the following program and ran it under DOS and UNIX.

PROGRAM 1

```
main(argc,argv)
int argc;
char *argv[ ];
{
    int i;
    for ( i = 0; i < argc, i++)
        printf("Argument is %s\n",argv[i]);
}
```

We ran this program with the parameter Hello World. Under both DOS and UNIX two statements each would be displayed: the program name and Hello World.

Now doesn't that prove that C under DOS and UNIX is the same. No. At least not to members of the other camp. They said they'd prove their point with one example. Pass, instead of the string Hello World, they said, a "*".

So that's exactly what we did. And what did we get? Under DOS we got the program name and the star, "*". But under UNIX there was a difference. Instead of the star we got a directory listing.

There's the proof that C under these two OS's is different? Not so fast. Lets first see what happened.

Under DOS, of course, C took the star as an argument and printed it. That's because the DOS shell, COMMAND.COM, took it for what it was: a star. The UNIX shell, however, is (what is termed) intelligent. It sometimes proceeds to deduce. In this case it interpreted the star to mean a directory listing. This directory listing was then passed to the program as an argument which proceeded to display the files on screen.

On the face of it, yes, the program worked differently and therefore we could say C is different under DOS and UNIX. But was it really the program that gave us this difference in output? Not at all. It was the shell. If the shell had not been built to interpret the star, the directory listing would never have appeared. And that is hardly the fault of the program.

So how do we overcome this problem? Simple. Enclose the star in inverted commas, "*".

If there is no difference between C under DOS and C under UNIX, why bother with this chapter?

Because UNIX is a multitasking, multiuser OS unlike DOS. And that is what we need to explore C through. Its ability to be used under UNIX for multitasking and in a multiuser environment.

Multi-tasking

Multitasking is essentially a way of using the computer efficiently by sharing both it and its resources among programs. There are many approaches to multitasking: those that use the computer efficiently, others that allow certain problems to be solved fast, and yet others that allow us to work with different jobs being run simultaneously.

In the days when mainframes reigned supreme it was essential that this expensive resource be used optimally. It was a colossal waste to have the CPU waiting while an I/O operation was being performed. This brought in the concept of multitasking.

OS's were designed to take away the CPU from a program that was waiting for an I/O operation and give it to another program that wanted it. If there were a lot of jobs running simultaneously it was now possible to keep the CPU busy most of the time. This kind of multitasking is also known as multi-programming. But there is no such thing as a free ride. This multitasking came at a cost: slow execution of programs.

The most basic form of multi-tasking is using interrupts and is known as serial multi-tasking.

One program is stopped temporarily while another is allowed to execute. At any given time only one task is run. You can liken this to a situation in which a human working on a computer stops his work to answer a ringing phone and then, having finished with the call, switches back to the computer.

This is possible even under DOS, though, by default DOS is considered a single tasking system. Most of us must have used Sidekick or some other such TSR. Once we load this into memory, a simple keystroke can take us from Sidekick to another program we may be running.

But serial multi-tasking makes the computer work less efficiently. If, for example, there was some calculation being done and we called in Sidekick, then all work on the calculations would stop as the computer responded to Sidekick. Wouldn't it then be far better to give Sidekick only a part of the computer's time ? So that even while we were in Sidekick the calculations would carry on being performed in the background.

Since all computers have a timer interrupt, we could use this to schedule CPU time between programs. These time periods are known as time-slices. And it is this concept that has been implemented in what are known as multitasking OS's. These are different from DOS which does not give time-slices to running programs. And if there are 5 programs running in DOS and even one goes haywire, the entire machine hangs. In any genuine multitasking environment this does not happen.

But merely giving equal time-slices may not be enough. There may be some programs that are relatively more important. For example, those that wait for user responses. In that case we would need to have some kind of priority scheme. Each program would receive a priority number based on which CPU time would be allotted. If there are programs with the same priority code, a round-robin scheduling would be done. UNIX favors interactive programs by giving them a higher priority.

At any one time, however, only one program has the CPU. And only if the system has more than one processor is it possible to have more than one task running at one time. This is called multi-processing.

This entire scheduling and intermingling of tasks can be left to the OS while we concentrate on getting the job done.

For most of us, just graduating from DOS, probably the most fascinating aspect will be the fact that we can have two programs in memory and not via serial multitasking.

Assume we had written a 10,000 line C program under DOS. Can you imagine the time that will be taken to compile and link it ? For the duration of this process the computer would become inaccessible. (Of course, if this happens around lunch time, it's fine.)

Background Process

Under UNIX there is no such problem. All we need to do is to compile and link in the background while we carry on doing whatever else we want in the foreground. Its like music playing in the background while we do something else - maybe write a program. Sounds like a real relief doesn't it ? It is.

PROGRAM 2

```
main()
{
  long i;
```

```
    for(i = 0; i<= 4000000; i++);
        printf("I is %d\n",i);
}
```

Key in the above program in whichever wordprocessor you have in UNIX. We have VI. (Frankly, this wordprocessor is a good reason not to use UNIX. It is high time someone came out with an integrated C environment -- like TURBO C's.) Compile it at the UNIX prompt by saying cc < program name >. The file generated will be a.out.

Execute it through the command a.out &. The & will make it a background process which is terminated only if the process ends, or is interrupted with a DEL. The UNIX prompt will come back on screen immediately. Load the editor again and wait. After some time a I is 4000000 will be displayed at the top left corner of the screen.

Isn't this more convenient than DOS's single tasking environment ? So how did this happen?

UNIX, being a multitasking OS, works on the basis of time slices. Each process that is run is given a little bit of time to perform. This switch between different processes happens so fast that we are never aware of it. Take the above example.

We first ran the program as a background process and then loaded the editor. Now the microprocessor kept alternating between the background process and the editor. Finally, after the *for* loop in the background process finished, the *printf( )* got activated.

If there were 10 processes running at one time, the microprocessor would keep switching between these 10 processes. At a given point in time only one process will be handled by the CPU. But because the switch happens so fast we get the feeling that the microprocessor works on a number of processes simultaneously.

Note: It's only programs that don't take input or print to screen that should be run as background processes.

UNIX is able to switch between processes because each process has an identification number. This identification number identifies more than just the process. It also identifies the variables and REGISTER values that are associated with this process. These variables are in a state of limbo when the process is suspended. And get activated again once the microprocessor resumes execution of the process.

Assume there are two processes running with a identification 1 and 2. And UNIX gives each a time-slice of 2 seconds. When the 2 seconds get over for the first process, all the variables and REGISTER values associated with it are saved somewhere in memory. This area is called the *swap area* and is the place in memory where the UNIX KERNEL writes suspended processes. This swapping, whether it takes place between disk or RAM depends on the size of memory. If there is not enough RAM a disk swap is done.

Now process number 2 begins to execute. Once its 2 seconds are over, its variables and REGISTER values are saved. UNIX at this point is aware of process number 1 which it had terminated temporarily. It goes to the location in memory at which this process is stored, restores the state of that process and then starts to execute it. This switch happens constantly every 2 seconds, till one of the processes finishes.

Process Identification

There is a UNIX function - *getpid( )* - that enables us to get the identification number of a process.

```
PROGRAM 3
main()
{
    int pid;
    pid = getpid();
```

```
    print("Process ID is %d\n",pid);
}
```

The *pid* value will depend on the number of processes already running. It will always be unique. This *pid* cannot be changed although it may be re-used once the process no longer exists. UNIX, itself, takes care of this.

Run the program listed below twice. Both times as a background process, i.e. suffix it with an ampersand and you will see two different ID numbers. Once both are running as background processes key the ps -e UNIX command and you will see that memory contains these two processes. If there were any others, they too would have been listed. You'll notice that even ps is listed as a process because that's what it is. Under the PID heading the identification number will be displayed.

```
PROGRAM 4
main()
{
    long i;
    printf("Process ID is %d\n",getpid());
    for(i = 0; i<= 4000000; i++);
        printf("I is %d\n",i);
}
```

Parent And Child

A process in UNIX is not a stand-alone. In the same way as a human being or animal is born from another, a process too has to come from the womb of another process. This results in a parent-child relationship existing between processes.

```
PROGRAM 5
main()
{
    int ppid;
    ppid = getppid();
    print("Parent Process ID is %d\n",ppid);
}
```

This program will give the ID number of its parent. So who is this parent? Not us, definitely.

When we boot the system, a special process called the swapper or scheduler is created with a PID of 0. The swapper manages memory allocation for processes and influences CPU allocation. (Remember the time- slicing we talked about earlier.) The swapper in turn creates three children: the process dispatcher, vhand and bdflush with the ID numbers 1, 2 and 3 respectively.

This is done by executing the file init which exists in the etc sub-directory. The process dispatcher now gives birth to the shell. From now on all processes initiated by us are children of the shell and in turn descendants of the process dispatcher. This gives rise to a tree-like structure, with ADAM as the swapper.

UNIX keeps track of all processes in an internal data structure called the PROCESS TABLE. A listing of the process table can be got using the ps -el command.

The 'fork( )'

Processes initiated by us can also create children in the same manner as the swapper and the process dispatcher did. These children processes are created using the *fork( )* function. It is by forking processes that we can exploit the multitasking capability of UNIX.

```
PROGRAM 6
main( )
{
   fork( );
   printf("Hello World\n");
}
```

Can you guess what the output of this program will be ?

The statement Hello World will be displayed twice on screen. The *fork( )* creates a child that is a duplicate of the parent process. The parent process in this case being the program listed above. Since now there are two identical processes in memory, the Hello World is printed twice.

The child process begins from the *fork( )*. All the statements after the call to *fork( )* will be executed twice. Once by the parent process and once by the child process. But had there been any statements before the *fork( )* they would have been only executed by the parent process.

PROGRAM 7

```
main()
{
   printf("This is to demonstrate the fork()\n");
   fork();
   printf("Hello World\n");
}
```

In this program, while the statement Hello World is printed twice, the statement This is to demonstrate the fork( ) will only be displayed once since it comes before the creation of the child process.

What would happen if we had two calls to the *fork( )* function, one below the other, in the same program.

PROGRAM 8

```
main()
{
   fork();
   fork();
   printf("Hello Worla\n");
}
```

Here instead of 2 processes, 3 processes will be created. This gives a total of 4 processes in memory: the parent, its 2 children and one grandchild.

The first call to the *fork( )* creates one child process. Now there are two processes. Both processes begin executing from the second call to the *fork( )* thus giving us a total of four processes. A diagram here would be helpful:

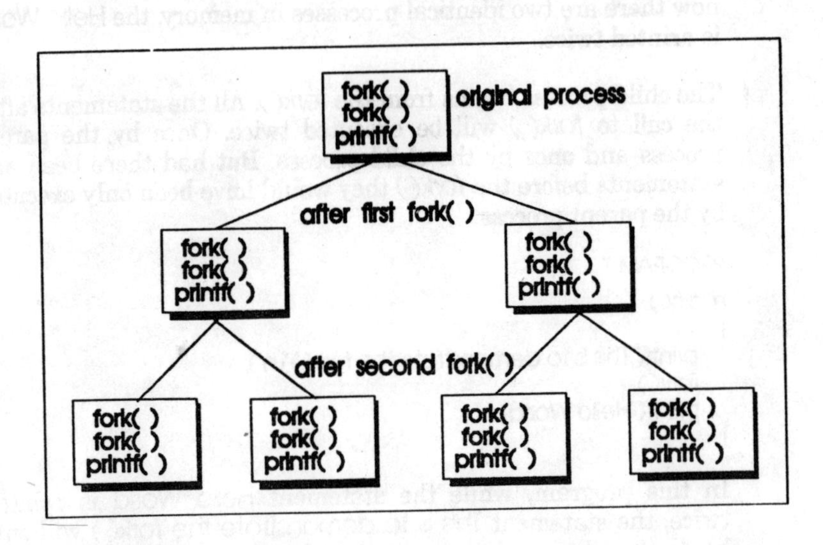

DIAGRAM 1.1

The progression with each *fork( )* that is added is 2 raised to the power of n, 2^n, where n is the number of calls to *fork( )*.

PROGRAM 9

```
main()
{
   fork();
   fork();
   fork();
   printf("Hello World\n");
}
```

The above example will create 8 processes.

Each of these children also has a PID number associated with it. This as we have explained above is how UNIX keeps track of the various processes in memory.

PROGRAM 10

```
main( )
{
    fork( );
    print("The PID is %d\n",getpid( ));
}
```

When we ran the above program, we got the numbers 63 and 64. The PID of the parent is 63 while that of the child process is 64.

But how do we know which PID is that of the parent and which PID is that of the child ? We can use the *fork( )* to find that out. To the parent process the *fork( )* will return the value of the child's PID. Whereas in the child process the value of the PID will always be 0.

PROGRAM 11

```
main( )
{
    int pid;
    pid = fork( );

    if( pid > 0)
        printf("Parent Process PID is %d\n",pid);
}
```

The moment a call is made to the *fork( )*, a child process is created. The child copy, too, gets a copy of the variable *pid*, but with a value of 0 by default. The parent process, however, is returned a value greater than 0 by the *fork( )*.

The variable *pid* of the parent process will always get the PID of the child process. This enables it to know who its child is.

The PID of the child will always be 0. Check it out.

PROGRAM 12

```
main( )
{
    int pid;
    pid = fork( );
```

```
    if( pid == 0)
        printf("Child Process\n");
}
```

The above program will result in two processes being created in memory. But the parent process will terminate as soon as the child process is created, since the *if* condition in it won't execute. The value of variable *pid* in the child process will be 0. Because, as we have stated earlier, although a duplicate child process is created, only the lines after the *fork( )* are executed. In the child process the statement *pid = fork( )* will never be executed. As a result, the variable *pid* in the child process will get a value of 0 by default.

But, sometimes, the *fork( )* may not create the child process due to some memory problem. In this case the variable *pid* of the parent process will reflect a -1, indicating an error.

PROGRAM 13

```
main( )
{
    int pid;
    pid = fork( );

    if( pid < 0)
        printf("Fork failed \n");
    else
        printf("Fork succeeded\n");
}
```

But it is not only the parent process that can register its child's PID. The child process too can figure out who its parent is. The *getppid( )* function will tell us this.

PROGRAM 14

```
main( )
{
    int pid;
    pid = fork( );
```

```
    if (pid == 0)
    {
        printf("I am the child, my process ID is %d\n",getpid( ));
        printf("The child's parent process ID is %d\n",getppid( ));
    }
    else
    {
        printf("I am the parent, my process ID is %d\n",getpid( ));
        printf("The parents parent process ID is %d\n",getppid( ));
    }
}
```

The *fork( )* function will result in two processes being in memory: a parent and its child. The *if..else* statements will be executed in both the processes.

In the child process, the variable *pid* will reflect a 0. Therefore we will get its (the child's), as well as its parent's PID number.

In the parent process, the *else* part will be executed. This will give us the parent's PID number, as well as it's parent's PID number. In this case, the parent of the parent process is the shell.

So we have a grandfather, father and son situation. Three generations, so to speak.

If you do a ps -el at the UNIX prompt, you'll see that the PID of the shell is the same as the value returned by the *getppid( )* function in the *else* part.

Orphan Process

Normally after a *fork( )*, the time slice is given to the child process. Now suppose the parent process were to terminate before the child process, what would happen? For one, we would have a fatherless child. But unlike as in real life where orphans sometimes remain just that for the rest of their lives, the creators of UNIX, being a kind bunch, arranged for a policy of adoption.

PROGRAM 15

```
main()
{
    int pid;
    pid = fork();

    if (pid == 0)
    {
        printf("I am the child, my process ID is %d\n",getpid());
        printf("The child's parent process ID is %d\n",getppid());
        sleep(20);
        printf("I am the child, my process ID is %d\n",getpid());
        printf("The child's parent process ID is %d\n",getppid());
    }
    else
    {
        printf("I am the parent, my process ID is %d\n",getpid());
        printf("The parents parent process ID is %d\n",getppid());
    }
}
```

A child process will be created when the *fork( )* statement is encountered.

If the *if* condition evaluates to a true, the statements in it will be executed. This means that the child process is active. The two calls to the *printf( )* function will print the child processes, as well as its parent's PID. At this point the child process will be put to *sleep( )*. This means that for 20 seconds the child process will remain inactive. It will not get the time slice in this period.

In the meanwhile, the parent process will be executed. This results in the parent processes and its parent's (the shell's) PID being displayed on screen. After which the parent process will terminate.

Now we have a parentless child process in memory. Once its sleep wears off, the next two *printf( )*s are executed. The first displays the same PID of the child as before. But the next will not print the PID of the parent process that gave birth to this child. Instead it will print the PID of the process dispatcher. Because it is the process dispatcher that immediately adopts an orphan.

Using the ps -el command you can check to see if the number printed is the same as that of the PID of the process dispatcher.

Let's verify if this really happens: by checking the status of the process table while the above program, with one minor change, is run as a background process.

PROGRAM 16

```
main( )
{
   int pid;
   pid = fork( );

   if (pid == 0)
   {
      printf("I am the child, my process ID is %d\n",getpid( ));
      printf("The child's parent process ID is %d\n",getppid( ));
      sleep(20);
      printf("I am the child, my process ID is %d\n",getpid( ));
      printf("The child's parent process ID is %d\n",getppid( ));
   }
   else
   {
      sleep(10);
      printf("I am the parent, my process ID is %d\n",getpid( ));
      printf("The parents parent process ID is %d\n",getppid( ));
      printf("Parent terminates\n");
   }
}
```

Here, if you notice, we have a *sleep( )* even in the *else* part. Now two sleeps will result in both processes being suspended for some time. Enough time for us to do a ps -el to check the PID of the child process.

Once the parent process terminates, re-run the ps -el command and see the change in the PID of the child's parent. At the same time observe the value of the child process in the second column. It will be a O signifying it is an orphan.

Zombies

Have you heard of the voodoo practices in the Caribbean and some places in South America ? The medicine men of tribes make use of the living dead or ZOMBIES as they are better known. These are people who have died but have been resurrected to accomplish certain desired tasks. Normally this is something that harms an enemy. Better make sure you don't fight with someone with this kind of power.

UNIX, too, has the concept of ZOMBIES for processes that are dead but have not been removed from the PROCESS TABLE. Of course, they aren't quite as scary as the real stuff.

Assume that we had a parent process create a child. Both would now have an entry in the PROCESS TABLE. Assume further that the child process terminated well before the parent does. Since the parent process is yet in action the child process cannot be removed from the PROCESS TABLE. It, therefore, exists in the twilight zone. And that's our ZOMBIE!

PROGRAM 17

```
main()
{
   if (fork() > 0)
   {
      printf(" parent\n");
      sleep(50);
   }
}
```

Run the program above as a background process, i.e. suffix the name with an ampersand sign. Once you are at the UNIX prompt, type **ps -el**. You will see in the PROCESS TABLE an entry with a Z for ZOMBIE in the second column and a <defunct> in the last column.

That was our child process which terminated as soon as it was created. You'll notice that in the program above the *fork()* creates a child process. The child is nothing but a duplicate of the parent process. Execution of both processes start from the line after the *fork()*. In this case that line is an *if* condition. This checks to see if the value returned by *fork( )* is greater than 0. Since this condition is not valid for a child process, the child process terminates. But, as the parent process is yet in memory because of the *sleep()*, the PROCESS TABLE remains unrectified.

A "Sleeping Beauty" Process

The second column of the PROCESS TABLE always shows the status of a process. That is, whether it is running (R), whether it is an orphan (O), or sleeping (S), or whether it is a zombie (Z).

So far we have seen a ZOMBIE and an ORPHAN being reflected. Let's now see a SLEEPping beauty.

PROGRAM 18

```
main()
{
   sleep(50);
   printf("The handsome prince kissed me\n");
}
```

Run this as a background process and its PID will be outputted to screen. Then do a ps -el to see the PROCESS TABLE and go to the entry with the PID just displayed. In the second column of this entry you will see an S.

A process in execution will reflect a R.

PROGRAM 19

```
main()
{
   for (; ;);
}
```

This program, too, has to be run as a background process. Since no limit is specified in the *for* loop, the process will never terminate.

Run the ps -el command at the prompt and an entry with the character R will be seen corresponding to the PID of this process.

But what happens if a process is first sleeping and then proceeds to execute. Initially it will reflect an S in the PROCESS TABLE and then as its mode changes, an R.

Run this program as a background process.

```
PROGRAM 20
main()
{
   printf("Run the ps -el command\n");
   sleep(50);
   printf("Run the ps -el command once more\n");
   for (; ;);
}
```

After the ps -el is run for the first time, a character S will be reflected in the second column of the PROCESS TABLE. The next time round it will reflect the character R.

What do you think the following program will do ?

```
PROGRAM 21
main()
{
   int i=0,j=0,pid;
   pid=fork();
   if(pid==0)
   {
      for(i=0;i<500;i++)
      printf("%d\t",i);
   }
   else
   if(pid>0)
   {
```

```
        for(j=0;j<500;j++)
        printf("%d..",j);
    }
}
```

Considering that UNIX operates on the basis of giving time slices to processes, first, any one of the processes will be executed. Suppose it is the child, then the value of variable *i* will be printed and a tab set.

The time slice will then work the parent process, which prints the value of variable *j* and two dots after it. This child..parent, child..parent switch will carry on till the variable *j* in both processes becomes 500.

Process Synchronization

This haphazard switching, as we have seen, results in confused output. How do we change this ? Basically, this calls for a kind of synchronization between processes, so that first the child process outputs and then the parent. It can't be vice versa. Why? Well, that's really quite logical. Can we ever ask a process initiated by us to wait till its parent, which is the UNIX shell, finishes ? Sounds silly, doesn't it ?

```
PROGRAM 22
main( )
{
    int i=0;pid;
    printf("Ready to fork\n");
    pid=fork( );

    if(pid==0)
    {
        printf("Child starts\n");
        for(i=0;i<1000;i++)
            printf("%d\t",i);
        printf("Child ends\n");
    }
    else
    {
```

```
        wait(0);
        printf("Parent process\n");
    }
}
```

Take the above program. Through it we create a child process and suspend the parent process with a *wait( )* function. The parameter passed to the *wait( )* function is a pointer to an integer.

Let's run through the program to make it clearer. The call to the *fork( )* creates a duplicate child process. Execution in both processes starts from the *fork( )*. Assume that at this point the time-slice was given to the parent process. As a result the statements within the *else* will be evaluated. This results in the parent process being suspended.

The call to the *wait( )* function results in a number of things happening. A check is first made to see if the parent process has any children. If it does not, a -1 is returned by *wait( )*. If the parent process has a child that has terminated (a zombie), that child's PID is returned and it is removed from the PROCESS TABLE.

However if the parent process has a child or children that have not terminated, it (the parent process) is suspended till it receives a signal. The signal is received as soon as the child dies. The last is what happens in our case.

Once the parent process is suspended by the *wait( )*, it is not reactivated till the variable *i* in the child process becomes 1000 and the execution ends.

After this, a signal is sent to the parent process which then resumes. But before it starts to execute, it checks to see if the process table contains any zombie children. If it does, they are removed.

Here is another program that drives home the message of process synchronization.

PROGRAM 23

```
main( )
{
   int i=0;pid;
   printf("Ready to fork\n");
   pid=fork( );

   if(pid==0)
   {
      printf("Child starts\n");
      for(i=0;i<1000;i++)
         printf("%d\t",i);
      printf("Child ends\n");
   }
   else
   {
      wait(0);
      for(i=0;i<1000;i++)
         printf("%d\t",i);
      printf("Parent process end\n");
   }
}
```

There is nothing essentially different between the above program and the previous one. We have just added one extra *for* loop to show what the parent is going to do once the child process ends.

But suppose a parent has created many children and wants to wait till all of them have terminated? One way of doing this is to put the parent to sleep for a certain amount of time. This time will be what it takes for the children to execute before they terminate.

PROGRAM 24

```
/* How to make parent wait for more than one child */
main( )
{
   int pid,dip;
   pid = fork( );
   if( pid == 0)
   {
      printf("1st child's process id is %d\n",getpid( ));
```

```
        printf("first-child dead\n");
    }
    else
    {
        dip = fork( );
        if (dip == 0)
        {
            printf("2nd child's process id is %d\n",getpid( ));
            printf("second-child dead \n");
        }
        else
        {
            sleep(15);
            printf("i am parent and i am dying \n");
        }
    }
}
```

The parent process *fork( )*s a child to start with. This first child executes and dies. The parent process is activated again and goes on to *fork( )* a second child. Hum do, Humare do. Now once again we have two processes in memory. But since the parent has been put to sleep the child process finishes. Finally, the parent process is given the time slice, after which it terminates.

If the first child process created had lots of lines of code, then, at some point, the time slice would have been given to the parent process - which would have forked another child. In that case we would have had the time-slice alternated between - the first child and the second one. The parent process, of course, would have been sleeping.

There are two problems here. Suppose both children's code was so long that the period of time that the parent process was put to sleep for ended. In that case all three processes would have started running concurrently. And further, suppose the parent process ended before the children did, we would have two orphans in memory.

The second problem is as follows: assume that both children finished executing and the parent process then started executing.

Assume further that the parent process had many lines of code to go through before it terminated. In that case, both dead children processes would be in the ZOMBIE state. That is, while they may not be in memory for the microprocessor to alternate between, they would yet exist in the Process Table. So what's the big deal if we have ZOMBIES ? Bad house-keeping.

How do we get out of this mess ? Elementary, my dear Watson. Instead of using *sleep( )*, use the *wait( )* function.

PROGRAM 25

```
main( )
{
    int pid,dip,cpid;
    pid = fork( );
    if( pid == 0)
    {
        printf(" 1st childs process id is %d\n",getpid( ));
        printf("first-child terminating from memory\n");
    }
    else
    {
        dip = fork( );
        if (dip == 0)
        {
            printf("2nd childs process id is %d\n",getpid( ));
            printf("second-child terminating\n");
        }
        else
        {
            cpid = wait(0) ;
            printf("Child with pid %d died\n",cpid);
            cpid = wait(0) ;
            printf("Child with pid %d died\n",cpid);
            printf("i am parent \n");
        }
    }
}
```

Here, instead of the *sleep( )*, we use two *wait( )*s. Both in the parent process. The *wait( )*, as we have seen earlier, returns a value. This value, if everything goes well, is the PID of the child process whose entry is removed from the Process Table.

In the above case we will see the PID of both child processes once the time slice is handed to the parent process. And this time slice will be handed to the parent process only when both child processes have terminated.

This is what we have said. And no doubt it is true. But seeing is believing. And for that we need to see the status of the Process Table. But this while the entire program is in memory. To do this we need to use the *sleep( )* function in conjunction with the *wait( )* while the process is run in the background.

PROGRAM 26

```
main( )
{
   int pid,dip;
   pid = fork( );
   if( pid == 0)
   {
      printf(" 1st childs process id is %d\n",getpid( ));
      printf("first-child terminating from memory\n");
   }
   else
   {
      dip = fork( );
      if (dip == 0)
      {
         printf("2nd childs process id is %d\n",getpid( ));
         printf("second-child terminating\n");
      }
      else
      {
         sleep( );
         printf("Child with pid %d died\n",wait(0));
         printf("Child with pid %d died\n",wait(0));
         printf("i am parent \n");
      }
   }
}
```

As soon as the process is loaded and we're returned to the UNIX prompt perform a ps -el to see the Process Table. Now look for the two ZOMBIES. They will have the word defunct in the last column.

Now if we put the *sleep( )* after the first two *printf( )*s in the parent process and run the program in the background we can see that both processes have been removed from the Process Table.

PROGRAM 27

```
main( )
{
   int pid,dip;
   pid = fork( );
   if( pid == 0)
   {
      printf(" 1st childs process id is %d\n",getpid( ));
      printf("first-child terminating from memory\n");
   }
   else
   {
      dip = fork( );
      if (dip == 0)
      {
         printf("2nd childs process id is %d\n",getpid( ));
         printf("second-child terminating\n");
      }
      else
      {
         printf("Child with pid %d died\n",wait(0));
         printf("Child with pid %d died\n",wait(0));
         printf("i am parent \n");
         sleep( );
      }
   }
}
```

After making the **above program** a background process, run the command ps -el to see the Process Table. You will not see any ZOMBIES as they have been already removed.

But the *wait( )* does more than just return the PID of a child process. It can also tell us in what manner the child process was terminated. For this information, however, we have to pass the *wait( )* an integer variable. Why an integer variable ?

Because, as we have said earlier, a *wait( )* will tell us in what manner the process was terminated - whether normally or abnormally. If it was terminated normally the high- order 8 bits of the integer variable passed to the *wait( )* will be updated, while the low-order 8 bits will be initialized to 0.

On the other hand, if it has been terminated abnormally it is the low-order 8 bits that are updated while the high-order 8 bits are initialized to 0. So any program that uses the *wait( )* can be queried to find out the mode of termination.

That's what the following program does.

PROGRAM 28

```
main( )
{
   int i,pid,exitstat,status;
   pid = fork( );
   if (pid == 0)
   {
      printf("enter exit stat : ");
      scanf("%d",&i);
      exit(i);
   }
   else
   {
      wait(&status);
      if ((status & 0xff) != 0)
      {
         printf("Signal interrupted \n");
      }
      else
      {
         exitstat = (int) status / 256;
         printf("Exit status from %d was %d \n",pid,exitstat);
      }
```

```
    }
}
```

When we run the above program, a child process is forked. In it we are asked to enter the exit state. Assume that we put 3. This 3 is stored in the integer variable *i*. The child process terminates and the time slice is handed to the parent process, which has been put in a *wait()* state.

To the address of variable *status* is passed the value that the child process has been terminated with. Since the termination was normal and with the value 3, variable *status* too reflects this number. Remember we have said that a termination normal or abnormal will assign a value to the variable passed to the *wait()* function. In this case the variable was *status*.

Now, when the parent process is executed, a check is made to see what the value of the variable *status* is. We AND it with a temporary integer, the lower 8 bits of which are all set ON. That is what the statement *if (status & 0xff)* does. The check is to see if the total value of lower 8 bits is equal to 0 or not after the ANDing.

Pictorially the ANDing would look like this:

The variable *status* will have some bits in the higher-order byte ON.

15							8	7							0
0	0	0	0	0	0	0	1	1	0	0	0	0	0	0	0

DIAGRAM 1.2

The temporary integer with which the ANDing takes place:

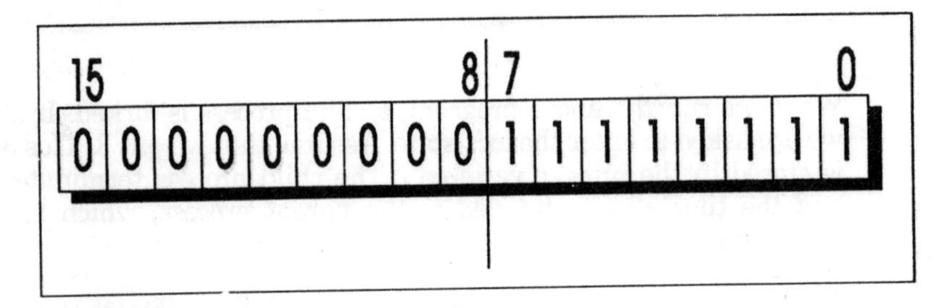

DIAGRAM 1.3

The ANDing will result in this output:

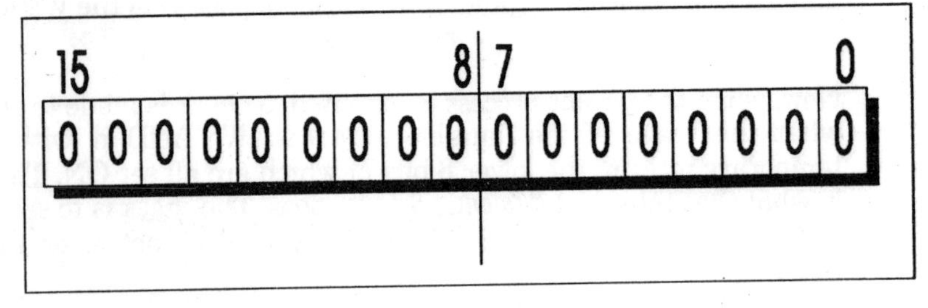

DIAGRAM 1.4

The ANDing will yield a value equal to 0 since the child process has been terminated normally. As a result, it is the statements within the *else* that will get activated. Here we divide the value of variable *status* by 256. This converts the higher order 8 bits to lower order 8 bits. And stores the result in variable *exitstat*. This result is 3 since the *exit( )* was called with a parameter of 3.

Finally the *printf( )* prints the PID of the child process and the value of the variable *exitstat*, which in our case is 3.

And what would happen if the program was terminated abnormally? To see that we need to make a slight change in the program above plus run it in the background.

PROGRAM 29

```
main( )
{
   int pid,exitstat,status;

   pid = fork( );
   if (pid == 0)
   {
      sleep(10);
      exit(3);
   }
   else
   {
      wait(&status);
      if ((status & 0xff) != 0)
      {
         printf("Signal interrupted \n");
      }
      else
      {
         exitstat = (int) status / 256;
         printf("Exit status from %d was %d \n",pid,exitstat);
      }
   }
}
```

We define this process to run in the background. Before we're brought back to the UNIX prompt, the PID of the parent process is displayed. Add a 1 to it and we'll get the PID of the child process. We now have a stalemate since the child process has been put to sleep and the parent process waits for the child to finish.

This stalemate is valid for 15 seconds since that is the sleep time we've defined for the child. Enough time to run the kill 9 (where 9 is the child's PID in our case) command. As soon as this command is executed the parent process will be activated. In it the *if* condition will be valid, i.e. the value of the lower 8 bits of the variable *status* will not be equal to 0 since the child process was terminated abnormally. As a result, the statements within the *if* are executed. And we get the message Signal Interrupted.

Core Dump

Probably one of the most frequent errors in UNIX is core dumped. This error would be displayed if, in a program, we tried to divide a number by 0.

PROGRAM 30

```
main( )
{
    int i,j = 0;
    i = 10/j;
    printf("Value of i is %d\n",i);
}
```

In this program, the *printf( )* will never get executed. And a Illegal instruction - core dumped message will flash on screen. The UNIX manual says that it is the 7th bit of a temporary 2-byte variable that is put ON to reflect a core dump or a Zombie. We decided to check this out, through the following program:

PROGRAM 31

```
main( )
{
    int i,pid,exitstat,status,j=0;
    pid = fork( );
    if (pid == 0)
    {
        i = 10/j;
    }
    else
    {
        wait(&status);
        if ((status & 0x80))
            printf(" our core dumped \n");
    }
}
```

After the *fork( )*, the child process is activated. It will terminate abnormally since we have tried to divide a value in it by 0. Since we have put the parent in a *wait( )* state, there will be a value passed to the variable *status* in the *wait( )*. This value will indicate an abnormal termination.

We are checking to see what the value of this variable is by performing an ANDing operation on it. A 0x80 signifies that the 7th bit is turned ON. And if it has been, we know that the UNIX manual did not lie. As if we doubted that in the first place.

Back To The 'fork( )'

The turning point in our lives.

Now that we have a basic understanding of processes let's explore the *fork( )* function in a bit more detail. To start with let's see how many processes we can have active at one time. In other words the maximum number of processes UNIX allows us to create.

PROGRAM 32

```
main( )
{
   int pid,i=1;
   for(;;)
   {
      pid = fork( );
      if (pid < 0)
         printf(" Maximum concurrent process are %d\n",i);

      if(pid == 0)
         i++;
      else
      {
         wait(0);
         exit(0);
      }
   }
}
```

Here we start a *for* loop and immediately fork a child. Now a check is made to see if the process is a child or a parent. If it is a child, variable *i* is incremented. And the child now *fork( )*s to create another process. In the bargain the child becomes a parent and is made to *wait( )*.

This newly forked child in turn forks another process, becomes a parent and *wait( )*s. This goes on till the limit is reached. At that point the value returned by variable *pid* is less than 0. From that point onwards, a backward movement starts taking place in which children start getting killed, one by one. First the last child, then the second last, and so on till the starter of the dynasty is himself terminated.

We know that a call to the fork statements results in the creation of a child process. This child process is an exact duplicate, but it starts executing from after the *fork( )* although a value is returned by *fork( )* in it. This value is 0 as we have seen. What would happen to a variable which is incremented in the child process but not in the parent process?

PROGRAM 33

```
main()
{
    int pid;
    int i = 10;
    pid = fork( );
    if(pid == 0)
    {
        printf("The initial value of variable i in the child process is %d\n",i);
        i += 10;
        printf("Value of variable i in Child process after
                incrementation is %d\n",i);
        printf("Child terminated\n");
    }
    else
    {
        wait(0);
        printf("value of i in parent process is %d\n",i);
    }
}
```

When a duplicate of a process is made, it is not only the lines but also the variables and their values that are copied. In the program after the *fork( )* there will be two processes in memory. Both will have a variable *i* with the value 10. The value of variable *pid* returned by the *fork( )* function will be greater than 0 in the parent process and equal to 0 in the child process. But hey, wait a minute, didn't we say that not only variables but their values are also copied exactly? So what went wrong?

In C, a statement is evaluated from right to left. In the case of *pid = fork( )*, first the function is executed. This creates a duplicate process. At the moment the child process is created the value returned by the *fork( )* to the child process is 0.

Now since the parent process is suspended by the *wait( )* function, only the child gets activated. That is, the statements within the *if* condition. Here the initial value of variable *i*, which is 10, is printed and then incremented to 20.

Once the child process terminates, a signal is sent to the parent process waking it. A *printf( )* gets executed. But here the value of variable *i* that's printed is 10. This is because the parent process has its own version of this variable: one which has remained unchanged.

From this it is clear that a change to the variable of one process will not be reflected in the other. Simply because they are two different variables, albeit with the same name.

In fact, even if we have variable *i* declared as a pointer it won't make a difference. The pointer variable *i* will remain distinct for the two processes.

PROGRAM 34

```
main( )
{
    int pid,*i;
    *i=10; /* Local Pointer */
    pid=fork( ):

    if(pid==0)
    {
```

```
        printf("In child initially i contains %d\n",*i);
        *i = (*i+10);
        printf("Child after incrementation %d\n",*i);
        printf("Child exiting\n");
    }
    else
    {
        wait((int*)0);
        printf("Parent after child exits i contains %d",*i);
    }
}
```

Here, in the child process, we change the value in the location that is pointed to by pointer variable *i*. However, once the parent process activates, the value at this location will still be 10. This was the value defined at declaration time.

But what if the variable is declared globally?

```
PROGRAM 35
int i = 10;
main( )
{
    int pid;
    pid = fork( );
    if(pid == 0)
    {
        printf("The initial value of variable i in the child process is %d\n",i);
        i += 10;
        printf("Value of variable i in Child process after
                incrementation is %d\n",i);
        printf("Child terminated\n");
    }
    else
    {
        wait(0);
        printf("value of i in parent process is %d\n",i);
    }
}
```

Here, by the very nature of its existence a change to it in one process should perforce reflect in the other. But this does not happen.

A *fork( )* will create a duplicate as we have seen. This means that even a global variable will be duplicated. So here again we will have two variables *i*. Each valid only for its own process.

UNIX is really strict about its duplication process. A change through the child process will not come through to the location pointed by the pointer in the parent process.

PROGRAM 36

```
int *i;
*i = 10;
main( )
{
   int pid;
   pid = fork( );
   if(pid == 0)
   {
      printf("The initial value of variable i in the child process is %d\n",i);
      i += 10;
      printf("Value of variable i in Child process after
            incrementation is %d\n",i);
      printf("Child terminated\n");
   }
   else
   {
      wait(0);
      printf("value of i in parent process is %d\n",i);
   }
}
```

The above program will still display the value 10 as being pointed to by the pointer variable *i* in the parent process.

How is this demarcation kept in memory by UNIX. It is something like this. A call to *fork( )* creates a child process which is stored in some area in memory. Once the parent processes time slice is over it is transferred to another part in memory called the swap area.

Next the child process is loaded in main memory. Once the time-slice of the child process is over, the latter is stored in the swap area and the parent process is transferred back to main memory. This swapping continues till both processes are terminated.

But what if the processes were too large to fit in the swap area? Then that part of the process that spills over is saved to the disk and swapping now takes place between main memory, swap memory and disk.

How do we find out if a process is run from a common place, i.e. main memory? All we need to do is see the address of a declared variable, i.e. where in memory it is stored.

PROGRAM 37

```
main( )
{
    int i,pid;
    i = 10;
    printf("Before fork I is %d\n",i);
    pid = fork( );
    if (pid == 0)
    {
        printf("In child i's address is %u\n",&i);
        i = 20;
        printf("i is %d \n",i);
    }
    else
    {
        printf("In Parent i's address is %u\n",&i);
        printf("I is %d\n",i);
    }
}
```

The variable *i* will be duplicated in the child process. In this child process the location where the variable *i* is stored is printed. In our machine it was 500.

When the time slice of the child process got over it was the parent process's turn to execute. Here, too, we printed the address of variable *i*. We got the same number, 500. However, the value of the variable remained 10 though we had changed it in the child process.

So, although the values change depending on the process, the locations of variables remain the same.

Sharing Data Between Processes Using Files

How can we have two processes share values or communicate with one another ? Through files is one way. No special files, just the same ones that we open in read/ write mode.

PROGRAM 38

```
#include <fcntl.h>
#include <stdio.h>
main( )
{
  int fp;
  char chr = 'A';
  int pid;
  pid=fork( );

  if(pid==0)
  {
    fp = open("baby",O_WRONLY,0666);
    printf("In child chr is %c\n",chr);
    chr = 'B';
    write(fp,&chr,1);
    printf("In child chr after change %c\n",chr);
    printf("Child exiting\n");
    close(fp);
  }
  else
  {
    wait((int*)0);
    fp = open("baby",O_RDONLY);
    read(fp,&chr,1);
    printf("chr after parent reads is %c",chr);
```

```
        close(fp);
    }
}
```

We declare a variable *chr* with the value *A*, after which a process is forked.

The child process is activated as the *wait( )* suspends the parent process. In the child process, a file baby is opened in the write mode. This file open is a low level one. The last parameter passed signifies a read/ write for all users.

Next, the value of variable *chr* is changed to *B* and then written to the file. The *write( )* function is also passed three parameters: the file handle, the address of the location where the character A is stored and the number of characters to write, in this case one.

As soon as the child process terminates, the parent gets active. Here the same file is opened once again, but in the read mode. In this process the value of variable *chr* is initially *A*. Remember, although we have changed it to a *B* in the child process, this new value is not reflected in the variable belonging to the parent process. However, this *A* is replaced with a *B*, which is read from the file baby. That is why the *printf( )* prints a *B*. Didn't both processes share the same value.

The file opened in the above program was done singularly. That is, at one time only one process had it opened. Only when the file was closed by the child process did the parent process reopen it.

However, if the file was opened before a call to the *fork( )*, it would be global. A file opened in this manner is accessible by both processes, unlike variables. So what would happen if we opened a file globally, created a child process, and proceeded to read the data from it into an array?

PROGRAM 39

```
#include <stdio.h>
#include <fcntl.h>
main( )
```

```
{
    int fp;
    char buff[11];
    int pid;
    fp = open("baby",O_RDONLY);
    pid=fork( );
    if(pid==0)
    {
        printf("Child begins %d\n", getpid( ));
        read(fp,buff,10);
        buff[10] = '\0';
        printf("Child read : ");
        puts(buff);
        printf("Child exiting\n");
    }
    else
    {
        read(fp,buff,10);
        buff[10] = '\0';
        printf("Parent read : ");
        puts(buff);
        printf("Parent exiting\n");
    }
}
```

A file, baby, is opened and a child process created. The file baby contains the line This is for all the lonely people, thinking that life has passed them by.

The child process is given the time slice. As a result the statements within the *if* are executed. 10 characters are read into the array *buff* , i.e. This is fo. The child process terminates after this string is displayed on screen.

Next the parent process gets the time slice. Here also 10 characters are read into the array *buff*. But this is the array variable that belongs to the parent process. In spite of that, when the *puts( )* executes we see r all the .

Hey, but shouldn't the parent process have also printed This is fo. So what went wrong ?

A file, unlike a variable, is never duplicated. When another process is created, the file handle is shared.

Included in the duplication of a child process is its FILE DESCRIPTOR TABLE. This table holds the integer value, also known as the file descriptor, of the file opened by the parent process. Since the file descriptor table is duplicated, all files open in the parent process when the *fork( )* is called, are also open in the child.

Besides the file descriptor table another entity known as the SYSTEM FILE TABLE is also used to control files. In this table are stored the file pointer and access mode. An entry of file opened is made into this table. And another entry of the same file is made in the file descriptor table. Both these entries are linked.

While each process has its own file descriptor table, the system file table is global and not duplicated when a process is created. Thus, not only the file, but also the file pointer and its access mode, are shared.

If we take the above example, we'll see that the child process moved this shared file handle 10 characters. So when the parent process began to execute, the file handle was on the 11th character. As a result, we saw the characters from then on.

Want to see if the file handle is really shared? Then try out this program.

PROGRAM 40

```
main( )
{
    int fp;
    char buff[11];
    fp = open("baby",O_RDONLY);
    pid=fork( );
    if(pid==0)
    {
        printf("File Handle is %d\n", lseek(fp,0l,1));
        read(fp,buff,10);
```

```
        buff[10] = '\0';
        printf("File Handle is now %d in the child process\n:",
        lseek(fp,0l,1));
    }
    else
    {
        wait(0);
        printf("File Handle in parent process is %d\n",lseek(fp,0l,1));
    }
}
```

We use the function *lseek( )*. It is passed three parameters: the file handle, the number of characters to move and from where to move, i.e. starting of file, current position of file pointer or end of file.

The first call to *lseek( )* prints the position of the file handle, in this case it will be at the beginning of the file. Next, 10 characters are read from the file. And the position of the file handle is printed once more. This will show a value of 11. Now the child process terminates and the parent process is handed the time slice. The value of the file handle printed by the *printf( )* will be 11. Hasn't it remained the same?

File Buffering

But so far we have been using low level file functions like *open( )* and *read( )*. What would happen if we used the high-level file functions like *fopen( )* and *fread( )* etc.?

```
PROGRAM 41
#include <stdio.h>

main( )
{
    FILE *fp;
    char buff[11];
    int pid;
    fp = fopen("baby","r");
    pid=fork( );
    if(pid==0)
```

```
    {
        printf("Initial Child file pointer %d\n", ftell(fp));
        fread(buff,sizeof(buff),1,fp);
        buff[10] = '\0';
        printf("Child read : %s",buff);
        printf("After child process reads data from file
                the file pointer is %d\n", ftell(fp));
        printf("Child exiting\n");
    }
    else
    {
        wait(0);
        printf("Initial Parent pointer %d\n", ftell(fp));
        fread(buff,sizeof(buff),1,fp);
        buff[10] = '\0';
        printf("Parent read : %s ", buff);
        printf("After Parent process reads data from file %d\n",ftell(fp));
        printf("Parent exiting\n");
    }
}
```

The file baby, which is opened by the function *fopen( )* has one line: This is for all the lonely people, thinking that life has passed them by. The *fork( )* creates a process. Now there are two processes in memory sharing the same file handle to the file baby.

Next, the child process is executed. It first prints the value of the file pointer, which is 0. This is done using the *ftell( )* function, which is passed the file handle *fp*. The *ftell( )* function only tells us what the value of the logical file pointer is and not the physical position which can be got through the *lseek( )* function. We cannot, unlike with the *lseek( )* function, move the file pointer through the *ftell( )* function.

The child process now reads 10 characters from the file into the array *buff* using the *fread( )* function. This function is passed four parameters: the array, the number of characters to read, how many times to read them and the file from which to read them.

Now the position of the file pointer is printed once more. It will be 11 since we have read 10 characters.

After this the parent process is given the time-slice. This proceeds to print the file pointer position. Hey, what happened ? Why is it showing 1024 ? Shouldn't it be 11 ?

When we use the *fread( )* function by default, it reads 1024 characters (whatever is the block size, ours was 1024) into the computer buffer. From this computer buffer (block) the number of characters we have specified in the 2nd parameter are transferred to the array variable, in this case *buff*. Since the *fread( )* function reads 1024 bytes, the file (physical) pointer is moved that many bytes, too. And this is reflected basically because the process is different.

Since the *fread( )* function in the child process reads 1024 bytes by default, when the parent process is given the time-slice, the file pointer is at the end of file. As a result, nothing is displayed on screen.

Of course, if the file baby had more than 1024 characters, 10 characters from the 1024th character onwards would have been displayed.

After figuring how the high-level file functions were operating, a thought struck us. Suppose, after printing the contents of the buffer in the child process, we put it to sleep. And then proceeded to the parent process, in which the next 10 characters were to be printed. After which once again the time slice would be handed back to the orphan child process. This would proceed to read 10 more characters and print them. But at this point where would the file handle be? Logically speaking it should show us 2048. But would that really be the case?

PROGRAM 42

```
#include <stdio.h>

main()
{
```

```
FILE *fp;
char buff[11];
int pid,i;
fp = fopen("book", "w+");

for (i=0;i<1024;i++)
   fprintf(fp, "A");

for (i=0;i<1024;i++)
   fprintf(fp, "B");

for (i=0;i<1024;i++)
   fprintf(fp, "C");

for (i=0;i<1024;i++)
   fprintf(fp, "D");
fclose(fp);

fp = fopen("book","r");
pid=fork( );

if(pid==0)
{
   fread(buff,sizeof(buff),1,fp);
   buff[10] = '\0';
   printf("after child read file pointer ftell-> %d %s\n",
   ftell(fp),buff);
   sleep(5);
   printf("in child after parent read file pointer ftell-> %d %s\n",
         ftell(fp),buff);

   fread(buff,sizeof(buff),1,fp);
   buff[10] = '\0';
   printf("after child 2nd time read file pointer %d %s\n",
        ftell(fp), buff);
}
else
{
   printf("initially in parent file pointer %d %s\n",
   ftell(fp),buff);
   fread(buff,sizeof(buff),1,fp);
   buff[10] = '\0';
   printf("after Parent read file pointer %d %s\n", ftell(fp),buff);
```

```
    }
}
```

To start with, we are creating a file with 1024 As, 1024 B's, 1024 C's and 1024 D's. That's a total file length of 4096 characters.

After reopening this file in *read* mode we fork a child process which reads 10 characters into the array *buff*. Next, we print the position of the logical file pointer using the *ftell( )* function. The value will be 11. Of course, the physical file pointer is at position 1024 at this point. The child process is then put to *sleep( )*.

The parent process gets the time slice. First, the value of the file pointer is read using *ftell( )*. This will show 1024, which is the logical as well as physical position. *ftell( )* has taken the value of the physical file pointer at this point. Remember we have said that an *fread( )* will actually read 1024 bytes at a time. But it's only when the process is a new one that the physical and logical value of the file pointer will match.

From the 1024th character onwards 10 characters are read into the array *buff* which belongs to the parent process. This will be the character *B*, 10 times over. The value of the logical file pointer is now 1035.

The parent process now terminates. And once more it is the child process that is handed the time slice. At this moment, the physical file pointer is at position 2048. The *ftell()* however prints 1035. Hey, what happened? Shouldn't it have shown 2048?

It would have if the temporary buffer into which the values read, using the *fread( )* , had not been full. Remember , when an *fread( )* is executed, by default, 1024 characters are read into a temporary buffer. From there, 10 characters are transferred to our array *buff*. Now it's because this buffer is full that the *ftell( )* shows a value 1035. Because *fread( )* reads only when the buffer is empty.

The second *fread()* in the child process now tries to read but fails as the buffer is full. The *printf()*, as a result, prints the next 10 *c*s from the buffer.

Want to see if the logical pointer, as shown by the *ftell()* function, is at a variance from the physical pointer? Then try out the next program.

Let's first see what the FILE structure defined in the stdio.h file looks like.

```
typedef struct {
    unsigned char *_ptr; /* pointer to the next character */
    int_cnt; /* total characters in buffer */
    unsigned char  *_base; /* pointer to logical buffer */
    char _flag; /* mode file opened in */
    char _file; /* file descriptor
}FILE;
```

PROGRAM 43

```
#include <stdio.h>

main()
{
    FILE *fp;
    char buff[11];
    int pid,dip;
    fp = fopen("book","r");
    pid=fork();
    if(pid==0)
    {
        fread(buff,sizeof(buff),1,fp);
        buff[10] = '\0';
        printf("after child read file pointer ftell-> %d lseek-> %d %s\n",
            ftell(fp), lseek(fp->_file, 0l, 1), buff);
        sleep(5);
        fread(buff,sizeof(buff),1,fp);
        buff[10] = '\0';
        printf("after child 2nd time read file pointer %d lseek->%d %s\n",
            ftell(fp), lseek(fp->_file, 0l, 1), buff);
    }
    else
```

```
    {
        printf("initially in parent file pointer %d lseek-> %d %s\n",
                  ftell(fp), lseek(fp->_file, 0l, 1), buff);
        fread(buff,sizeof(buff),1,fp);
        buff[10] = '\0';
        printf("after Parent read file pointer %d lseek->%d %s\n",
                  ftell(fp), lseek(fp->_file, 0l, 1), buff);
    }
}
```

The program is the same as the one above except that we have added the *lseek( )* function. Now each *printf( )* will also print the value of the physical file pointer. For every problem there has to be a solution around. To overcome the above problem all we need to do is use the *fflush( )* function.

PROGRAM 44

```
#include <stdio.h>

main( )
{
    FILE *fp;
    char buff[11];
    int pid,dip;
    fp = fopen("book","r");
    pid=fork( );
    if(pid==0)
    {
        fread(buff,sizeof(buff),1,fp);
        buff[10] = '\0';
        printf("after child read file pointer ftell-> %d lseek-> %d %s\n",
                  ftell(fp), lseek(fp->_file, 0l, 1), buff);
        sleep(5);
        fflush(fp);
        fread(buff,sizeof(buff),1,fp);
        buff[10] = '\0';
        printf("after child 2nd time read file pointer %d lseek->%d %s\n",
                  ftell(fp), lseek(fp->_file, 0l, 1), buff);
    }
    else
    {
        printf("initially in parent file pointer %d lseek-> %d %s\n", ftell(fp),
```

```
        lseek(fp->_file, 0l, 1), buff);
    fread(buff,sizeof(buff),1,fp);
    buff[10] = '\0';
    printf("after Parent read file pointer %d lseek->%d %s\n",
          ftell(fp), lseek(fp->_file, 0l, 1), buff);
  }
}
```

The *fflush( )*, which is called in the child process after the *sleep( )*, is passed the file handle. It proceeds to empty the temporary buffer created at the time the *fread( )* was called. Now that the buffer has been emptied, the *fread( )* will read 1024 characters from 2048 onwards. These will be all the Cs. As a result, the final *printf( )* prints 10 Cs.

Similarly, when we use the *fwrite( )* high level file function, a write is performed not to the file but to a buffer. It is only when the buffer is filled or the file is closed that the write to the file takes place. This write from the buffer to the file is known as flushing.

PROGRAM 45

```
#include <stdio.h>
#include <fcntl.h>

main()
{
   char *p = "hello world";
   FILE *fp ;

   fp = fopen("tamper","w");
   fwrite(p,11,1,fp);
   fork( );
}
```

Into the file tamper, opened in write mode, we write the string hello world. Then, a call to the *fork( )* creates a child. And immediately, both parent and child processes are terminated.

If you see the contents of the file tamper using the cat command, you'll see in it hello world written twice. Hey, how is that possible? Surely, the child process is being created after the *fwrite( )*? And isn't it true that the child process begins to execute from the *fork( )* onwards?

Yes, all these questions are valid. But the answer has nothing to do with any of them. It lies in the way the *fwrite( )* function behaves. Instead of writing directly to the file, it writes to a buffer. This buffer is 1024 bytes long. *fwrite( )* transfers the contents of the buffer to the file if, either the buffer gets full, or the file is closed.

In our case, the file is closed by default, as the process terminates. However, since just before the process terminates a *fork( )* is performed, the buffer, which holds the string, is also duplicated. As a result, when the file closes, the values of both buffers are written to it.

This *fwrite( )* function in the above program, if replaced by the *write( )* function, will ensure that this duplication will not take place.

```
PROGRAM 46
#include <stdio.h>
#include <fcntl.h>

main( )
{
    char *p = "hello world";
    int fp ;

    fp = open("tamper",O_CREAT,0666);
    write(fp,p,11);
    fork( );
}
```

Now the contents of the file tamper will show only one line since it was a low level write that was performed.

You'll have noticed that we've passed three parameters to the *open( )* function: the name of the file, an instruction that it be created and a write permission.

Note: A low level function resorts to what is known as **kernel** buffering which anticipates reads, postpones writes and keeps frequently accessed data in fast internal memory. This is opposed to user buffering which is what happens when we use high level file buffering.

So far we have opened the file globally. But what if the file were opened in the child process? Would the parent be able to access it?

PROGRAM 47

```
#include <stdio.h>

main()
{
    int pid;
    FILE *fp;

    pid = fork();
    if(pid == 0)
    {
        fp = fopen("txt","w");
        fputc('a',fp);
    }
    else
    {
        fputc('b',fp);
    }
    fclose(fp);
}
```

The file is opened and a character written to it only when the child process is run. In the parent process, however, the character will not be written since it isn't aware that a file has been opened. It is not that an entry of the file is not made in the SYSTEM FILE TABLE. It is just that the file pointer variable *fp* belonging to the parent process is not pointing at this file in memory. You'll notice that this pointer variable has not been initialized anywhere in the parent process.

An error Bus error - Core dumped is flashed and the process terminated.

However, what if the file was opened immediately after the call to *fork( )*? This would mean that both copies of the file pointer would be initialized and pointing to the same file. A write performed through both processes should then be registered.

PROGRAM 48

```
#include <stdio.h>

main( )
{
   int pid ;
   FILE *fp;

   pid = fork( );
   fp = fopen("txt","w") ;

   if(pid == 0)
   {
      fputc('a',fp);
   }
   else
   {
      fputc('b',fp);
   }
   fclose(fp);
}
```

And though that does happen, we don't see it in the file. We only see one character, depending on the process that was performed last.

Assume now that the child process was performed first. The *fputc( )* function would write the character *a*. After which the file would be closed. Next the parent process would open the file - remember that each process begins to execute from the call to the *fork( )*. Since the file has just been opened, the file pointer will be on the first character, which in our case is the *a* written by the child process. Hence the *fputc( )* will overwrite the *a* with a *b*.

The way out of this kind of situation would be to open the file in append mode, and not in write mode, which is what we have done. In append mode, the file pointer is immediately positioned at the end of file.

PROGRAM 49

```
#include <stdio.h>

main( )
{
   int pid ;
   FILE *fp;

   pid = fork( );
   fp = fopen("txt","a") ;
   if(pid == 0)
   {
      fputc('x',fp);
   }
   else
   {
      fputc('y',fp);
   }
   fclose(fp);
}
```

Now if we use the command cat txt, we'll see both an x and a y.

The 'exec( )' Function

Ask any person working with computers what his prime concern is and he will say memory. We have come a long way from the days when the computer had only 16 KB of main memory or RAM. Now we have machines that boast of over 64 MB of RAM. But this has not stopped people from desiring more and more memory. There never seems to be enough of it. And if we're going to run a program that is tens of thousands lines long, we're going to reach the limit sooner or later.

In C, we have a way to work around this. Remember, in the beginning of this chapter we said that UNIX believes that small and simple is beautiful. And that small programs can be built that handle only one task. That these in turn can call others and those others will call others and so on till we have a synergy of small processes that come to life, execute, bring another process to life and die in this process of creation.

So, at a point in time we have only one process in memory. Since a copy of the program is not made like with the *fork( )* function, won't this help in freeing memory?

There is a family of functions that enables us to create another process. But once the other process is initiated, the parent process can never be given control again since its memory space is overwritten by the new process.

It's like a GOTO in BASIC, where execution begins from the line specified in the GOTO and there is no returning. This new process, however, has the same PID as the original process. Not only the PID but also the parent process ID, current directory, and file descriptor tables - if any are open - also remain the same.

There are two examples listed below. Not too difficult, and which will explain the concept of the *exec( )* function adequately.

Note : Compile the following programs in this manner:

cc -o<object filename> <source filename.c>

eg. cc -oex1 ex1.c
eg. cc -oex2 ex2.c

This is necessary because when we compiled normally, we did so by just saying cc <source filename.c>. And the resultant file was always a.out. But to explain the *exec( )* family we need to resort to two programs since one is calling another. If we were to resort to the old method of compiling we would always find the program EX1.C which becomes a.out being overwritten by the a.out got from compiling EX2.C. By compiling in the new manner shown we'll get two executable files, ex1 and ex2.

```
PROGRAM 50
EX1.C
main()
{
    printf("Before exec my ID is %d \n",getpid());
    printf("My parent process's id is %d\n",getppid());

    printf("exec starts\n");
    execl("/usr/guest/ex2","ex2",(char *)0);
    printf("this will not print\n");
}
```

Wait, don't run this program till you have compiled the one below.

```
PROGRAM 51
EX2.C
main()
{
    printf("After the exec my process id is %d\n",getpid());
    printf("My parent process's id is %d\n",getppid());

    printf("exec ends\n");
}
```

Let's see what happens when we run the first program.

Its PID will be printed on screen. And a call made to the second program, ie. EX2.C through the *execl()* function. This function is passed three parameters, but the second parameter can be further subdivided to reflect many parameters. In the above case we pass three parameters: the path where the file EX2 will be found, the filename itself and a NULL to terminate, since all the parameters are taken as one string.

The execution of this function will result in the program EX2 being loaded into the same memory space where the process EX1 was. This process prints its PID, which remains the same and then exits. But it will not return to the process that activated it since, in the first place, it doesn't exist any longer in memory.

What do we mean by saying that the second parameter passed to the *execl( )* function can be subdivided ? Whenever we call another program we invariably pass it some values. These are used by the program as its input. Suppose we wanted the process that was being created to be given some input, this is how we'd do it:

PROGRAM 52

EX1.C

```
main(argc,argv)
int argc ;
char *argv[ ] ;
{
   printf("Before exec my ID is %d \n",getpid( ));
   printf("exec starts\n");
   execl(argv[1],argv[2],argv[3],argv[4],(char *)0);
   printf("this will not print\n");
}
```

PROGRAM 53

EX2.C

```
main(argc,argv)
int argc ;
char *argv[ ];
{
   printf("After exec my ID is %d \n",getpid( ));
   printf("Child is %s and its arguments are : %s %s
\n",argv[0],argv[1],argv[2]);
   printf("exec ends\n");
}
```

Run the program EX1 as shown: ex1 /usr/guest/ex2 ex2 Hello World.

The pointer array variable argv will be assigned all the parameters passed. The second parameter, which is the filename will have a further division of two parameters to reflect the two strings Hello and World.

Next, the *execl( )* function is executed with these parameters. This process in turn prints its PID which is the same as that of its parent process. The string ex2 Hello World is displayed by this process and the process terminates.

It is not only programs written by us that we can execute in this way. Even a shell command like ls can be similarly executed. After all, ls too is nothing but a program. The only difference is that it hasn't been written by us.

But why would we want to run a shell command like ls through a call to the *exec( )* function?

You must have noticed that when we do a ls -l at the UNIX prompt, the screen fills with data columns but there are no headings to signify what each data column is. If we found this particularly painful we can always write a program that prints the headings and then uses *exec( )* to call the ls command

PROGRAM 54

EX1.C

```
main(argc,argv)
int argc ;
char *argv[ ] ;
{
   printf("Before exec my ID is %d \n",getpid( ));
   printf(" File-PermNo.of linksGroupOwnerSizeDateName\n");
   printf("exec starts\n");
   execl(argv[1],argv[2],argv[3],argv[4],(char *)0);
   printf("this will not print\n");
}
```

PROGRAM 55

EX2.C

```
main(argc,argv)
int argc ;
char *argv[ ];
{
   printf("After exec my ID is %d \n",getpid( ));
   printf("Child is %s and its arguments are : %s %s\n",
```

```
        argv[0],argv[1],argv[2]);
    printf("exec ends\n");
}
```

The program will be run like this: ex1 /bin/ls ls -l. This will output all the files in the directory.

But suppose the program we are trying to execute through the *execl( )* function does not exist? Won't this give an error? Sure, it will.

For example, take the above programs. Assume that the file ex2 was deleted by mistake. If we now run ex1, the *execl( )* function will not execute properly as it wont find the file ex2. As a result a -1 will be returned signifying an error. And of course the statement *printf("this will not print\n");* will be executed. This happens since control is never handed to ex2, which does not exist at all.

This error can be trapped to display our own message in conjunction with UNIX's message.

Note: Remember to delete the program EX2.

PROGRAM 56

```
main()
{
    printf("executing ex2\n");
    execl("/usr/guest/ex2","ex2",(char *)0);
    perror("execl failed to run EX2");
}
```

We'll get the message execl failed to run EX2 as specified by us, as well as the UNIX message :No such file or directory. The *perror( )* function prints our message, a colon and then the UNIX message. It can be used for all UNIX error messages.

If we don't want to print our own message, all we need to do is specify the *perror( )* function without any parameters: *perror(" ");*.

Terminal And File Buffering

Even when we use the *exec( )* function, buffering takes place. We've said that when we do a *exec( )*, the process is replaced in memory by the one that has been called. Along with the process, the buffers which so far contained data from the previous process are also emptied and filled with the new process' data.

Which is why the next program doesn't work in quite the way we expect.

PROGRAM 57

EX1.C

```
main()
{
   printf("The cat jumped over the wall");
   execl("/usr/guest/ex2","ex2",(char *)0);
}
```

PROGRAM 58

EX2.C

```
main( )
{
   printf("The clock went dong");
}
```

The line The cat jumped over the wall will never be printed. Let's see why not. Normally, in a UNIX system the terminal is line-buffered. Before anything is printed on screen it is first stored in this buffer. Unless this buffer is full, or physically flushed by us, its contents will not be displayed. The statement The cat jumped over the wall will not fill the entire buffer. Nor is it being flushed physically by us and as a result, will not be displayed immediately.

Now the *exec( )* spawns the ex2 process. This act of creation will not only replace the space in memory where the ex1 was, but will also destroy all the buffers. As a result, the line The cat.. is lost. The line The clock.. will however be displayed as the process terminates. This results in the contents of the buffers being displayed on screen.

A physical flush of buffers can be done by specifying a *\n*.

PROGRAM 59

EX1.C

```
main( )
{
   printf("The cat jumped over the wall\n");
   execl("/usr/guest/ex2","ex2",(char *)0);
}
```

PROGRAM 60

EX2.C

```
main( )
{
   printf("The clock went dong");
}
```

The other way of doing a physical flush is by using the function *fflush( )*.

PROGRAM 61

EX1.C

```
main( )
{
   printf("The cat jumped over the wall");
   fflush(stdout);
   execl("/usr/guest/ex2","ex2",(char *)0);
}
```

PROGRAM 62

EX2.C

```
main( )
{
   printf("The clock went dong");
}
```

Here the *fflush( )* function is passed a parameter which signifies the terminal.

Instead of redirecting output to the terminal, what if we were to re-direct it to a file?

PROGRAM 63

EX1.C

```
main( )
{
   printf("The cat jumped over the wall");
   execl("/usr/guest/ex2","ex2",(char *)0);
}
```

PROGRAM 64

EX2.C

```
main( )
{
   printf("The clock went dong");
}
```

Run the program like this: ex1 > temp, where temp is the file the output should be re-directed to. When you do a cat temp to see the contents of the file, you'll see only the line The clock went dong.

What if we were to put a *\n*.

PROGRAM 65

EX1.C

```
main( )
{
   printf("The cat jumped over the wall\n");
   execl("/usr/guest/ex2","ex2",(char *)0);
}
```

PROGRAM 66

EX2.C

```
main( )
{
```

```
    printf("The clock went dong");
}
```

This re-directs the output to a file, as done previously. However the cat temp will yet show only the line The clock ...

But haven't we said that if we do a physical flush, we'll get both lines. True, that's what we've said and that's also what we've seen. But that was when the output was being directed to the terminal where line-buffering was taking place. Whereas, when we re-direct output to a file, block-buffering takes place. A block is 1024 bytes.

The first time we ran the program, ie. without the \n, the 1024 bytes were never exhausted. As a result, the buffer did not get flushed. The creation of EX2 resulted in the buffer contents being destroyed.

The second time, too, ie. in the program above, the 1024 bytes were not filled. The \n just results in another buffer position being filled.

The only way out of this kind of a predicament is to use the *fflush( )* function.

PROGRAM 67

EX1.C

```
main( )
{
    printf("The cat jumped over the wall\n");
    fflush(stdout);
    execl("/usr/guest/ex2","ex2",(char *)0);
}
```

PROGRAM 68

EX2.C

```
main( )
{
    printf("The clock went dong");
}
```

Here *stdout*, the parameter passed to the *fflush( )* function, is the file to which we re-direct the output.

The 'execv( )' Function

In a couple of the programs above we've **predefined** the number of arguments that we'll pass. The parameters passed are hard coded. This results in inflexibility. Suppose tomorrow we decide to pass more parameters, then what?

For that we have another function *execv( )*.

PROGRAM 69

```
main()
{
    char *temp[3];
    temp[0] = "ls";
    temp[1] = "-l";
    temp[2] = (char *)0;
    execv("/bin/ls",temp);
    printf("this will not print\n");
}
```

The *execv( )* function takes only two **parameters**, the program **we want** to execute and the array of pointers that holds all the **parameters** we want passed.

In this case the array of pointers, *temp*, has been defined with three elements: the *ls*, the *- l* option for it, and the NULL terminator. Isn't this simpler than using *execl( )* if we want many parameters passed ?

Now if we **want more** parameters passed, all we need to do is add them to the **array of pointers**, *temp*.

The 'execvp( )' Function

In all the programs that use the **two** *exec( )* function seen so far we've always specified the path. **But**, there is a function that allows us to omit this, too.

PROGRAM 70

EX1.C

```
main( )
{
   char *tem[4] ;
   tem[0] = "ex2" ;
   tem[1] = "hello" ;
   tem[2] = "world" ;
   tem[3] = (char *)0 ;
   printf("I am parent my pid is %d\n",getpid( ));
   execvp(tem[0],tem);
   printf("this will not print\n");
}
```

PROGRAM 71

EX2.C

```
main(argc,argv)
int argc ;
char *argv[ ];
{
   printf("I am child after execl my process id is %d \n",getpid( ));
   printf("Child is %s and its arguments are : %s %s \n",
         argv[0],argv[1],argv[2]);
   printf("exec ends\n");
}
```

As in the last program we define an array of pointers and assign them some values. A call is made to the *execvp( )* function with two parameters, the file to be executed and the array of pointers which holds the other values to be passed.

The file to be executed, in this case ex2, prints the PID which will remain the same. And then the arguments ex2 and Hello World are printed.

If you notice we have not passed the path name. The *execvp( )* takes the default path.

onment Block

At the UNIX prompt, type set and you'll get all the environment variables like path, prompt, etc. We can write a program, too, to see these environment variables.

PROGRAM 72

```
main(argc,argv,envp)
int argc;
char *argv[ ];
char *envp[ ];
{
   int i;
   for(i=0;envp[i];i++)
       printf("%s\n",envp[i]);
}
```

Besides the *argc* and *argv* we also define a new parameter, *envp*. This is also an array of pointers and will point to, by default, all the variables we have defined in the environment.

The *printf( )* in the *for* loop will now display all the environment variables.

But this is not the only way we can program to find out the values in the environment block. C has another special variable called *environ* that we can use to access the environment variables. This *environ* is a pointer to a pointer which points to a character.

PROGRAM 73

```
extern **environ;
main()
{
   int i;
   for(i=0;environ[i];i++)
       printf("%s",environ[i]);
}
```

environ is the special variable. The *printf( )* in the *for* loop will print the values this pointer points to, which are nothing but the environment variables.

The Environment Block And The Child Process

We know that when we fork a process, a duplicate of the parent is made. This child process has a copy of the variables defined in the parent process. But besides this, the values of the variables in the environment block of the parent process are also duplicated. Check it out:

```
PROGRAM 74
main( )
{
   extern **environ;

   int pid,i;
   pid = fork( );
   if (pid == 0)
   {
      printf("\nln child environmental block is at %u\n",*environ);
      for(i=0; environ[i]; i++)
         printf("%s\n", environ[i]);
   }
   else
   {
      wait(0);
      printf("\nln parent environmental block is at %u\n",*environ);
      for(i=0; environ[ i ]; i++)
         printf("%s\n", environ[ i ]);
   }
}
```

We use the defined **array of** pointers, variable *environ*. The process forks a child. **The** ***wait( )*** in the *else* part ensures that the time-slice is given to **the child process**. As a result the statements within the *if* are executed. **In them**, we first print the address of *environ.* And then use a *for* loop to print all the variables defined in the environment block.

After the child process terminates, it is the waiting parent process' turn. This process is swapped into main memory from the swap area. The address of the environment block is printed. This remains the same as that shown by the child process. Finally, the *for* loop prints the values of the variables in the environment block. This will be the same as those printed in the child process.

The environment variables between the spawning and the spawned processes remain the same. But sometimes we may need to change these variables for the spawned process. In that case we need to pass this spawned process the new environment variables. One way of doing this is by using the *execve( )* function.

```
PROGRAM 75
ZZZ.C
main( )
{
   int i;
   char *env[5], *av[2];

   env[0] = "NAME=STEFF";
   env[1] = "COMPANY=PUMA";
   env[2] = "ADDRESS=NEWYORK";
   env[3] = "TEL=387-305-02";
   env[4] = (char *)0;

   av[0] = "zzz1";
   av[1] = (char *)0;
   printf("executing zzz1\n");
   execve("/usr/zzz1",av,env);
   perror("execve failed");
}
```

Don't run the program just yet.

```
PROGRAM 76
ZZZ1.C
extern **environ;
main(argc,argv,envp)
int argc;
char *argv[ ];
char *envp[ ];
{
   int i;
   for(i=0;envp[i];i++)
      printf("%s\n",envp[i]);
   for(i=0;environ[i];i++)
      printf("%s",environ[i]);
}
```

Note: Compile both the above programs separately so that you get two executable files.

Let's see what ZZZ is doing. In it, we've defined two arrays of pointers. To *env* we assign the values of the new environment variables. This variable *env* is known in UNIX jargon as a SYMBOL TABLE. If we want to change the environment block, we need to define the SYMBOL TABLE. Because, normally, there isn't room in THE ACTUAL ENVIRONMENT BLOCK for any new variables or longer values. And if the pointer *environ* is then made to point to this new environment, it will be passed on to any program subsequently invoked.

To *av* we assign the filename to spawn and a NULL terminator, the second parameter because the parameters by the *exec( )* family of functions are taken as a string as we have mentioned earlier.

Finally, we call the *execve( )* function with three parameters: the path, the filename and the new environment variables.

The program ZZZ1 is then spawned using the *execve( )* function. The environment variables from the spawning process, ZZZ, are passed to the array of pointers *envp*. This, we have seen earlier, points to the environment block variables.

The first *for* loop will now print these new environment variables. The second *for* loop is a check to make sure the environment block has really changed. It also emphasizes the fact that both *environ* and *envp* point to the same location.

Really speaking the *execve()* function is quite useless. We can, if we want the spawned process to have a different environment block, change it using the *execl()* function, too. How?

PROGRAM 77

ZZZ.C

```
char *env[ ]={"Hello","mosad",(char *)0};

main()
{
    extern **environ;
    environ = env;
    printf("Now exec will start\n");
    execl("/usr/guest/deep/ZZZ1","ZZZ1",(char *)0);
    perror(" ");
}
```

PROGRAM 78

ZZZ1.C

```
main()
{
    extern **environ;
    int i;
    for(i=0;environ[i];i++)
        printf("%s\n",environ[i]);
}
```

In ZZZ we declare an array of pointers *env* with some values. The array of pointers *environ*, by default, points to the default values in the environment block. We change this pointer to point to the new variables. By doing this, we have in effect changed the environment block.

Now when the *execl()* spawns the new process, in this case ZZZ1, the copy of the new environment block will be a reflection of the spawning process' environment block. And this we have just changed.

The point is, if we change the environment block just before a call to the *execl( )* function, the spawned process will reflect these new values in its environment block.

So where is the need for the *execve( )* function?

This is not to say that we can't change the environment block variables if a child process is created by a *fork( )*. We can. All we need to do is define another array of pointers, assign them new values and make sure that the first line in the child process initializes the predefined variable *environ* with this new array of pointers.

PROGRAM 79

```
main( )
{
  extern **environ;
  int pid,i;
  char *env[3];
  env[0] = "COMPANY=IBM";
  env[1] = "CITY=USA";
  env[2] = (char *) 0;

  pid = fork( );
  if (pid == 0)
  {
     environ = env;
     printf("\nln child environmental block is at %u\n",*environ);
     for(i=0; environ[i]; i++)
        printf("%s\n", environ[i]);
  }
  else
  {
     wait(0);
     printf("\nln parent environmental block is at %u\n",*environ);
     for(i=0; environ[i]; i++)
        printf("%s\n", environ[i]);
  }
```

```
}
```

In this program, we first define an array of pointers *env*. To this we assign some values. The *fork( )* creates a child process. In it, the first thing we do is assign the predefined variable *environ* to *env*. So *environ*, which was pointing to the environment block, is now pointing to these values. This new location is what the first *printf( )* will print. The *for* loop in the child process will print these new environment variable values.

The child process terminates and the parent process is reactivated. The *printf( )* in the *for* loop will first print the address of the environment block. This will be different from that printed in the child process since, in the child process, we had redefined *environ* to point to a different location. The values of the environment block printed by the *for* loop will be the original ones.

That should also have been enough proof that there are two separate environment blocks for the parent and child processes. But for the Doubting Thomases, here's further proof.

PROGRAM 80

```
main( )
{
   extern **environ;
   char *temp[ ];
   char *env[3];
   int pid,i;

   env[0] = "COMPANY=IBM";
   env[1] = "CITY=USA";
   env[2] = (char *) 0;

   temp = environ;
   pid = fork( );
   if (pid == 0)
   {
      environ = env;
      printf("\n\n child environment block is at %u\n",*environ);
      for(i=0; environ[i]; i++)
```

```
        printf("%s\n", environ[i]);
      printf("\nPrevious Environment Variables were; block is at %u \n",
        *temp);

      for(i=0; temp[i]; i++)
        printf("%s\n", temp[i]);
   }
   else
   {
      wait(0);
      printf("\nIn parent environmental block is at %u\n",*environ);
      for(i=0; environ[i]; i++)
        printf("%s\n", environ[i]);
   }
}
```

We define two arrays of pointers, *env* and *temp*. To *env* we assign the new values we want passed to the child process' environment block. *temp* is assigned the same location as the predefined array of pointers *environ*. So now we have two variables pointing to the same environment block.

The forked child process now executes. That is, the statements within the *if* are executed. The first thing we do is change the location to which *environ* points. We make it point to the same location that the array of pointers *env* points. These are the new values we want the environment block of the child process to reflect. This new address is printed. As well as the new variables in it.

After that's done, we print the location to which *temp* points. This is the address of the *environ* variable before it was assigned *env*. The values *temp* points to are now printed. That is, the variables of the unchanged environment block. The child process then terminates.

Next, the parent process proceeds to print the address and values of its environment block, both of which have remained unchanged.

Doesn't this prove that there are two different environment

blocks, one for the child and one for the parent. And that though they occupy the same memory space as the previous process during swapping, if it (the environment block) is changed the predefined variable *environ* will point elsewhere.

But it's not that we can't change the values in the environment block on the fly that is while the program is executing. While a process is running we can use the *putenv( )* function to make changes to its environment block.

But this new value: is it put into the new environment block or assigned to the old one? (The old one referred to is the environment block before the *environ = env* statement.)

To find that out we wrote the following program:

```
PROGRAM 81
main( )
{
    extern **environ;
    int pid,i;
    char **temp;
    char *env[3];
    env[0] = "COMPANY=IBM";
    env[1] = "CITY=USA";
    env[2] = (char *) 0;

    temp = environ;
    pid = fork( );
    if (pid == 0)
    {
        environ = env;
        putenv("NAME=JOKER");
        printf("\nln child environment block is at %u\n",*environ);
        for(i=0; environ[i]; i++)
            printf("%s\n", environ[i]);
        printf("\nPrevious Environment Variables were; block is at %u \n",
            *temp);

        for(i=0; temp[i]; i++)
            printf("%s\n", temp[i]);
```

```
    }
    else
    {
        wait(0);
        printf("\nln parent environmental block is at %u\n",*environ);

        for(i=0; environ[i]; i++)
            printf("%s\n", environ[i]);
    }
}
```

There is nothing different in the above program from the two immediately prior to it. Except for the call to the *putenv( )* function. This function is passed a string.

Now, when the *for* loop prints the values of the environment block, you'll notice that one of them is NAME=JOKER.

Here's still more proof that there are two different copies of the environment block.

PROGRAM 82

```
main( )
{
    extern **environ;
    int pid,i;
    char *temp[ ];
    char *env[3];
    env[0] = "COMPANY=IBM";
    env[1] = "CITY=USA";
    env[2] = (char *) 0;
    temp = environ;
    pid = fork( );
    if (pid == 0)
    {
        environ = env;
        printf("\nln child environment block is at %u\n",*environ);
        for(i=0; environ[i]; i++)
            printf("%s\n", environ[i]);
        printf("\nPrevious Environment Variables were; block is at %u \n",
            *temp);
        for(i=0; temp[i]; i++)
```

```
        {
            *temp[i] = (char *) 0;
            printf("%s\n", temp[i]);
        }
    }
    else
    {
        wait(0);
        printf("\n\n parent environmental block is at %u\n",*environ);
        for(i=0; environ[i]; i++)
            printf("%s\n", environ[i]);
    }
}
```

Here, we first define two arrays of pointers besides *environ*. To the array *env* we assign the values for the new environment block. And to *temp* we assign the location of the environment block as pointed to by *environ*.

In the forked child process we specify *environ* to point to *env*. This changes the environment block for the child process.

The *for* loop, which results in the changed environment block values being printed, will show variable *NAME=JOKER*. Whereas in the second *for* loop, we first assign zero's to every byte that *temp* points to, and then print it.

Once again in the parent process we print the variables in the environment block. These are as before.

If we have two blocks for a process, one old and the other current, we can get the process to switch from one to another.

PROGRAM 83

```
main( )
{
    extern **environ;
    int pid,i;
    char *temp[ ];
    char *env[3];
    env[0] = "COMPANY=IBM";
```

```
        env[1] = "CITY=USA";
        env[2] = (char *) 0;
        temp = environ;
        pid = fork( );
        if (pid == 0)
        {
           environ = env;
           printf("\nIn child environment block is at %u\n",*environ);
           for(i=0; environ[i]; i++)
              printf("%s\n", environ[i]);
           printf("\nPrevious Environment Variables were; block is at %u \n",
              *temp);

           environ = temp;
           printf("\nIn child environment block is at %u\n",*environ);
           for(i=0; environ[i]; i++)
              printf("%s\n", environ[i]);
        }
        else
        {
           wait(0);
           printf("\nIn parent environmental block is at %u\n",*environ);
           for(i=0; environ[i]; i++)
              printf("%s\n", environ[i]);
        }
}
```

You'll notice in the child process that we first change the *environ* to point to the new SYMBOL TABLE. After printing the values we once more make *environ* point to its original location - which is also what *temp* is pointing to. The next *for* loop then prints the values from the original environment block.

The 'exec( )' Called Through A 'fork( )'

We may want to use the *exec( )* function without killing the main process. In that case we would need to resort to forking. This would result in a child process through which the *exec( )* function could be called. This call would result in the child process being replaced. But the parent process would still be in memory and therefore executed once it gets the time slice. The combination of *exec( )* and *fork( )* provides a very powerful tool.

PROGRAM 84

```
main( )
{
   int pid ;
   pid = fork( ) ;
   if(pid == 0)
   {
      printf("exec starts\n");
      execl("/bin/ls","ls","-l",(char *)0);
      printf("Execl did not work\n");
   }
   else
   {
      wait(0) ;
      printf("Parent : ls is completed in child\n");
   }
}
```

Here we create a child process in which a call to the *execl( )* function is made. This gives control to the ls shell program, which gives a directory listing. However, once that is over, control is not handed back to the child process (which has anyway been replaced in memory by the ls program - now ls is the child process).

The parent process, which has been in a *wait( )* state so far, is now activated. And as a result we see the line Parent : ls is completed in child on screen.

So where could we use this concept of using the *exec( )* in a forked child process ? There are a number of places. Let's take some of them here.

To start with, let's understand how the shell works. The shell, as we know, is a process running in the background. When a call is made to it, it (the shell) creates a child process through a call to the *fork( )*. It is from this child process that an *exec( )* call runs the commands we specify.

Let's take an example. Suppose at the UNIX prompt we said ls -l. What would happen? The shell, which has been waiting patiently for us to key in some command, will call a function that looks like this:

PROGRAM 85

```
#include <time.h>
main(argc,argv)
int argc;
char *argv[ ];
{
   int pid;
   if((pid=fork( ))==0)
   {
      execvp(argv[1],&argv[1]);
      perror(" program failed");
   }
   else
   {
      wait(0);
   }
}
```

Compile this program and run it by keying in a.out ls -l.

In this function a *fork( )* is executed in the child process and a call to one of the members of the *exec( )* family is made. In our case we use *execvp( )*. This function requires two parameters: the program to run -- in this case ls as signified by *argv[1]* -- and the pointer to the arguments, ie. ls -l, as signified by *&argv[1]*.

So, we'd get the directory listing, after which we will be returned to the shell. In this way we could run any program, from which it is imperative to return to the shell.

So that's what the shell does. But where can we use it? Well, if we wanted to find out how much time one process was taking to run, using the shell would be an ideal way to find out. All we need to do is get the time before the *fork( )* takes place. Run the command we want through the child process while the parent is waiting. And when the command is over and the parent process wakes up, note the time again. The difference between the two times will give us an approximate idea of the time taken.

PROGRAM 86

```
#include <time.h>
main(argc,argv)
int argc;
char *argv[ ];
{
   int pid;
   long a,b;
   time(&a);
   if((pid=fork( ))==0)
   {
      execvp(argv[1],&argv[1]);
      perror(" program failed");
   }
   else
   {
      wait((char*)0);
      time(&b);
      printf(" time taken : %ld seconds \n",(b-a));
   }
}
```

So, with which command or program do we check the program? The ls -l command has been used once too often. Why not try VI or whatever editor you're using?

Run the program in the following manner: a.out vi test. This gets you the VI editor. Wait for some time and then exit. Before you returned to the UNIX prompt you'll see the time you spent in VI.

From the one track attitude of DOS to the broader perspective of UNIX - we have a traveled a long way. We have exposed UNIX's true colors - its chameleon like ability to switch roles so effcrtlessly. From one task to another and another and another, all without pausing to catch its breath or blowing its trumpet.

Versatility - that's what UNIX is all about. And while we have explored one face of UNIX a lot is yet hidden. Though we have been able to use UNIX's versatility we still haven't reached out to peoples and worlds beyond us. Oysters we have remained.

UNIX : The Multi-User Operating System

Why do we have civilization ? Because no man is an island. Because man is a social animal. Because man is a thinking animal. Because man likes to talk. Because man likes to listen. Because man likes to relate. Because man is afraid of himself.

Whatever be the reason the world has "progressed" because of this need in man to have and maintain relationships around him.

Although the writing and coding for this book has been fun, it has also been educative and interesting. Discussing, arguing, analyzing, exchanging ideas and of course arriving at compromises - this to us was more what the book was all about. A cementing of relationships.

And as we started working on UNIX the sense of involvement reached a new high, bonds were strengthened and the spirit of working together towards a common goal became more meaningful.

For UNIX is more than just a multi-tasking OS. It also has the facility to enable many users to access the machine it is housed in at one time. And not just access the machine at the same time but also interact with each other. That's what relationships are all about anyway.

But while many users are allowed to access it there is no guarantee that UNIX will respond in a given amount of time. Much like human beings, isn't it ?

Booting Up

To really understand how UNIX is able to take care of different users simultaneously we need to start at the beginning. And the beginning as with any other Operating System is always the switching on of the computer. And it is the special steps that UNIX takes that will give us an insight into its ability to work with simultaneous users.

The process that takes place when we switch on the computer is known as "booting".

The first thing that happens is that the file unix residing in the root directory is loaded into memory. This file is also known as the kernel when in memory. And is the very center of UNIX. It does all low level jobs like controlling processes and hardware devices, as well as keeps track of files and scheduling processes. Which is why it's also called SCHEDULER. All other normal OS functions are taken care of by UTILITY programs that have been coded by not just the UNIX development team but a number of third parties too.

These UTILITIES of course finally talk to the kernel. This communication is called SYSTEM CALL INTERFACE.

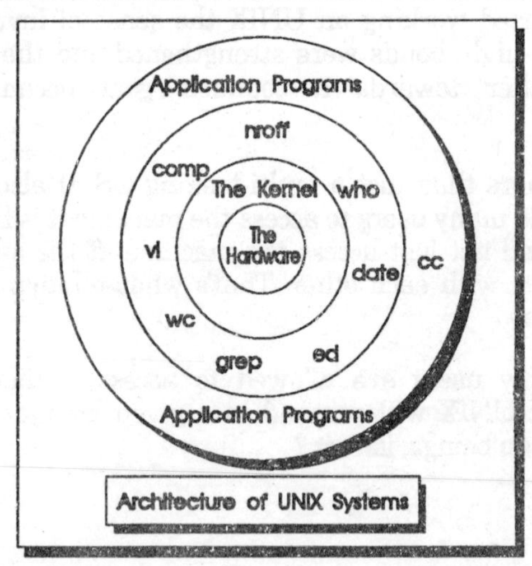

DIAGRAM 2.1

Once the kernel is loaded into memory, it proceeds to initialize various data structures like the PROCESS TABLE that we've explored in the previous chapter. The kernel is also a process and lasts as long as the microprocessor is not halted. It has a PID of 0.

The kernel then creates various processes that ultimately allows us to login. The first one is the INIT process. This is a program stored in a file called /etc/init. Its main purpose is to allow the creation of other processes. It is given a PID of 1 and is active till the kernel is alive.

The difference between INIT and the kernel is that while the kernel can access CPU features like memory management and time-slices, as well as hardware devices directly, INIT can't.

Now that INIT is active it proceeds to create a process that will allow us to login to the UNIX system. INIT decides which of the many terminals that may be attached can be used to login. The data for ascertaining which terminals can be used for login is stored in the file /etc/inittab.

This file tells UNIX which program to execute. This program is normally getty. getty in turn reads data from the /etc/gettydefs file, displays the login : prompt on screen and waits for input. After which it spawns the login program, which takes the login name we have keyed in as a parameter.

This parameter is then looked up in the /etc/passwd file. If a match is found it takes us to the home directory, executes the shell and we get the shell prompt, usually a $ sign.

We opened the /etc/inittab in our wordprocessor after running the su command, which made us a super-user. For a super-user there are no permissions or rights (like whether some file in the computer is accessible by us or not) involved. This is what the file looked like:

```
bchk::bootwait:/etc/bcheckrc </dev/console >/dev/console 2>&1
brc::bootwait:/etc/brc 1> /dev/console 2>&1
mt:23:bootwait:/etc/brc </dev/console >/dev/console 2>&1
```

```
is:2:initdefault:
r0:0:wait:/etc/rc0 1> /dev/console 2>&1 </dev/console
r1:1:wait:/etc/rc1 1> /dev/console 2>&1 </dev/console
r2:23:wait:/etc/rc2 1> /dev/console 2>&1 </dev/console
r3:3:wait:/etc/rc3 1> /dev/console 2>&1 </dev/console
co:12345:respawn:/etc/getty console console
c1:23:respawn:/etc/getty cons1 virtcon1
c2:23:respawn:/etc/getty cons2 virtcon2
c3:23:respawn:/etc/getty cons3 virtcon3
m0:23:off:/etc/getty ttym00 1200 # For modem on COM1 - incoming
only
M0:23:off:/etc/getty ttyM00 1200 # For modem on COM1 - incoming
& outgoing
00:23:respawn:/etc/getty tty00 9600 # Standard serial getty for COM1
01:23:respawn:/etc/getty tty01 9600 # Standard serial getty for COM2
02:23:orf:/etc/getty tty02 9600 # Gettys for tty02-09 for multi-port cards
03:23:off:/etc/getty tty03 9600
04:23:off:/etc/getty tty04 9600
05:23:off:/etc/getty tty05 9600
06:23:off:/etc/getty tty06 9600
07:23:off:/etc/getty tty07 9600
08:23:off:/etc/getty tty08 9600
09:23:off:/etc/getty tty09 9600
```

Notice the two lines starting with 00 and 01. They signify that we have two terminals attached to our serial ports COM1 and COM2. And these two nodes or terminals have the number tty00 and tty01. From tty02 downwards, the terminals have not been attached. Further notice the word getty just before the terminal number. This is the next program that is spawned by init. The respawn means that when a logout or a CTRL D is executed, the getty program is to get re- executed. That's why we get the login message again whenever we do a CTRL D.

In UNIX, besides the terminals, we have a console which is the terminal attached to the main UNIX box. In our case it is c0. But over and above this genuine console we also have what are known as virtual consoles. Notice the lines beginning with c1,c2,c3.

What do we mean by virtual consoles? Assume that your machine had, save for the console, no other terminals attached to it and that you were running a rather large program on this console. What if, in the middle you wanted to kill this process?

Simple. All you need to do is kill the process from another terminal. But we don't have any other terminals. Ha ! Problem. That's where the concept of virtual consoles comes in. All we need to do is press the Alt-F2 key to move on to the first virtual console. From here we can issue a kill process command. An Alt-F1 will now take us back to the main console. Similarly we can move to the other two virtual consoles by pressing Alt-F3 or Alt-F4 keys. A virtual console is like a terminal except that it has no physical manifestation.

We decided to try an experiment. We changed the getty specified towards the end of the 00 to login. Why ? We said that in any case since getty itself calls login, why not do it ourselves. Guess what happened? We got an error message at the console.

"INIT : Command is re-spawning too rapidly. Check for possible errors. id: 00 "/etc/login tty00 9600 # Standard Serial getty for COM1"

Why did we get this re-spawning error?

Under normal circumstances the INIT, after reading data from the inittab file proceeds to create the getty process by forking a child process through which the getty program is *exec( )*ed. This getty program in turn reads the data from a file called /etc/gettydefs, which tells it to display the login : message and waits for us to enter some word and press enter.

If the user has a password, this is prompted for . getty then *exec( )*s the login process. Which means that the login name we keyed in is looked up in the /etc/passwd file. If this name is found, the shell is executed and we get the prompt.

But before executing the shell, login checks the user ID and group ID attached to this login name (these details are also got from the /etc/passwd file). It then sets the user and group ID of the shell to these ID's. Suppose it did not do this what would happen? The user, assume that it was us would be logged in as a super-user.

However, in the above case we changed the word getty to login. This resulted in the login process being created and executed directly. There was no question of it getting a parameter since it is the getty program that takes in our input.

As a result, as soon as the login was spawned, finding no entry in the /etc/passwd file, it died and control was once more handed to the init process. The init process again proceeds to read the data from the inittab file which tells it to *fork()* a child process through which to *exec( )* login. login, of course, is not passed any parameter and the cycle goes on....

After making this change there was no way we could login. We thought we had lost the terminal. What did we do? Well, we first thought of calling the engineer. But we said why not experiment a little more.

So we reopened the inittab file at the console and changed the login to getty once more. However a ps -el yet did not show our terminal.

When in doubt, reboot. That's exactly what we did. And hey presto, we got our terminal back. With so much luck on our side we decided to try one more experiment.

We opened the file /etc/gettydefs and changed the #login related to our terminal to #enter your login name. We can find out which terminal is ours by checking the baud rate. Key in the command stty at the prompt and it will show you the baud rate. In our case, the baud rate was 9600 and this was one of the entries in the gettydefs file, too. (You can view this file using the editor). Our terminal entry looked liked this:

```
9600# B9600 OPOST ONLCR TAB3 BRKINT IGNPAR ISTRIP IXON IXANY
ECHO
ECHOE ECHOK ICANON ISIG CS8 CREAD # B9600 OPOST ONLCR
TAB3 BRKINT
```

```
IGNPAR ISTRIP IXON IXANY ECHO ECHOE ECHOK ICANON ISIG CS8
CREAD
#login : #4800
```

Check the 9600#. It's the same baud rate we got through the stty command. The login towards the end is the message we see on screen.

This change, fortunately, did not result in any problem. Instead of the login message we just got the enter your login message. Of course, after we keyed in the login name, getty spawned the actual login process. Which in turn checked what we had keyed into the passwd file. That's how we got to the prompt.

The login name we specify enables UNIX to know which user it is communicating with. And this, it finds out through a User ID which corresponds to the login name. This login name and its corresponding user ID plus a password, where specified, are stored in a file called /etc/passwd.

Most of the time a login name has a password connected with it. As soon as the login name is keyed in the password is prompted for. What we key in is not echoed on screen. A check is made in the /etc/passwd to ensure that the password is legitimate. This password is stored in an encrypted form in the /etc/passwd file.

This file looks something like this:

```
root::0:3:0000-Admin(0000):/:/bin/sh
guest::100:1:guest:/usr/guest:
vmci:defghtAL:101:1:vmci:/usr/vmci:
```

Each line in the file describes a different user. And contains the following information: user name, encrypted password, user ID, group ID, two unused fields, user's full name and other personal data, home directory and the name of the program to execute when user logs in, which is normally the shell (in that order). The colons act as separators.

UNIX Copyright

If the password is correct, the login process *exec( )*s the program that is specified in the /etc/passwd file. This is normally the C shell or the Bourne shell. But before we are brought to the UNIX prompt, the UNIX version number plus the copyright and trademark are displayed on screen. This information can also be retrieved by using the *uname( )* system call.

PROGRAM 87

```
#include <sys/utsname.h>
#include <stdio.h>

main()
{
    struct utsname name;
    uname(&name);
    printf("Current sys name : %s\n", name.sysname);
    printf("node name : %s\n", name.nodename);
    printf("release : %s\n", name.release);
    printf("version : %s\n", name.version);
    printf("Hardware used : %s\n", name.machine);
}
```

UNIX has, in the header file utsname.h, a predefined structure called *utsname*. We declare a structure called *name* to look like this predefined structure.

The function *uname( )* is passed the location where this structure begins in memory, i.e. a pointer to the structure. The function then proceeds to fill the structure with the relevant information.

Finally, the members of this structure are printed. And we're back at the shell. Can you guess what the output of this program will be if run from different terminals?

Note: Bet you're wondering what happens if two different users login under the same login name and password. Nothing. They can both work simultaneously because the two terminals are different.

What is the shell?

It is merely an interface between the user and the kernel. Much like the COMMAND.COM file in DOS.

User Details

Remember, we said above that the /etc/passwd file contains data about a user, his ID, password, etc. Well, we can write a program to print these details on screen. All we need to do is fill a predefined structure with the details from the passwd file.

PROGRAM 88

```
#include <pwd.h>

main( )
{
   struct passwd *pass;
   int uid;
   uid = getuid( );
   pass = getpwuid(uid );
   printf("Login name : %s\n", pass->pw_name);
   printf("Encrypted Password : %s\n", pass->pw_passwd);
   printf("User ID : %d\n", pass->pw_uid);
   printf("Group ID : %d\n", pass->pw_gid);
   printf("Password Age : %s\n", pass->pw_age);
   printf("Comment : %s\n", pass->pw_comment);
   printf("Miscellany : %s\n", pass->pw_gecos);
   printf("Login dir : %s\n", pass->pw_dir);
   printf("Shell : %s\n", pass->pw_shell);
}
```

We define a pointer to a structure *pass* and an integer *uid*. *pass* is assigned the location in the /etc/passwd file where the specific user details are stored. The function *getpwuid( )* is passed the user ID, which is the value returned by the *getuid( )* function.

Assume that we'd logged in as UNIX. The user ID related to it, say 100, would have been returned by the *getuid( )* function and passed to the *getpwuid( )* function. Which in turn returns the location in memory where this entry is stored.

The *printf( )*s print the various details.

We can also use another function to read an entry from the passwd file: the *getlogin( )* function.

```
PROGRAM 89
#include <pwd.h>
main( )
{
    struct passwd *pass;
    pass = getpwnam( getlogin( ) );
    printf("Login name : %s\n", pass->pw_name);
    printf("Encrypted Password : %s\n", pass->pw_passwd);
    printf("User ID : %d\n", pass->pw_uid);
    printf("Group ID : %d\n", pass->pw_gid);
    printf("Password Age : %s\n", pass->pw_age);
    printf("Comment : %s\n", pass->pw_comment);
    printf("Miscellany : %s\n", pass->pw_gecos);
    printf("Login dir : %s\n", pass->pw_dir);
    printf("Shell : %s\n", pass->pw_shell);
}
```

The *getlogin( )* function returns a pointer to a string containing the login name. This pointer is passed to the *getpwnam( )* function, which returns the location where the entry is stored in memory. It works in basically the same way as the *getpwuid( )* function.

So far, we have got details of only one user, i.e. us. What if we want the details of the entire passwd file. We could open the file directly. But we could also write a program.

In this program we would go through each line and read all the characters that come before the first colon because that is where the user name comes. These characters would be stored in an array. The address where this array is stored in memory is then passed to the *getpwnam( )* which returns the entry in the passwd file.

PROGRAM 90

```
#include <pwd.h>
#include <stdio.h>

main( )
{
   struct passwd *pass;
   FILE *fp ;
   int i = 0 ,ch;
   char name[10];
   fp = fopen("/etc/passwd","r");
   while( (ch = fgetc(fp)) != EOF)
   {
      memset(name,'\0',10);
      i = 0 ;
      while(ch != ':')
      {
         name[i] = ch ;
         i++;
         ch = fgetc(fp) ;
      }
      while( (ch = fgetc(fp)) != 0x0a);

      pass = getpwnam( name);

      printf("Login name : %s\n", pass->pw_name);
      printf("Encrypted Password : %s\n", pass->pw_passwd);
      printf("User ID : %d\n", pass->pw_uid);
      printf("Group ID : %d\n", pass->pw_gid);
      printf("Password Age : %s\n", pass->pw_age);
      printf("Comment : %s\n", pass->pw_comment);
      printf("Miscellany : %s\n", pass->pw_gecos);
      printf("Login dir : %s\n", pass->pw_dir);
      printf("Shell : %s\n", pass->pw_shell);
      printf("\n\n\n");
      getchar( );
   }
}
```

Here, we define a pointer to a structure called *pass*. To the pointer pointing to a data structure called FILE we then assign the address returned by *fopen( )*.

Now the main loop begins. This executes till the end of file is reached.

The *memset( )* function assigns all the elements of the array *name* with a *\0*. This is a string terminator. Why do we do this? Because a login name can be any number of characters between 1 and 8. By putting a *\0* we make sure that the string is terminated at some point or the other.

The next *while* loop keeps filling the array name with characters till a colon is reached. This colon will signify that the end of the user name has been reached.

The final *while* loop reads each character till end of line is reached. As a result we will now be on the next user name. This we are doing since we want to know all the users.

Once this is done the *getpwnam( )* function is passed the starting address of array *name*. The pointer returned by this function relates to the entry for this login name in the passwd file. The *printf( )*s finally print these members from the structure.

This entire program works till end of file is reached, at which point it ends.

Group ID

There are two IDs associated with each user: his user ID and a group ID. An user ID is pretty straightforward. It identifies each user individually. A group ID does not identify each user individually but considers him as belonging to a clique. There may be several users who are members of one group, by which they have access to files owned by that group. But a user cannot be a member of more than one group.

This is much like a club that has a number of members. All have access to the same facilities. Any person who is not a member cannot avail of the facilities of the club.

The group ID has other details linked to it. Like the group name, the password and names of all other members. These details are stored in a file called group. This file in our computer looked like this:

```
root::0:root
other::1:
bin::2:root,bin,daemon
sys::3:root,bin,sys,adm
adm::4:root,adm,daemon
mail::6:root
rje::8:rje,shqer
daemon::12:root,daemon
sysviz:NONE:13:sysviz
```

Let's write a program to access the details from this file. We won't get all the entries. Only those corresponding to our ID number.

PROGRAM 91

```
#include <grp.h>

main()
{
   int i;
   struct group *grp;
   grp = getgrgid( getgid( ) );
   printf("Group Name : %s\n", grp->gr_name);
   printf("Group Password : %s\n", grp->gr_passwd);
   printf("Group ID : %d\n", grp->gr_gid);
   printf("Group Members : ");
   for(i=0;grp->gr_mem[i];i++)
      printf("\n : %s", grp->gr_mem[i]);
}
```

We define a pointer to a structure that looks like group. This structure is defined in the header file grp.h.

The *getgid( )* function returns the numeric ID of the group we belong to. This ID is passed as a parameter to the function *getgrgid( )* which returns the starting location of our entry in the group file. The group file consists of four colon-separated bits of information: the name, password, ID and all the members of the group. The last data, members, is a pointer to a pointer which points to an array of characters.

The *printf( )*s finally prints all these data items.

There is a function which we can use to print all the entries in the group file. While the above program just gave us the entry in the group file connected with us, the program below gives us all the entries. This enables us to find out which other groups there are, and the members of these groups.

PROGRAM 92

```
#include <grp.h>
#include <stdio.h>

main( )
{
    int i;
    struct group *grp;
    while((grp = getgrent( )) != NULL)
    {
        printf("\n");
        printf("Group Name : %s\n", grp->gr_name);
        printf("Group Password : %s\n", grp->gr_passwd);
        printf("Group ID : %d\n", grp->gr_gid);
        for(i=0;grp->gr_mem[i];i++)
            printf("\n : %s", grp->gr_mem[i]);
    }
}
```

The *while* loop, used in conjunction with the *getgrent( )* function, is used to traverse the entire file till the end is reached. The function *getgrent( )* returns a pointer to a structure that looks like *group*. This pointer is assigned to the pointer variable *grp* which itself points to a structure that looks like *group*.

And, of course, the *printf( )* prints all the details.

All Those Currently Logged In, Please Stand Up

While both the passwd and group file give us information as to the various users and which groups they belong to, they don't tell us who is currently logged in. This information is available in two ways: by using the who command at the UNIX prompt and through writing a program to access this information (which is stored in the utmp file). This file consists of three members: terminal name, user ID and time logged in.

PROGRAM 93

```
#include <sys/types.h>
#include <stdio.h>
#include <utmp.h>
#include <pwd.h>
#define UTMP "/etc/utmp"
#define NAMELEN 8

main( )
{
   FILE *fp;
   struct utmp u;
   struct passwd *p;
   char temp[NAMELEN + 1];
   fp = fopen(UTMP,"r");
   while(!feof(fp))
   {
      fread(&u,sizeof(u),1,fp);
      if (u.ut_name == NULL)
         continue;

      strncpy(temp,u.ut_name,NAMELEN);
      p = getpwnam(temp);

      if (p == NULL)
         continue;

      printf("%-10.8s %-10.8s %-30.30s %s\n",
```

```
            u.ut_name,u.ut_line,p->pw_gecos,ctime(&u.ut_time));
    }
    fclose(fp);
    exit(0);
}
```

One of the header files is utmp.h, in which the structure of file *utmp* is defined.

We open the file utmp in read mode and start a *while* loop that executes till the end of file is reached. In this loop, we first read one entry from the utmp file into the structure *u* which we have defined above. This structure looks like the *utmp* structure defined in the utmp.h header file.

Next, we check to see if the member *ut_name* has some name assigned to it. This name will be assigned it when we use the *fread( )* function. If the member *ut_name* doesn't have a name attached to it, which means a certain user for whom that entry is reserved has not logged in, we go back to the beginning of the *while* loop and read the next entry. If that user has logged in, we proceed further down.

The user name in the member *ut_name* is string copied to the array *temp*. The starting address of this array is then passed to the *getpwnam( )* function which returns a pointer to a structure that looks like the *passwd* structure. This value is assigned to the pointer variable *p* which is a pointer to a structure that looks like *passwd*. If this entry does not exist in the *passwd* file, we get a NULL and the continue takes us back to the top of the *while* loop. Else we proceed.

In which case the *printf( )* prints *ut_name* and *ut_line* (both of which are members of the structure *u*), followed by *pw_gecos* (is a member of the structure that pointer *p* points to), which is the user's full name and other personal data.

The last data item it prints is *ut_time*, a member of the structure *u*. The location where this item is stored is passed to the *ctime( )*

function, which converts it to ASCII format. Thus we get on screen a string value in terms of month, date and time.

Time

One of the finest examples of human thought is the concept of time. If you really think about it there is nothing like time. Or what we know as a day is quite different on other planets. But can you imagine what a confused existence we would lead had time not been introduced. How would we tell someone to meet us on a particular day at a particular time? Thank God for time and the finiteness it brings to our lives. So what if its every tick means a moment of our life gone. We all have to die some day, time or no time.

One of the first clocks built was based on the sun. It was called the sun dial. Depending on the shadow cast by the dial, we figured out how far the day had progressed. But how about the night, or what if the sun didn't show itself for months, like in the polar regions? We have come a long way since then, what with clocks that work on batteries and some that even work on the pulse.

Most computers too,. from the AT onwards, have a clock. This clock is known as a Real Time Clock. It works on batteries, and from it we can tell what the day and the time is.

UNIX provides us with some functions that we can use to print the time, day, month and year on screen.

PROGRAM 94

```
#include <time.h>
#include <sys/types.h>

main( )
{
    long t;
    time(&t);
    printf("Time %ld\n", t);
}
```

The function *time( )* assigns to the address of the variable passed to it, the clock time as a number. But this doesn't make much sense to us. To convert this number to a time form we understand, we need to use another function: *localtime( ).*

PROGRAM 95

```
#include <time.h>
#include <sys/types.h>

main()
{
    long t;
    struct tm *tp;
    time(&t);
    tp = localtime(&t);
    printf("Time %d:%d:%d\n", tp->tm_hour, tp->tm_min, tp->tm_sec);
}
```

We define a pointer to a structure that looks like *tm.* This prototype structure is defined in the header file time.h.

The *time( )* function is passed the location where variable *t* begins in memory. This function places the time in long integer form in this variable.

Next, the function *localtime( )* is passed the starting address of this variable *t.* It structures the value in this variable in a manner that fits the structure that *tp* points to. And returns the time as per the local time zone.

The *printf( )* prints the values from three members of this structure: the hour, minutes and seconds.

However, this structure has more members than just the hours, minutes and seconds. It can even show the month and year for example.

PROGRAM 96

```
#include <time.h>
#include <sys/types.h>
```

```
main( )
{
   long t;
   struct tm *tp;
   time(&t);
   tp = localtime(&t);
   printf("\nTime : %d:%d:%d\n", tp->tm_hour, tp->m_min,
         tp->tm_sec);
   printf("Day of month : %d\n", tp->tm_mday);
   printf("Month : %d\n", tp->tm_mon+1);
   printf("Year : %d\n", tp->tm_year+1900);
   printf("Day of the Week : %d\n", tp->tm_wday+1);
   printf("Day of the Year : %d\n", tp->tm_yday+1);
}
```

Here, we essentially do the same thing as in the last program, with the exception of printing five more members of the structure.

We add a 1 to the month, day of the week and year because all three values start from 0.

The world is divided into different time zones. At any given time, while one part of the globe experiences day, the other part experiences night. The central point is GMT or Greenwich Mean Time, situated in England. Countries to the West of Greenwich see the sun some time later than countries to its East. This is why India is approximately 12 hours ahead of the USA.

UNIX was born on January 1, 1970, at the stroke of midnight GMT. Since then its internal clock has been ticking every second. This GMT can be obtained from the structure *tm* by using the *gmtime( )* system call.

PROGRAM 97

```
#include <time.h>
#include <sys/types.h>

main( )
{
   long t;
```

```
    struct tm *tp;
    time(&t);
    tp = gmtime(&t);
    printf("\nTime: %d:%d:%d\n", tp->tm_hour,
          tp-> m_min, tp-> tm_sec);
    printf("Day of month : %d\n", tp->tm_mday);
    printf("Month : %d\n", tp->tm_mon+1);
    printf("Year : %d\n", tp->tm_year+1900);
    printf("Day of the Week : %d\n", tp->tm_wday+1);
    printf("Day of the Year : %d\n", tp->tm_yday+1);
}
```

Instead of the *localtime( )* function, we use *gmtime( )*. This function is passed the starting location of the variable *t* and returns the time as per GMT. Notice that this time is different from that displayed by the last program.

What if we want to see the time in ASCII format. That is day, month, date, time and year.For this we need to use the *asctime( )* system call.

PROGRAM 98

```
#include <time.h>
#include <sys/types.h>

main()
{
    long t;
    struct tm *tp;
    char *ts;
    time(&t);
    tp = localtime(&t);
    ts = asctime(tp);
    printf("Time is : %s\n",ts);
}
```

We assign the pointer to a structure *tp*, that looks like *tm*, the address returned by the *localtime( )* function. We then pass this address to the *asctime( )* system call. This converts the address to a string and returns a pointer to it. The string is then printed.

And time runs on (or out, whatever is your state of mind) while we move to other less esoteric and abstract topics.

Process Group ID

Indian culture has always maintained a need for strong family ties. We have many generations living together in the same house. Grandfather, father and son, sometimes even a great grandfather.

But slowly, as western values seep through, a metamorphosis is taking place. Increasingly more young married and non-married people opt to live on their own, away from their parents. And very few come back to the secure fold they have left.

It isn't just family ties that are beginning to fall apart, but even ties based on caste and religion. This is especially true in what are known as cosmopolitan centers. New worlds are being created as people move away from the familiar. A sure sign that the human race is constantly evolving, though the cynics may say otherwise.

In UNIX so far, we have seen processes that are always attached to their parents. For example:

PROGRAM 99

```
main( )
{
    int i,pid;
    pid = fork( );
    if (pid == 0)
        for(i = 0; i<= 10000; i++);
    else
        for(i = 0; i<= 10000; i++);
}
```

When we run this program we get two processes in memory, both of which run till their respective *i*s reach the 10000 limit. During the entire operation the child will always belong to the parent, which in turn will always belong to the UNIX shell, which in turn belongs to init, the father of all processes.

But if we want this child to move away from the shadows of his parent process we can get him to do so. The child in that case would be a leader in his own right.

Besides a PID, a process also has a GPID (Group Process ID). This GPID is inherited by a child from its parent. Basically all processes created by us belong to the group of which the shell is the leader.

PROGRAM 100

```
main( )
{
   printf("The Process Group ID is %d\n",getpgrp( ));
   printf("My Process ID is %d\n",getpid( ));
   printf("The Process ID of Parent is %d\n", getppid( ));
}
```

The *getpgrp( )* function will give the ID of the Group the process belongs to. This will be the same as the value returned by the *getppid( )* function. Both mean the shell.

A child process created by our program will also get the same Group ID as its parent. A matter of inheritance.

PROGRAM 101

```
main( )
{
   int pid;
   pid = fork( );

   if (pid == 0)
   {
      printf("The Process Group ID is %d\n",getpgrp( ));
      printf("My (child) Process ID is %d\n",getpid( ));
      printf("The Process ID of Parent is %d\n", getppid( ));
   }
   else
   {
```

```
        printf("The Process Group ID is %d\n",getpgrp());
        printf("My (parent) Process ID is %d\n",getpid());
        printf("The Process ID of Parent is %d\n", getppid());
    }
}
```

Let's see what happens when we run this program. The first thing it does is creates a child process. Now we have two processes, parent and child. Depending on the one UNIX gives the time-slice to, the *if* or *else* condition is evaluated.

If it is the child process that is given the time slice then the statements within the *if* condition are executed. The *getpgrp( )* function will return a value that matches the Group the parent process belongs to -- in this case the shell. The *getpid( )* function will return the child processes PID. And the *getppid( )* will return its parent's PID.

In the *else* part the *getpgrp( )* function will return the Group ID which is the same as the one returned to the child process -- that of the shell . The *getpid( )* function will return the PID of this (parent) process. And the *getppid( )* function will return the PID of the parent's parent, i.e. the child's grandfather. In this case it is the shell itself. This PPID is also the same value as returned by the *getpgrp( )* function.

From this it is clear that a parent and its child belong to the same Group.

Although the starting Group leader is the shell, it needn't always remain so. A process can initiate its own group if it so desires. From then on all child processes created by it will be considered belonging to its group and not the shell.

PROGRAM 102

```
main()
{
    printf("The Group PID is %d\n", getpgrp());
    printf("The PID is %d\n", getpid());
    printf("The Parents PID is %d\n", getppid());
```

```
    setpgrp();
    printf("After the setgroup\n");
    printf("The Group PID is %d\n", getprgp());
    printf("The PID is %d\n", getpid());
    printf("The Parents PID is %d\n", getppid());
}
```

The value returned by the first *getpgrp()* will match that of the shell. After the *setpgrp()* function performs, the value returned by the second *getpgrp()* will be different. It will now be the same as the PID of the process itself. It is the *setpgrp()* function that disassociates a process from its parents group. After the disassociation, the process is given a Group ID that matches its PID. Now this process has become the Group leader.

So far we have understood the *setpgrp()* to disassociate a process from its parent and set up a group of its own. But it does more than that. It also disassociates the process from the terminal that it was executed from. So, from now onwards, whatever we do at this terminal will not be signaled to this process.

For example, suppose we pressed a CTRL-D, which, as we have seen earlier, terminates a process running in the background, the process which has now become its own group leader won't terminate. Since this CTRL D only effects those background processes that are linked to the terminal it (the CTRL D) is done on. And this process as we know is not associated with this terminal any more.

Let's write two programs that will explain this better. The first program will be an ordinary program that will run in the background. This, of course, will be terminated the moment a CTRL D is pressed.

PROGRAM 103

```
main()
{
    for(;;);
}
```

Run this program by suffixing it with an ampersand to make it a background process. Once the UNIX prompt is displayed type ps -el. This will show us an entry related to this process in the Process Table. Now press CTRL and D simultaneously and you will get the login message. Login once again and key in ps -el. And presto, the entry disappears from the Process Table.

But if we'd added a *setpgrp( )* just before the *for* loop, this process would have been disassociated from both its parent (the shell) and the terminal.

PROGRAM 104

```
main( )
{
   setpgrp( );
   for(; ;);
}
```

Run this program as a background process, i.e. by suffixing it with an ampersand. Run the ps -el command once you are back at the prompt. And you will see an entry for this process in the Process Table. Now do a CTRL D, which will give us the login message on screen. Login again and run the ps -el command. You'll find that the entry for the process will yet be a part of the Process Table.

So why would we want to run a process in this manner, i.e. not connected to any terminal and in a group by itself? Suppose we were trying to run a batch process that would take a number of hours to complete and we wanted to make sure this carried on even when we went home. By disassociating the process from the terminal we can ensure that the process will continue to do its work even if the terminal has been switched OFF.

This kind of thing is possible because while individual terminals are put OFF when not in use, the main machine or console is always kept ON.

Another way of doing this (disassociating a process from the terminal) is by using the nohup system call. This ensures that the program this system call is used on becomes blind to all signals like the CTRL D.

PROGRAM 105

```
main()
{
    for(; ;);
}
```

Compile this program and run it with the nohup system call:

```
nohup a.out&
```

Run the ps -el to see the entry for this process in the Process Table. Then do a CTRL D and login again. Run the ps -el command and you will see the process in the Process Table.

There is one difference here. If you notice the listing of the contents of the Process Table related to our process, you will see that the terminal we have run this program from still exists as an entry.

Another Way Of Implementing A Background Process

So far we have always said that to run a process in the background we have to suffix it with an ampersand. But there is another way of implementing a background process.

All we need to do is initiate a process that forks a child and kill the parent before the child terminates.

PROGRAM 106

```
main()
{
    int pid;
    pid = fork( );
    if (pid == 0)
        for( ; ;);
}
```

When you are returned to the prompt, run the ps -el **command** and you'll see the entry for this process in the Process Table. A CTRL D will, of course, kill this process.

Why, Background Processes

There is a comic strip character called Hagar the Horrible. Whenever Hagar's wife wants him to buy something from the market, she ties a piece of string around his finger as a reminder.

Hey, can't we use background processes as **reminders** ? For example suppose after a specified number of **seconds we want** a message displayed on screen.

PROGRAM 107

```
main(argc,argv)
int argc;
char *argv[ ];
{
   int i,pid;
   pid = fork( );
   if ( pid == 0)
   {
     i=atoi(argv[2]);
     sleep(i);
     printf("%s\n",argv[1]);
   }
}
```

We don't need to run this program by suffixing it with an ampersand. Killing the parent before the child terminates ensures that it becomes a background process.

We have to pass two parameters to the program: **the message** and the time period after which we want it **displayed**. For example:

```
a.out "Tea is Ready" 4
```

Another use of a background process would be if we had to copy a large file. The file being large would take some time to copy. And there isn't any point in blocking our work while this process is going on.

```
PROGRAM 108
#include <stdio.h>

main()
{
   FILE *fpi,*fpo;
   int ch,pid;
   pid = fork( );
   if ( pid == 0)
   {
      fpi=fopen("bigfile","r");
      fpo=fopen("outfile","w");
      while((ch = getc(fpi)) != EOF)
           putc(ch,fpo);
      printf("\7\7\7\7\7\7\7\7\7\7\7\7");
   }
}
```

In the child process, we transfer the contents of one file to another, byte by byte. At the end of the process we get to hear beeps. That's what the *printf( )* does.

Most supervisors are nosy by nature. Guess it is learnt on the job. The next program is dedicated to the nosy supervisor. Every 10 seconds it will tell him the number of users logged in.

```
PROGRAM 109
main( )
{
   int pid ;
   pid = fork( );
   if ( pid == 0)
   {
      for(;;)
      {
         sleep(10);
         printf(" The number of users logged in are : ");
         system("who | wc -l");
```

```
        }
    }
}
```

The *system( )* function is passed a pointer to a string. This string in our case is the who command. When this command executes, we get the number of users logged in.

Just who displays the user's login name, the terminal the user is attached to and login date and time. The | pipe indicates that the output of who is to become the input of the wc command. The wc command counts the number of lines, words and characters of a file. When we define it as who | wc we get the number of lines, words and characters as shown by the who command. Since we only want to know the number of users logged in a -l is specified. This tells us the number of lines, which corresponds to the number of users.

A Tribute to Cuckoo's Nest

There were a group of German hackers who illegally logged into networks in the US. They were out to steal military secrets and pass them on to the Eastern bloc. This entire electronic espionage game has been written about in a book called "Cuckoo's Nest", written by the guy who tracked these hackers down.

He realized there was someone logging in with a certain password which had been discontinued but had not been deleted. This someone was then exploring the system and through it entering some army network installations.

To find out when the hacker logged in and what he did, a small program was written. This program kept checking to see if the hacker had logged in, at which moment it would be reported.

If we have a similar problem or we want to monitor someone's logging in, we too can write a program to do this.

PROGRAM 110

```
/* give name of person and program will report you as soon as he
login*/

#include <sys/types.h>
#include <stdio.h>
#include <utmp.h>
#define UTMP "/etc/utmp"

main(argc,argv)
int argc;
char *argv[ ];
{
   FILE *fp;
   struct utmp u;
   for(;;)
   {
      fp = fopen(UTMP,"r");
      while(!feof(fp))
      {
         fread(&u,sizeof(u),1,fp);
         if (u.ut_name == NULL)
            continue;
         if (strcmp(argv[1],u.ut_name) == 0)
         {
            printf("\n\7\7\7%s has login\n",argv[1]);
            exit(0);
         }
      }
      fclose(fp);
      sleep(5);
   }
}
```

Run this program by suffixing it with an ampersand so that it becomes a background process. We could have used the other method too, as shown by the last three programs. We used this because we did not want to increase the lines of code as understanding the program may have then become more difficult.

We start a *for* loop that will run continuously. In it we open the file /etc/utmp in read mode. This file contains all information about users currently logged in to the system. This file is indexed by terminal number, and if a terminal is not in use the entry will be a NULL.

The *while* loop will work till the end of file is reached. In it, we read a record from the file into the structure *u*. We then compare the value in the member *ut_name* with NULL. If it is a NULL, it means that no one has logged in from that terminal and so we go back to the beginning of the *while* loop.

Else we compare this name with that passed by us as an argument at the command line when we activated this program. This name is that of the user we want to check for. If these two names match, a message is flashed and the program terminates.

This entire procedure is repeated every five seconds till the user logs in. Whenever a user logs in, an entry is made in the /etc/utmp file. That is why we check this file every 5 seconds.

Now that we have seen what are background processes and how we can use them, keep this concept in the background as we move on to another topic.

UNIX's View Of Disks And Devices

There was a time when men were few and roamed the earth singly. In time, as life evolved men came together to live as families. Families merged to create communities. And with the advent of communities came various institutions: the barter system, social rules, councils, etc. All these created structures around which man's existence was built. And as mankind flourished, old structures died making way for the new. But the concept of structures remained. A necessary "evil" keeping man together bonded for life and saving him from an isolated existence.

Everything man has done has some organization: a structure. There is no arbitrariness, even if sometimes it may seem so.

There are always rules and laws that guide him and his work. A way of passing legacies through the ages.

And so it is with Operating Systems. They too have well-defined structures in whose boundaries only, can ideas be realized. UNIX, like all OS's, is arranged in a definite manner on disk. Like DOS, which we saw in the last chapter was organized on disk into Boot Sector, File Allocation Table and Root Directory, UNIX too has a Boot (Block) Sector, a Super Block (like the FAT) and the Data Area.

Let's take this up in more detail.

Essentially, UNIX is made up of files. In fact, every aspect of UNIX is looked at as a file. When we write some data to be displayed on screen for example, the data is actually written to a screen file and then a certain device driver in the kernel is activated. This controls the particular device, in our case the screen. And the contents of the screen file are displayed on screen. Files that relate to hardware are known as "special files".

We have one UNIVERSAL file and that is unix itself. But this file is broken up into many other smaller file systems. By default, i.e. when we install UNIX, there is one Root and two User File systems created. Normally file systems correspond to physical sections of the disk. Basically the Root File System and the many User File Systems.

These File Systems are further broken up into directories (which are also viewed by UNIX as files) and files. These directories can further have sub-directories and files giving rise to a hierarchical tree-like structure.

In DOS, we sometimes divide the disk into two logical sections C and D. Each of these logical drives has its own set of directories and files. To move from one drive to another we just need to specify the drive at the DOS prompt and press enter.

But while we are at one drive we can access a file from another drive. Now both these drives are always available by default. In

UNIX there is a slight difference. While the Root file system and the two user file systems that are created by default are loaded, access to any other file system is only possible if they are explicitly mounted. Mounting means nothing but loading them into memory. And considering that File Systems are viewed by UNIX as files, if a time comes for them to be accessed they, like any other file, have to be in memory.

For example, the floppy drive. This too is considered by UNIX as a file. Any read or write to a floppy drive is first done in a "special file", from which a transference is then done to the floppy itself. But to be able to access the floppy drive through the file connected to it, it (the file) has to be mounted, i.e. in memory.

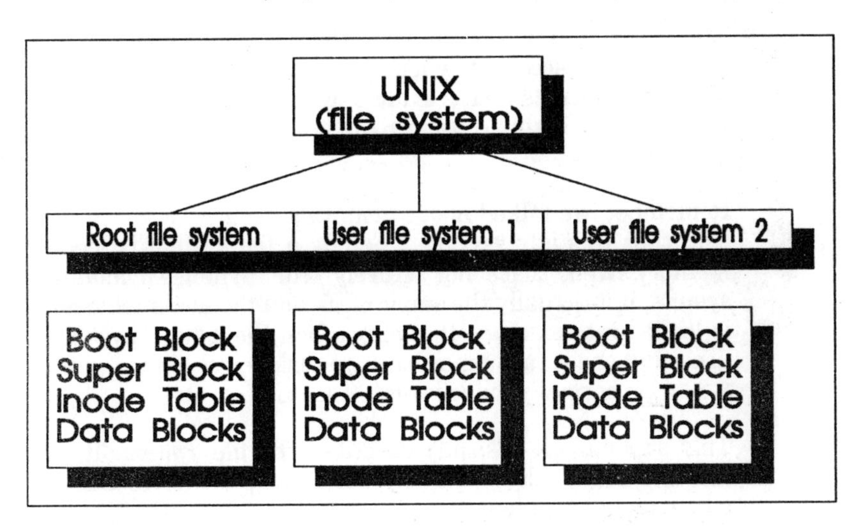

DIAGRAM 2.2

Root File System

Contains the file /unix which is loaded into memory when the computer is switched on. Also contains the root directory and the /bin, /etc, /dev and /tmp directories. In the same way the User

File systems, too, contain directories and files. Now let's see what the sub-divisions of each File System are all about:

Boot Block

Starts at logical block 0 but, physically, is wherever this disk partition actually begins. Consists of a hardware specific boot program that loads the file unix, which is also known as the kernel, at system startup time. The boot block of the user file systems will consist of the bootstrap loader program that loads that file system into memory.

Super Block

The super block is the center of the UNIX file system and is the area that is accessed whenever a disk manipulation is done. However, since its access is done frequently, a copy of it is kept in RAM. And it is this copy in RAM that changes are registered in initially.

Remember, we talked about mounting earlier. At which point we said that this is a process whereby a file system is loaded into memory. Well, that's not entirely true. When we mount a file system, it is actually the super block and the inode table only that is loaded into memory. It is only when the *sync( )* system call is used that the actual super block on disk is written to. A call to the *sync( )* is normally made every 30 seconds.

This super block basically describes the file system. It is much like the FAT (File Allocation Table) in DOS. It consists of the following information:

1. The size of the file system: how much space the file system will occupy on disk.

2. The size of the inode section of the file system which follows the super block: each inode stands for one file. By specifying a number we define the maximum number of files we can have in each file system.

3. The number of unallocated blocks in the data section: like the clusters in DOS. A file occupies a minimum of 1 block. Even if it has only one character in it. A block size can be 512 bytes or 1024 bytes.

4. The block numbers of some of the unallocated blocks.

5. The last time the super block was written to.

6. The file system type: this tells the size of a logical block.

To see what the super block consists of we need to make use of two predefined structures - *filsys* and *mnttab*.

PROGRAM 111

```
#include <stdio.h>
#include <fcntl.h>
#include <sys/types.h>
#include <mnttab.h>
#include <sys/fs/s5param.h>
#include <sys/fs/s5filsys.h>

struct filsys superblk;
struct mnttab mounttab;

main( )
{
   int fd;
   fd = open("/etc/mnttab",O_RDONLY);
   while( read(fd,&mounttab,sizeof(mounttab)) == sizeof(mounttab) )
   {
      printf("\n Mountab details : \n");
      printf("\t Device : %s\n",mounttab.mt_dev);
      printf("\t File system : %s\n",mounttab.mt_filsys);
      showblok(mounttab.mt_dev);
   }
   close(fd);
}

showblok(df)
char *df;
{
```

```
    int fdsb,i;
    printf("\n--- File System : %s\n",df);
    fdsb = open(df,O_RDONLY);
    sync( );
    lseek(fdsb,512l,0); /* skipping first sector */
    read(fdsb,&superblk,sizeof(superblk));
    printf(" \t Size of the inode table : %8d \n", superblk.s_isize);
    printf(" \t File system buffer size : %8ld\n",512*superblk.s_type);
    printf(" \t Total free blocks : %8d \n",superblk.s_type*superblk.s_tfree);
    printf(" \t Total free i-nodes : %8d\n",superblk.s_tinode);
    printf(" \t Size of the entire file system : %8d\n",superblk.s_fsize);
    printf(" \t inode free : ");
    for(i = 0 ; i < 4 ; i++ )
        printf(" %8d : ",superblk.s_inode[i]);
    printf("\n");
    printf(" \t Number of free inodes : %8d\n",superblk.s_ninode);
    printf(" \t file system name : %s\n",superblk.s_fname);
    printf(" \t Time of last update : %s\n",ctime(&superblk.s_time));
    close(fdsb);
}
```

filsys and *mnttab* are two predefined structures (their members can be viewed in the sys/fs/s5filsys.h and mountab.h header files, respectively). We define *superblk* and *mounttab* to look like them. The *while* loop proceeds to read a certain number of bytes from the mnttab file, which has been opened in the read only mode.

This file consists of data regarding the various file systems. The *while* loop continues till the end of file is reached (which means it has read details of all file systems; if there are 3 file systems the *while* loop will perform thrice).

In the loop reached after printing the value of the members of the *mounttab* structure we call the *showblk( )* function with a parameter. This parameter is the member *mt_dev* from the structure *mounttab*. *mt_dev* is actually a pointer to the name of the device on which the details of the super block of this file system are stored.

In the *showblk( )* function, this parameter is defined as a pointer to a character. This character is actually the first character of the name of the device, which is nothing but a "special file". We open this "special file" in read only mode. After which the *sync( )* function is called. This writes whatever is on memory to disk. Thus updating the disk.

Why do we need to do this?

We know that a copy of the super block is made in memory and it is this copy that is always updated when a change occurs. Similarly, any other file that is open is also manipulated in memory. Therefore, at any given moment in time the data on disk is always out of sync with that in memory. To get both disk and memory aligned we need to use the sync system call. Most times this system call is done every 30 seconds by UNIX itself.

The record pointer is now positioned on the 513th byte because the first 512 bytes are the boot block. The 513th byte onwards is the start of the super block. This super block is read into the structure *superblk*. And finally its details are printed on screen.

There is one thing about the answers given by UNIX commands: they are cryptic. Take the df command for example. While it tells you the amount of free space on disk, it does so in a very unfriendly manner. So what's to stop us writing our own df? Nothing. After all we do know C well by now. Plus, we're reasonably familiar with the super block, where the details we want are stored.

To do this we need to use the predefined structure *ustat*. This contains basically four members: the file system name, free blocks, free inodes and the name of the pack (this refers to a removable disk pack).

We'll write this program to receive a parameter at the command line. This parameter will be the number of the device, eg. 1 for dsk01, 2 for dsk02 etc.

PROGRAM 112

```
#include <sys/types.h>
#include <ustat.h>

main(argc,argv)
int argc;
char *argv[ ];
{
   struct ustat thebuf;
   int dev,i;
   for(i=1; i<argc; i++)
   {
      dev = atoi(argv[i]);
      printf("Device number : %d\n",dev);
      if(!ustat(dev, &thebuf))
      {
         printf("Name of the file system : %s \n",thebuf.f_fname);
         printf("Number of free blocks : %ld\n",thebuf.f_tfree);
         printf("Number of free inodes : %d\n",thebuf.f_tinode);
      }
      else
         printf("Cannot get statistics on devices %d\n",dev);
   }
}
```

We define the structure *thebuf* which looks like *ustat*, which is the predefined structure we mentioned above.

In the *for* loop, we first convert the character passed as parameter to an integer and then print it.

The *ustat( )* system call is passed this number and the address of the structure in memory. It fills this structure with the details of free blocks and free inodes. And this is what is printed on screen.

Inode Table

Directories on most UNIX systems consist of series of 16-byte entries, one for each file or sub-directory. The first 2 bytes reflect the inode number of the file or directory. And the next 14 bytes contain the filename.

The ls system call lists the files in the current directory. We can simulate this command. All we have to do is read the series of 16-byte entries in the directory.

PROGRAM 113

```
#include <stdio.h>
#include <sys/types.h>
#include <sys/dir.h>

main(argc, argv)
char *argv[ ];
int argc;
{
   FILE *fp;
   struct direct dir;
   fp = fopen(argv[1],"r");
   printf("\n\nDirectory listing of %s\n\n",argv[1]);
   while ( fread(&dir, sizeof(dir), 1, fp ) != EOF )
   {
      if ( dir.d_ino == 0 )
         continue;
      printf("Inode number : %d of file : %s\n",dir.d_ino,dir.d_name);
   }
   fclose(fp);
   exit(0);
}
```

Note: Run this program like this: a.out <directory name>.

eg. a.out . (the . stands for the current directory).

To start with we define a structure *dir* to look like *direct*, which is a predefined structure in the sys/dir.h header file. Next we open the directory specified. Remember, we can do this because a directory in UNIX is nothing but a file.

A number of bytes, as defined by the structure size, are read from the file into the structure. This structure contains two members, the inode number and the file name. These two members are printed on screen.

This *while* loop continues till all the entries in the directory are read and printed.

The inode number that's printed is stored in the inode table located below the super block. UNIX takes this inode number, looks for it in the inode table. The next 64 bytes following the inode number give us the status of the file.

These 64 bytes which are in the Inode Table contain a description of the file:

1. user and group id of its owner.

2. its protection - read / write permission.

3. where on disk it is stored.

4. its size.

5. time of creation, last use and last modification.

6. number of links to the file. We can have more than one name refer to the same file by making a link to that file. In a directory we have a structure that contains the name of the file and a pointer to the file itself. This pointer is an integer called the i-number (index number) of the file. It is this index number that is used to access this file. When we link files with different names it is by assigning them the same i-number.

7. a tag indicating its (the file's) type: directory, regular file or special file.

We can use the *stat()* system call to print all these details.

PROGRAM 114

```
#include <sys/types.h>
#include <sys/stat.h>
#include <pwd.h>
#include <grp.h>
#include <time.h>
```

```
struct passwd *getpwuid( );
struct group *getgrgid( );

main(argc,argv)
int argc;
char *argv[ ];
{
   struct stat thebuf;
   char *path;
   int i;
   for(i=1;i<argc;i++)
   {
      path = argv[i];
      printf("Path : %s\n",path);

      if(!stat(path,&thebuf))
      {
         printf("File mode st_mode : %o\n",thebuf.st_mode);
         printf("Inode number st_ino : %d\n",thebuf.st_ino);
         printf("Device Id st_dev : %d\n",thebuf.st_dev);
         printf("Special Device Id st_rdev : %d\n",thebuf.st_rdev);
         printf("Number of links st_nlink: %d\n",thebuf.st_nlink);
         printf("User id st_uid : %d",thebuf.st_uid);
         printf("(%s)\n",getpwuid(thebuf.st_uid)->pw_name);
         printf("Group id st_gid : %d",thebuf.st_gid);
         printf("(%s)\n",getgrgid(thebuf.st_gid)->gr_name);
         printf("Size in bytes st_size : %ld\n",thebuf.st_size);
         printf("Last access st_atime : %s",ctime(&thebuf.st_atime));
         printf("Last modification st_mtime : %s",
               ctime(&thebuf.st_mtime));
         printf("Last status st_ctime: %s",ctime(&thebuf.st_ctime));
         printf("\n");
      }
      else
         printf("cannot get statistics on %s \n ",path);
   }
}
```

Note: Run this program like this: a.out <filename>.

eg. a.out /usr/inode.c

We define two pointers to structures that look like the predefined structures *passwd* and *group*.

In the *for* loop the stat system call is passed two parameters, the path and the address of the structure in which to assign the details of the inode. The *for* is given to take care of wild cards.

And, finally, the various members of this structure are printed. The user name and group name that this file or sub-directory belongs to are stored in the *passwd* and *group* structures. We already have two pointer functions that look like these structures. To them we pass the members *st_uid* and *st_gid* belonging to the *thebuf* structure. And display the members *pw_name* and *gr_name*.

This process is like having a function that points to a structure. When we pass this function a parameter, the value of this parameter is looked for in the structure. When it is found, the corresponding *pw_name* or *gr_name* are printed on screen.

Another way of getting the inode details of a directory or file is to go directly to the inode table and search for the inode required. For this, we don't need to use the stat system call.

There are a couple of things to keep in mind before you run this program:

1. You have to be a super-user. To become one, just type su at the prompt and key in the right password when asked.

2. Get the inode number of the directory or file you want to run this program for - the inode number can be got by executing - ls -i.

3. Get the file system name where this file or directory is stored. This is done through the df.

4. And finally when you execute the program state the complete pathname, the file system name and the inode number as parameters.

```
<path & filename> <file system> <inode>
eg. /usr/vmci/inoddet /dev/dsk/0s3 3380
```

There are three things we need to do to get the details of the inode specified. Go to the start of the super block from which we get the size of the block. The block, as we have said before, is the minimum space a file occupies. Once we get the block size, we travel to the end of the super block, which means to the start of the inode table. Here the inode number starts from 1. And each inode is a 64-byte chunk. To get to the one we want we need to multiply one less than it (the inode) by 64. And position the pointer at this location. From here the next 64 bytes will contain information about our inode.

PROGRAM 115

```
#include <stdio.h>
#include <fcntl.h>
#include <sys/types.h>
#include <sys/fs/s5param.h>
#include <sys/fs/s5filsys.h>
#include <sys/ino.h>
#include <time.h>

struct filsys SB;
struct dinode I;
int fs;
int inode;

#define SECTOR 512
int block;
long iaddr;

main(argc, argv)
int argc;
char *argv[];
{
   int i,j;

   fs =open (argv[1], O_RDONLY);
   lseek (fs, 512, 0);
   read (fs, &SB, sizeof (SB));
```

```
  if (SB.s_type == 1)
      block = 512;
  else
      block = 1024;

  inode = atoi(argv[2]);
  iaddr = (inode - 1) * sizeof(I);

  lseek (fs, (long) block * 2 + iaddr, 0);
  read (fs, &I, sizeof(I));

  printf("*** inode %d\n", inode);
  printf(" mode bits:m %8o\n", I.di_mode);
  printf(" number of links: %8d\n", I.di_nlink);
  printf(" owner user ID number: %8d\n", I.di_uid);
  printf(" owner group ID number: %8d\n",I.di_gid);
  printf("number of bytes in file: %8d\n",I.di_size);
  printf(" time last accessed: %s ", ctime(&I.di_atime));
  printf(" time last modified :%s ", ctime(&I.di_mtime));
  printf(" time created :%s ", ctime(&I.di_ctime));

  close(fs);
  exit(0);
}
```

We open the file system in read only mode. And then move the pointer 512 bytes forward so as to position it at the beginning of the super block. Next, we read the super block into the predefined structure *SB*. One of its members *s_type* will tell us whether the block size is 512 or 1024 bytes.

After converting the inode number, which is passed as a string to an integer, we subtract 1 from it and then multiply it by the block size, i.e. 512 or 1024. The 1 is minused because inodes start from 0, like array members.

Now that we've got the inode number we need to move the pointer to it. The details of this inode is in the inode table, whereas the pointer is at this moment pointing to the super block. The super block is two blocks in size, i.e. either 1024 or 2048 bytes.

To get to its end we have to move the pointer by these many bytes. But since we also want the pointer to point to the inode concerned we add the value of variable *iaddr* (which is nothing but the number of bytes to skip in order to position the pointer at the specified inode) to it.

From this byte onward, the next 64 bytes are read into the predefined structure *I*. The members of which (the structure I) contain details about the inode and that's what we print on screen.

So what's the purpose of storing all this information in the inode table?

Considering that UNIX is a multi-user system, all these different users and the work they do have to be monitored at some level. More importantly, the system also needs to be monitored. For example, on a single-user system we can always take the necessary steps ourselves when there is no disk space free. But on a multi-user system this is a system administrator's job.

Can you imagine what a time he'll have when suddenly one day he wakes up to find there is no space free on the disk? He'll probably have hundreds of users haranguing him through the day. And then to start housekeeping steps would be time-consuming, which means some more complaints.

To avoid this kind of a nightmare it would be ideal if he kept track of the amount of disk space free. Once a certain limit is reached, a message like "can only hold 500 files more" should be flashed. This will give him ample time to warn all users to take backup measures and start deleting unwanted files.

So how do we ascertain how many more files can be accommodated at a given point in time? Simple. Check the number of inodes free. Each inode means one file, and if there are 30 inodes free we know we can have 30 more files. And if 30 is the warning point we've decided upon, that's when the message will be flashed on screen.

A program that constantly monitors how much file space is available would have to run in the background. This is because the disk is being used constantly, the system being a multi-user one.

The next program constantly updates a member in a structure that reflects the number of blocks free.

PROGRAM 116

```
#include <sys/types.h>
#include <ustat.h>

main(argc,argv)
int argc;
char *argv[ ];
{
   int dev;
   int inodeno;
   struct ustat thebuf;
   if( argc < 3 )
   {
      printf(" Usage : a.out <device no> <no of inode>\n");
      exit(1);
   }
   dev = atoi(argv[1]);
   inodeno = atoi(argv[2]);
   for(;;)
   {
      ustat(dev, &thebuf);
      if (thebuf.f_tinode < inodeno)
      {
         printf("\nYou are going to run out of Inodes.");
         printf("\nFree Inodes %d\n",thebuf.f_tinode);
         exit(0);
      }
   }
}
```

Run the program with two parameters: the file system and the number of inodes to warn for.

We start a *for* loop that never terminates. In this loop we call the *ustat()* function with two parameters, the device number and the address of the structure which is to be filled up with the details concerning that device.

The member *f_tinode* will always reflect the number of inodes free. If this number is less than the one we are checking for, a message will be flashed on screen.

In a similar manner, we can find out how many blocks are free -- though a block is not a clear indication of how many files we can accommodate. It just tells us how much disk space is free.

PROGRAM 117

```
/* file system statistics warn block shortage*/
#include <sys/types.h>
#include <ustat.h>

main(argc,argv)
int argc;
char *argv[ ];
{
   int dev;
   int noblk;
   struct ustat thebuf;
   if(argc < 3 )
   {
      printf("Usage : a.out <device no> <no of block>\n");
      exit(1);
   }
   dev = atoi(argv[1]);
   noblk = atoi(argv[2]);
   for(;;)
   {
      ustat(dev, &thebuf);
      if (thebuf.f_tfree < noblk)
      {
         printf("You are going to run out of Blocks\n");
         printf("Free blocks %d\n",thebuf.f_tfree);
         exit(0);
      }
   }
```

```
}
```

There is only one difference between this and the previous program, and that's the structure member we are checking. In this case the member is *f_tfree*. This will always indicate the number of blocks free. Once this number becomes less than the value, we pass this program as a parameter a message will be flashed on screen.

Another bit of detail that could prove immensely valuable is the data and time stamp. Once again this is to do with the nature of UNIX itself. While 'we' are logged in, there will always be some others logged in too. And maybe at this point (when we have logged in) we don't want these others to modify any common file.

So how do we ensure that the moment someone opens this common file(s) we are notified? Well, one way is store the time the file was last updated in an array and then keep checking it with the present time-stamp of this file. The moment this file is accessed, there will be a time mismatch and we'll get a warning message on the screen.

PROGRAM 118

```
#include <stdio.h>
#include <sys/types.h>
#include <sys/stat.h>
#define MAXFILE 10

main(argc,argv)
int argc;
char *argv[ ];
{
    struct stat fs;
    int j,retval;
    long last_mtime[MAXFILE + 1];
    if ((argc < 2) | | (argc > 11))
    {
        printf("Usage is %s filename ...\n",argv[0]);
        printf("Maximum 10 files\n");
        exit(0);
    }
```

```
    for (j = 1; j < argc ; j++)
    {
        retval = stat(argv[j], &fs);
        if (retval < 0)
        {
            perror(" ");
            exit(1);
        }
        last_mtime[j] = fs.st_mtime;
    }
    for(;;)
    {
        for (j = 1; j< argc; j++)
        {
            retval = stat(argv[j], &fs);
            if ((last_mtime[j] != fs.st_mtime) | | (retval < 0))
            {
                printf("Lookout %s has ",argv[j]);
                printf("been deleted or changed\n");
                exit(0);
            }
            sleep(5);
        }
    }
}
```

Once again this has to be run as a background process so that a check can be conducted continuously.

We can pass a maximum of 10 files as parameters at the command line. The first *for* loop goes through all these files to get the time-stamp which it stores to an array element. The *stat( )* function is passed two parameters the address of the filename and a pointer to the structure *fs*. As a result all the members of the structure are filled with the details of the file. The value assigned to the member *st_mtime* is stored in the corresponding array element.

Now that we have got the base time we need to check it with whatever is the latest time-stamp of the file. This is done in the second *for* loop. Here once again the *stat( )* function is called to fill the structure *fs* with the details of the file. And the value of the corresponding element of the array *last_mtime* is compared with that of the member *st_mtime*. If they are not equal means the file has been opened.

Data Blocks

Data Blocks contain the data for all files, as well as the free blocks in the file system. This is where the actual data, which we know in terms of files, is stored. Each file is assigned a minimum of two blocks, and the number of these blocks is stored in the inode of that file.

Actually, in the inode table there is an array of 13 elements that is assigned to hold the block numbers of each file. UNIX, by default, assumes that a file will go up to a maximum of 10 blocks. The next 3 bytes (elements) are in case the file exceeds these 10 blocks.

So what happens if a file goes beyond the expected 10 blocks?

Then the 11th element of the array, which points to a chunk of 256 bytes that hold the addresses of 256 blocks is used. And it is in these 256 more blocks that the rest of the file is stored.

And what happens if these 256 blocks are also exhausted? Then the 12th element of the array is activated. This holds the address of another 256 bytes which in turn point to another 256 bytes which hold the addresses of 256 blocks where the rest of the file is stored.

And if this is exhausted? Then it's the 13th element's turn to swing into action. This holds the address of 256 bytes which in turn hold the addresses of another 256 bytes, which in turn hold the addresses of another 256 bytes, which finally point to 256 blocks that will hold the file.

And if even this gets exhausted, then you ought maybe to distribute your data over different disks.

There are five different kinds of files that we can have in this data area: block, special, ordinary, FIFO (first in first out) and directory files. We can determine a file's type by typing in:

```
ls -l /usr/vmci/c_lang
```

where c_lang is the name of the file.

Another way of finding this out is through a program.

PROGRAM 119

```
#include <sys/types.h>
#include <sys/stat.h>
#include <pwd.h>
#include <grp.h>
#include <time.h>
struct passwd *getpwuid( );
struct group *getgrgid( );

main(argc,argv)
int argc;
char *argv[ ];
{
   struct stat thebuf;
   char *path;
   int i;
   for(i=1;i<argc;i++)
   {
      path = argv[i];
      if(!stat(path,&thebuf))
      {
         printf("\nFile mode of %s is : %o which is ",
               argv[1], thebuf.st_mode);
         switch ( thebuf.st_mode & S_IFMT )
         {
            case S_IFDIR : printf("a directory\n");
               break;
            case S_IFCHR : printf("a charachter special file\n");
               break;
            case S_IFREG : printf("an ordinary file \n");
               break;
            case S_IFBLK : printf("a block special file \n");
```

```
                break;
              case S_IFIFO : printf("a FIFO file \n");
                break;
            }
        }
        else
            printf("Cannot get statistics on %s \n ",path);
    }
}
```

We call the *stat( )* function, which is then passed two parameters, the filename and the address of the structure that will be assigned the necessary details from the inode. The member *st_mode* is then queried for the type of file it is, and the appropriate *printf( )* is activated.

Let's examine these file types in more detail:

Block Files: are called such because the transfer of data between them and the RAM takes place in blocks. For example, when we want to copy a file to the disk, the data in this file is first transferred to a buffer. When this buffer is full, its entire contents are copied to the disk as one chunk. The size of the block can be 512 or 1024.

Special Files: also known as character files. A good example is the screen. We have mentioned before that when we write to the screen, the data is first written to a file and the screen device driver activated. This proceeds to reflect data in the file on screen. Data to the file and to the screen is reflected one character at a time.

Ordinary Files: these are our data or program files.

FIFO (first in first out) Files: are used for inter-process communication. They are also known as PIPE files. We can write at one end and read from the other.

Directory Files: these house further sub-directories or files, and thus give rise to a tree-like structure.

Considering that a directory is nothing but a warehouse of some other information (a file) , UNIX offers users a lot of functions that permit a view of the directory's contents.

Writing some code to list directories could be the start of our own UNIX shell. The essence of this code is in the header file, dirent.h. This contains predefined structures that we can use to read the directories.

To start with, let's see how we can get the first entry in a directory to be displayed on screen. By the first entry we don't mean the . and .. sub-directories.

PROGRAM 120

```
#include <sys/types.h>
#include <dirent.h>

main(argc,argv)
int argc;
char *argv[ ];
{
   DIR *dirname;
   struct dirent *preaddir;
   dirname = opendir(argv[1]);
   preaddir = readdir(dirname);
   preaddir = readdir(dirname);
   preaddir = readdir(dirname);
   printf("Opened %s\n",argv[1]);
   printf("The first entry in this directory is %s\n",preaddir-> d_name);
   closedir(dirname);
}
```

Note: This program has to be passed a parameter at the command line. The parameter is the name of the directory we want to read a file from.

We define a pointer to a structure, *dirname*, that looks like the predefined structure *DIR*. There is also another pointer to a structure, called *preaddir*.

The directory that we want the first file read from is passed as a parameter at the command line to this program. This directory is opened using the *opendir( )* function and the pointer returned by this function is assigned to *dirname*.

The *readdir( )* function reads the name of the first file from this opened directory. The *readdir( )* function is passed the starting location of this directory as a parameter. A call is made thrice to this function since we don't want to display the . and .. sub-directories. The third call to this function gets the first entry, whose name is stored in the member *p_name* of the structure *preaddir*.

The *closedir( )* function closes this open directory.

That was only one entry. But using the same functions in a loop we can get the entire directory listing. A simulation of the ls command.

PROGRAM 121

```
#include <stdio.h>
#include <sys/types.h>
#include <dirent.h>

main(argc,argv)
int argc;
char *argv[ ];
{
   DIR *dirname;
   struct dirent *rdir;
   dirname=opendir(argv[1]);
   while(1)
   {
      rdir = readdir(dirname);
      if ( rdir == NULL )
      {
         closedir(dirname);
         exit(0);
      }
      printf("Found entry in %s :- %s\n",argv[1],rdir->d_name);
   }
```

```
    closedir(dirname);
    exit(0);
}
```

We open the directory file using the *opendir( )* function. In the *while* loop we read each entry using the *readdir( )* function which returns a pointer. If no pointer is returned we exit from the program, else the name of the entry is displayed.

But each entry consists of more than just the name. There is also the inode number, the length of the record, etc. This too can be displayed, through the program shown below.

PROGRAM 122

```
#include <stdio.h>
#include <sys/types.h>
#include <dirent.h>

main(argc,argv)
int argc;
char *argv[ ];
{
    DIR *dirname;
    struct dirent *dir ;
    dirname=opendir(argv[1]);
    while((dir = readdir(dirname))!= NULL)
    {
        printf(" Entry found : %s \n",dir->d_name);
        printf(" inode number of entry : %d \n",dir->d_ino);
        printf(" length of this record : %d \n",dir->d_reclen);
        printf(" file descriptor : %d\n",dirname->dd_fd);
        printf(" offset in block : %d \n",dirname->dd_loc);
        getchar( );
    }
}
```

The *while* loop performs till the end of file is reached. In the loop the *readdir( )* function keeps reading the details of each file into the structure, whose members are then printed.

The length of the record signifies how many bytes each entry (file) occupies in the directory file. The file descriptor is nothing but a handle that is returned when we do an *open( )* on the file. And the offset in the block signifies that details of that particular entry start in the directory file.

One of the real useful tools that NORTON UTILITIES provides under DOS is the FileFind. Through this you can check to see if a file exists on the disk or floppy. In UNIX writing a program like this is real kid's stuff. All we need to do is open the directory in which we want to look for the file. This file that we want to look for can be passed as a parameter to the program.

PROGRAM 123

```
#include <stdio.h>
#include <sys/types.h>
#include <dirent.h>

main(argc,argv)
int argc;
char *argv[ ];
{
   DIR *dirname;
   struct dirent *rdir;
   if ( argc < 3 )
   {
      printf("Usage is :%s <path to search> <filename>\n",argv[0]);
      exit(0);
   }
   dirname=opendir(argv[1]);
   while( (rdir = readdir(dirname)) != NULL )
   {
      if(strcmp(rdir->d_name,argv[2]) == 0 )
      {
         closedir(dirname);
         printf("Found entry %s\n",argv[2]);
         exit(0);
      }
   }
   printf("Could not locate entry %s within %s\n",argv[2],argv[1]);
   closedir(dirname);
}
```

We have to specify two parameters to the program: the path to search in and the name of the file to search for.

The directory where we think the file resides is opened and a *while* loop performed which reads each entry using the *readdir( )* function. A string compare is done with the filename read and that passed by us at the command line. If they match, an entry found message is flashed.

A directory, as we know, consists of files and sub-directories. In DOS, a simple dir *. command gives us a listing of all sub-directories. In UNIX we have to write a program to do this. This program will open a directory, read all entries in that directory into an array. Then a *for* loop goes through the entire array and checks to see if it can open that entry as a file. If it cannot, we know that it isn't a directory.

PROGRAM 124

```
extern int errno;

#include <stdio.h>
#include <sys/errno.h>
#include <sys/types.h>
#include <dirent.h>

main(argc,argv)
int argc;
char *argv[ ];
{
   Int i = 0,j,k;
   char *names[ ];
   char newname[100];
   DIR *dirname;
   struct dirent *rdir;
   if (argc < 2)
   {
      printf("Usage %s <path>\n",argv[0]);
      exit(0);
   }
   dirname=opendir(argv[1]);
   printf("Major directory : %s \n",argv[1]);
```

```
        while( (rdir = readdir(dirname)) != NULL )
        {
            names[i] = rdir->d_name;
            i++;
        }
        closedir(dirname);
        for(j=k=0 ; j < i; j++)
        {
            strcpy(newname, argv[1]);
            strcat(newname, "/");
            strcat(newname, names[j]);
            dirname = opendir(newname);
            if (errno == ENOTDIR)
            {
                errno = 0;
                continue;
            }
            else
            {
                k++;
                printf("->%s \n",names[j]);
            }
        }
        printf("Number of directories within %s is %d\n",argv[1],k);
}
```

After opening the directory passed as a parameter to the program, the *while* loop proceeds to read each entry and assign the names of the file/sub-directory to the array of pointers *names*.

Since the *opendir( )* expects the entire pathname we string copy and string concatenate it to the filename/sub- directory name. The *opendir( )* is then used on that entry. If the entry is a file, it will return an error to the predefined variable *errno*. Else, since it is a directory, we print the name.

But there is a cleaner way of writing the above program -- by making use of the *stat( )* function.

PROGRAM 125

```
extern int errno;
#include <stdio.h>
```

```
#include <sys/errno.h>
#include <sys/types.h>
#include <sys/stat.h>
#include <dirent.h>

main(argc,argv)
int argc;
char *argv[ ];
{
   int i = 0,j,retval=0,cntsub=0;
   char newname[100];
   char *names[100];
   DIR *dirname;
   struct stat statbuff;
   struct dirent *rdir;
   if (argc < 2)
   {
      printf("Usage %s <path>\n",argv[0]);
      exit(0);
   }
   dirname=opendir(argv[1]);
   printf("Subdirectories within %s \n",argv[1]);
   while( (rdir = readdir(dirname)) != NULL )
   {
      strcpy(newname,argv[1]);
      strcat(newname,"/");
      strcat(newname,rdir->d_name);
      if ( stat(newname,&statbuff) >= 0 )
      {
         retval = statbuff.st_mode & S_IFMT;
         if (retval == S_IFDIR )
         {
            cntsub++;
            printf("%s\n",rdir->d_name);
         }
      }
   }
   printf("Number of subdirectories is %d\n",cntsub);
   closedir(dirname);
}
```

We first open the directory that we pass as a parameter. Then, in the *while* loop, the filenames are read one at a time. A string copy and string concatenate add the pathname to the file/sub-directory. And finally this is passed as a parameter to the *stat( )* function along with the address of the *statbuff* structure.This structure is filled with the necessary details.

By ANDing the member *st_mode* with the predefined variable *S_IFDIR*, which is defined in the sys/stat.h header file, we get to know whether an entry is a directory or not.

There is a function which can be used to reposition the pointer at the beginning of a directory file. This could come in handy if we want to see the directory listing again.

PROGRAM 126

```
#include <stdio.h>
#include <sys/types.h>
#include <dirent.h>

main(argc,argv)
int argc;
char *argv[ ];
{
   DIR *dirname;
   struct dirent *rdir;
   long dirpos;
   dirname=opendir(argv[1]);
   while(1)
   {
      rdir = readdir(dirname);
      if ( rdir == NULL )
      {
         break;
      }
      printf("%s\n",rdir->d_name);
   }
   printf("Once more ! Press <enter>\n");
   seekdir(dirname,0l);
   getchar( );
   while(1)
   {
      rdir = readdir(dirname);
      if ( rdir == NULL )
```

```
        {
           break;
        }
        printf("%s\n",rdir->d_name);
    }
    closedir(dirname);
    exit(0);
}
```

The first *while* loop reads each entry and prints it till a NULL is encountered.

The *seekdir( )*, which is passed two parameters, the directory name and the position to move the pointer to, now repositions the pointers. An Enter will activate the second *while* loop, which prints the directory entries again.

File Permissions

The US stands for capitalism. And capitalism means private ownership. What better way to ensure privacy of your files in a multi-user system like UNIX than to introduce the concept of ownership.

So we have files which, like processes, belong to the user that created them. But then, since a user normally belongs to some group, we also have the file belonging to the group. Every user and group we know has an ID, and it is this ID that is attached to the file.

We can get the ID of the user and the group that the file belongs to by using the *stat( )* function.

PROGRAM 127

```
/* file statistics */
#include <sys/types.h>
#include <sys/stat.h>
#include <pwd.h>
#include <grp.h>
struct passwd *getpwuid( );
struct group *getgrgid( );
```

```
main(argc,argv)
int argc;
char *argv[ ];
{
   struct stat thebuf;
   char *path;
   int i;
   for(i=1;i<argc;i++)
   {
      path = argv[i];
      printf("Path : %s\n",path);

      if(!stat(path,&thebuf))
      {
         printf("User id st_uid : %d",thebuf.st_uid);
         printf(" User Name --> %s \n",
               getpwuid(thebuf.st_uid)-> pw_name);
         printf("Group id st_gid : %d",thebuf.st_gid);
         printf(" Group Name --> %s\n",
               getgrgid(thebuf.st_gid)->gr_name);
         printf("\n");
      }
      else
         printf("cannot get statistics on %s \n ",path);
   }
}
```

At the command line we can pass the names of as many files as we want as parameters. But we have to pass a minimum of 1 name, of course.

In the *for* loop, which performs as many times as there are files, the stat function is called with two parameters, the name of the file and the address of the structure *thebuff*. The function fills this structure with the necessary details concerning the file.

The two members *st_uid* and *st_gid* which signify the user and group IDs are then printed. We pass the two functions *getpwuid( )* and *getgrgid( )* these two members as parameters. This gives us the respective user and group names.

So what happens if a user from another group wants to access a file that does not belong to him or his group? Or, what if some member of a group wants access to a data file belonging to the group but which he does not have any rights over?

This takes us into the realm of permissions and user IDs.

As with any kind of ownership, file ownership gives the owner certain rights. The owner can choose the permissions connected with the file. These permissions indicate how different users can access a file. There are essentially three kinds of users: first - the file's owner; second - anyone who belongs to the same group that the file belongs to; and third - everyone else not connected with the file or the group that the file belongs to.

And for each of these categories there are three basic file permissions: read, write and execute.

Do a ls -l at the prompt and you will get a listing of all the entries in the directory you are in. The first column of this list indicates the permissions for each file and each type of user.

The first slot indicates the type of file it is: directory, special file, etc. The next three slots give the rights of the file owner. It would normally be rw and an x, if executable. The three slots that come after that indicate the permissions of the group the file belongs to. And the final three slots indicate the permissions for the rest of the world.

Lets take an example:

-rw-rw-r--

A - indicates no permission. A r indicates a read, a w indicates a write and an x indicates a executable file.

The above example means that the file owner and the members of the group the file belongs to, both have read/ write permission whereas anyone else, i.e. someone from another group, only has read permission.

A superuser, of course, is like a GOD. He does not need any permissions. He has access to all files.

So what happens when a certain user tries to access a file?

UNIX first checks to see if the ID of the user matches the ID of the owner of the file. If it does, it checks to see what permissions the owner has. And accordingly allows access to the file.

But if the IDs don't match, UNIX checks to see if the Group ID of the user matches the Group ID of the file. If it does, then a check is made to see what permission a group member has. If the user has asked for a write when only a read permission is valid, access will be denied.

If even the group ID is not valid then the permissions for all others are checked. If these others have no appropriate permissions, an error indicating that the OS is unable to access the file is flashed.

These permissions aren't valid only for files but directories, too. After all, a directory in UNIX is nothing but a file. A user can only access a directory if he has the required permissions.

For example, assume that we want to delete a file called mother_c in a directory called /unix_5. Even if we don't have read/write permissions over the file, as long as we have read/write rights over the directory, we can do so. All that the delete function will do is go to the file entry in the directory file and remove the filename and inode number related to it.

Data Security And The 'suid' Bit

In dBASE, one of the most common grouses is that a database file can be accessed by anybody. This leads to a real security problem. In UNIX, though, we can use the permissions discussed above to make sure that no one can access a datafile except through the valid programs.

Assume that we have a data file that we don't want accessed except through a program. All we need to do is first change its permission status so that nobody but its owner can access it. We could do this by using the chmod UNIX command.

eg. chmod 0600 mother_c

Here 0600 means read/write permission for only the owner. mother_c is the filename.

How did we get the value 0600? We looked up the manual. Each of the three sets of permissions: read, write, execute can be viewed as one octal value. So 06 signifies the permission for the owner, 0 for the group and 0 for the others. Both the 0's mean no access at all.

Well, that took care of uncontrolled access to the data file. But we still do want the others to read/write to it albeit in a manner dictated by us. For this we need to write a program. And it is through this program and this program only, that another user can access the mother_c file.

But there is one problem here: any other user who runs the program will certainly have a different user ID. Because of this the data file won't be opened since it can only be accessed by the owner, whereas the guy running this program is someone else.

How do we solve this? Simple. Get the user ID of a process, (which reflects the user who has activated a process) to change to the ID of the owner of the data file. This is possible because every process has two IDs: a real user ID and an effective user ID. And it is actually the effective user ID that UNIX checks to see what permissions are valid for the user.

Let's understand this a little more explicitly. Every file has a real user ID. This reflects the owners ID, ie. the person who has created the file. When the program or file is activated, the kernel checks the effective user ID. This latter is always the real user ID , unless changed.

```
PROGRAM 128
main( )
{
   printf("User Id : %d\n",getuid( ));
   printf("Effective User Id : %d\n", geteuid( ));
}
```

Both the user IDs will reflect the person who activates this program. If we activate this process it will be our ID.

By changing this effective user ID to reflect another user we can get permissions over files that belong to him. For example, say there is a user Man_1 and another user Man_2 with user ID's 100 and 200, respectively. Assume that user Man_1 created a data file which only he is allowed to read and write to.

```
PROGRAM 129
#include <fcntl.h>

main( )
{
   int fd,i;
   printf("User-ID %d\n", getuid( ));
   printf("Effective User-ID %d\n", geteuid( ));
   fd = open("mother_c", O_CREAT | O_APPEND | O_RDWR,0600);
   if ( fd == -1 )
   {
      printf("Could not open testfile\n");
      exit(0);
   }
   write(fd, "Hello World\n", 15);
   close(fd);
}
```

The file mother_c will belong to whoever created it. In this case let's assume that it is Man_1 who has the user ID 100. The second parameter passed to the *open( )* will give only the owner, ie. Man_1, the permissions to create (since first time round it has to be created) read/write and append the file.

The file is being created with a Hello World in it.

Now let's assume that user Man_2, whose user ID is 200, logged in on another machine. When he runs the program above (make sure that the permissions of this program file are such that he can run it), the ID of the process will be 200. As a result user Man_2 won't be able to access the data file mother_c because access rights over this file only belong to Man_1.

Thus we need to change the effective user ID (which is 200) of the process to 100. This the ID of the data file mother_c. Once that is done, UNIX will think the process is being run by Man_1, and therefore allow the program to access the data file mother_c.

This can be done only by (the user) Man_1. He has to change what is known as the suid bit of the program file (not data file) after he makes this program executable. This can be done by using the chmod command which we have seen before.

```
chmod u+s <name of program file>
```

If you do a ls -l you will see an s in the permission bit in the owner section.

Now when Man_2 runs the program, the user ID that will be printed will be 200. But the effective user ID will be 100. UNIX is therefore fooled into thinking that user Man_1 is running the program. Now, since user Man_1 has total rights over the data file mother_c, an access to this file will be allowed. And isn't this what we want? That a data file should be accessed only through a specific program or by its owner.

By changing the effective user ID of the program it is not that its actual permissions are changed. This change is only valid till the process is in memory. The real user ID will always remain the same. If you don't believe us, try out the next program:

PROGRAM 130

```
#include <unistd.h>

main(argc, argv)
int argc;
```

```
char *argv[ ];
{
   if( !access(argv[1], F_OK) )
      printf("File %s Exists\n", argv[1]);
   if( !access(argv[1], R_OK) )
      printf("You have Read permission\n");
   if( !access(argv[1], W_OK) )
      printf("You have Write permission\n");
   if( !access(argv[1], X_OK) )
      printf("You have Execute permission\n");
}
```

When you run this program, pass it the filename mother_c. You'll see the actual permissions you, as a user, are allowed. If you have logged in as Man_1, the *printf( )* will print read and write permissions. And if you've logged in as Man_2, it will only print a file exists message.

The *access( )* function signifies the permission.

Well, now we're getting possessive about this data file mother_c. We don't want all those others, including Man_1, to access it any more. Instead, we only want the user Man_2 to access it from here on. So what do we do?

Transfer its ownership rights to the new user, that is Man_2. This will ensure that from that point on nobody can access this data file. And this won't be possible even if an attempt is made to access the file through the program which till now allowed us to do so. Total transfer of ownership, that's what it's all about.

PROGRAM 131

```
extern errno;

main( )
{
   int i;
   system("ls -l mother_c ");
   i = chown("mother_c",200,1);
   printf("Chown -> Ret : %d\n", i);
```

```
    if (i == -1)
        perror(errno);
    system("ls -l mother_c");
}
```

First we do a ls to ascertain the owner of the data file mother_c. The owner we know was Man_1, and that's what we'll see on screen.

The *chown( )* function is passed three parameters: the name of the file, the new owner's ID -- which in this case is 200 for Man_2 -- and the group ID of this new owner. It may be that the new owner belongs to another group. We have seen that a user doesn't have only an user ID but also a group ID. This group ID tells us which group he belongs to.

The second call to the ls command will now show the file belonging to user Man_2.

The 'sticky' Bit And The 'Utilize Memory Efficiently' Syndrome

One thing about files that can be executed (programs) is that for each user that activates, there will be one copy in memory. Can you imagine what an overhead this is in terms of response time? But the creators of UNIX were not fools. They attached one more permission to a file: save-text-image or, as it is more commonly known, the sticky bit.

Do a ls -l in the directory /usr/bin where the wordproceesor VI is stored. In the permission rights of VI you will see a t. This means that the sticky bit is on.

Now when VI is run for the first time, a copy of it is made in memory. From then on, no matter how many users run this program, they will be working with the same copy. Although the data for each user, of course, is different.

Actually a shareable program like VI is not loaded into memory but into the special area called the swap area. So whenever someone else runs this program, UNIX does not search for it in the directory but simply swaps it into memory.

We can make any executable file that is commonly used, a one copy in memory only file by setting its sticky bit on. For this we need to use the chmod command.

chmod u+t <filename>

There is one problem, though. If there are too many such files that fill the swap area, they could halt your system.

Links

System overhead and response time is a very important aspect of any multitasking - multi-user system. The idea is to make UNIX perform optimally. After all, you can't keep users waiting. The fact that UNIX has been written in C enhances the concept of a good response time considerably. How?

C, as we know, is nothing but functions. Programs written in C adopt a modular approach: one function does just one task, and nothing more.

Take VI, for example. To us it is a complete wordprocessor. True, but it can also be used as a line editor. That's what the program edit does. Essentially what happens is that VI also calls some function that allows editing on individual lines, among other things. By calling this function independently of VI we are able to edit only individual lines. What has happened is that only part of the VI program, and not the entire program, is loaded into memory. Since this will take less space it also reduces response time.

It is like having two computers: one at home and one in the office. Assume the floppy drive of the computer at home got damaged when you needed it most. There is no point in taking the office computer home. Just remove the latter's drive and attach it to the computer at home. The idea is to use just the part you need instead of carrying the whole baggage.

This sort of thing is possible in UNIX because of what are known as links.

Do a ls -lisa vi and then another ls -lisa edit and you will see the following two lines (at least this is what we got):

187 318 -rwxr-xr-t 5 bin bin 160326 Dec 13 1989 vi
187 318 -rwxr-xr-t 5 bin bin 160326 Dec 13 1989 edit

Notice the number 187 in the first column. This is the inode number and signifies that both filenames point to the same inode. Further, the value 5 after the permissions set signifies that there are five other filenames that point to the same inode. (Remember one inode means one file).

There are three programs shown below that demonstrate how two files are linked. Compile this program by typing in cc man.c -o ln1. Then type ln ln1 ln2 at the prompt. And finally, ln ln1 ln3.

If you do a ls -lisa ln* at the prompt, you will see that all three files have the same inode number.

PROGRAM 132

MAN.C

```
main(argc,argv)
int argc;
char *argv[ ];
{
   if (strcmp(argv[0],"ln1")==0)
      printf("This is in ln1\n");
   if (strcmp(argv[0],"ln2")==0)
      printf("This is in ln2\n");
   if (strcmp(argv[0],"ln3")==0)
      printf("This is in ln3\n");
}
```

If you run the ln1 program the first *if* statement will be executed. ln2 will execute the second *if* and ln3 the third *if*.

Not to say that the command line command ln is the only way to link files. You can also link files through programs using the *link( )* function.

The program above MAN.C has already been compiled to output ln1. When you run the program below, pass it two parameters: ln1 and ln2. One word of caution: make sure that both ln2 and ln3, created above, are deleted; else the program will return an error.

PROGRAM 133

```
extern errno;

main(argc,argv)
int argc;
char *argv[ ];
{
   int i;
   i = link(argv[1], argv[2]);
   printf("Created Link -> Ret : %d\n", i);
   if (i == -1)
      perror(errno);
}
```

The *link( )* function links the two files passed as parameters to it. Ans ls -lisa ln* will show the two files with the same inode number.

Now we're stuck. We'll have two/three files that are linked to each other for life. Ha, fooled you. We can unlink them too.

PROGRAM 134

```
extern errno;

main(argc,argv)
int argc;
char *argv[ ];
{
   int i;
   i = unlink(argv[1]);
   printf("Deleted Link -> Ret : %d\n", i);
   if (i == -1)
      perror(errno);
```

}

Run this program with a parameter which is the file you want to unlink, eg. ln1. Do an ls -l ln* and you won't see the ln1 file that you have just unlinked. It has been removed from the directory.

Does this mean that the *unlink()* does what the rm command, ie. the remove file, does. Well, yes and no. While rm immediately removes a file, *unlink()* waits till the file is closed.

PROGRAM 135

```
#include <fcntl.h>

extern errno;

main()
{
   int i,fd;
   char buff[20];

   fd = open("temp",O_RDWR);
   i = unlink("temp");
   printf("Deleted Link -> Ret : %d\n", i);
   if (i == -1)
      perror(errno);
   i = write(fd, "Hello World", 12);
   printf("Write -> Ret : %d\n", i);
   i = lseek(fd, 0L, 0);
   printf("Seek -> Ret : %d\n", i);
   i = read(fd, buff, 12);
   if (i == -1)
      perror(errno);
   printf("Read -> Ret : %d\n", i);
   printf("\"%s\"\n", buff);
   close(fd);
}
```

We open a file temp. For our example assume it is linked to some other file, it does not matter which. Next we call the *unlink()* with temp as parameter. The value returned by the function to variable *i* is 0, signifying that the *unlink()* has been successful, (it was so in our case).

Also, the *write( )*, which prints the string Hello World to the file; the *lseek( )*, which takes the file pointer to the beginning of the file; and the *read( )*, which reads the contents of the file into the array *buff*, are all successful.

As a result, when the *printf( )* prints the contents of the array, Hello World is displayed on screen. This happens in spite of the file actually being *unlink( )ed*.

However, once the program terminates, an ls temp will not list the file.

"And the world has come together as one ... ", as Bob Geldof had the world humming.

From the solitariness that DOS imposed we have broken out into a new world. A world that gives you as much as you put in and maybe more. Where the only thing that stands between you and the beyond is your imagination. And the power and need to communicate.

"There comes a time when we heed a certain call
When the world must come together as one"

UNIX. Have you heeded its call?

On Files

Railway bookings in major cities in the country today have been computerized. People can queue up in front of one of the several booking windows and reserve a seat on a train headed to any destination. This, of course, is if the tickets are available.

Assume that there was one ticket left for a train from Bombay to Delhi. Now, if two people, A and B, went to two different windows to reserve seats for themselves on this train, the booking clerks at both windows query the database for the ticket situation.

A's clerk queries the database first. He finds one seat left and allocates it to A. But he fouls up: he doesn't register the allocation in the database immediately. In the meantime, B's clerk queries the database and finds that there is one ticket left. Remember while the ticket has been allocated earlier, the database has not been notified that this allocation has taken place. As a result the same ticket will now be allocated to B, too. And that, dear reader, is the overbooking we hear so much about.

To overcome this kind of situation, the ideal step would be to lock the file. This would disallow anybody else from accessing the data. If the person catering to A for example accessed the file first and locked it. He could issue the reservation, change the file to show that no more seats are available and exit. The person catering to B would have been waiting for the lock to be lifted in the meantime. The moment the lock is lifted, he will get access to the database and find that there is no ticket available. Hence there will be no overbooking.

Unlocked Confusion

To start with, let's see how running two processes which have access to the same file could result in a mess up of data. Run these programs one after the other, both times in the background. To run both the following programs do this at the prompt:

```
$<first>&
$<second>&
```

PROGRAM 136

```
#include <fcntl.h>
#include <unistd.h>
main( )
{
   int fd,i;
   fd = open("locktest",O_APPEND | O_CREAT,0666);
   for(i= 0 ;i<=2000;i++)
      write(fd,"A",1);
}
```

PROGRAM 137

```
#include <fcntl.h>
#include <unistd.h>
main( )
{
   int fd,i;
   fd = open("locktest",O_APPEND | O_CREAT, 0666);
   for(i= 0 ;i<=2000;i++)
      write(fd,"B",1);
}
```

Once both these processes are in memory the time slice will be alternated between them. As a result, since both processes have read write access to the same file, the data they write will be all jumbled up. And that's exactly what happens. First come some *A*'s, then some *B*'s and so on so forth. This, as is obvious from both the *for* loops in the two programs, will happen 4000 times.

Both the programs do essentially the same thing. They open the same file in append mode and then write to it for the same number of times, but with different alphabets, A and B.

One at a Time Please

So what's the way out of this confusion? Simple. Just ensure that at one time only one process is allowed to write to the file. In other words, let the first process lock the file; and only when it has finished allow the second process to access it.

PROGRAM 138

```
#include <fcntl.h>
#include <unistd.h>
main( )
{
   int fd,i;
   fd = open("locktest",O_APPEND | O_RDWR | O_CREAT,0666);
   lockf(fd,F_LOCK,0);
   for(i= 0 ;i<=2000;i++)
      write(fd,"A",1);
}
```

PROGRAM 139

```
#include <unistd.h>
#include <fcntl.h>
main( )
{
   int fd,i;
   fd = open("locktest",O_APPEND | O_RDWR | O_CREAT,0666);
   lockf(fd,F_LOCK,0);
   for(i= 0 ;i<=2000;i++)
      write(fd,"B",1);
}
```

Here, too, both processes have to be run in the background, and one after the other.

The time slice is first given to the first process. This results in the file being opened in append mode. The *lockf( )* function is then passed three parameters: the file descriptor, F_LOCK, which locks the file, and a 0 which means that the entire file is to be locked. The *lockf( )* function locks the file so that only this process can write to it. Now this process proceeds to write its "A"s to the file.

When the time slice is handed to the second program, the latter will be unable to write as it finds the file locked. So it keeps waiting till the lock is removed.

Once the first program finishes writing all its **2000 "A"s**, it will terminate. As a result, the lock will be removed. **And the** second program will start writing to the same file. Since **it, too, opens** the file in append mode, the file pointer will be **positioned right** at the end. As a result the "B"s won't overwrite the "A"s.

Do a cat on the file to see the results.

From now on all the programs that have been listed to explain file locking will create a child process. This, we hope, makes it easier to understand, rather than having to run two processes each time.

Let's start with another example of a file lock. But with a parent and child process.

PROGRAM 140

```
/* parent has locked child will wait */
#include <fcntl.h>
#include <unistd.h>
main( )
{
   int fd,pid;
   fd=open("locktest",O_RDWR);
   lockf(fd,F_LOCK,0);
   printf("process %d locked file\n",getpid( ));
   pid = fork( );
   if (pid == 0)
   {
      lockf(fd,F_LOCK,0);
      printf("Process %d locked file \n",getpid( ));
      printf("Chile Process over\n");
   }
   else
   {
      sleep(5);
      printf("Process %d over\n",getpid( ));
```

```
    }
}
```

Here we open the file in read write mode and then lock it. Next, a child process is forked. As usual the child process gets the time slice. But it can't proceed as the file it is trying to lock has already been locked by the parent process.

The time slice is given to the parent process which is put in a *sleep( )* state. Now for 5 seconds the child process waits at the *lock( )* while the parent process sleeps. At the end of the 5 seconds, the parent process wakes, prints its PID and terminates. Now the child process proceeds to lock the file since its wait is over. And then prints the child process' PID before terminating.

Explicit Unlocking

So far an unlock has been performed by default. For example, in the last program, the moment the parent process terminated, the file was unlocked. But what if the parent process didn't terminate. And we yet wanted the child process to have access to the file. That's where the explicit unlocking for a file comes in. The function is the same save that instead of F_LOCK we specify F_ULOCK.

PROGRAM 141

```
/* explain unlock */
#include <fcntl.h>
#include <unistd.h>
main( )
{
   int fd,pid;
   fd=open("locktest",O_RDWR);
   lockf(fd,F_LOCK,0);
   printf("process %d locked file\n",getpid( ));
   pid = fork( );
   if (pid == 0)
   {
      printf("Process %d running\n",getpid( ));
      lockf(fd,F_LOCK,0);
      printf("Process %d locked file \n",getpid( ));
```

```
        printf("Child Process over\n");
    }
    else
    {
        sleep(5);
        printf("Process %d unlocking \n",getpid( ));
        lockf(fd,F_ULOCK,0);
        sleep(5);
        printf("Process %d over\n",getpid( ));
    }
}
```

We open the file locktest in read write mode and then lock it. A *fork( )* now creates a child process. And although the child process is given the time slice and prints its PID, it keeps waiting because of the lock on the file by the parent process.

The time slice is thus given to the parent process which promptly goes to sleep. Now there is one process that's sleeping and one that's waiting for a file to become accessible. The *sleep( )* finishes and the parent's PID is printed. An unlock is done (observe the second parameter passed to the function). And the parent is put back to sleep.

Now it's the child process' turn to execute. With all locks lifted, it proceeds to lock the file, print its PID and terminate. In time the parent process wakes, prints its PID and terminates.

A Sign to Ease the Suspense

But a child process that keeps waiting could be quite painful. Over and above that is the fact that a wait like the one above could get quite misleading with us not knowing what's really happening.

The best way out would be to have some value returned which would indicate to us whether the file has been already locked or not. If it has not been, then of course the current process will lock it. Else we can carry on with some other operation.

PROGRAM 142

```
/* Explain tlock i.e non blocking */
#include <fcntl.h>
#include <unistd.h>
main( )
{
    int fd,pid,retval;
    fd=open("locktest",O_RDWR);
    lockf(fd,F_LOCK,0);
    printf("process %d locked file\n",getpid( ));
    pid = fork( );
    if (pid == 0)
    {
        printf("Process %d running\n",getpid( ));
        retval = lockf(fd,F_TLOCK,0);
        if (retval == -1)
            printf("the file has been already locked\n");
        else
            printf("Process %d locked file\n",getpid( ));
        printf("Process %d over\n",getpid( ));
    }
    else
    {
        sleep(5);
        printf("Process %d over\n",getpid( ));
    }
}
```

Once again we lock the file before forking. In the child process which gets the time slice an attempt is made to lock the file using the *lockf( )* function. But since it is already locked a value of -1 is returned indicating that the file is locked. This return value is a result of the **F_TLOCK parameter** being passed to *lockf( )* function.

The statements within the *if* are executed and the child process terminates. In time the parent process too terminates.

F_TLOCK does two things. It checks to see if a file is locked, if it isn't, it proceeds to lock it else it returns a value indicating file already locked. F_TLOCK ensures that atomicity is maintained. What do we mean by that?

Suppose a check to see if the file is locked returns file not locked. But just before the file is subsequently locked, the time slice is taken away from this process; and the next program it is given to locks the file. When the time slice is returned to the first program it too will proceed to lock the file. Hey, problem, problem.

F_TLOCK is somewhat intelligent. It makes sure that the time slice is never given to another process at the critical moment. If it finds the file unlocked it will make sure it locks the file. And only then can the time slice be snatched away.

F_TEST Will Tell Us

If all we are interested in is merely checking to see if a file is locked, the parameter to pass is F_TEST.

PROGRAM 143

```
/* explain test returns 0 if it is not locked*/
#include <fcntl.h>
#include <unistd.h>
main( )
{
   int fd,pid,retval;
   fd=open("locktest",O_RDWR);
   lockf(fd,F_LOCK,0);
   printf("process %d locked file\n",getpid( ));
   pid = fork( );
   if (pid == 0)
   {
      printf("Process %d running\n",getpid( ));
      retval = lockf(fd,F_TEST,0);
      if (retval != 0)
         printf("the file has been already locked\n");
      printf("Process %d over\n",getpid( ));
   }
   else
   {
      sleep(5);
      printf("Process %d over\n",getpid( ));
   }
}
```

The basic program is the same. The only difference being F_TEST. If *lockf( )* in the child process now returns a value other than a 0 it means that the file has already been locked.

It is the *lockf( )* in the child process that keeps the latter waiting for the parent process to release the file. What would happen if this function was not called? Would a read or write take place? But before you run the next program to find out, create a file called test with 10 bytes worth of data.

PROGRAM 144

```
#include <fcntl.h>
#include <unistd.h>
main()
{
    int fd,pid;
    char buff[11];
    fd=open("test",O_RDONLY);
    lockf(fd,F_LOCK,0);
    pid = fork( );
    if (pid == 0)
    {
        read(fd,buf,10);
        buff[10] = '\0';
        printf("Buf is %s \n",buf);
    }
    else
    {
        sleep(5);
        printf("Parent Process over\n");
    }
}
```

After opening the file we lock it and then fork a child process. The time slice is handed to the child process. Since there is no *lockf( )* here the process does not wait. The *read( )* does not care whether the file is locked or not. It proceeds to do its work. It reads 10 bytes which are then printed.

So how do we make sure that a read does not take place if a file has been locked? Because if it did and the other user was writing to the file we would not get the updated version of data. To overcome this read inconsistency we can use the F_TEST parameter.

PROGRAM 145

```
#include <fcntl.h>
#include <unistd.h>
main( )
{
    int fd,pid;
    int i;
    char buf[11];
    fd=open("test",O_RDWR);
    lockf(fd,F_LOCK,0);
    pid = fork( );
    if (pid == 0)
    {
        for(;;)
        {
            if (lockf(fd,F_TEST,0) == 0 )
            {
                read(fd,buf,10);
                break;
            }
        }
        buf[10] = '\0';
        printf("Buf is %s \n",buf);
    }
    else
    {
        sleep(5);
        printf("Parent Process over\n");
    }
}
```

The child process is put in a *for* loop that is unending. In it, a check is made to see if the file test is locked. If it is we're taken back to the beginning of the loop.

The parent process wakes up after a period of 5 seconds. As a result the file lock is released. The *if* condition proves true and the *read( )* gets activated. The child process then prints the values read before it terminates.

Read Inconsistency

However, there's one problem here. What if, as soon as the *if* condition was proved true but before the *read( )* started, the time slice ended and another process which was activated locked this file? In that case the next time slice round this process would again be reading some false data because the other process may be writing to the file. So what do we do in a case like this?

Simple. Take the *if* and all the statements within it as one logical unit. So when the *if* is evaluated to a true all statements within it have to get executed.

Remember that ticketing example we explained right in the beginning. Well, now let's see how we can actually implement it. But we'll do this real slowly, a step at a time.

To start with, there has to be a unique number to identify each ticket. Whenever a person accesses the computer for a ticket he gets the ticket number that has not been issued. For example, if 10 tickets have been already issued, a request for a ticket will yield ticket number 11. But what if 2 people accessed at the same time?

If there was no lock, both would get the same ticket number -- that is 11 -- since the person who accessed first, time slicewise, would not have issued it in the meantime. To circumvent this, we could have a common file that had only one bit of data: the next ticket number to get.

Now the first person to access this number will immediately increment it and write it back to the file. Now the second user will see the new number. Which in turn he will increment, and so on and so forth.

To start with let's first create a file that will hold the latest number.

PROGRAM 146

```
#include <fcntl.h>
main( )
{
    int fd,seqno,ctr;
    fd = open("seq",O_CREAT | O_RDWR | O_TRUNC,0666);
    seqno = 0;
    write(fd,&seqno,sizeof(int));
}
```

We open a file called seq in read write mode. If it already exists, it is truncated. In this file we then write a 0.

The next step would be to have a process that opens this file, reads its value, increments this value and then writes the incremented value back. That's what the next program does.

PROGRAM 147

```
#include <fcntl.h>
#include <unistd.h>
main( )
{
    int fd,seqno,ctr;
    fd = open("seq",O_RDWR);
    if (fd < 0)
    {
        perror("first creat the seq file and then run ");
        exit(1);
    }
    for(ctr = 0; ctr < 20; ctr++)
    {
        lseek(fd,0l,0);
        read(fd,&seqno,sizeof(int));
        printf("Process id %d seqno is %d\n",getpid( ),seqno);
        seqno++;
        lseek(fd,0l,0);
        write(fd,&seqno,sizeof(int));
    }
}
```

We open the file seq in read write mode. If it does not exist, the process terminates. Else the *for* loop is activated. It runs 20 times.

In this *for* loop an *lseek( )* is done to position the pointer at the beginning of the file. And the data is read into the variable *seqno* which is then printed with the PID. The value in this variable is incremented and written back to the file. The *lseek( )* repositions the file pointer back to the beginning.

```
Process id 935 seqno is 0
Process id 935 seqno is 1
Process id 935 seqno is 2
Process id 935 seqno is 3
Process id 935 seqno is 4
Process id 935 seqno is 5
Process id 935 seqno is 6
Process id 935 seqno is 7
Process id 935 seqno is 8
Process id 935 seqno is 9
Process id 935 seqno is 10
Process id 935 seqno is 11
Process id 935 seqno is 12
Process id 935 seqno is 13
Process id 935 seqno is 14
Process id 935 seqno is 15
Process id 935 seqno is 16
Process id 935 seqno is 17
Process id 935 seqno is 18
Process id 935 seqno is 19
```

If this program is run only by one user at a time, there isn't a problem. A sequence will always be maintained. But this is hardly the case in a multi-user system. Run this program twice one after the other, both times in the background, and see what happens.

Note: remove the seq file and then re-run the program that creates it.

This is the output we saw:

```
Process id 936 seqno is 0
Process id 936 seqno is 1
Process id 936 seqno is 2
Process id 936 seqno is 3
Process id 936 seqno is 4
Process id 936 seqno is 5
Process id 936 seqno is 6
Process id 936 seqno is 7
Process id 936 seqno is 8
Process id 936 seqno is 9
Process id 936 seqno is 10
ProcessProcess id 937 seqno is 6
Process id 937 seqno is 7
Process id 937 seqno is 8
Process id 937 seqno is 9
Process id 937 seqno is 10
Process id 937 seqno is 11
Process id 937 seqno is 12
Process id 936 seqno is Process id 937 seqno is 13
Process id 937 seqno is 14
Process id 937 seqno is 15
Process id 937 seqno is 16
Process id 937 seqno is 17
Process id 937 seqno is 18
Process id 937 seqno is 17
Process id 936 seqno is 18
Process id 936 seqno is 19
Process id 936 seqno is 20
Process id 936 seqno is 21
Process id 936 seqno is 22
Process id 936 seqno is 23
Process id 936 seqno
```

Everything went haywire. The sequence that should have been maintained is not there at all. All because we left out one important step: that of locking the file.

PROGRAM 148

```
#include <fcntl.h>
#include <unistd.h>
main( )
{
```

```
    int fd,seqno,ctr;
    fd = open("seq",O_RDWR);
    for(ctr = 0; ctr < 20; ctr++)
    {
        lockf(fd, F_LOCK,0);
        read(fd,&seqno,sizeof(int));
        printf("Process id %d seqno is %d\n",getpid( ),seqno);
        seqno++;
        lseek(fd,0l,0);
        write(fd,&seqno,sizeof(int));
        lockf(fd, F_ULOCK,0);
    }
}
```

Here, notice what we're doing. In the *for* loop we lock the file, read from it, increment the value and write the changed value back to the file. And because the file is locked no other process can read or write to it. After the incremented value is written, the file is unlocked so that some other process may get access to it.

Run this program twice, both times in the background, and you will see that this time round there is no confusion of data. Because the file lock - unlock takes care to ensure this.

Range Locking

We need not always lock the whole file. We can, if we want only to lock a part of it. This small part is normally known as a record. To the *lockf( )* function we normally specify the last parameter as a 0. 0 signified the entire file. By specifying a number here we can lock only that many bytes.

Create the file locktest with at least 20 characters worth of data.

PROGRAM 149

```
/*
range locking i.e explain till now it was file level lock this  is like record
or it is range locking
*/
#include <fcntl.h>
#include <unistd.h>
```

```
main( )
{
   int fd,pid,retval;
   fd=open("locktest",O_RDWR);
   lockf(fd,F_LOCK,10l);
   printf("Parent locked 1-10 chars\n");
   pid = fork( );
   if (pid == 0)
   {
      retval = lockf(fd,F_TLOCK,10);
      if (retval == -1)
         printf("Char 1-10 are already locked\n");
      else
         printf("Child locked 1-10 char\n");
      lseek(fd,10l,0);
      retval = lockf(fd,F_TLOCK,10l);
      if (retval == -1)
         printf("Char 11-20 are already locked\n");
      else
         printf("child locked 11-20 cahrs\n");
      printf("Child process over\n");
   }
   else
   {
      sleep(5);
      printf("Parent Process over\n");
   }
}
```

When you run this program the locktest file is opened and the first 10 bytes are locked through a call to the *lockf( )* function. This function is passed three parameters: the file handle, F_TLOCK, signifying that the file should be locked, and a 10 for the number of bytes to lock.

The *fork( )* creates a child process which is given the time slice. It then tries to lock the first 10 bytes of the file. But since they are already locked, the call fails.

An *lseek( )* moves the pointer 10 bytes forward. Another call to the *lockf( )* now results in the next 10 bytes being locked successfully since the parent process has only locked the first 10 bytes. The child process now terminates.

In time the parent process wakes and terminates too.

Action Stations....Deadlock !!!

What is this deadlock? Some new anarchic weapon? Not at all, merely a Catch-22 situation that we have forced ourselves into. Let's see how?

PROGRAM 150

```
#include <fcntl.h>
#include <unistd.h>
main( )
{
   int fd,pid;
   fd=open("locktest",O_RDWR);
   lockf(fd,F_LOCK,10l);
   printf("Parent locked 1-10 chars\n");
   pid = fork( );
   if (pid == 0)
   {
      lockf(fd,F_LOCK,10l);
      printf("Child process over\n");
   }
   else
   {
      wait(0);
      printf("Parent Process over\n");
   }
}
```

We open a file locktest in read write mode and lock ten bytes. A child process is forked and gets the time slice. In it we try to lock 10 bytes but these have already been locked. So no go.

Now we have the child process waiting for the parent to unlock the file. But in the parent there is a *wait( )* which is waiting for the child process to get over. And while each waits for the other life goes on.

But if a deadlock occurs in the way shown below, UNIX is smart enough to recognize it and do the needful.

PROGRAM 151

```
#include <fcntl.h>
#include <unistd.h>
main( )
{
    int fd,pid,retval;
    fd=open("locktest",O_RDWR);
    lockf(fd,F_LOCK,10l);
    printf("Parent locked 1-10 chars\n");
    pid = fork( );
    if (pid == 0)
    {
        lseek(fd,10l,0);
        retval = lockf(fd,F_LOCK,5l);
        if (retval == -1)
            perror("in child 11-15 chars ");
        else
            printf("11-15 chars locked in child\n");
        lseek(fd,0l,0);
        retval = lockf(fd,F_LOCK,5l);
        if (retval == -1)
            perror("in child 1-5 chars ");
        else
            printf("1-5 chars locked in child\n");
        printf("Child process over\n");
    }
    else
    {
        sleep(1);
        lseek(fd,10l,0);
        retval = lockf(fd,F_LOCK,5l);
        if (retval == -1)
            perror("in parent 10-15 chars ");
        else
            printf("Parent 10-15 chars locked\n");
        printf("Parent Process over\n");
    }
}
```

The parent process opens the file *locktest*, locks the first 10 bytes and creates a child process.

The child process moves the pointer to the 11th byte from where it locks the next 5 bytes. Another *lseek( )* now moves the pointer back to the beginning of the file where a lock is attempted on the first 5 bytes. But this fails as these bytes have been locked by the parent process. As a result, the child process waits at this function call.

Now the time slice is handed to the parent process which wakes, moves the pointer to the 11th byte and tries to lock the next 5 bytes. But this is unsuccessful as they have already been locked by the child process.

At this point normally we would expect a deadlock to occur since the child is waiting for the parent, which in turn is waiting for the child. But UNIX does not allow this to happen. It realizes a deadlock has occured here. So it prints an error message Deadlock situation detected/avoided and terminates the parent process.

This results in the lock on the first 10 bytes being lifted. The child process can now lock these bytes -- which it does -- before terminating.

Note: a deadlock will not only be the case between two parent-child processes. It is also vaild for two totally unrelated processes that are trying to work with the same resources.

System Lock Table

Whenever a file is locked, an entry is made in a table called the system lock table. This table is filled with all the details regarding a locked file. A file can be locked only if there is place available in the system lock table.

Suppose we locked a file and then unlocked a small part in the middle: would that mean for the two extreme locked areas there would be two entries in the system lock table? Yes, in this table there will be two different entries. Unfortunately, there is no way of actually seeing this table. But we can see how two extreme sections can be locked.

That's what the next program does.

PROGRAM 152

```
#include <fcntl.h>
#include <unistd.h>
#include <errno.h>
main()
{
    int fd;
    int i,retval,pid;
    char ch;
    fd=open("test",O_RDWR);
    lockf(fd,F_LOCK,100) ;
    pid = fork( ) ;
    if (pid == 0)
    {
        printf("Child trying to lock\n");
        lseek(fd,25l,0);
        lockf(fd,F_LOCK,25l);
        printf("Child successfully locked\n");
        printf("Child process over\n");
    }
    else
    {
        sleep(5);
        printf("Parent unlocked\n");
        lseek(fd,25l,0);
        lockf(fd,F_ULOCK,25l);
        sleep(5);
        printf("Parent process over\n");
    }
}
```

We open a file and then lock the first 100 bytes. A *fork( )* then creates a child process.

In the child process, which is handed the time slice first, an *lseek( )* moves the pointer 25 bytes forward. An attempt is made to lock the next 25 bytes. But it fails as they are already locked. This results in the child process waiting at this point.

The time slice is handed to the parent process which immediately goes to *sleep( )*. So at this point the child and the parent are both waiting. After the 5 seconds the parent process moves the file ponter to the 26th byte. Then it unlocks the next 25 bytes before going back to *sleep( )*.

When the time slice is handed to the child process it locks these 25 bytes and terminates. Now at this point we have the first 25 bytes and the last 50 bytes locked. This lasts till the parent process is in memory.

There is one problem with the *lockf( )* function. If a file is opened in read only mode, another process which has opened the file in write mode has access to it. A test for a lock in that process will yield a not true.

PROGRAM 153

```
#include <fcntl.h>
#include <unistd.h>
main()
{
   int fd,pid;
   int i;
   char buf[11];
   fd=open("test",O_RDONLY);
   lockf(fd,F_LOCK,0);
   pid = fork( );
   if (pid == 0)
   {
      for(;;)
      {
         if (lockf(fd,F_TEST,0) == 0)
         {
            read(fd,buf,10);
            break;
         }
```

```
        }
        buf[10] = '\0';
        printf("Buf is %s \n",buf);
    }
    else
    {
        sleep(5);
        printf("Parent Process over\n");
    }
}
```

We open a file in read only mode, lock it and then fork a child process. In this child process an attempt is made to check whether the file is locked. However, this *if* returns a not locked, ie. a 0, even though the file is locked. A 0 is returned because the file is opened in read only mode and therefore the *lockf( )* does not really lock it. As a result, 10 bytes from the file are read and printed. In time the parent process wakes and terminates.

More Control Over a File

And it is to counter this problem that we need to use the *fcntl( )* function. To understand this function we need to understand the related structure which is defined in the fcntl.h header file.

```
struct flock {
    short l_type;
    short l_whence;
    long l_start;
    long l_len; /* len = 0 means until end of file */
    short l_sysid;
    short l_pid;
};
```

This structure holds information that the *fcntl( )* function needs to lock the file it is being asked to. The following program will make this clearer.

PROGRAM 154

```
#include <fcntl.h>
main( )
```

```
{
    int fd,pid,retval;
    struct flock lockp,lockc;
    fd = open("test",O_RDONLY);
    lockp.l_type = F_RDLCK;
    lockp.l_whence = 0;
    lockp.l_start = 10;
    lockp.l_len = 15;
    retval = fcntl(fd,F_SETLK,&lockp);

    printf("in parent fcntl returned %d\n",retval);
    pid = fork( );
    if (pid == 0)
    {
        printf("In child\n");
        lockc.l_type = F_RDLCK;
        lockc.l_whence = 0;
        lockc.l_start = 10;
        lockc.l_len = 15;
        retval = fcntl(fd,F_SETLK,&lockc);
        printf("in child fcntl returned %d\n",retval);
        printf("Child process over\n");
    }
    else
    {
        sleep(5);
        printf("Parent process over\n");
    }
}
```

We define two structures *lockp* and *lockc* that look like the structure *flock*. And then open the file test in read only mode.

Next, we assign some of the members of the *lockp* structure some values. *l_type* with F_RDLCK means a read lock on the file. *l_whence* is similar to the last parameter of *lseek( )* with a 0 signifying the start of the file, a 1 for the current position of the file pointer and a 2 for the end of the file.

l_start indicates which byte and from *l_whence*. In our case, the 10th byte from the start of the file. Finally *l_len* gives the number of bytes to lock. In this case we are assign a value of 15. So, from the 10th byte onward, the next 15 bytes will get locked.

A call is then made to the *fcntl( )* function which is passed three parameters: the file handle, F_SETLK, and the starting address of the *lockp* structure. It then proceeds to lock the number of bytes specified, in our case 15.

A *fork( )* then creates a child process. In it we assign values to the members of the structure *lockc* in much the same way as we did for the *lockp* structure. Here, too, since we're assigning a F_RDLCK to the *l_type* member when a call is made to the *fcntl( )*, the specified bytes in the file are locked. So both processes have locked the same 15 bytes. This was possible because a read lock had been specified.

Finally, the child process terminates, and then the parent process. But while we can have two or more read locks on a file at the same time, the same is not true if on a read locked file a write lock is attempted.

PROGRAM 155

```
#include <fcntl.h>
main( )
{
    int fd,pid,retval;
    struct flock lockp,lockc;
    fd = open("test",O_RDWR);
    lockp.l_type = F_RDLCK;
    lockp.l_whence = 0;
    lockp.l_start = 10;
    lockp.l_len = 15;
    retval = fcntl(fd,F_SETLK,&lockp);
    printf("in parent fcntl returned %d\n",retval);
    pid = fork( );
    if (pid == 0)
    {
        printf("In child\n");
        lockc.l_type = F_WRLCK;
        lockc.l_whence = 0;
        lockc.l_start = 10;
```

```
        lockc.l_len = 15;
        retval = fcntl(fd,F_SETLK,&lockc);
        printf("in child fcntl returned %d\n",retval);
        printf("Child process over\n");
    }
    else
    {
        sleep(5);
        printf("Parent process over\n");
    }
}
```

Here the parent process assigns a **F_RDLCK** to the file test, which is opened in read write mode. As a result, a call to the *fcntl( )* function commits a read lock on this file.

In the *fork( )*-created child process a write lock is attempted on the same number of bytes in the file. But this fails. And the child process terminates. After 5 seconds the parent process wakes and terminates.

Even if another write lock is attempted on an already writelocked file, it will be unsuccessful. That's what the next program shows.

PROGRAM 156

```
#include <fcntl.h>
main( )
{
    int fd,pid,retval;
    struct flock lockp,lockc;
    fd = open("test",O_RDWR);
    lockp.l_type = F_WRLCK;
    lockp.l_whence = 0;
    lockp.l_start = 10;
    lockp.l_len = 15;
    retval = fcntl(fd,F_SETLK,&lockp);
    printf("in parent fcntl returned %d\n",retval);
    pid = fork( );
    if (pid == 0)
    {
        printf("In child\n");
        lockc.l_type = F_WRLCK;
```

```
        lockc.l_whence = 0;
        lockc.l_start = 10;
        lockc.l_len = 15;
        retval = fcntl(fd,F_SETLK,&lockc);
        printf("in child fcntl returned %d\n",retval);
        printf("Child process over\n");
    }
    else
    {
        sleep(5);
        printf("Parent process over\n");
    }
}
```

There is no change in this program save that both *l_type* members are being assigned a F_WRLCK. The child process terminates since it can't lock the specified number of bytes. And after 5 seconds so does the parent process.

If a lock is unsuccessful and we don't want the child process to terminate, but want instead to keep it waiting, then the second parameter to the *fcntl( )* function has to be F_SETLKW.

PROGRAM 157

```
/* locking with block */
#include <fcntl.h>
main( )
{
    int fd,pid,retval;
    struct flock lockp,lockc;
    fd = open("test",O_RDWR);
    lockp.l_type = F_WRLCK;
    lockp.l_whence = 0;
    lockp.l_start = 10;
    lockp.l_len = 15;
    retval = fcntl(fd,F_SETLK,&lockp);
    printf("in parent fcntl returned %d\n",retval);
    pid = fork( );
    if (pid == 0)
    {
        printf("In child\n");
        lockc.l_type = F_WRLCK;
```

```
        lockc.l_whence = 0;
        lockc.l_start = 10;
        lockc.l_len = 15;
        fcntl(fd,F_SETLKW,&lockc);
        printf("Child process over\n");
    }
    else
    {
        sleep(5);
        printf("Parent process over\n");
    }
}
```

The entire program is the same. But in the child process we pass F_SETLKW as the second parameter to the *fcntl( )* function. As a result, the child process keeps waiting till the parent process releases its lock on the file. This, of course, happens only after a period of 5 seconds.

The *fcntl( )* function can be used to unlock a file too. Here's how:

```
PROGRAM 158
#include <fcntl.h>
main( )
{
    int fd,pid,retval;
    struct flock lockp,lockc;
    fd = open("test",O_RDWR);
    lockp.l_type = F_WRLCK;
    lockp.l_whence = 0;
    lockp.l_start = 10;
    lockp.l_len = 15;
    retval = fcntl(fd,F_SETLK,&lockp);
    printf("in parent fcntl returned %d\n",retval);
    pid = fork( );
    if (pid == 0)
    {
        printf("In child\n");
        lockc.l_type = F_WRLCK;
        lockc.l_whence = 0;
        lockc.l_start = 10;
        lockc.l_len = 15;
```

```
        retval = fcntl(fd,F_SETLKW,&lockc);
        printf("in child fcntl returned %d\n",retval);
        printf("Child process over\n");
    }
    else
    {
        sleep(5);
        lockp.l_type = F_UNLCK;
        lockp.l_whence = 0;
        lockp.l_start = 10;
        lockp.l_len = 15;
        printf("Parent unlocking\n");
        retval = fcntl(fd,F_SETLK,&lockp);
        printf("in parent fcntl returned %d\n",retval);
        sleep(5);
        printf("Parent process over\n");
    }
}
```

We open a file test in read write mode and assign some values to the members of structure *lockp*. We then call the *fcntl( )* function (with the file handle *fp*), F_SETLK and the starting address of the structure *lockp*. As a result the file gets write locked.

Next, a *fork( )* creates a child process. In this some members of the *lockc* structure are initialized. An attempt is then made to write lock the test file using the *fcntl( )* function. But since it has been already locked the attempt is unsuccessful. The child process thus waits at this point.

In time the parent process, which has been put to sleep for 5 seconds, wakes and proceeds to unlock the file. Notice the value F_UNLCK that is being assigned to the member *l_type* of structure *lockp*. The *fcntl( )*, as a result, unlocks this file. The parent process is then put back to sleep.

The child process is given the time slice. It locks the file since at this point the file is unlocked. And terminates. After 5 seconds the parent process too terminates.

We can find out what type of locking has been performed by passing the F_GETLK value to the *fcntl( )* function. Of course, in this case the process won't wait till the lock is removed but merely give the details of the kind of lock it is. It will then terminate the process.

PROGRAM 159

```
/* use of getlock */
#include <fcntl.h>
main( )
{
  int fd,pid,retval;
  struct flock tlock,glock;
  printf("In parent pid is %d\n",getpid( ));
  fd = open("test",O_RDWR);
  tlock.l_type = F_WRLCK;
  tlock.l_whence = 0;
  tlock.l_start = 5;
  tlock.l_len = 55;
  retval = fcntl(fd,F_SETLK,&tlock);
  printf("in parent fcntl returned %d\n",retval);
  pid = fork( );
  if (pid == 0)
  {
    printf("In child pid is %d\n",getpid( ));
    tlock.l_type = F_RDLCK;
    tlock.l_whence = 0;
    tlock.l_start = 10;
    tlock.l_len = 25;
    retval = fcntl(fd,F_GETLK,&tlock);
    printf("in child fcntl returned %d\n",retval);
    printf("%d Process has locked this section\n",tlock.l_pid);
    printf("Lock type is %d\n",tlock.l_type);
    printf("whence is %d\n",tlock.l_whence);
    printf("start is %d\n",tlock.l_start);
    printf("len is %d\n",tlock.l_len);
    printf("Child process over\n");
  }
  else
  {
    sleep(5);
    printf("Parent process over\n");
```

```
    }
}
```

In the parent process we write lock the file and then fork a child process. In the child process we assign some values to the members of the structure *t_lock*. These values signify whether the particular part of the file is locked or not. This structure as well as the value F_GETLK is passed to the *fcntl()* function.

fcntl() interprets this to mean that only information is wanted as to the kind of lock that has been performed on the file. It subsequently proceeds to assign this information to the members of the structure *tlock*. These are then printed.

These members will have the values that the file has been locked with in the parent process -- that is, F_WRLCK for a write lock, a 0 to signify from the beginning of file, a 5 to say from the 5th byte onwards and a 55 to mean the next 50 bytes.

After these values are printed, the child process terminates and in time, so does the parent process.

Remember somewhere above in the *lockf()* we showed how a lock need not stop another process from reading a file. This is because the *read()* is not worried whether a file has been locked or not. Well, the same is true for a *fcntl()* locked file.

PROGRAM 160

```
/* use of getlock */
#include <fcntl.h>
main()
{
   int fd,pid,retval;
   char buff[16];
   struct flock tlock;
   fd = open("test",O_RDWR);
   tlock.l_type = F_WRLCK;
   tlock.l_whence = 0;
   tlock.l_start = 5;
   tlock.l_len = 55;
   retval = fcntl(fd,F_SETLK,&tlock);
```

```
    printf("in parent fcntl returned %d\n",retval);
    pid = fork( );
    if (pid == 0)
    {
        printf("In child process\n");
        retval = read(fd,buf,15);
        buf[15] = '\0';
        printf(" retval is %d buf is %s\n",retval,buf);
    }
    else
    {
        sleep(5);
        printf("Parent process over\n");
    }
}
```

We open a file test and lock 55 bytes from the 5th byte onwards. A *fork( )* now creates a child process in which we read 15 bytes into the array *buf*. The *read( )* performs successfully even though the file has been locked. The *buf* is then printed on screen. The child process terminates and, in time, so does the parent.

Don't get misled by these two commands for locking and unlocking. Although they work differently they use the same system lock table. So, if a file is locked, say, through the *fcntl( )* function, an attempt to lock it through the *lockf( )* will yet be unsuccessful.

PROGRAM 161

```
/*from her onwards till 26 comb starts*/
#include <unistd.h>
#include <fcntl.h>
main( )
{
    int fd,pid,retval;
    struct flock lockp,lockc;
    fd = open("test",O_RDWR);
    lockp.l_type = F_WRLCK;
    lockp.l_whence = 0;
    lockp.l_start = 2;
```

```
    lockp.l_len = 5;
    retval = fcntl(fd,F_SETLK,&lockp);
    printf("in parent fcntl returned %d\n",retval);
    pid = fork( );
    if (pid == 0)
    {
        printf("In child\n");
        lseek(fd,2l,0);
        retval = lockf(fd,F_TLOCK,5);
        printf("in child lockf returned %d\n",retval);
        printf("Child process over\n");
    }
    else
    {
        sleep(5);
        printf("Parent process over\n");
    }
}
```

We lock bytes 2 to 7 in the file test using the *fcntl( )* function. A *fork( )* then creates a child process in which the file pointer is moved by two bytes. An attempt is made also to lock the bytes from 2 to 7, ie. the same 5 bytes which have already been locked, but using the *lockf( )* function.

However, since these bytes have already been locked the *lockf( )* is unsuccessful. The child process does not wait since we have specified the second parameter to the *lockf( )* function as F_TLOCK. Instead, it terminates immediately. Later, so does the parent process.

Of course, if we want the child process to wait till the parent process removes its lock on the file, we can pass the F_LOCK value to the *lockf( )* function.

PROGRAM 162

```
#include <unistd.h>
#include <fcntl.h>
main( )
{
    int fd,pid,retval;
```

```
    struct flock lockp,lockc;
    fd = open("test",O_RDWR);
    lockp.l_type = F_WRLCK;
    lockp.l_whence = 0;
    lockp.l_start = 2;
    lockp.l_len = 5;
    retval = fcntl(fd,F_SETLK,&lockp);
    printf("in parent fcntl returned %d\n",retval);
    pid = fork( );
    if (pid == 0)
    {
        printf("In child\n");
        lseek(fd,2l,0);
        lockf(fd,F_LOCK,5);
        printf("Child process over\n");
    }
    else
    {
        sleep(5);
        printf("Parent process over\n");
    }
}
```

We lock bytes 2 to 7 of the file in the parent process using the *fcntl( )* function and then attempt to lock it in the child process, too. However, since these bytes are already locked the attempt is unsuccessful. As a result the child process is put in a waut state. Once the parent process terminates, the child process is able to lock this file.

Considering that both the *lockf( )* and *fcntl( )* functions deal with the same system file table, a lock by one of these can be removed by the other. If you don't believe us, try out the next program.

PROGRAM 163

```
#include <unistd.h>
#include <fcntl.h>
main( )
{
    int fd,pid,retval;
    struct flock lockp,lockc;
    fd = open("test",O_RDWR);
```

```
    lockp.l_type = F_WRLCK;
    lockp.l_whence = 0;
    lockp.l_start = 2;
    lockp.l_len = 5;
    retval = fcntl(fd,F_SETLK,&lockp);
    printf("in parent fcntl returned %d\n",retval);
    pid = fork( );
    if (pid == 0)
    {
        printf("In child\n");
        lseek(fd,2l,0);
        lockf(fd,F_LOCK,5);
        printf("Child process over\n");
    }
    else
    {
        sleep(5);
        printf("parent unlocking\n");
        lseek(fd,2l,0);
        lockf(fd,F_ULOCK,5);
        sleep(5);
        printf("Parent process over\n");
    }
}
```

We lock 2 to 7 bytes of the file test in the parent process using the *fcntl( )* function. A *fork( )* now creates a child process which tries to lock the same bytes in the file. However, if the attempt is unsuccessful, it results in the child process waiting at the call to *lockf( )*.

Meanwhile, the parent wakes, moves the file pointer to the 2nd byte, unlocks the next 5 bytes using the *lockf( )* function and goes to sleep. As a result, when the time slice is handed to the child, the latter sees that these bytes have been locked and its call to the *lockf( )* function performs successfully. The child process terminates and, after a while, so does the parent process.

So far we have always been locking bytes from the beginning of the file. Here is one example that shows how to lock bytes at the end of a file.

PROGRAM 164

```
/* whence explanation */
#include <unistd.h>
#include <fcntl.h>
main( )
{
    int fd,pid,retval;
    struct flock lockp,lockc;
    fd = open("test",O_RDWR);
    lockp.l_type = F_WRLCK;
    lockp.l_whence = 2;
    lockp.l_start = -10;
    lockp.l_len = 5;
    retval = fcntl(fd,F_SETLK,&lockp);
    printf("in parent fcntl returned %d\n",retval);
    pid = fork( );
    if (pid == 0)
    {
        printf("In child\n");
        lseek(fd,0l,0);
        retval = lockf(fd,F_TLOCK,-5);
        printf("in child lockf returned %d\n",retval);
        printf("Child process over\n");
    }
    else
    {
        sleep(5);
        printf("Parent process over\n");
    }
}
```

We open a file test in read write mode and assign a 2 to the member *l_whence* of structure *lock_p*. This 2 means end of file. Further, a -10 is assigned to the member *l_start*.

Now when we call the *fcntl( )* function and pass it this structure, it will first move the file pointer to the end of file. It then takes the pointer 10 bytes back and, from this 10th last byte, locks the next 5 bytes.

Assume that we had 50 bytes in the file. The pointer would be first moved to the end of the file, then moved to the 40th byte, and from the 40th byte the next 5 bytes will be locked.

Permissions and File Locking

You'll remember that we ran a program earlier that locked a file, but in spite of that a *read( )* read the number of characters specified. As we said then a *read( )* (or *write( )*) does not care if a file is locked or not. So, does this mean that we have to live with this quirk? Not at all.

We know that every file has associated with it a set of permissions. These can be seen when we do a ls -l. These permissions are for the user-group-everyone. And basically project read write and a execute status. This is what we can make use of to lock a file so that even a *read( )* won't be able to perform.

So which is the bit in the permissions that we can fool around with? Considering that it is a data file, we don't need the group-execute bit, do we? So, why not turn it off? And turn the set-group-ID on? In which case the file is given a permission l to imply a lock.

The set-group-ID being on means that any person in the group who runs the program will do so as the owner. But if the file is a data file there is no question of running it. And if that is the case isn't it rather stupid to have the execute bit on?

UNIX System V realized this and decided to take advantage of it by allowing this execute bit to be turned on for locking purposes. But if the group-execute bit is off, the set-group-ID cannot be switched on. Try it and see.

Create a file called test with read-write, read- write, read-write permissions, ie. 0666 as the last parameter to the *open( )* function. Then do a chmod g+s test on the file at the UNIX prompt.

The g+s means set the group ID on. However UNIX, instead of following our wishes, flashes an error: chmod: Warning: Execute permission required for set-ID on execution for test.

So what is the way out? Create the file with the set-group-ID on and the group-execute bit off. This 16-bit integer that needs to be operated on in this manner is devised in the following manner.

The first 3 bits are for the permissions for the others. The next 3 bits are for the group permissions and the next 3 bits are for user permissions.

After that, the next 3 bits are for the stick bit, set-group-Id and set-user-ID. That leaves us with 4 bits, of which 3 bits are for the FIFO, character special file and directory file, and finally, the 4th bit is for whether it is a regular file or not.

We need to have a read-write on for all users. So this will evaluate to a 666. The set-group-ID needs to be also set, and gives us a value of 2. Finally, a 1 indicates that it is a regular file. Therefore, if we open a file with this value we will have the group-execute bit off and the set-group-ID on while giving evevrybody read-write access to it.

PROGRAM 165

```
#include <fcntl.h>
main( )
{
  int fd,i;
  umask(0);
  fd = open("test",O_CREAT | O_RDWR,0102666);
  if (fd < 0)
  {
    perror( " ");
    exit(0);
  }
  write(fd,"Hello world 123",15);
}
```

Note: make sure the file test does not exist.

We create this file with a value 0102666, which means what we have explained above. At the UNIX prompt, when you do a ls -l you will see an l in the group-execute bit permission. This is how it looks:

-rw-rwlrw- 1 vmci other 15 Apr 2 17:26 locktest

Now that we have created a file with a locked permission, let's move on to see whether a *read( )* works on it.

PROGRAM 166

```
#include <fcntl.h>
#include <unistd.h>
main( )
{
   int fd,pid;
   fd = open("test",O_RDWR);
   pid = fork( );
   if (pid == 0)
   {
      sleep(2);
      write(fd,"AAAAAAAAAA",10);
      printf("child process over\n");
   }
   else
   {
      lockf(fd,F_LOCK,0);
      sleep(5);
      printf("Parent Process over\n");
   }
}
```

We open the file test with read-write permissions and fork a child process. The child being put to sleep means the parent gets the time slice.

The parent proceeds to lock the file. And promptly goes to *sleep( )*. When the child awakes it tries to write to the file, but since it finds the file locked it proceeds to wait for the lock to be released. (Remember this file has been created with a locked permission by the last program. Therefore the *write( )* is not able to write to it.) This lock is released only when the parent wakes and terminates. The output is Parent process over and then Child process over.

A cat test at the prompt will show it to contain the "A"s written by the *write( )* in the child process.

What if we opened the file in read only mode?

PROGRAM 167

```
#include <fcntl.h>
#include <unistd.h>
main( )
{
   int fd,pid;
   pid = fork( );
   if (pid == 0)
   {
      sleep(2);
      fd = open("test",O_RDWR);
      write(fd,"AAAAAAAAAA",10);
      printf("child process over\n");
   }
   else
   {
      fd = open("test",O_RDONLY);
      lockf(fd,F_LOCK,0);
      sleep(5);
      printf("Parent Process over\n");
   }
}
```

A *fork( )* and the child process is immediately put to sleep. As a result the parent gets to open the file in read only mode. A *lockf( )* is now attempted. But does not really lock the file as it is opened in read only mode (this we have seen before). Now it is the parent's turn to *sleep( )*.

The time slice is once more handed to the child. It opens the file in read write mode and successfully writes to it before terminating. This is because the file is not locked. Thus the child process here gets over before the parent process terminates.

But isn't this a problem? We have some process having read access to the file while at the same time another is able to write to it? That's where *fcntl( )* comes in.

PROGRAM 168

```
#include <fcntl.h>
#include <unistd.h>
main( )
{
   int fd,pid;
   struct flock lockp;
   pid = fork( );
   if (pid == 0)
   {
      sleep(2);
      fd = open("test",O_RDWR);
      write(fd,"AAAAAAAAAA",10);
      printf("child process over\n");
   }
   else
   {
      fd = open("test",O_RDONLY);
      lockp.l_type = F_RDLCK;
      lockp.l_whence = 0;
      lockp.l_start = 0;
      lockp.l_len = 10;
      fcntl(fd,F_SETLK,&lockp);
      printf("Parent locked\n");
      sleep(5);
      printf("Parent process over\n");
   }
}
```

A *fork( )* creates a child which is put to *sleep( )*. In the parent the file is opened in read only mode. Members of the *lockp* structure are assigned values. And a call is made to the *fcntl( )* function to lock 10 bytes of this file with a read lock. Now it is the parent's turn to *sleep( )*.

The time slice is given to the child process. It proceeds to open the file in read write mode. But the *write( )* is not successful since the file has been locked. As a result only when the parent process terminates is the lock on the file released and the *write( )* performed successfully.

Thus, this time the parent process terminates before the child process.

Conclusion

As the world gets increasingly networked, as countries get electronically linked, computer professionals will have to converge on one burning issue - data security. Infact there will come a day when, like the Systems Administrator there will be a more specialized breed whose sole job will be to police these networks.

Until that happens the onus of data integrity and security will lie with us, the programmers.

Communicating Across Processes

One of the most important factors in making the world a global village is the level of sophistication that communications technology has reached. We have telephones and fax machines and telexes and, of course, modem-linked computers, not to mention ever-ubiquitous cinema and music.

Man has come a long way from being an island. And yet one gets the feeling that despite all the improvement in communications technology, people are interacting less and less. You have TV sets that constantly generate a kind of me and my fantasy world situation. Most science fiction writers too have painted a pessimistic view of the future in which man's overdependence on machines features prominently. There is also the new work ethos that has started in the US, where people work from home and are connected to their offices or clients through some technology like the phone or his computer modem. If this work style catches on, we are soon going to have a world where humans stop interacting directly.

But then, as most scientists feel, if we have something to create, we can't help but make it see the light of day and to hell with the social implications. And while this is a natural progression of humanity, what we need to be aware of and constantly remind ourselves of is that we need to interact with people if we are to grow. And a technologically imposed isolation is not the way to go about it. In fact we should remember why in the first place we have built these bridges of communication, and try to utilize them meaningfully.

Communication takes place if there is something to share. Ideas, thoughts, feelings, beliefs, cultures and just about every other facet that goes to make a human being. Through computers so far we have shared data - data linked to business, science and now as satellite communications make their mark news, views and what have you.

Communication in UNIX plays a very important role. We can send files to be printed at some distant location as well as have them accessed by different people logged on at different terminals. More than just sharing data actual communication can also take place in the form of a computer based conference, as you will see towards the end of this chapter.

Processes in computer memory are said to be communicating when one process passes data to another or vice-versa. But why do we need to have processes communicating in the first place? Because processes working in tandem considerably reduce the strain on the machine. Picture having one giant program in memory. Can you imagine the response time? Wouldn't it be better to split it up into smaller programs with all of them acting as and when needed. Of course, all these small programs have to mutually agree as to what the communication protocol to be followed will be.

And for these processes in memory to communicate with each other they need to be able to share data effectively. UNIX provides a number of ways to share or communicate data: signals, pipes and FIFO's.

Signals

Besides verbal communication, all of us depend a lot on non-verbal communication. This is conscious as well as unconscious. Most of us must have come across a situation when a member of the opposite sex looked at us with what we understood as interest. The dilation of her pupils or a longer than necessary stare were indicators or signals of her interest (of course, the dilations, etc, may have been caused because the person found us weird). Many books have been written on the subject of reading the signals people send us.

These signals, imaginary or real, tell us a lot about the person's frame of mind, and in turn shape our responses. Anger may reproduce anger, love, love, etc. All in all, signals indicate something which we can use to formulate our reactions. Take the signals on roads, for example. A red means halt and a green means proceed.

In UNIX too we can use SIGNALS in the very same manner. "To respond or not to respond", that is for the process that receives the signal to decide.

Processes can send each other signals. For example say Process A has finished processing some data, it may send a signal to Process B. Process B will also receive the output of the processed data from Process A. Based on this output it has to decide what response to give.

There are many different types of signals, each with some mnemonic name: SIGINT, for example. These names, which are defined in the signal.h header file are symbolic for some positive integer.

Suppose we run a process that takes inordinately long, thus leading us to believe that something is wrong. To terminate it, we either press the DEL or CTRL \ keys. This results in us being brought back to the shell.

What happens is that the part of the kernel looking after keyboard interrupts realizes that the DEL key has been pressed. The kernel then sends a signal called SIGINT to all processes associated with the terminal. And they terminate. The shell, too, because it is a process, receives this signal but ignores it.

PROGRAM 169

```
#include <signal.h>

main( )
{
   printf("Use DEL key for exiting\n");
   for(; ; );
```

```
}
```

Compile and run this program. Then press the DEL key. The program terminates because the pressing of the DEL key forces the kernel to send a SIGINT signal which is interpreted as "terminate a program".

Signal Handling

By default UNIX already understands some signals like the one generated by the kernel when the DEL key is pressed. These signals have some default code attached to them, which is activated whenever the signal is sent. But this very signal can be reset by us to perform some other task, that is execute some other code.

The function that UNIX provides us to handle signals with is *signal( )*. This function expects two parameters: the key and the name of the function that is to be activated when the key is pressed.

PROGRAM 170

```
#include <signal.h>

void abc( );
main( )
{
   printf("Press <DEL> key.\n");
   signal(SIGINT, abc);
   for(; ; );
}

void abc( )
{
   printf("You have pressed the <DEL> key.\n");
}
```

The first parameter we have passed the *signal( )* function is the signal sent when the DEL key is pressed. SIGINT is defined in the signal header file as 2.

The second parameter is the name of the function to run when the signal related to the DEL key is sent. This is the function *abc( )*, which prints a message on the screen.

The *for* loop now ensures that the program is up and running constantly.

Essentially what has happened is that since we're redefining the signal sent by the DEL key to do some other task, its default task -- terminating a program -- does not perform.

However, if you press the DEL key once more, the program does terminate. Does this mean that since there was one call to the *signal( )* function it worked only once? If so then three calls should terminate the program only if the DEL key is pressed thrice.

PROGRAM 171

```
#include <signal.h>

void abc( );
main( )
{
   printf("Press <DEL> key.\n");
   signal(SIGINT, abc);
   signal(SIGINT, abc);
   signal(SIGINT, abc);
   for(; ; );
}

void abc( )
{
   printf("You have pressed the <DEL> key.\n");
}
```

Not at all. It did not work in the way we thought. The program yet terminated on the second instance of the DEL key being pressed. So where's the problem?

Whenever *signal( )* is called, the second parameter, which is the function, passed to it is stored in memory. Whenever the specified key is pressed, this function is executed and then immediately cleared from memory. As a result further calls can't execute it. Instead the default code is executed. This terminates the program. The default code is always defined as SIG_DFL, no matter which signal is sent.

PROGRAM 172

```
#include <signal.h>

main()
{
   printf("Press Delete Key to terminate \n");
   signal(SIGINT, SIG_DFL);
   for(; ;);
}
```

The SIG_DFL stands for the default code. This is the code that is activated when the signal SIGINT is sent.

Isn't it a lot like the TSRs we did in DOS, where an interrupt function was replaced with another user-defined function that got called. After this function terminated, the actual function in the ROM BIOS was called.

But this gives a half-baked signal form. Shouldn't it be that once a key is defined to run some code, it should remain so forever, or at least till we explicitly release it? Of course, but the question remains as to how to get this done? Simple. After the function is executed and cleared from memory restore it by using the same method, that is, another call to the *signal( )* function.

PROGRAM 173

```
#include <signal.h>

void abc( );
main()
{
   signal(SIGINT, abc);
   printf("Press <DEL> key.\n");
   for(; ;);
}
```

```
void abc( )
{
   printf("You have pressed the <DEL> key.\n");
   signal(SIGINT, abc);
}
```

Check out the call to *signal( )* in the *abc( )* function. It reinitializes the function in memory. It's a kind of recursion. We press the DEL key - a signal is sent - *abc( )* is executed and cleared from memory - but the call to *signal( )* reloads it into memory. Press the DEL key and the same procedure takes place. And so on and so forth.

The shell is a process, too. But a signal sent by a DEL key pressed at the prompt does not terminate it. This is a real bias. Why should we have one set of rules for some process and another set for another process? And how does UNIX implement this?

What the shell does is ignore the SIGINT signal sent when the DEL key is pressed. And what UNIX can do we can. That, after all, is the magic of UNIX.

PROGRAM 174

```
#include <signal.h>

main( )
{
   signal(SIGINT, SIG_IGN);
   for( ; ;);
}
```

The second parameter SIG_IGN passed to the *signal( )* function results in the code that ignores the signal. When the DEL key is pressed it is this code that is executed. Now we're stuck: this process is going to execute for life. But there's a way out. Just press a CTRL \\. This does the same thing the DEL key does ordinarily, i.e. terminates a process.

The CTRL \ sends another signal like the DEL key did. It results, as you must have seen, in a QUIT - core dumped being flashed on screen. This creates a file called core on disk which contains an image of the process that was terminated, and is normally used for debugging purposes. A simple cat core will print the contents of the file on screen, but we doubt you will be able to make much sense of this outpouring.

The signal sent when CTRL \ is pressed is SIGQUIT and the code name is *sigkey*. Check it out.

PROGRAM 175

```
#include <signal.h>

void sigkey( );
main( )
{
    printf("Press <Ctrl \\> key.\n");
    signal(SIGQUIT, sigkey);
    for( ; ;);
}

void sigkey( )
{
    printf(" Received Signal\n");
}
```

The first time we press the CTRL \ combination, the process does not terminate. The second time round it terminates. For the same reasons as mentioned for the DEL key (in the first program).

We can have our program handle more than one signal, too. Take the next example: here we define two signals to be considered, SIGINT and SIGQUIT. These signals are normally sent by the DEL and CTRL \ keys, respectively.

PROGRAM 176

```
#include <signal.h>

void sigkey( );
main( )
```

```
{
   signal(SIGINT, sigkey);
   signal(SIGQUIT, sigkey);
   for( ; ;);
}

void sigkey(signo)
int signo;
{
   printf("You have Killed the process with Signal No is %d.\n", signo);
}
```

Whenever the *sigkey( )* function is called it is also passed a parameter which signifies the signal sent.

Assume that we pressed the DEL key. The *sigkey( )* function is called and prints the signal value, which is 2. And the main program starts its *for* loop again. If the CTRL \ is pressed now, the *sigkey( )* function is called once again. But this time the value printed will be 3.

Now another DEL or CTRL \ will terminate the program. In fact, if we had pressed the DEL or CTRL \ one after another then, too, the program would have terminated. Because, as we have seen earlier, the code is cleared from memory.

Illegal Instruction Handling

Whenever we try to execute an Illegal Instruction UNIX gives us an error message. One example of an illegal instruction is trying to divide a number by 0. This error when generated sends a signal. This signal like the ones we saw above can also be trapped to run our code instead of the default.

The predefined word for the signal sent in this case is SIGILL.

PROGRAM 177

```
#include <signal.h>

void sigkey( );
main( )
```

```
{
    int i=0, j=50;
    signal(SIGILL, sigkey);
    j = j / i;
}

void sigkey(signo)
int signo;
{
    printf("the process received a Signal %d.\n", signo);
    exit(0);
}
```

We pass SIGILL and the name of the function to execute. When an attempt is made to divide variable *j* by 0, the function *sigkey( )* is executed. The signal number is printed and the program terminates.

If we did not pass *sigkey( )* as the parameter but instead called the default function then we would get the error we normally get whenever we try to divide a number by 0.

PROGRAM 178

```
#include <signal.h>
void sigkey( );

main( )
{
    int i=0, j=50;
    signal(SIGILL, SIG_DFL);
    j = j / i;
}

void sigkey(signo)
int signo;
{
    printf("the process received a Signal %d.\n", signo);
    exit(0);
}
```

Here, the *sigkey( )* function will never get activated. Instead we get the default error message Illegal Instruction - core dumped.

About 'SIGHUP'

Most of us today have some hangup or the other. It's cool to be cool, which means, essentially, a no-hangup guy. UNIX uses this phrase, hangup, somewhat differently -- to mean a signal that is sent by the kernel to a terminal when the terminal is disconnected. This results in all the background processes related to that terminal being terminated.

Whenever we do a CTRL D at the UNIX prompt, this hangup signal, which is defined as SIGHUP in the signal header file, is sent to all background processes warning them that they are about to be terminated.

But assume that out of the 10 background processes we have, we want one to remain active even after the SIGHUP signal is sent. Then all the process has to do is ignore the signal. Here's how:

PROGRAM 179

```
#include <signal.h>

main( )
{
   signal(SIGHUP,SIG_IGN);
   for( ; ;);
}
```

Run this program as a background process. Then do a CTRL D. Log in again and do a `ps -el`. You'll see that this process is yet active and connected to your terminal. Remember we did something similar in the multi-user topic, when we disassociated a process from the terminal.

Suppose we ran the following program:

PROGRAM 180

```
#include <fcntl.h>

main( )
{
```

```
   int fd ;
   fd = open("t.c",O_RDONLY);
   lseek(fd,0l,5);
}
```

A Bad system call - core dumped message is generated because the lseek is passed a value 5 as the third parameter. This third parameter cannot have a value greater than 3.

The signal sent, that activates the code that displays the error message, is SIGSYS. And is always generated by the kernel when a process passes an invalid argument to a system call. We can reinitialize this signal to run our own code.

PROGRAM 181

```
#include <fcntl.h>
#include <signal.h>

void abc( );
main( )
{
   int fd ;
   signal(SIGSYS,abc);
   fd = open("t.c",O_RDONLY);
   lseek(fd,0l,5);
}

void abc( )
{
printf("Illegal use of system call\n");
exit(0);
}
```

To the function *signal( )* we pass SIGSYS and the name of the function we want executed. The SIGSYS signal is sent whenever a system call is used incorrectly.

Now when the *lseek( )* is called, since there is an error in the third parameter, the SIGSYS signal will be generated. This results in function *abc( )* being called. This function prints our error message instead of the default error message, and the process terminates.

About 'SIGCLD'

Have you ever wondered how a process that has terminated is removed from the Process Table, or how the shell knows that a process has died? It's something like this: the moment the process dies it sends a signal to its parent. Assume that its parent was the shell. The shell, on receiving the signal, proceeds to delete its entry from the table. The signal sent is SIGCLD.

Even if a forked child process dies, it intimates the parent by sending the same signal.

PROGRAM 182

```
#include <stdio.h>
#include <signal.h>

void abc( );
int pid,i;
main( )
{
   pid = fork( );
   if (pid == 0)
      sleep(1);
   else
   {
      signal(SIGCLD,abc);
      for(i=0;i<1000;i++)
         printf("%d..\t",i);
      printf("\nparent exiting\n");
   }
}

void abc( )
{
   printf("\nI is %d\n",i);
   printf("Child died\n");
   getchar( );
}
```

The program above first forks a child and puts it to sleep. In the parent process, we call the *signal( )* function to handle the SIGCLD signal. The *for* loop executes till the parents time slice runs out.

The child process wakes up and terminates immediately, sending a signal, SIGCLD. Since this signal has been set to our function *abc( )* it gets executed. This prints a message to the effect that the child has died. And the parent process starts to execute from where it left off.

About 'SIGALRM'

"Joann please remind me to ring up the Secretary General of the UN after half an hour". And what if there is no Joann to remind us? Then we can always depend on the UNIX machine on our desk. All we have to do is set the *alarm( )*.

The *alarm( )* function sets up a process alarm clock. Signals are used to tell the process that the clock's timer has expired. After the call, the process carries on. Whenever we want to place a time limit on some activity we can use the alarm system call. If the process takes longer than the alarm set, it is interrupted by the SIGALRM signal and the process terminates.

PROGRAM 183

```
main( )
{
   alarm(5);
   for( ; ;);
}
```

If the program is run in the foreground, 5 seconds later a message Alarm Call is flashed on screen. When it is run in the background, the message is only flashed on screen after another system call is made: for example, ps -el. This is because while the alarm is sent, the message is not printed on screen but saved to some buffer in memory. It is only when a system call is made that the buffer contents are emptied on screen.

The ps -el system call will not show this process in the Process Table even though it's in an endless *for* loop. Because after the signal SIGALRM is sent, the process is terminated.

The *sleep( )* function which we use so often is written using *alarm( )* and one more function *pause( )*. The *pause( )* basically waits for a signal to be sent before it terminates. And the *alarm( )* waits for the time period specified to elapse. The moment the time period elapses, a signal, the SIGALRM, is sent. This terminates the *pause( )*.

The *sleep( )* function probably looks like this:

```
#include <signal.h>
sleep(i)
int i;
{
   alarm(i);
   pause( );
}
```

The program below makes use of the signal SIGALRM sent by the kernel when it receives an alarm call. Normally it sends its own message: Alarm Call. But this time we trap SIGALRM to instead call our function.

PROGRAM 184

```
#include <signal.h>

main( )
{
   void abc( );
   signal(SIGALRM,abc);
   alarm(30*60);
   pause( );
}

void abc( )
{
   printf("Time to ring the Sec.Gen. my boy \n");
}
```

Note: This program has to be run in the background else the foreground will be occupied, and that hardly serves our purpose.

The *pause( )* is necessary to keep the process active. We could have, if we wanted, included an infinite *for* loop but this would have meant wasting CPU time. Because a *for* loop will attract CPU attention, whereas a *pause( )* does not.

The *alarm( )* informs the kernel when the specified time (30*60) is up. The kernel in turn generates a SIGALRM which results in the *abc( )* function being called, and this prints a reminder. Sorry, Joann, but you aren't needed any more.

However, a ps -el will yet show this program in memory since the error message has been generated through our function, which does not have a termination statement in it.

An explicitly defined *exit( )*, as shown below, will terminate the process and hence remove it from the Process Table.

PROGRAM 185

```
#include <signal.h>

main( )
{
   void abc( );
   signal(SIGALRM,abc);
   alarm(30*60);
   for( ; ; );
}

void abc( )
{
   printf("Time to ring the Sec.Gen. my boy \n");
   exit(0);
}
```

Here, the moment the time is up and *alarm( )* notifies the kernel about it, the signal SIGALRM is sent. This results in the *abc( )* function being called, which, after printing the message, *exit( )*s.

Another way of terminating the program would be to call *alarm( )* again, but this time in the user-defined function. Because a call to the SIGALRM's default code terminates the program.

PROGRAM 186

```
#include <signal.h>

main( )
{
   void abc( );
   signal(SIGALRM,abc);
   alarm(30*60);
   for( ; ; );
}

void abc( )
{
   printf("Time to ring the Sec.Gen. my boy \n");
   alarm(5);
}
```

Here, you'll notice that we call SIGALRM with our code. *abc( )* executes as a result of the time up signal sent by the *alarm( )*. But in *abc( )* there is yet another call to *alarm( )*. Once the time is up, the kernel will send the SIGALRM signal. But since the code of *abc( )* has been cleared from memory, the default code is called.

Better still to have a Joann that can always be called upon to remind us of various tasks. For that we need to pass the program different messages and time periods at the command line.

PROGRAM 187

```
#include <signal.h>
#include <stdio.h>

char msg[100];
main(argc,argv)
int argc;
```

```
char *argv[ ];
{
    int tim;
    void abc( );
    tim = atoi(argv[2]);
    strcpy(msg,argv[1]);
    signal(SIGALRM,abc);
    alarm(tim);
    for(;;);
}

void abc( )
{
    printf("%s\n",msg);
    exit(0);
}
```

We can pass this program two parameters at the command line: the message and the time. Make sure the message is not longer than 100 characters.

Both parameters are converted. On *argv[1]* a *strcpy( )* is done, copying its contents to the array, and on *argv[1]* an *atoi( )* is done, converting the string to an integer and assigning it to the variable *tim.*

Once the time limit is up, *alarm( )* will signal the kernel, which in turn will generate the SIGALRM signal. Once this happens, the *abc( )* function is executed. This prints the message and terminates the process.

KILL!!

So far we've seen that a process calls the *signal( )* function to handle signals sent by the kernel. But beyond just using signals for a kernel to process communication, we can also use them for a process to process communication.

Here the operation of sending a signal is performed by the system call *kill( )*. It expects two parameters, the PID of the process to which the signal is to be sent and the signal that is to be sent.

This signal is defined in the signal.h header file. We have already seen some of these signals, for example, SIGINT.

So we have a process that sends a signal and a process that receives the signal. And depending on the signal sent, the receiving process proceeds to take some action. Normally, this kind of communication is between a child and parent because the PID of the child is known to the parent and vice-versa. We could also have two unrelated processes communicating with each other by saving their PIDs to a file. The restriction here is that the processes should belong to the same process group.

PROGRAM 188

```
#include <signal.h>

void abc( );
main( )
{
   int pid;
   pid = fork( );
   if(pid == 0)
   {
      signal(SIGINT,abc);
      sleep(2);
   }
   else
   {
      kill(pid,SIGINT);
      sleep(5);
      printf("Parent exiting\n");
   }
}

void abc( )
{
   printf("Signal is received by child \n");
}
```

In the forked child process we make a call to the *signal( )* function to handle a certain signal, SIGINT. The *sleep( )* ensures that the time slice is handed to the parent process.

The parent process calls the *kill( )* function with its child's PID and the SIGINT. This as we have seen earlier is the signal sent when the DEL key is pressed.

Once this signal is received by the child process, the *abc( )* function gets executed.

Open Signals

There are two other signals, SIGUSR1 and SIGUSR2, that can be used. They are not mapped to any keys but generate the values 16 and 17.

PROGRAM 189

```
#include <stdio.h>
#include <signal.h>

void abc( );
int pid,i;
main( )
{
   pid = fork( );
   if (pid == 0)
   {
      sleep(1);
      kill(getppid( ),SIGUSR1);
      exit(0);
   }
   else
   {
      signal(SIGUSR1,abc);
      for(i=0;i<1000;i++)
         printf("%d..\t",i);
      printf("parent exiting\n");
   }
}

void abc( )
{
   printf("\nI is %d\n",i);
}
```

The forked child process is immediately put to sleep. And the parent process is activated. In it the *signal( )* function is called to handle the SIGUSR1 signal.

In the *for* loop some values get printed before the time slice is handed once more to the child process. The child process calls the *kill( )* function with the parent's PID and the signal SIGUSR1. This results in the *abc( )* function getting executed.

The *abc( )* function prints the value of *i*. The child process terminates and the parent process starts its *for* loop from where it left off.

Using both SIGUSR1 and SIGUSR2 two processes can send and receive signals. Here's how:

PROGRAM 190

```
#include <stdio.h>
#include <signal.h>

int pid;
main( )
{
   void abc( ), def( );
   pid = fork( );
   if (pid == 0)
   {
      signal(SIGUSR2,abc);
      sleep(1);
      printf("Hello Papa\n");
      kill(getppid( ),SIGUSR1);
      sleep(5);
   }
   else
   {
      signal(SIGUSR1,def);
      sleep(5);
   }
}

void abc( )
```

```
{
   sleep(1);
   printf("Bye Papa\n");
   exit(0);
}

void def( )
{
   sleep(1);
   printf("Hello Baby \n");
   kill(pid,SIGUSR2);
}
```

We define both the child and parent processes to handle signals. Since the parent process is put to *sleep( )* for a longer time, the child process gets executed first. This process prints Hello Papa and emits a signal SIGUSR2.

In the parent process we've defined the function *def( )* to be related to the SIGUSR2 signal. And it is this function that is activated. This process prints Hello Baby and transmits the SIGUSR1 signal. Which in turn results in the *abc( )* function being called.

So we have one process signaling another process and the code executed as a result in turn signals the first process.

A signal, like that sent by the press of the DEL key is not only received by one process but all processes running on that terminal. Run the following example and you'll see what we mean.

PROGRAM 191

```
#include <signal.h>

void sigkey( );
main( )
{
   signal(SIGINT,sigkey);
   fork( );
   fork( );
```

```
    fork( );
    for(;;);
}

void sigkey( )
{
    printf("You have interrupted the process \n");
}
```

Can you imagine what the output will be? After initializing the *signal( )* function to handle the SIGINT signal, the forking starts. This will create 8 processes, all of which will have the signal handler set on.

The pressing of the DEL key will generate the SIGINT signal, as a result of which the *sigkey( )* function will be called. This will be called 8 times since there are 8 processes. Point proven!

However, the processes are not killed. Consequently, we're not returned to the UNIX prompt. To overcome this just press the DEL key again.

Not to say that we can't blind some processes to signals sent.

PROGRAM 192

```
#include <signal.h>

void sigkey( );
main( )
{
    int pid;
    printf("Press < Del > key to exit\n");
    signal(SIGINT,sigkey);
    fork( );
    fork( );
    pid = fork( );
    if (pid > 0)
    {
        printf("Hello, I am parent and my PID is %d \n",getpid( ));
        signal(SIGINT,SIG_IGN);
    }
    alarm(10);
```

```
    for(;;);
}

void sigkey( )
{
    printf("You have Killed the child process with
            pid %d and Parent PID %d \n",getpid( ),getppid( ));
}
```

In this program all parent processes will execute the statements within the *if*. Within this condition the signal is defined to ignore SIGINT. When a DEL key is pressed the parent process will ignore the signal but its children will get terminated.

However, after the 10 seconds specified to the *alarm( )* have elapsed, all processes will be killed.

Though signals are useful for communication they exist more for the purpose of handling errors generated. For actually transmitting data from one process to another we need to use another mechanism - PIPES.

Pipes

A pipe is a one way communication channel. Input from one end becomes output at the other end. By using pipes we can have characters being passed from one task to another.

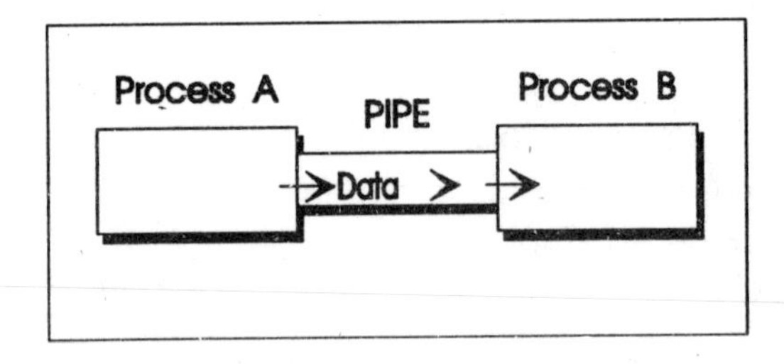

DIAGRAM 4.1

The simplest example of a pipe can be shown at the UNIX prompt itself:

```
cat abc.c | more
```

This gives us a page by page view of the file. The contents of the file are passed to more which only shows one page at a time.

Another example is:

```
who | wc -l
```

This gives us a count of all the users logged in. The program wc -l takes as input the lines that are printed by the who command and prints the number.

However, both cat and who are under the impression that their data is going to the standard output. Similarly, both more and wc are under the impression that their input comes from the keyboard.

If either cat or who were passing their data too quickly, their execution is halted. This gives the command on the other side of the pipe time to catch up.

In a program, a pipe is created using the system call *pipe( )*. It is passed an array with two elements as parameter. The *pipe( )* function will return in these two elements two file descriptors.

PROGRAM 193

```
main( )
{
   int p[2];
   pipe(p);
   printf("p[0] is %d p[1] is %d\n",p[0],p[1]);
}
```

We pass the array *p* to *pipe( )*, i.e. the starting address of this array. And the values of the two file descriptors which are returned in this array are then printed. The first file descriptor is where data is read from (input end); the second is for writing (output end).

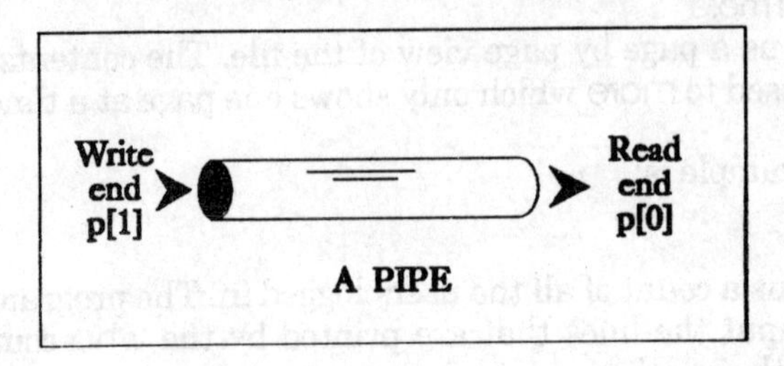

DIAGRAM 4.2

These file descriptors are common or public to all processes. And there is therefore a limit to how many pipes we can have at one time.

Run the next program and you will know how many that is.

PROGRAM 194

```
main()
{
   int p[2],retval,i=0;
   while(1)
   {
      retval = pipe(p);
      if (retval == -1)
      {
         printf("Max no of pipes that can be opened
                concurrently are %d\n",i);
         break;
      }
      i++;
      printf("%d     %d\n",p[0],p[1]);
   }
}
```

In the *while* loop, the *pipe()* results in two file descriptors being returned. If the value returned to *retval* is -1, then the statements within the *if* are executed. This will print the value of variable *i*, which tells us how many pipes can be open at one time.

Once the limit is reached the loop is exited from and the program terminates.

Now let's get down to the real thing. Let's actually see how a pipe in pipe out takes place.

```
PROGRAM 195
#include <stdio.h>
#define MSGSIZE 16

main( )
{
    char *msg1="hello,world #1";
    char *msg2="hello,world #2";
    char *msg3="hello,world #3";
    char inbuf[MSGSIZE];
    int p[2],j;

    pipe(p);
    write(p[1],msg1,MSGSIZE);
    write(p[1],msg2,MSGSIZE);
    write(p[1],msg3,MSGSIZE);

    for(j=0;j<3;j++)
    {
        read(p[0],inbuf,MSGSIZE);
        printf("%s\n",inbuf);
    }
    exit(0);
}
```

We define three pointers to characters *msg1*, *msg2* and *msg3*. Also, two arrays: *inbuf* to be filled with characters and *p* that will hold the two file descriptor values returned by the *pipe( )* call.

A call to *pipe( )* with *p* as parameter results in two file descriptors being returned to the elements 0 and 1 of the array *p*.

Three calls are made to the *write( )* function. The parameters passed are - the file descriptor, the pointer to the message and the length of the message -- which 16. The message gets written at the write end of the pipe.

The *for* loop then proceeds to read these three messages one by one from the first element of the array *p* -- that is, the read end of the pipe -- into the array *inbuf*. And the contents of the array are then printed on screen.

From this it is clear that any write to the write end will immediately be reflected at the read end.

But the above program does not really make much sense because the process is the same. And pipes, as we know, are supposed to help two different processes communicate by unidirectionally passing data from one to the other.

But then, having two processes would mean that the pipe has to be shared between them. A kind of globalization of the pipe.

PROGRAM 196

```
main( )
{
   int p[2],pid;
   pipe(p);
   pid = fork( );
   if (pid == 0)
      printf("In child p[0] is %d p[1] is %d\n",p[0],p[1]);
   else
      printf("In Parent p[0] is %d p[1] is %d\n",p[0],p[1]);
}
```

We fork a child process. In both the parent and child processes we print the value of the elements in the array *p*. Since a *fork( )* creates an identical process with lines of code and variables matching, the *pipe( )* function returns two copies of the file descriptors. But the pipe itself is not forked. It remains one. Still, both processes can access it.

Both the child and the parent processes will print the same file descriptor values, thereby proving that the pipe is a shared over processes.

Diagrammatically, a shared pipe between two processes looks like this:

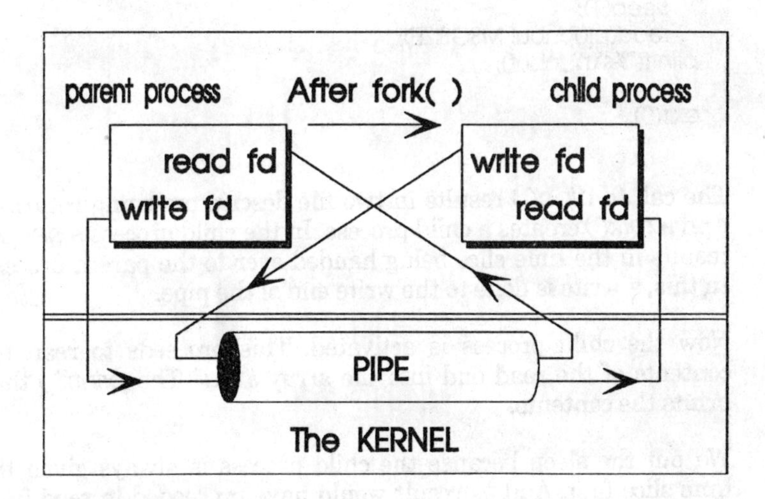

DIAGRAM 4.2.1

Each process has a write end and a read end available to it. Thus, altogether, there are four file descriptors in memory, albeit their values are the same.

So how do we pass values from one process to the other, using this mode of communication.

PROGRAM 197

```
#include <stdio.h>
# define MSGSIZE 16

main( )
{
    char *msg1="hello,world";
```

```
    char inbuf[MSGSIZE];
    int p[2],j,pid;
    pipe(p);

    pid=fork( );
    if (pid > 0)
       write(p[1],msg1,MSGSIZE);
    else
    {
       sleep(1);
       read(p[0],inbuf,MSGSIZE);
    printf("%s\n",inbuf);
    }
    exit(0);
}
```

The call to *pipe( )* results in two file descriptors being returned. And a *fork( )* creates a child process. In the child process a *sleep( )* results in the time slice being handed over to the parent process. In this, a write is done to the write end of the pipe.

Now the child process is activated. This proceeds to read the contents of the read end into the array *inbuf*. The *printf( )* then prints the contents.

We put the sleep because the child process is always given the time slice first. And as result would have proceeded to read from an empty read end.

But we found that this *sleep( )* was not necessary. The moment UNIX finds that the read end is empty, it does not read the data into the array but waits instead for a write to take place. Remove the *sleep()* and run the program. The result will be the same.

But by opening pipes as shown above, it is very easy for both the processes to write to the write end of the pipe. And haven't we mentioned that pipes are for one way communication?

PROGRAM 198

```
#include <stdio.h>
# define MSGSIZE 16
```

```
main( )
{
    char *msg1="hello,world #1";
    char inbuf[MSGSIZE];
    int p[2],j,pid;
    pipe(p);
    pid=fork( );
    if (pid > 0)
    {
        write(p[1],msg1,MSGSIZE);
    }
    else
    {
        write(p[1],msg1,MSGSIZE);
        for ( j=0;j<=1;j++)
        {
            read(p[0],inbuf,MSGSIZE);
            printf("%s\n",inbuf);
        }
    }
    exit(0);
}
```

Here we have two calls to the *write( )*: one in the parent process where it really belongs, and one in the child process. Both write the message to the write end of the pipe. Only the child process prints the contents of the read end.

But pipes are meant for one-way processes. To ensure that only a one-way process takes place we need to take certain precautions. The ball, as they say, is in our court.

What we should do is in the parent process first close the read end of the pipe. And in the child process close the write end of the pipe. This will make sure that the child can't write to, and the parent can't read from the pipe. It will also save entries for the two file descriptors we are closing up. (Thus making space for one more pipe to be opened if need be.)

Diagrammatically it will looks like this:

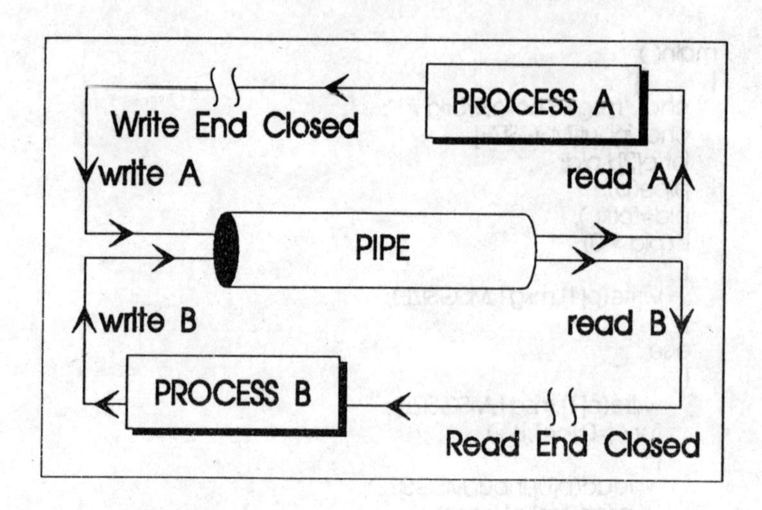

DIAGRAM 4.2.2

PROGRAM 199

```
#include <stdio.h>
#define MSGSIZE 16

main( )
{
   char *msg1="hello,world #1";
   char inbuf[MSGSIZE];
   int p[2],pid,j;
   pipe(p);
   pid=fork( );
   if(pid>0)
   {
      close(p[0]);
      write(p[1],msg1,MSGSIZE);
   }
   if(pid==0)
   {
      close(p[1]);
      read(p[0],inbuf,MSGSIZE);
      printf("%s\n",inbuf);
```

```
    }
    exit(0);
}
```

Here, you'll notice that we're closing the read end that is related to the parent process and the write end that is related to the child process. Which is why we get the diagram shown above. As a result, the parent process will no longer be able to read from the pipe while the child process will no longer be able to write to the pipe.

The advantage of doing this is that two file descriptors which would have otherwise been unused are now given back to the system. Look at the last and second last diagrams and you will see how the two descriptors are being cut off.

This *close( )* plays an important part in ensuring that a process does not hang. There are a lot of permutation and combination games we can play with the *close( )* on pipes.

PROGRAM 200

```
main( )
{
    int pid, p[2];
    int retval;
    char *buff="hello";
    char inbuff[5];
    pipe(p);
    pid = fork( );
    if (pid == 0 )
    {
        printf("Child Exiting\n");
    }
    else
    {
        retval = read(p[0],inbuff, 5);
        printf("Value returned : %d \n",retval);
    }
}
```

First we make a call to the *pipe( )* function. This returns two file descriptors. A *fork( )* then creates a child process. Both processes now have a copy of the two file descriptors.

The child process terminates immediately (we know **that it is** normally given the time slice first after a *fork( )*). **Since** this process terminates both the read and write ends of the child process are closed by default.

Now all that we have in memory is a parent process. The parent process can do both a read and write to the file since we haven't closed one of these ends. But in our code we have specified that the parent process can only do a read. And since we haven't closed its write end explicitly, the read keeps waiting for some data to be passed to it. That's why the process hangs.

A DEL will bring you back to the prompt.

So how do we ensure that the process does not hang if a situation like the one above occurs? Simple. Just do a *close( )* before the *read( )* so that the write end for the parent is closed.

PROGRAM 201

```
main( )
{
   int pid, p[2];
   int retval;
   char *buff="hello";
   char inbuff[5];
   pipe(p);
   pid = fork( );
   if (pid == 0 )
   {
      printf("Child Exiting\n");
   }
   else
   {
      close(p[1]);
      retval = read(p[0],inbuff, 5);
      printf("Value returned : %d \n",retval);
```

```
    }
}
```

Here, if you notice, we close the write end of the parent, thereby ensuring that the parent process can't write to the pipe. The termination of the child process has already closed its gateway to the pipe -- both the read and the write ends.

And our closing the write end of the parent releases the *read( )* in the parent process. UNIX realizes that there is no write end open and therefore a read is pointless. As a result, the process terminates.

What would happen if the child process was put to *sleep( )* for some time? Would the parent process terminate if its write end was closed?

PROGRAM 202

```
main( )
{
    int pid, p[2];
    int retval;
    char *buff="hello";
    char inbuff[5];
    pipe(p);
    pid = fork( );
    if (pid == 0 )
    {
        sleep(5);
        printf("Child Exiting\n");
    }
    else
    {
        close(p[1]);
        retval = read(p[0],inbuff, 5);
        printf("Value returned : %d \n",retval);
    }
}
```

We put the child process to *sleep( )* for 5 seconds. As a result, the parent process got executed. In it, the write end is closed. But instead of terminating, the parent process waits at the *read( )* because the write end of the child process has not been closed. The *read()* senses that one write end is yet open and that it may get data from there. So it waits.

However, once the child process is activated, the parent process terminates. This results in its write and read ends getting closed. The *read( )* in the parent process senses this and knows there is no point in waiting. So it terminates.

The *read( )* does not differentiate between processes. If a write end is open in any of the two processes, whether it is the parent or the child, the *read( )* will keep waiting. Waiting for Godot? No, just for the DEL key.

PROGRAM 203

```
main( )
{
  int pid, p[2];
  int retval;
  char *buff="hello";
  char inbuff[5];
  pipe(p);
  pid = fork( );
  if (pid == 0 )
  {
     close(p[1]);
     sleep(5);
     printf("Child Exiting\n");
  }
  else
  {
     retval = read(p[0],inbuff, 5);
     printf("Value returned : %d \n",retval);
  }
}
```

Here we first close the write end related to the child process and then put this process to sleep. Thus the time slice is handed to the parent processes.

In the parent process, we do not close off the write end. As a result, the *read( )* is blocked. After 5 seconds the child process executes and immediately terminates. So the time slice is once more handed back to the parent process, where the *read( )* is waiting expectantly.

Please don't torture it too much. Press the DEL key to terminate the process.

Closing the write end in both the child and parent processes, however, results in the parent terminating if the child has been put to *sleep( )*.

PROGRAM 204

```
main( )
{
   int pid, p[2];
   int retval;
   char *buff="hello";
   char inbuff[5];
   pipe(p);
   pid = fork( );
   if (pid == 0 )
   {
      close(p[1]);
      sleep(5);
      printf("Child Exiting\n");
   }
   else
   {
      close(p[1]);
      retval = read(p[0],inbuff, 5);
      printf("Value returned : %d \n",retval);
   }
}
```

A close of the write end is first performed in the child process, after which the *sleep( )* results in the time slice being handed to the parent process. Here, too, we close the write end.

Since both write ends are closed and the time slice is with the parent process, it terminates immediately. After the 5 seconds, it is the child process' turn to terminate.

That was what the *read( )* does. Now it's time to see how the *write( )* functions on pipes.

PROGRAM 205

```
main()
{
    int pid, p[2];
    int retval;
    char buff[10];
    pipe(p);
    pid = fork( );
    if (pid == 0)
    {
        printf("Child Exiting\n");
    }
    else
    {
        retval = write(p[1], buff, 1);
        printf("Retval = %d\n",retval);
        printf("Parent Exiting\n");
    }
}
```

The child process is terminated as soon as it gets the time- slice. As a result, its two pathways to the pipe are closed. However, the parent process, which is indulging in a *write( )*, yet has its read end open. Therefore the *write( )* returns a value 1, signifying that it has been successful. And then the parent process terminates.

But if we were to close the read end in the parent process also, the write would fail -- as is shown by the next program.

PROGRAM 206

```
main()
{
    int pid, p[2];
    int retval;
```

```
    char buff[10];
    pipe(p);
    pid = fork( );
    if (pid == 0)
    {
        printf("Child Exiting\n");
    }
    else
    {
        close(p[0]);
        retval = write(p[1], buff, 1);
        printf("Retval = %d\n",retval);
        printf("Parent Exiting\n");
    }
}
```

As soon as the child process terminates, the parent process gets into action. The first thing it does is to close the read end. The *write( )* senses this and realizes some foo' does not know his UNIX too well, so why bother to write and the process terminates.

Whenever the *write( )* (if it is being used on pipes) returns a -1, the **kernel** sends a terminate signal called SIGPIPE. We can capture this signal and stop it from terminating the process if we want. Here's how:

PROGRAM 207

```
#include <signal.h>

void abc( );
main( )
{
    int pid, p[2];
    int retval;
    char buff[10];
    pipe(p);
    signal(SIGPIPE,abc);
    pid = fork( );
    if (pid == 0)
    {
        printf("Child Exiting\n");
```

```
    }
    else
    {
        close(p[0]);
        retval = write(p[1], buff, 1);
        printf("Value returned : %d \n",retval);
        printf("Parent Exiting\n");
    }
}

void abc( )
{
    printf("parent failed");
}
```

We call *signal( )* to handle the SIGPIPE signal. To it we assign our own function *abc( )*. After the child process terminates, the time slice is handed to the parent process. In it, the read end is being closed. The *write( )* consequently returns a -1 since it does not sense any read ends open for it.

This error returned by *write( )* results in the kernel generating the SIGPIPE signal. But instead of calling the actual code, it calls our function, which merely prints a message, then returns control to the line after the *write( )* in the parent process. Which prints the return value of the *write( )*.

All that the *write( )* needs is one read end open. It does not matter in which process this is open.

PROGRAM 208

```
#include <signal.h>

void abc( );
main( )
{
    int pid, p[2];
    int retval;
    char buff[10];
    pipe(p);
    pid = fork( );
    if (pid == 0)
```

```
    {
        sleep(5);
        printf("Child Exiting\n");
    }
    else
    {
        close(p[0]);
        retval = write(p[1], buff, 1);
        printf("Value returned : %d \n",retval);
        printf("Parent Exiting\n");
    }
}
```

Here we first put the child process to sleep. Thus, the time slice is handed to the parent process. In it we close the read end. But the *write( )* will not return an error as the read end of the child process is yet open. The parent process terminates. And in time the child process too terminates.

But normally a message may take some time coming. Does this mean that if the *read( )* encounters an empty pipe it should keep waiting there. If that happens then when will a *write( )* take place? To overcome this we need to make sure that an empty pipe does not block the process from moving on.

The following program pipes data from one process to another. The process that is doing the read will keep taking in data as long as a bye, meaning end of conversation is not encountered. However, since we are specifying a O_NDELAY to the *fcntl( )* function, even if the pipe is empty the *read( )* function won't block the process. The next statement will get executed.

PROGRAM 209

```
#include <fcntl.h>
#define MSGSIZE 16

char *msg1="hello";
char *msg2="bye";
main()
{
    int pfd[2];
```

```
    pipe(pfd);
    fcntl(pfd[0],F_SETFL,O_NDELAY);
    if (fork( ) == 0)
        child(pfd);
    else
        parent(pfd);
}

parent(p)
int p[2];
{
    int nread;
    char buf[MSGSIZE];
    close(p[1]); /* close the write end - here it is unused */
    for(;;)
    {
        nread=read(p[0],buf,MSGSIZE);
        if (nread == 0)
        {
            printf("Pipe empty\n");
            sleep(1);
        }
        else
        {
            if(strcmp(buf,msg2)==0)
            {
                printf("End of conversation\n");
                exit(0);
            }
            else
                printf("MSG=%s\n",buf);
        }
    }
}

child(p)
int p[2];
{
    int count;
    close(p[0]);
    for(count=0;count<3;count++)
    {
        write(p[1],msg1,MSGSIZE);
```

```
        sleep(3);
    }
    write(p[1],msg2,MSGSIZE);
    exit(0);
}
```

This program has two user-defined functions related to it: *parent( )* and *child( )*.

In the main part of the program we define an array *pfd* which is passed to the *pipe( )* function. The *pipe( )* function returns two file descriptors to the elements of the array.

A call is made to the *fcntl( )* function with three parameters. The first parameter is the file descriptor - in our case it is the read end of the pipe, the second parameter is F_SETFL which is a flag that can be set. And it is the third parameter which tells what the flag is set to and what action is to be taken. In our case we don't want to be blocked at the *read( )*. Which is why we specify a O_NDELAY.

After the call to the *fcntl( )* function, a check is made to see if the value returned by the *fork( )* is a 0 or not. This will tell us if the process is a child process or a parent process. And accordingly, the *parent( )* or *child( )* function is called with the array that holds the file descriptors returned by the *pipe( )* function.

The *parent( )* function is passed the array that contains the two file descriptors returned by the *pipe( )* function. In this process we close the write end and start an endless *for* loop. In this loop a *read( )* is done on the read end of the pipe. If it returns a 0, we know that no message or data has been passed. As a result we get a message saying pipe empty.

However, if some data has been passed we string compare this data to the string pointed to by the *msg2* pointer, i.e. bye. If this compare proves true, i.e. the string *read( )* at the read end is a bye, we know that it is the end of conversation. The process then terminates. Else the message sent is printed on screen.

The *child( )* function is passed the array that holds the two descriptors returned by *pipe( )*. In this function we close the read end. And start a *for* loop that executes thrice. In this loop the message Hello is written to the write end of the pipe and then this function is put to *sleep( )*.

As a result the time slice is handed to the parent process, which in turn calls the *parent( )* function. The parent function which reads from the read end sees this message and proceeds to print it. However, since the child process is put to sleep for 3 seconds, the parent process keeps making a call to the parent function which is not able to read any thing from the read end of the pipe as there is no message there. So it prints pipe empty.

After 3 seconds, the time slice is once more handed to the child process that calls the child function. This writes the same message once more and goes to sleep. The parent function reads and prints it. And this goes on till the *for* loop is over, in which case a bye is written to the read end. The parent function reads this bye and prints end of conversation before terminating.

Another way of not getting blocked at the read is to not call it at all in the first place if the write end of the pipe is empty. But there has to be some way of determining whether the pipe is empty or not, for this we need to use the *fstat( )* function.

The *fstat( )* function takes two parameters, the read end of the pipe, i.e. the file descriptor connected to the read end, and a structure. The structure's members are assigned certain values by the *fstat( )* function. These values tell us about the status of the pipe.

PROGRAM 210

```
#include <sys/types.h>
#include <sys/stat.h>

main()
{
    int pid, p[2];
    struct stat pinfo;
```

```
    char buff[10];

    pipe(p);
    pid = fork( );
    if (pid != 0)
    {
       sleep(5);
       write(p[1], "Hello World", 12);
       printf("Parent Exiting\n");
    }
    else
    {
       for(;;)
       {
          fstat(p[0], &pinfo);
          if (pinfo.st_size == 0)
             abc( );
          else
          {
             read(p[0], buff, 12);
             printf("Buff : %s\n", buff);
             printf("Child Exiting\n");
             exit(0);
          }
       }
    }
}

abc( )
{
   printf("Pipe Empty, I can do any thing now\n");
   sleep(1);
}
```

We have defined a structure *pinfo* that looks like the predefined structure *stat*.

We first do a *pipe( )*, and then fork a child process. In the child process we start a never-ending *for* loop. In this loop we first call the *fstat( )* function with the file descriptor connected to the read end and the starting address of the structure *pinfo*.

Then the member *st_size* of this structure is queried. This member will tell us whether the read end of the pipe is empty or not. If it is empty the *abc( )* function is called. This prints the pipe empty message and the function is put to *sleep( )*. This is necessary to give the guy who is going to write to the write end some breathing space.

After 5 seconds are up, the parent process wakes up, writes Hello World to the write end and terminates. In the child process the query returns a value other than a 0. Hence the statements within the *else* are executed. These read the contents of the read end into an array and print them, after which even this process terminates.

'lseek( )' And Pipes

An *lseek( )*, as we know, can be used to shift the file pointer to any byte we want in a file. Try out the next program.

Assume that there is a file xxx (or, better still, create this file) with the line Hello World in it.

```
PROGRAM 211
#include <fcntl.h>

main( )
{
   int fd,rd;
   char msg[11];
   fd=open("xxx",O_RDONLY);
   lseek(fd,2l,0);
   rd = read(fd,msg,11);
   printf("%d\n",rd);
   printf("%s\n",msg);
}
```

Here the *lseek( )* will position the pointer on the second location from the beginning of the file. The *read( )* will then proceed to read 11 characters . However , since we start from location 2 *read( )* will only read 9 characters. And it is this value that the *printf( )* will print.

Let's try an *lseek( )* on pipes to see what happens. Why ? Because after all pipes are nothing but files, aren't they?

PROGRAM 212

```
#include <stdio.h>
#define MSGSIZE 16

main( )
{
   char *msg1="hello,world #1";
   char inbuf[MSGSIZE];
   int p[2],j,pid;
   pipe(p);
   pid=fork( );
   if (pid > 0)
   {
      write(p[1],msg1,MSGSIZE);
   }
   else
   {
      printf("%d\n",lseek(p[0],0L,2));
      read(p[0],inbuf,MSGSIZE);
      printf("%s\n",inbuf);
   }
   exit(0);
}
```

Hey what happened! How did the entire message get read by the *read( )* function? That's because the *lseek( )* does not work on pipes. Pipes, as we know, channelize data in a unidirectional flow. And because of this unidirectional movement an *lseek( )* does not work on them.

Many Processes and One Pipe

It is also possible to have different processes communicating to one process using the same pipe. A many to one situation.

PROGRAM 213

```
#include <stdio.h>

main( )
{
    int p[2],j,pid;
    char msg[20];
    pipe(p);
    pid = getpid( );
    fork( );
    fork( );
    if (pid == getpid( ))
    {
        for(j=0;j<3;j++)
            wait((int *)0);
        for(j=0;j<3;j++)
        {
            read(p[0],msg,12);
            printf("%s\n",msg);
        }
    }
    else
        write(p[1],"hello world",12);
}
```

The call to *pipe( )* opens one pipe. In *pid* we get the PID of the current process. This process then *fork( )*s a child. And then the process and its child *fork( )* another process each. Thus, we now have four processes in memory: one grandfather, his two sons and one grandson.

The *if* structure checks to see if the process is the grandfather or any of his offspring. And if it is the grandfather process that has the time slice, the statements within the *if* are executed. The first *for* loop, which executes thrice, makes the grandfather wait so that its three offspring processes have executed.

These offspring processes, as is shown by the *else*, print a message into the write end of the pipe. When all three offspring processes finish writing, the parent process finally wakes and proceeds to execute. It *read( )*s, 12 characters at a time thrice, from the read end into the array *msg* and prints them on screen.

Sorting Using Pipes

An ls -li at the prompt would give us a directory listing, but in an unsorted manner. However, by using the | pipe we can get a sorted listing: ls -li | sort.

Let's see how this works. Any command at the shell results in the shell forking a child process. In our case the shell forks a child which, because of the pipe, forks once more. So we have a grandfather in the shell, a father which takes care of the ls -li command and its child which takes care of the sort command. The father process writes to the write end of the pipe and the child process reads from the read end of the pipe.

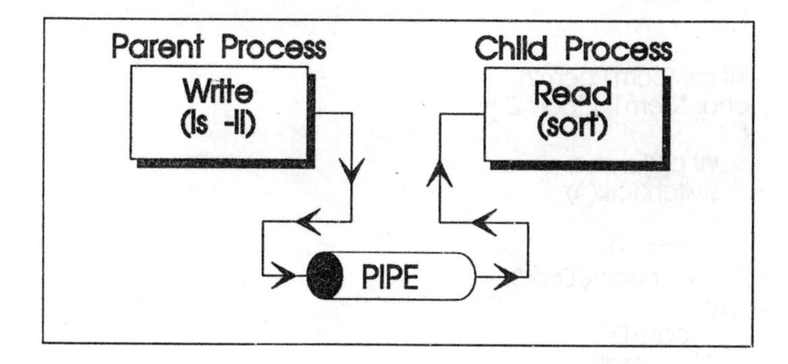

DIAGRAM 4.3

We could do this sort through a program, too. But for this we need to use the *dup( )* function. The *dup( )* function is passed one parameter: either the file descriptor connected to the write end or the one connected to the read end.

It in turn returns a new file descriptor that refers to the same end of the pipe. This value is the lowest number available: either 0, 1 or 2, which refer to the standard input, standard output and standard error, respectively. By doing a *dup( )* we can couple a pipe end to a standard device. For example, by doing a *dup( )* on the read end we couple it to the standard input.

PROGRAM 214

```
main( )
{
    char *one[3],*two[2];
    int ret;
    one[0]="ls";
    one[1]="-li";
    one[2]= (char*)0;

    two[0]="sort ";
    two[1]=(char)0;

    ret=join(one,two);
    printf("join returned %d\n",ret);
    exit(0);
}

int join(com1,com2)
char *com1[ ],*com2[ ];
{
    int p[2],status;
    switch(fork( ))
    {
        case -1:
            perror("Error");

        case 0:
            break;

        default:
            wait(&status);
        return(status);
    }

    if(pipe(p)<0)
        perror("pipe call in join");
    switch(fork( ))
    {
```

```
        case -1:
            perror(" 2nd fork call in join");
        case 0:
            close(1);
            dup(p[1]);
            close(p[0]);
            close(p[1]);
            execl("/bin/ls",com1[0],com1[1],com1[2]);
            perror(" 1st execvp call in join");

        default:
            close(0);
            dup(p[0]);
            close(p[0]);
            close(p[1]);
            execl("/bin/sort",com2[0],com2[1]);
            perror(" 2nd execvp call in join");
    }
}
```

We define two pointers to arrays and assign their elements some values. A call is then made to the *join( )* function which is passed these two pointers to arrays as parameters.

In the *join( )* function we fork, and then check to see what value is returned by the fork. If it is -1, we know that the *fork( )* did not work else we should now have two processes in memory.

If it is 0, we know that it is the child process that has been given the time slice and is executing. This gets us out of the case statements and into the *if*.

In the *if*, we first *pipe( )* and then do a *fork( )*. This latter results in another process being created in memory. So now in memory there is a grandfather, father and child.

Once more we check whether it is the father that has the time slice or the child.

Assume it is the child process. The first thing we do then is close the standard output. Then we do a *dup( )* to the write end. This gets us a duplicate file descriptor, which is the write end of the pipe and also the standard output. Therefore anything written on the screen will instead go to the write end. For example, ordinarily an ls -li will display the directory contents on screen. But here, instead of displaying the directory contents on screen, these will be redirected to the write end. That is just what happens when the *execl( )* executes. The output of the ls goes to the write end of the pipe.

Now the time slice is handed to the parent process. In it the standard input is first closed. Next a call to the *dup( )* is made. This gives us another descriptor that also points to the read end instead of the standard input (keyboard). Now whatever is read will be from the read end, and this is then dumped on screen in a sorted manner. A call to the *execl( )* runs the sort command. This results in the output of ls -li being sorted and printed on screen.

So far we have created only unidirectional pipes providing a oneway flow of data. What do we do for a two way flow? Create two pipes, one for each direction.

Then, basically, a few steps have to be followed. Create two pipes. Fork. Parent closes read end of pipe 1 and write end of pipe 2. Child closes the write end of pipe 1 and read end of pipe 2.

Diagrammatically this looks like:

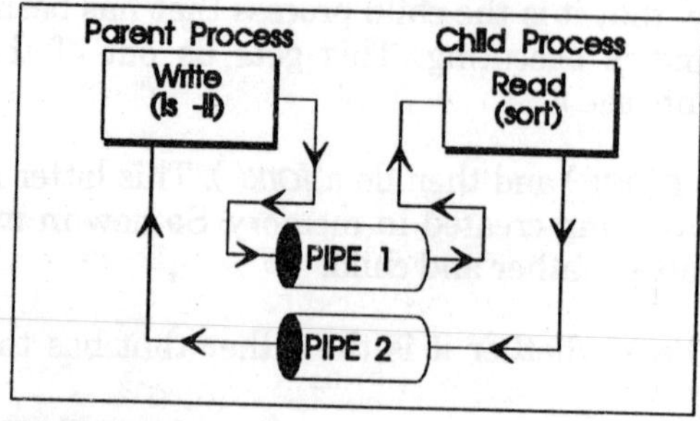

DIAGRAM 4.4

PROGRAM 215

```
#include <stdio.h>
```

```
main()
{
   int pp[2],pc[2],j,pid;
   char msg1[20];
   char msg2[20];
   char msg3[20];
   pipe(pp);
   pipe(pc);
   pid = fork( );
   if (pid == 0)
   {
      close(pp[1]);
      close(pc[0]);
      write(pc[1],"Hello Daddy",12);
      read(pp[0],msg2,12);
      printf("%s\n",msg2);
      write(pc[1],"Thankyou Papa",14);
   }
   else
   {
      close(pp[0]);
      close(pc[1]);
      read(pc[0],msg1,12);
      printf("%s\n",msg1);
      write(pp[1],"Hello Baby ",12);
      read(pc[0],msg3,14);
      printf("%s\n",msg3);
   }
}
```

We open two pipes *pp* and *pc*. A *fork( )* then creates a child process.

In the child process we close the write end of pipe *pp* and the read end of pipe *pc*. Next, we write Hello Daddy to the write end of pipe *pc*. And read from the read end of pipe *pp*. But at this point there will be no data to read. As a result the process is blocked. The time slice is given to the parent process.

In the parent process we close the read end of pipe *pp*. And the write end of pipe *pc*. Next, we read from the read end of pipe *pc* the message that is waiting and which has been sent by the child process. This message is read into the array *msg1*. After this message is printed a *write( )* is executed. This writes a message to the write end of pipe *pp*. And the parent process now gets blocked at the second *read( )*.

The time slice is once more given to the child process that was blocked at the *read( )*. But now the *read( )* works because a message has been sent to it. This message is printed and another call is made to the *write( )*, which writes Thankyou Papa to the write end. The child process then terminates.

In the parent we have been blocked at the second *read( )*. But here too a message is now received. As a result, the *read( )* works, assigns the message to the array and prints it. And the process then terminates.

The 'popen( )'

The standard I/O library provides a function, *popen( )*, that creates a pipe and initializes a process that either reads from the pipe or writes to it.

popen( ) expects two parameters: a shell command eg. ls - l and an r or w that tells the calling process to either read or write to the pipe. *popen( )* returns a FILE pointer which is used for input or output depending on whether we have specified r or w.

Here's a program that demonstrates the *popen( )* function.

PROGRAM 216

```
#include <stdio.h>

main( )
{
   int n,fd ;
   char line[200] ;
   fd = popen("ls -l","r");
   while((fgets(line,200,fd))!= NULL)
      printf("%s",line);
```

}

We make a call to the *popen( )* function with two parameters, the ls -l command and an r to perform a read. The read is done on the ls file (remember all commands are basically files in UNIX).

The *fgets( )* reads a line at a time from this file and prints it on screen. This *while* loop performs till the end of file is reached.

Named Pipes

While pipes are a powerful interprocess communication they are not without drawbacks.

Firstly, pipes can only be used on processes that have a common ancestry like a parent and child process. And, secondly, they are not permanent. A process creates them and the termination of the process leads to their destruction.

To overcome these deficiencies a variation on these pipes has been implemented known as NAMED PIPES or FIFOs. These named pipes basically function in the same way as pipes: acting as one way communication channels. But unlike pipes, a named pipe is a permanent fixture. UNIX treats it just likes a file, giving it a size, owner and access permissions. It can be opened, closed or deleted like any other file.

Similar to pipes, named pipes too can be initiated either at the UNIX prompt or through a program. The system call to do this is the same, mknod.

Let's take an example of a named pipe at the prompt.

At the prompt type in: /etc/mknod testpipe p. Here mknod is the call that creates a named pipe. The command mknod exists in the /etc directory. testpipe is the name we give the named pipe that we create. And the p at the end signifies a pipe.

Do a ls -l testpipe* and you'll see a p in the permissions column. Now let's see how we can use this named pipe.

Do a cat < testpipe &. This results in the cat program being made into a background process. Why are we making it a background process? Well, had we not, the cat would have kept waiting to read something. But since the pipe is empty, the program would hang. By making it a background process we ensure that the program does not hang.

But this process is unable to read from the named pipe testpipe. Why? Because in the first place this pipe has not even been opened. A name pipe can only be opened if there is someone waiting at both its ends. In this case cat tries to read from it, but there is no corresponding process trying to write to it. As a result the pipe is not opened at all.

So what we need here is some way of writing to the pipe. And that is what a ls -l > testpipe at the prompt, will do. The moment we give this command at the prompt, the pipe is opened in the background process for a read and in this (the ls) process for a write. The output of the ls -l is now outputted to the pipe instead of to the screen. But since, at the read end of the pipe, a cat is being performed we see the output on screen.

This ls -l > testpipe could have been given on some other distant terminal which is running a user not connected in any way with us. But the output would be displayed on our screen because the cat < testpipe & was running on our terminal as a background process. Doesn't this make named pipes global variables, unlike ordinary pipes which can only be shared between parent-child processes only.

UNIX, we know, is based on a client-server relationship. On the server machine we have the OS and all other files. This is the main machine on which all processing is done. All other machines connected to this main machine are known as nodes or clients. They are merely a screen and keyboard connection. All commands or programs specified at these nodes are actually run on the server.

Probably one of the most common uses of named pipes is for communicating between a client and server. We keep a process that has opened a named pipe running in the background. This process waits for some other process to write to the named pipe. Once something is written, the message is printed on screen.

Basically, there will be two programs that run hand in hand. One that waits for something to be written to a name pipe and one that can be used to write something to the named pipe. Of course, the write program has to be aware of the named pipe it can write to. And the program that keeps the named pipe ready and waiting to receive information has to be active. The read program will have to be run on the server while the write program can be run by any client. This is what client-server communication is all about.

PROGRAM 217

```
#include <fcntl.h>
#include <stdio.h>
#define MSGSIZ 63

main( )
{
   int fd;
   char msgbuf[MSGSIZ+1];

   if((fd = open("testfile",O_RDWR)) <0)
      perror("pipe open failed");

   for(;;)
   {
      if(read(fd,msgbuf,MSGSIZ+1) > 0 )
         printf("message received:%s\n", msgbuf);
   }

}
```

Here we open the same named pipe we had created at the command line. The file is being opened in the read write mode. In the never ending *for* loop, a *read( )* is activated. The moment a message is read from the pipe it is printed by the *printf( )* function.

Now we need a program that will write messages to the pipe.

PROGRAM 218

```
#include <fcntl.h>
#include <stdio.h>
#include <errno.h>
#define MSGSIZ 63

main(argc, argv)
int argc;
char *argv[ ];
{
   int fd, j, nwrite;
   char msgbuf[MSGSIZ];
   if(argc <2)
   {
      printf("Usage:<Filename> <message> <message> ....\n");
      exit(1);
   }
   if((fd = open("testfile",O_WRONLY)) < 0 )
      perror("fifo open failed");

   for(j = 1; j <argc; j++)
   {
      strcpy(msgbuf, argv[j]);
      if(( nwrite = write(fd, msgbuf, MSGSIZ+1)) <= 0)
         perror("message write failed");
   }
   exit(0);
}
```

This program, when it is run, has to be passed a message or messages. It is this message that will be read and printed by the receiving program.

We open the testfile pipe in write only mode. In the for loop, which executes as many times as there are messages passed to the program, we first string copy the message into an array and write this message into the named pipe. This results in the (previous) program getting the message and printing it on screen.

We can, if we want, create the named pipe in the program itself. The function is the same: *mknod( )*. That's what we're doing below.

```
PROGRAM 219
#include <fcntl.h>
#include <stdio.h>
#define MSGSIZ 63

main( )
{
   int fd;
   char msgbuf[MSGSIZ+1];

   if(mknod("myfifo",010666,0) < 0)
      perror("myfifo failed");

   if((fd = open("myfifo",O_RDWR)) <0)
      perror("fifo open failed");

   for(;;)
   {
      if(read(fd,msgbuf,MSGSIZ+1) > 0 )
      printf("message received:%s\n", msgbuf);
   }
}
```

Note: run this program as a background process on the server.

We define two variables: *fd* as an integer and *msgbuff* as an array.

Next, we make a call to the *mknod( )* function with three parameters: the name of the named pipe to create, the permissions to attach to this pipe -- the 010 signifies that it is a pipe and the 666 signifies a read write permission. And the last 0 stands for a special device: block or character device. If the *mknod( )* fails we get an error.

We then open the newly created named pipe *myfifo* in read write mode. And then start an unending *for* loop. In the loop, a read from the named pipe takes place. But this happens only if there is something written there in the first place. In which case, the data is printed on screen. But if we ever want this *read( )* to read some data we need to write something to the named pipe.

And that's where the next program comes in. Whenever we want to send a message to the named pipe specified, we just run this program with the message as a parameter.

PROGRAM 220

```
#include <fcntl.h>
#include <stdio.h>
#include <errno.h>
#define MSGSIZ 63

main(argc, argv)
int argc;
char *argv[ ];
{
   int fd, j, nwrite;
   char msgbuf[MSGSIZ];
   if(argc <2)
   {
      printf("Usage:<Filename> <message> <message> ....\n");
      exit(1);
   }
   if((fd = open("myfifo",O_WRONLY)) < 0 )
      perror("fifo open failed");

   for(j = 1; j <argc; j++)
   {
      strcpy(msgbuf, argv[j]);
      if(( nwrite = write(fd, msgbuf, MSGSIZ+1)) <= 0)
            perror("message write failed");
   }
   exit(0);
}
```

We open the named pipe *myfifo* in write only mode.

Now the *for* loop executes as many times as there are messages. In the loop, each message is string copied into the array *msgbuf* and written into the file. This results in each message being printed on screen.

There is one problem with the above set. Actually only with the program that is constantly alive in the background. The problem is that if the program is run once there is no stopping it being run once more. No doubt a ps -el would help in determining whether it has already been run or not. But a solution could be incorporated in the program too.

That's what we've done in the next program. We open a file *lock* in exclusive mode the moment the program is run. So that the second time round, when the program attempts to open the *lock*, an error will be generated.

PROGRAM 221

```
#include <fcntl.h>
#include <stdio.h>
#include <errno.h>
#define MSGSIZ 63
#include <signal.h>

void term( );
extern int errno ;

main( )
{
   int fd;
   char msgbuf[MSGSIZ+1];

   signal(SIGTERM,term);

   if((fd = open("lock",O_RDWR | O_CREAT | O_EXCL,0600)) <0)
   {
      if(errno == EEXIST )
      {
         printf("Server Has Been Already Loaded\n");
         exit(1) ;
      }
```

```
    }

    mknod("myfifo",010644,0);

    fd = open("myfifo",O_RDWR | O_EXCL);

    for(;;)
    {
        if(read(fd,msgbuf,MSGSIZ+1) > 0 )
            printf("Message received : %s\n",msgbuf);
    }
}

void term( )
{
    unlink("lock");
    exit(0);
}
```

In the program we call *signal( )* to handle the SIGTERM signal. The moment this signal is sent the *term( )* function executes. This function deletes the file *lock*.

Assume we ran this program on the server, it would start to open the file *lock* in exclusive mode. Next it would create a named pipe *myfifo* in read write mode. Now the never-ending *for* loop will get control. In it, the *read( )* will try to read any message that may be sent to this pipe. And print it.

If another attempt is made to run the program, an error will be generated as the file *lock* has already been opened.

Since this process is run in the background we can remove it through the kill command at the prompt: kill <PID>. The PID of this process can be got by doing a ps -el. The moment we do a kill the SIGTERM signal is sent. This results in the function *term( )* getting activated. And the *lock* file being deleted.

The sending program remains the same as previously.

Want to try a fun application involving named pipes? Then run the next program as a background process. What it expects is a message, too, but with a difference. The message has to be a system command eg. ls -l.

PROGRAM 222

```
#include <fcntl.h>
#include <stdio.h>
#include <errno.h>
#define MSGSIZ 63
#include <signal.h>

void term( );
extern int errno ;
main( )
{
    int fd;
    char msgbuf[MSGSIZ+1];
    signal(SIGTERM,term);

    if((fd = open("lock",O_RDWR I O_CREAT I O_EXCL,0666)) <0)
    {
        if(errno == EEXIST )
        {
            printf("Server Has Been Already Loaded\n");
            exit(1) ;
        }
    }

    mknod("myfifo",010644,0);

    fd = open("myfifo",O_RDWR);

    for(;;)
    {
        if(read(fd,msgbuf,MSGSIZ+1) > 0 )
        {
            system(msgbuf);
            system("echo ");
            system("echo ———————————");
            system("echo ");
        }
```

```
    }
}
void term()
{
    unlink("lock");
    exit(0);
}
```

This program, too, has been written in a way that ensures it can't be loaded again. That's why the *lock* file is being opened in the exclusive mode.

We then create a pipe, *myfifo*, using the *mknod( )* function and open it in read mode.

The *for* loop then starts executing endlessly. If it reads a message from the named pipe, a *system( )* call is immediately made with this message as parameter. Since this process runs on the server, the command will be executed there. If the message was an ls, we would get a listing of all files.

Remember the program that will actually write to this pipe is the same as the one we have seen previously.

Conclusion: Signals And Pipes

We yet have a long way to go before we can add some suave and polish to our methods of communication. What we have seen here is just the raw and primitive methods that UNIX has implemented. And while these may do when the needs are simple, for more effective and intense communication we will have to look elsewhere.

While signals,pipes and named pipes are ways by which processes can communicate they are rather primitive. Take named pipes for example they suffer from one problem - a reader process is mandatory. Which means that even if we are willing to wait till someone communicates with us its of no use. This kind of compulsion acts as a severe restriction. A lot like us humans isn't it, compel somebody to do a task and the chances are he will make a mess of it. The more refined method of inter process communication is through Message Queues, Semaphores and Shared Memory.

Message Queues

A message queue is much like any other queue. All messages will be dumped into this queue. And the various listeners can now pick up these messages from the queue.

Do a ipcs at the prompt and you will see output that looks like this - IPC stands for Inter Process Communication.

```
IPC status from /dev/kmem as of Mon Mar 25 12:16:20 1991
T              ID   KEY   MODE   OWNER   GROUP
Message Queues:
Shared Memory:
Semaphores:
```

Creating a Message Queue

This shows that at present there have been no IPC's created. All IPC's are created using functions. Message queue s for instance are created using the *msgget( )* function. It takes two parameters the name of the message queue also known as key. And flag which can be one or both of the following - IPC_CREAT which means that the message queue is to be created if it does not exist. If the queue does exist this keyword is ignored. IPC_EXCL which forces an error when used with IPC_CREAT when a queue already exists.

Finally *msgget( )* returns an integer that is the message queue identifier.

PROGRAM 223

```
#include <sys/types.h>
#include <sys/ipc.h>
#include <sys/msg.h>
main( )
```

```
{
   int msqid;

   msqid = msgget((key_t)10,IPC_CREAT);
   printf("Message queue successfully created with key %d\n",msqid);
}
```

Here we are calling msgget with 10 which is the name we are giving the queue and the create mode - IPC_CREAT. If the queue is created the *msgget( )* returns its value to the *msqid* variable. If we were to run the above program once again the IPC_CREAT parameter is ignored and we are just returned the ID number of the queue .

If you do a ipcs now to see the status of IPC's you will get the following output -

```
IPC status from /dev/kmem as of Mon Mar 25 12:25:33 1991
T          ID  KEY          MODE       OWNER    GROUP
Message Queues:
q           0  0x0000000a   ---------  vmci     other
Shared Memory:
Semaphores:
```

Check the values under the various column headings. A "q" signifying its a message queue . A 0 under ID - this is the value we were returned by the *msgget( )* function. Under *KEY* we have a number in hex for 10 that was the name we gave our queue . *MODE* defines the permissions for user who can access this queue . The *OWNER* is the person who owns this queue . This is normally the user who created the queue in the first place but this owner ID can be changed. And *GROUP* signifies the group the owner of the queue belongs to. If you only want to see all message queues in memory run the ipcs -q. This is what you will see.

```
IPC status from /dev/kmem as of Mon Mar 25 12:54:35 1991
T          ID  KEY          MODE       OWNER    GROUP
Message Queues:
q           0  0x0000000a   --------   vmci     other
```

There is a predefined structure, *ipc_perm*, in the sys/ipc.h header file that hold all this information. The structure has the following members -

```
struct ipc_perm
{
   ushort uid; /* owners user id */
   ushort gid /* owners group id */
   ushort cuid; /* creators user id */
   ushort cgid; /* creators group id */
   ushort mode; /* access modes */
   ushort seq; /* slot usage sequeue nce number */
   key_t key; /* key */
};
```

Whenever a new message queue is created the *uid, gid, cuid and cgid* are all set to the effective user and group ID's. The former two ID's are called the owner ID's while the latter two are called the creator ID's. While the creators ID can never be changed a owner ID can through certain system calls.

Now if we were to run this program again do you think we would get another queue or an error ? All that would happen is that the IPC_CREAT would get ignored. And we would be returned the same message queue identifier. In fact try running the program as shown below -

PROGRAM 224

```
#include <sys/types.h>
#include <sys/ipc.h>
#include <sys/msg.h>

main( )
{
  int msqid;

  msqid = msgget((key_t)10,0);
  printf("Message queue successfully created with key %d\n",msqid);
}
```

When this program is run it will return a message queue identifier. Because the queue already exists.

Notice the absence of the IPC_CREAT.

If we use the IPC_EXCL flag and the queue already exists we will be notified immediately. This flag has to be ORed with the IPC_CREAT flag. If the queue that we are trying to create exists an error will be flashed else the queue will be created and its identifier passed back to the calling program.

PROGRAM 225

```
#include <sys/types.h>
#include <sys/ipc.h>
#include <sys/msg.h>
main( )
{
   int i,msqid;
   key_t key = 10;
   msqid = msgget(key,IPC_CREAT | IPC_EXCL);
   if (msqid < 0)
      perror("msgget failed");
   else
      printf("Message queue successfully created with key %d\n",
            msqid);
}
```

Here if you have noticed we are defining a variable *key* of type *key_t*. *key_t* is defined in the types.h header file and is basically an *int*.

We are passing the variable *key* which has the value 10 and an ORed *IPC_CREAT | IPC_EXCL* to the *msgget( )* function. If the value returned by this function is less than 0 it means that the function failed to create a message queue. Else it will return the message queue identifier of the message queue created.

In our case we will get an error as the message queue we are trying to create already exists. We have created a message queue with this name in the previous program.

If we want to see the above program actually create a queue we need to kill the message queue first. We can kill a message queue using the ipcrm -q <id number> command. Try killing the message queue we have just created using this command. And then run the ipcs - q command to verify that it has actually been killed. Then run the above program again. This time it should create a queue . Verify this by running the ipcs -q .

Queue Permissions

Use of the IPC_EXCL and/or IPC_CREAT does not guarantee us exclusive use of the IPC channel. All they do is create a channel. Other users can access this channel if they have the right permissions. The IPC_EXCL cannot be used on its own, it has to be used in conjunction with the IPC_CREAT.

So far the queue we have created was not defined with any permissions. As a result any user had access to it. If you remember when we did a ipcs we saw our message queue but under the column heading MODE there were just dashes. Because at that time we had not specified any permissions for the queue.

To specify permissions we need to OR the IPC_CREAT with a certain value which signifies the permission. For example -

PROGRAM 226

```
#include <sys/types.h>
#include <sys/ipc.h>
#include <sys/msg.h>

main( )
{
   int i,msqid;
   key_t key = 15;
   msqid = msgget(key,IPC_CREAT | 0644);

   if (msqid < 0)
      perror("msgget failed");
   else
```

```
    printf("Message queue successfully created with key %d\n",msqid);
}
```

We are creating a message queue with the name 15. It is created in the read write mode for owner and read only mode for all others. The *0644* signifies these permissions. This queue is now available to every user on the system but only for a read. The *else* part is activated if the call to the *msgget()* function is successful.

Note : a execute permission for a message queue does not make sense since it is not code.

Run the ipcs -q to see the details regarding this queue . This is what the output looks like -

```
IPC status from /dev/kmem as of Mon Mar 25 12:54:35 1991
T          ID  KEY          MODE        OWNER  GROUP
Message Queues:
q           0  0x0000000a   ---------   vmci   other
q           1  0x0000000f   -rw-r--r--  vmci   other
```

Notice the permissions under the *MODE* column. That's what the *0644* did.

Whenever a new IPC channel is created the low order 9 bits of the of the second parameter passed to the *msgget()* function, i.e. the flag argument initialize the *mode* word in the *ipc_perm* structure.

The member *mode* of this structure is then subsequently queried whenever a user tries to access this IPC channel. If the rights of the user match those in the *mode* he is allowed access. This is necessary as the *mode* can be modified. For example a owner process can set the *mode* for its input messages so that the read permission bits are OFF. Thus if another process with its read bits ON tries to use this message queue an error will be returned by the *msgget()* function.

PROGRAM 227

```
#include <sys/types.h>
#include <sys/ipc.h>
```

```
#include <sys/msg.h>

main( )
{
   int i,msqid;
   key_t key = 15;
   msqid = msgget(key,IPC_CREAT | 0666);

   if (msqid < 0)
      perror("msgget failed");
   else
      printf("Message queue successfully created with key %d\n",
               msqid);
}
```

Here if you notice we have changed the permissions of access to the queue the previous program created. We are trying to access it with a *0666* which signifies a read write for everybody - owner, user, group members and all others. This permission mismatch (since the queue has been created with a 0644) results in an error being returned by the *msgget( )* function which fails to allow us to access this queue.

This is a real hindrance since we may know the queue to have certain permissions but these may be changed by some other process. As a result even though by default we may have rights over the queue it will become inaccessible. But any process can overcome this test easily by specifying the flag parameter as 0.

PROGRAM 228

```
#include <sys/types.h>
#include <sys/ipc.h>
#include <sys/msg.h>

main( )
{
   int i,msqid;
   key_t key = 15;
   msqid = msgget(key,IPC_CREAT | 0);

   if (msqid < 0)
      perror("msgget failed");
```

```
    else
        printf("Message queue successfully created with key %d\n",
                msqid);
}
```

This time round however the error wont occur. Because we are ORing the IPC_CREAT with a 0. As a result the check with the *mode* in the *ipc_perm* structure is bypassed since a bitwise ORing with a 0 keeps the number as it was.

UNIX's Queue Numbering System

UNIX has a very funny numbering system for message queues, or so it seems on the face of it. If queues are created without any being killed in between the numbering starts from 0 and increments by 1.

PROGRAM 229

```
#include <sys/types.h>
#include <sys/ipc.h>
#include <sys/msg.h>
#define PERMS 0666

main( )
{
    key_t i;
    int msqid;

    for(i = 0; i <50; i++)
    {
        msqid = msgget(i,PERMS | IPC_CREAT);
        if (msqid < 0)
        {
            perror("msgget failed\n");
            exit(1);
        }
        printf("msqid = %d\n",msqid);
    }
}
```

When this program is run 50 message queues will be created. Each of them will have a identifier one greater than the previous and one less than the next. If you do a ipcs -q you will see queue s numbering from 0-50. So far so good. Now delete all these queues using the ipcrm -q <number>. You will have to do it 50 times (or write a program calling this command using the *system( )* function). Then run the following program -

PROGRAM 230

```
#include <sys/types.h>
#include <sys/ipc.h>
#include <sys/msg.h>
#define PERMS 0666

main( )
{
   key_t key = 100;
   int i,msqid;

   for(i = 0; i < 50; i++)
   {
      msqid = msgget(key,PERMS | IPC_CREAT);
      if (msqid < 0)
      {
         perror("msgget failed\n");
         exit(1);
      }
      printf("msqid = %d\n",msqid);
      if (msgctl(msqid, IPC_RMID, 0) < 0)
      {
         perror("msgctl failed\n");
         exit(1);
      }
   }
}
```

The message queue identifier returned by the *msgget( )* function is printed and the message queue killed using the *msgctl( )* function.

The *msgctl( )* function is passed three parameters, the message queue identifier, what we want done to this message - in this case we want to kill the queue that's what the IPC_RMID signifies. And a 0 which should always be passed if the second parameter is IPC_RMID.

So we create a message queue which is killed immediately. But hey, why are the message queue identifiers incrementing in 50's?

Whenever a message queue is created with the same name, that's what we are doing (the name is 100), the identifier value returned by the *msgget( )* function is incremented by the maximum number of table entries that can be held by the table,(in our case it is 50), each time the entry is reused.

Therefore when the first queue created, which was given the identifier 0, was deleted the next queue which also had the same name, *100*, was given an identifier with a value 50 and the one after that 100 and so on so forth.

Tabularly it looks something like this.

Message Queue Identifiers

KEY	I	II	III	IV	V
100	0	50	100		
200	1	51	101		
300	2	52	102		
400	3	53	:		
:	:	:	:		
:	49	:	:		
.	.	.	.		

DIAGRAM 4.5

So assume a message queue with the name *100* as in the previous program was given the identifier 0. If this queue is killed and a new queue with the same name is created its identifier will be 50.

If this one is killed too and a new queue but with the same name is created once more its identifier will now be 100 and so on so forth.

If the identifier of a message queue is 1 and it is killed only to be created again (with the same name, say 200), then its new identifier will be 51 and if killed and created once again it will 101. (This is what the second line in the above table shows).

Note the name of a queue is what we define, whereas the identifier to the queue is what the function *msgget( )* returns.

Information About The Queue

For every message queue we create the system maintains information about these queues in the following structure.

```
struct msqid_ds {
struct ipc_perm msg_perm; /* operation permission struct */
struct msg *msg_first; /* ptr to first message on q */
struct msg *msg_last; /* ptr to last message on q */
ushort msg_cbytes; /* current # bytes on q */
ushort msg_qnum; /* # of messages on q */
ushort msg_qbytes; /* max # of bytes on q */
ushort msg_lspid; /* pid of last msgsnd */
ushort msg_lrpid; /* pid of last msgrcv */
time_t msg_stime; /* last msgsnd time */
time_t msg_rtime; /* last msgrcv time */
time_t msg_ctime; /* last change time */
};
```

ipc_perm - is the structure dealing with user, group ID's and permissions. We have seen this one before.

**msg_first* - is a pointer to the structure that contains the first message in the queue .

**msg_last* - is a pointer to the structure that contains the last message in the queue .

msg_bytes - the number of bytes worth of information that has been written to the queue .

msg_qnum - the number of messages on queue .

msg_qbytes - the maximum number of bytes of information that can be held in the queue .

msg_lspid - the PID of the last message sent. This depends on the PID of the process that is sending the message.

msg_lrpid - the pid of the last message received. This too depends on the PID of the receiving process.

msg_stime - the time the last message was sent at.

msg_rtime - the time the last message was received at.

msg_ctime - the last time the structure was made a change to.

The *msgctl( )* function that we have seen in the above program has two other variations besides the one that we saw. In the program below we are making use of this function to access the members of the structure explained above.

We have to pass the name of the message queue we want to know the details about or create, at the command line.

PROGRAM 231

```
#include <sys/types.h>
#include <sys/ipc.h>
#include <sys/msg.h>
#include <stdio.h>

main(argc,argv)
int argc;
char *argv[ ];
{
   int qid;
   struct msqid_ds qstatus;
   qid = msgget((key_t) atoi(argv[1]),IPC_CREAT);
```

```
    if (qid == -1)
    {
        perror("msgget Failed") ;
        exit(1);
    }
    if ( msgctl(qid, IPC_STAT, &qstatus) < 0 )
    {
        perror("msgctl failed");
        exit(1);
    }
    printf("Real User ID of Queue creator : %d\n",
                qstatus.msg_perm.cuid);
    printf("Real Group ID of Queue creator : %d\n",
                qstatus.msg_perm.cgid);
    printf("Effective User ID of Queue creator : %d\n",
                qstatus.msg_perm.uid);
    printf("Effective Group ID of Queue creator : %d\n",
                qstatus.msg_perm.gid);
    printf("Permissions : %o\n",
                qstatus.msg_perm.mode);
    printf("\nMessage queue id : %d\n\n", qid);
    printf("%d message(s) on queue \n\n", qstatus.msg_qnum);
    printf("Last Msg. send by Process : %3d at %s\n",
                qstatus.msg_lspid, ctime( &(qstatus.msg_stime)));
    printf("Last Msg. recv by Process : %3d at %s\n",
                qstatus.msg_lrpid, ctime( &(qstatus.msg_rtime) ) );
    printf("Current no of bytes on queue %d\n",qstatus.msg_cbytes);
    printf("Max no of bytes allowed on queue %d\n",
                    qstatus.msg_qbytes);
}
```

In the program we have defined a structure *q_status* that looks like the predefined structure *msqid_ds.* Next we are creating a queue using the *msgget( )* function. The message queue identifier which is returned is stored in the variable *qid.*

A call to the *msgctl( )* function with the three parameters - message queue identifier, IPC_STAT and the starting address of the structure qstatus fills this structure with all the information about the message queue .

We are finally printing the individual members of this structure.

The second variation of the *msgctl( )* function is its use in changing the values of some of the members of the above structure. We can only change four members - *msqid_ds.msg_perm.uid*, *msqid_ds.msg_perm.gid* , *ms_qid.msg_perm.mode* (these are members of the *ipc_perm* structure, which itself is a member of this structure) and *msg_qbytes*.

PROGRAM 232

```
#include <sys/types.h>
#include <sys/ipc.h>
#include <sys/msg.h>
#include <stdio.h>

main(argc,argv)
int argc;
char **argv;
{
   int qid;
   struct msqid_ds qstatus;
   qid = msgget((key_t) atoi(argv[1]),IPC_CREAT);
   if (qid == -1)
   {
      perror("msgget Failed") ;
      exit(1);
   }
   if ( msgctl(qid, IPC_STAT, &qstatus) < 0 )
   {
      perror("msgctl failed");
      exit(1);
   }
   printf("Real User ID of Queue creator: %d\n",
            qstatus.msg_perm.cuid);
   printf("Real Group ID of Queue creator : %d\n",
            qstatus.msg_perm.cgid);
   printf("Effective User ID of Queue creator : %d\n",
            qstatus.msg_perm.uid);
   printf("Effective Group ID of Queue creator : %d\n",
            qstatus.msg_perm.gid);
   printf("Permissions : %o\n", qstatus.msg_perm.mode);
   printf("\nMessage queue id : %d\n\n", qid);
   printf("%d message(s) on queue \n\n", qstatus.msg_qnum);
```

```
   printf("Last Msg. send by Process : %3d at %s\n",qstatus.msg_lspid,
ctime(&(qstatus.msg_stime)) );
   printf("Last Msg. recv by Process : %3d at %s\n",qstatus.msg_lrpid,
ctime( &(qstatus.msg_rtime)));
   printf("Current no of bytes on queue %d\n",qstatus.msg_cbytes);
   printf("Max no of bytes allowed on queue
%d\n",qstatus.msg_qbytes);

   qstatus.msg_qbytes = 5120;
   qstatus.msg_perm.mode = 0644;
   qstatus.msg_perm.uid = 101;
   qstatus.msg_perm.gid = 3;

   if ( msgctl(qid, IPC_SET, &qstatus) < 0 )
   {
      perror("msgctl failed");
      exit(1);
   }

   printf("Real User ID of Queue creator : %d\n",
                qstatus.msg_perm.cuid);
   printf("Real Group ID of Queue creator : %d\n",
                qstatus.msg_perm.cgid);
   printf("Effective User ID of Queue creator : %d\n",
                qstatus.msg_perm.uid);
   printf("Effective Group ID of Queue creator : %d\n",
                qstatus.msg_perm.gid);
   printf("Permissions : %o\n", qstatus.msg_perm.mode);
   printf("\nMessage queue id : %d\n\n", qid);
   printf("%d message(s) on queue \n\n", qstatus.msg_qnum);
   printf("Last Msg. send by Process : %3d at %s\n",
                qstatus.msg_lspid, ctime( &(qstatus.msg_stime) ) );
   printf("Last Msg. recv by Process : %3d at %s\n",
                qstatus.msg_lrpid, ctime( &(qstatus.msg_rtime)));
   printf("Current no of bytes on queue %d\n",qstatus.msg_cbytes);
   printf("Max no of bytes allowed on queue %d\n",
                qstatus.msg_qbytes);
}
```

With the help of the *msgctl( )* we fill details regarding this message queue into the structure *qstatus*. The *printf( )*'s show the values of the members of this structure.

Next we change the values of the 4 members which are modifiable. And then printing the values of all the members of the structure once again to verify that this change has taken place.

In each message queue there may be many messages. For each message sent to a message queue an entry is made concerning details about it in the structure listed below. If you noticed in the *msqid_ds* structure we had a pointer as the first member - well that pointer which was pointing to the first message in a queue was actually pointing at this structure -

```
struct msg {
    struct msg *msg_next; /* ptr to next message on q */
    long msg_type; /* message type */
    short msg_ts; /* message text size */
    short msg_spot; /* message text map address */
};
```

**msg_next*- is a pointer to the next message in the queue.

msg_type- is the type of a message - a priority setting.

msg_ts- is the length of the message.

msg_spot- this is the address where the data is.

Details about all messages we send are put in this structure.

Sending A Message

So far we have seen what the message queue is made up of but a message we yet haven't sent. After all that's what we really need the queue for. Like most things in UNIX, this too is very simple. All we need to do is call the right function with the required parameters.

PROGRAM 233

```
#include <sys/types.h>
#include <sys/ipc.h>
#include <sys/msg.h>
```

```
#include <stdio.h>

main( )
{
   int qid,len;
   struct msqid_ds qstatus;
   struct {
      long mtype;
      char mtext[15];
   } message;

   printf("My process id is %d\n",getpid( ));
   qid = msgget((key_t) 10,IPC_CREAT | 0666);
   if (qid == -1)
   {
      perror("msgget Failed") ;
      exit(1);
   }
   strncpy(message.mtext,"Hello World\n",15);
   message.mtype = 1;
   len = strlen(message.mtext);
   if (msgsnd(qid,&message,len,0) == -1)
   {
      perror("msgsnd failed ");
      exit(1);
   }
   if ( msgctl(qid, IPC_STAT, &qstatus) < 0 )
   {
      perror("msgctl failed");
      exit(1);
   }
   printf("\nMessage queue id : %d\n\n", qid);
   printf("%d message(s) on queue \n\n", qstatus.msg_qnum);
   printf("Last Msg. send by Process : %3d at %s\n",
              qstatus.msg_lspid, ctime( &(qstatus.msg_stime) ) );
   printf("Last Msg. recv by Process : %3d at %s\n",
              qstatus.msg_lrpid, ctime( &(qstatus.msg_rtime) ) );
}
```

We are defining two structures one that looks like *msquid_ds* and another called *message*. We are then printing the PID of the process. After which a message queue is being created with the *msgget( )* function.

We are then string copying a message into the member *mtext* of the structure *message*. And assigning a 1 to the member *mtype* of the same structure. This is the priority given to the message.

Finally the message is sent using the *msgsnd( )* function to which we are passing 4 parameters - the message queue identifier, the starting address of the structure *message* , the length of the message which has been saved to the variable *len*. And a 0.

A call is made to the *msgctl( )* function to fill the structure *qstatus* with the details of the message queue . And the value of its members are printed.

As many times as we run this program that many messages will be saved into the queue.

So how many message can be saved to a queue ? Put the *msgsnd( )* in a loop - a sure way of finding out.

PROGRAM 234

```
#include <sys/types.h>
#include <sys/ipc.h>
#include <sys/msg.h>
#include <stdio.h>

main( )
{
   int qid,len,i;
   struct {
      long mtype;
      char mtext[15];
   } message;
   qid = msgget((key_t) 10,IPC_CREAT | 0666);
   if (qid == -1)
   {
      perror("msgget Failed") ;
      exit(1);
   }
   strncpy(message.mtext,"Hello World\n",15);
   message.mtype = 1;
   len = strlen(message.mtext);
```

```
    for(i=0;i<10000;i++)
    {
        printf("I is %d\n",i);
        if (msgsnd(qid,&message,len,0) == -1)
        {
            perror("msgsnd failed ");
            exit(1);
        }
    }
}
```

Here too we are defining a structure *message*. And creating a message queue with read write status. A string copy is done and a message assigned to the member *mtext*. While it is given a priority of 1 by the assignation of a 1 to member *mtype*.

In the *for* loop we are first printing the value of variable *i* and then sending a message through the *msgsnd( )* function to the just created message queue .

The *for* loop in our case executed for 35 times - signifying that we could send only 35 messages to the queue . And then the machine hung.

So far we have just been saying that the last parameter to pass to the *msgsnd( )* is a 0. But exactly what does it mean ? Processes normally wait until there is room for a message to be stored. This is a result of the 0. But by specifying a IPC_NOWAIT as the last message we can have the process terminate immediately if there is no more room left.

PROGRAM 235

```
#include <sys/types.h>
#include <sys/ipc.h>
#include <sys/msg.h>
#include <stdio.h>

main( )
{
    int qid,len,i;
    struct {
```

```
        long mtype;
        char mtext[15];
    } message;
    qid = msgget((key_t) 10,IPC_CREAT | 0666);
    if (qid == -1)
    {
        perror("msgget Failed") ;
        exit(1);
    }
    strncpy(message.mtext,"Hello World\n",15);
    message.mtype = 1;
    len = strlen(message.mtext);
    for(i=0;i<10000;i++)
    {
        printf("I is %d\n",i);
        if (msgsnd(qid,&message,len,IPC_NOWAIT) == -1)
        {
            perror("msgsnd failed ");
            exit(1);
        }
    }
}
```

Before you run this program just erase the message queue because it already exists in a full state (a result of the last program).

There is nothing different about this program except that we have specified a IPC_NOWAIT as the last parameter to the *msgsnd()* function. As a result when the message queue gets full we will be brought back to the prompt immediately.

And Now To Receive A Message

But what good is sending a message that is not received. Its like writing a book that no one will read. Or worse still talking to the wall. That reminds me of an interesting book I read where an experiment was tried out on a person. They kept him in a small room in pitch darkness. This room besides having no light was totally soundproof. Infact no external stimuli could come in. Can you imagine living in this room for days on end ? We would go mad and that's exactly what happened to the guy in the book.

Anyway lets get back to receiving messages that are sent. The first program is rather pointless because it is sending the message as well as receiving it. Much like being your own broadcaster - receiver. But it serves as a good illustration. So here goes.

PROGRAM 236

```
#include <sys/types.h>
#include <sys/ipc.h>
#include <sys/msg.h>
#include <stdio.h>

main( )
{
   int qid,len;
   struct {
      long mtype;
      char mtext[15];
   } message,buff;

   qid = msgget((key_t) 11 ,IPC_CREAT | 0666);
   if (qid == -1)
   {
      perror("msgget Failed") ;
      exit(1);
   }
   strncpy(message.mtext,"Hello World\n",15);
   message.mtype = 1;
   len = strlen(message.mtext);
   if (msgsnd(qid,&message,len,0) == -1)
   {
      perror("msgsnd failed ");
      exit(1);
   }
   if(msgrcv(qid,&buff,len,0,0) == -1)
   {
      perror("msgrcv failed ");
      exit(1);
   }
```

```
    printf("message is %s \n",buff.mtext);
}
```

This time we are defining two structures *message* and *buff*. After which we are creating a message queue with read write permissions.Now a string copy is done so that a message is copied to the member *mtext*, which is given the priority 1. This message is then sent to the message queue .

Now its receiving time folks and for that we need to use the *msgrcv( )* function. To this too we are passing four parameters - the message queue identifier, the starting address of the *buff* structure, the length of the message and as usual we would rather you ignored the two 0's for the time being.

And the message is printed on screen.

Message In A Bottle

Ok guys now its time to come out of the womb and communicate with the big bad world. Sending a message, not to be read by us but by someone waiting out there somewhere. Waiting and waiting for a message in a bottle, sorry on the network.

PROGRAM 237

Send.C

```
#include <sys/types.h>
#include <sys/ipc.h>
#include <sys/msg.h>
#include <stdio.h>

main( )
{
    int qid;
    struct {
        long mtype;
        char mtext[25];
    } message;
    qid = msgget((key_t) 10,IPC_CREAT | 0666);
    if (qid == -1)
```

```
    {
        perror("msgget Failed") ;
        exit(1);
    }
    strcpy(message.mtext,"Good Morning World\n");
    message.mtype = 1;
    if (msgsnd(qid,&message,21,0) == -1)
    {
        perror("msgsnd failed ");
        exit(1);
    }
    strcpy(message.mtext,"Good Afternoon World\n");
    message.mtype = 2;
    if (msgsnd(qid,&message,21,0) == -1)
    {
        perror("msgsnd failed ");
        exit(1);
    }
    strcpy(message.mtext,"Good Evening World\n");
    message.mtype = 3;
    if (msgsnd(qid,&message,21,0) == -1)
    {
        perror("msgsnd failed ");
        exit(1);
    }
}
```

We are giving this program a name because we are going to be using it later down the line too.

Basically all its doing is creating a message queue with read write permissions and writing three messages to it with different priority numbers.

Now that we have a message queue with some messages lets write a program that receives them.

PROGRAM 238

Receive.C

```
#include <sys/types.h>
#include <sys/ipc.h>
#include <sys/msg.h>
```

```
#include <stdio.h>

main( )
{
    int qid,i;
    struct {
        long mtype;
        char mtext[25];
    } buff;
    qid = msgget((key_t) 10,IPC_CREAT | 0666);
    if (qid == -1)
    {
        perror("msgget Failed") ;
        exit(1);
    }
    for(i=0;i<3;i++)
    {
        if(msgrcv(qid,&buff,21,0,0) == -1)
        {
            perror("msgrcv failed ");
            exit(1);
        }
        printf("message is %s \n",buff.mtext);
    }
}
```

Here too we are creating a queue with the same name *10*. But since it has already been created (by the send.c program)we are just returned the identifier.

In the *for* loop which executes thrice we are receiving each message through the *msgrcv( )* function. And printing it.

Hey, are we psychic or what, else how else can you explain the loop executing thrice which is also the actual number of messages sent by the previous program. Actually no, its just that we had planned it out from before.

Run this program once more. It waits this time, since there is no message in the queue . To avoid this we need to modify it slightly.

PROGRAM 239

Receive.C

```
#include <sys/types.h>
#include <sys/ipc.h>
#include <sys/msg.h>
#include <stdio.h>

main( )
{
    int qid,i;
    struct {
        long mtype;
        char mtext[25];
    } buff;
    qid = msgget((key_t) 10,IPC_CREAT | 0666);
    if (qid == -1)
    {
        perror("msgget Failed") ;
        exit(1);
    }
    for(i=0;i<3;i++)
    {
        if(msgrcv(qid,&buff,21,0,IPC_NOWAIT) == -1)
        {
            perror("msgrcv failed ");
            exit(1);
        }
        printf("message is %s \n",buff.mtext);
    }
}
```

Here we have just specified a IPC_NOWAIT as the last parameter to the *msgrcv( )* function. In much the same way as we did with the *msgsnd( )* function above.

If this program were run again the program would terminate immediately instead of hanging. This is the result of not waiting if there are no messages in the queue to read.

All the parameters passed to *msgrcv( )* function are extremely important. Take for example the third parameter which defines the length of the message. If its value was less than the message sent there would be no truncation, instead we would get an error message. Check it out -

PROGRAM 240

Receive.C

```
#include <sys/types.h>
#include <sys/ipc.h>
#include <sys/msg.h>
#include <stdio.h>

main( )
{
    int qid,i;
    struct {
        long mtype;
        char mtext[25];
    } buff;
    qid = msgget((key_t) 10,IPC_CREAT | 0666);
    if (qid == -1)
    {
        perror("msgget Failed") ;
        exit(1);
    }
    for(i=0;i<3;i++)
    {
        if(msgrcv(qid,&buff,15,0,IPC_NOWAIT) == -1)
        {
            perror("msgrcv failed ");
            exit(1);
        }
        printf("message is %s \n",buff.mtext);
    }
}
```

Here if you notice we have specified the third parameter as 15 while the length of the messages sent are more than 15 (the send.c program listed above), infact they are 21 characters long.

When we run this program the following error message is flashed -

msgrcv failed : Arg list too long.

But where there is a problem there has to be a solution. Lets see what UNIX gives us to overcome this problem.

PROGRAM 241

Receive.C

```
#include <sys/types.h>
#include <sys/ipc.h>
#include <sys/msg.h>
#include <stdio.h>

main( )
{
    int qid,i;
    struct {
        long mtype;
        char mtext[25];
    } buff;
    qid = msgget((key_t) 10,IPC_CREAT | 0666);
    if (qid == -1)
    {
        perror("msgget Failed") ;
        exit(1);
    }
    for(i=0;i<3;i++)
    {
        if(msgrcv(qid,&buff,15,0,IPC_NOWAIT | MSG_NOERROR) == -1)
        {
            perror("msgrcv failed ");
            exit(1);
        }
        printf("message is %s \n",buff.mtext);
    }
}
```

What UNIX says is if you OR the last parameter, be it IPC_NOWAIT or a 0, with MSG_NOERROR he will ignore any length that is overshot and instead print only the defined number of characters.

Run the send.c program and then run this program. The output will be -

"message is Good Morning"
"message is Good Afternoon"
"message is Good Evening".

Notice the absence of the word world at the end of each message. It has been truncated because the size 15 defined in the *msgrcv( )* function was less then the actual size of the string.

A Sense Of Priority

That leaves us with one of the most important parameter to explain - the fourth one. This signifies the priority number. And only those messages which are sent with the matching priority number are displayed on screen.

PROGRAM 242

Receive.C

```
#include <sys/types.h>
#include <sys/ipc.h>
#include <sys/msg.h>
#include <stdio.h>

main( )
{
    int qid,i;
    struct {
        long mtype;
        char mtext[25];
    } buff;
    qid = msgget((key_t) 10,IPC_CREAT | 0666);
    if (qid == -1)
    {
        perror("msgget Failed") ;
        exit(1);
    }
    for(; ;)
    {
        if(msgrcv(qid,&buff,21,1,IPC_NOWAIT | MSG_NOERROR) == -1)
        {
            perror("msgrcv failed ");
            exit(1);
```

```
        }
        printf("message is %s \n",buff.mtext);
    }
}
```

Here we are passing the fourth parameter as 1. Now if we were to run the program send.c again only the first message, message is Good Morning World, is printed because it too has a priority of 1. No matter how many times you run the send.c program only the message with the matching priority will displayed on screen.

By writing a program in such a way as to pass priority numbers from the command line we can get only those messages we want displayed on screen.

PROGRAM 243

Receive.C

```
#include <sys/types.h>
#include <sys/ipc.h>
#include <sys/msg.h>
#include <stdio.h>

main(argc,argv)
int argc;
char **argv;
{
    int qid;
    struct {
        long mtype;
        char mtext[25];
    } buff;
    qid = msgget((key_t) 10,IPC_CREAT | 0666);
    if (qid == -1)
    {
        perror("msgget Failed") ;
        exit(1);
    }
    for(;;)
    {
        if(msgrcv(qid,&buff,21,atoi(argv[1]),
            IPC_NOWAIT | MSG_NOERROR)==-1)
```

```
        {
            perror("msgrcv failed ");
            exit(1);
        }
        printf("message is %s \n",buff.mtext);
    }
}
```

Here whatever number we pass at the command line will be taken as the fourth parameter, ie. the priority number. And only that message will be printed.

Run the send.c program and then run this program with a 1 as parameter and you will see only the Good Morning message printed.

This parameter passed can be used with one variation. If we were to pass a -2 for example, we would get not only messages with a priority of 2 but also messages with a priority of 1. And if we were to specify a -3 we would get messages with a priority of 1,2 and 3. This is an ideal way to flush the queue , all we need to do is specify a really larger number like -1000 and we should get all messages in the queue on screen, emptying it in the bargain.

The Queue For Telecommunication

Probably one of the greatest inventions besides the wheel was the telephone. What it has done for communications is stupendous. Of course we in the city of Bombay won't agree, what with the regularity with which our phones conk off. Maybe we could resort to using UNIX instead. How ? That's exactly what we intend to show you now.

From now on the next few programs are to be viewed as pairs, after all telephonic conversations cannot be without a person to talk or listen to.

We have 'man1' and 'man2'. 'Man1' sends first and receives later (hits first and talks later), while 'man2' receives first and talks later (that's the stuff psycho-analysts are made off).

PROGRAM 244

Man1.C

```
#include <sys/types.h>
#include <sys/ipc.h>
#include <sys/msg.h>
#include <stdio.h>

main( )
{
    int qid,len;
    struct {
        long mtype;
        char mtext[100];
    } send,recv;
    qid = msgget((key_t) 10,IPC_CREAT | 0666);
    if (qid == -1)
    {
        perror("msgget Failed") ;
        exit(1);
    }
    strcpy(send.mtext,"Hello how are you\n");
    send.mtype = 1;
    len = strlen(send.mtext);
    if (msgsnd(qid,&send,len,0) == -1)
    {
        perror("msgsnd failed ");
        exit(1);
    }
    if(msgrcv(qid,&recv,100,2,0) == -1)
    {
        perror("msgrcv failed ");
        exit(1);
    }
    printf("%s \n",recv.mtext);
}
```

After defining two structures *send* and *recv* we are creating a message queue in the read write mode with the *msgget( )* function. Next we are string copying a message into the member *mtext* of the *send* structure. This message is given the priority 1. The message is then sent using the *msgsnd( )* function. It is passed the queue identifier, the starting address of the structure *send* the length of the message and a 0 which means that the process should wait till a message is sent.

When a message is sent by the guy at the other end of the line the *msgrcv( )* will get activated. It is passed 5 parameters - the queue identifier, the starting address of the structure *recv*, the length of the message, the priority number which will tell it which message to read and finally the last parameter - a 0 for making the program wait till a message is read.

When this program is run on terminal 1 it creates a message queue and writes a message to it with the priority 1. It then waits to read a message from this queue but only those messages which have a priority 2.

Now lets see what the guy on the other side is doing. That is terminal 2.

PROGRAM 245

Man2.C

```
#include <sys/types.h>
#include <sys/ipc.h>
#include <sys/msg.h>
#include <stdio.h>

main( )
{
   int qid,len;
   struct {
      long mtype;
      char mtext[100];
   } send,recv;
   qid = msgget((key_t) 10,IPC_CREAT | 0666);
   if (qid == -1)
   {
      perror("msgget Failed") ;
      exit(1);
   }
   if(msgrcv(qid,&recv,100,1,0) == -1)
   {
      perror("msgrcv failed ");
```

```
        exit(1);
    }
    printf("%s \n",recv.mtext);
    strcpy(send.mtext,"I am ok what about you\n");
    send.mtype = 2;
    len = strlen(send.mtext);
    if (msgsnd(qid,&send,len,0) == -1)
    {
        perror("msgsnd failed ");
        exit(1);
    }
}
```

Here we are as usual first defining two structures and then creating a queue . But since this queue has already been created by 'man1' this program will just be returned the queues identifier.

In this program we are first reading or receiving a message using the *msgrcv( )* function. Notice the last two parameters passed. The second last parameter signifies that it will read only those messages with a priority of 1. And that's exactly the message priority of the message sent by the man1 program. The last parameter makes sure that the process waits till a message is received. Only after a message is received can we send a message from this program.

That's where the subsequent statements come in. A string copy fills the member *mtext* with the string which is assigned a priority of 2. That is exactly the priority number for messages that man1.c is looking for. We are then sending this message.

Lets see how these two programs would work. On terminal 1 man1 would be run and on terminal 2 'man2'. 'man1' would send a message first which would be read by 'man2', Then it in turn would send a message which would be read by the waiting 'man1'.

There is one limitation here. We can only send and receive one message. Which means we now need to write a program that allows us to send and receive more than 1 message. A logical progression, wouldn't you say ?

PROGRAM 246

```
#include <sys/types.h>
#include <sys/ipc.h>
#include <sys/msg.h>
#include <stdio.h>

main( )
{
    int qid,len ;
    struct {
        long mtype ;
        char mtext[100] ;
    } send,recv;

    qid = msgget((key_t) 10,IPC_CREAT | 0666) ;
    if (qid == -1)
    {
        perror("msgget Failed") ;
        exit(1);
    }
    for(;;)
    {
        init(send.mtext) ;
        for (;;)
        {
            fflush( stdin ) ;
            gets(send.mtext) ;
            if (send.mtext[0] == '\0')
                continue ;
            break ;
        }
        send.mtype = 1 ;
        len = strlen(send.mtext) ;
        send.mtext[len] = '\0' ;
        if (msgsnd(qid,&send,len+1,0) == -1)
        {
            perror("msgsnd failed ");
            exit(1);
        }
```

```
        if (strcmp("bye", send.mtext) == 0)
        {
            exit(0);
        }
        init(recv.mtext);
        if(msgrcv(qid,&recv,100,2,0) == -1)
        {
            perror("msgrcv failed ");
            exit(1);
        }
        if (strcmp("bye", recv.mtext) == 0)
            exit(0);
        printf("%s\n",recv.mtext);
    }
}

init(str)
char *str;
{
    int i;
    for(i=0 ;i < 100 ;i++)
        str[i] = ' ';
}
```

Structures two : *send* and *recv* followed by the creation of a message queue . And then with a *for* loop that goes on forever we have the framework for what we want to accomplish - a continuous conversation.

In the *for* loop first a call to the user defined function *init( )*. This initializes the member *mtext* with spaces so that a message a little shorter than the last does not reflect characters that don't belong to it. And now another *for* loop. In which first the standard input (keyboard) buffers are flushed, that's what the *fflush( )* function is doing. And then *gets( )* waits for us to key in a message. If we just happen to press a return without keying in a message we come back to the *gets( )*. And otherwise we are taken out of the *for* loop. In which case the priority for this message is set to 1 and it is sent using the *msgsnd( )* function to the message queue. A string compare is done to see that the message is not a bye in which case the program would terminate. Not like in ordinary conversations where a bye does not necessarily mean end of conversation. Once the message is sent the member *mtext* is reinitialized to spaces- the call to the *init( )* function does this.

Now a call to the *msgrcv( )* function waits for a message to be read from the message queue . A 0 as the last parameter ensures a wait till a message is received. No point in carrying on talking without getting some feedback. Once the message is received a check is made to see if the guy on the other side is bidding us adieu. If so the process terminates else we start all over again.

Now for the program on the other side.

PROGRAM 247

```
#include <sys/types.h>
#include <sys/ipc.h>
#include <sys/msg.h>
#include <stdio.h>
main( )
{
   int qid,len;
   struct {
      long mtype;
      char mtext[100];
   } send,recv;
   qid = msgget((key_t) 10,IPC_CREAT | 0666);
   if (qid == -1)
   {
      perror("msgget Failed") ;
      exit(1);
   }
   for(;;)
   {
      init(recv.mtext);
      if(msgrcv(qid,&recv,100,1,0) == -1)
      {
         perror("msgrcv failed ");
         exit(1);
      }
      printf("%s\n",recv.mtext);
      if (strcmp("bye",recv.mtext) == 0)
         exit(0);
```

```
        init(send.mtext);
        for(;;)
        {
            fflush(stdin);
            gets(send.mtext);
            if (send.mtext[0] == '\0')
                continue;
            break;
        }
        send.mtype = 2;
        len = strlen(send.mtext);
        send.mtext[len] = '\0';
        if (msgsnd(qid,&send,len+1,0) == -1)
        {
            perror("msgsnd failed ");
            exit(1);
        }
        if (strcmp("bye",send.mtext) == 0)
            exit(0);
    }
}

init(str)
char *str ;
{
    int i;
    for(i = 0 ; i < 100 ; i++)
        str[i] = ' ';
}
```

If you notice this program is identical to the previous one in every respect save one. The message is first received and then only can we send one.

One more point to note though and that is the priority numbers of both the message received and that of the one sent. Here the priority of the message received is 1 and that's the priority of the message sent by the previous program. While that of the message sent is 2 which is the priority of messages that are to be read by the previous program. This is the way a program can distinguish which messages belong to it.

So far what we have seen is a one-to-one conversation. Hardly satisfying when one feels that the whole world ought to listen to those pearls of wisdom. Like in the days of old when courts were held in which the king expounded to his courtiers on every topic which he generally didn't know enough about. Of course once in a while the courtiers were allowed to respond.

Lets rewrite history and create a dumb king only fit to give one standard answer. Sounds sadistic ?

PROGRAM 248

```
#include <sys/types.h>
#include <sys/ipc.h>
#include <sys/msg.h>
#include <stdio.h>

main( )
{
   int qid,len;
   struct {
      long mtype;
      int pid;
      char mtext[100];
   } recv;

   struct {
      long mtype;
      char mtext[100];
   } send;

   qid = msgget((key_t) 10,IPC_CREAT I 0666);
   if (qid == -1)
   {
      perror("msgget Failed") ;
      exit(1);
   }
   if(msgrcv(qid,&recv,100,1,0) == -1)
   {
      perror("msgrcv failed ");
      exit(1);
   }
   printf("%s \n",recv.mtext);
```

```
        strcpy(send.mtext,"I am ok what about you\n");
        send.mtype = recv.pid;
        len = strlen(send.mtext);
        if (msgsnd(qid,&send,len,0) == -1)
        {
            perror("msgsnd failed ");
            exit(1);
        }
}
```

This time we are defining two structures but a little differently. In the structure *recv* from which we will be reading the messages we have one more member *pid*. This will tell us who (which of the courtiers) has responded. The structure *send* remains the same.

The message queue is created and the king waits for one of his subjects to ask for something or tell his tale of woe. That's what the *msgrcv( )* function is waiting for. The *msgrcv( )* function is passed the starting address of the structure *recv*, which it fills with the message sent , the priority of the message and the process identity of the message sender. (Notice the last parameter to *msgrcv( )* is 0 which means keep waiting till a message is received).

But to make sure he answers the subject that asked him the question in the first place, we assign the member *mtype* of the structure *send*, the process identifier of the process from where the question came. This PID has been saved to the structure *mrecv*.

A call to the *msgsnd( )* function now ensures that the kings message is sent to the process that asked him and no other.

So far we have sent and received messages according to priority numbers. But this time since it is a matter of a many to one communication we are using the PID instead. Basically we are replacing the priority number with the PID. So a *msgrcv( )* always knows who has sent the message and the *msgsnd( )*

makes use of this knowledge to send the message to the message sender.

But if the king has such meaningless a answer do you think his subjects are really going to ask him anything meaningful. On the contrary.

One thing though the subject has to make sure is to explicitly state who he is. And that's why he sends his PID. Which is of course what the king uses to answer the right person.

```
PROGRAM 249
#include <sys/types.h>
#include <sys/ipc.h>
#include <sys/msg.h>
#include <stdio.h>

main()
{
  int qid,len;
  struct {
    long mtype;
    int pid;
    char mtext[100];
  } send;

  struct {
    long mtype;
    char mtext[100];
  } recv;

  qid = msgget((key_t) 10,IPC_CREAT ! 0666);
  if (qid == -1)
  {
    perror("msgget Failed") ;
    exit(1);
  }
  strcpy(send.mtext,"Hello how are you\n");
  send.mtype = 1;
  send.pid = getpid( );
  len = strlen(send.mtext);
  if (msgsnd(qid,&send,len,0) == -1)
```

```
    {
        perror("msgsnd failed ");
        exit(1);
    }
    if(msgrcv(qid,&recv,100,getpid(),0) == -1)
    {
        perror("msgrcv failed ");
        exit(1);
    }
    printf("%s \n",recv.mtext);
}
```

In this program the *send* structure has a member *pid*. To this we save the PID of the process. An attempt is made to create the message queue which if the previous program was run, would already exist.

A string copy assigns the member *mtext* of structure *send* with the message. A priority of 1 is given to the message and the PID of the process is assigned to the member *pid*. Now its sending time folks and a call is made to the *msgsnd( )* function. This function is passed the queue identifier, the starting address of the structure *send* ,the length of the message and a 0 to keep it waiting till the message is sent.

Which means its time to wait for a reply - accomplished by the call to the *msgrcv( )* function. This function is passed the queue identifier, the starting address of the structure *recv*, a 100 signifying maximum length of the message to be received, the PID of the present process which now behaves like the priority number and a 0 to keep the function in a wait state. Its bad manners to hang up on the king, you could risk getting your head chopped. Once the message is received it is printed.

Now that we know how the king differentiates between his subjects let us allow him a little more intelligence. Let us give him the ability to at least do one useful task. Now what could that be ? How about allowing him to give phone numbers, like an information agency ?

So we will have one program that queries for the phone numbers of some person and the king program that gives the phone number. The query can be from any terminal and since the data is globally accessible the modus operandi will work fine.

```
PROGRAM 250
#include <sys/types.h>
#include <sys/ipc.h>
#include <sys/msg.h>
#include <stdio.h>
char *name[ ] = { "onion" , "ennui" , "ashes" , "aegis" , "realm" };
char *nos[ ] = { "651145" ,"522387" , "5124058" , "587305" ,"235064" };

main( )
{
    int i,qid,len;
    struct {
        long mtype;
        int pid;
        char mtext[100];
    } recv;

    struct {
        long mtype;
        char mtext[100];
    } send;
    if (fork( ) > 0)
        exit(0);
    setpgrp( );
    qid = msgget((key_t) 10,IPC_CREAT I 0666);
    if (qid == -1)
    {
        perror("msgget Failed") ;
        exit(1);
    }
    for(;;)
    {
        init(recv.mtext);
        msgrcv(qid,&recv,100,1,0);
        for(i = 0 ; name[i] ; i++)
        {
            if( strncmp(recv.mtext , name[i],5 ) == 0)
```

```
                {
                    init(send.mtext);
                    strcpy(send.mtext,nos[i]);
                    send.mtype = recv.pid;
                    len = strlen(send.mtext);
                    msgsnd(qid,&send,len,0);
                    break ;
                }
            }
        }
}

init(str)
char *str ;
{
    int i;
    for(i = 0 ; i < 100 ; i++)
        str[i] = ' ';
}
```

We are defining two global array of pointers - *name* and *nos*.

So how else have we changed this program. Well the structures and their members have remained the same. But a *fork( )* creates a child process after which the parent is promptly killed. The call to the *setpgrp( )* ensures that the resulting orphan now becomes a group leader in his own right and therefore not linked to any terminal.

So we now have a king process which even the gods can't kill. Try doing a CTRL D and you will see what we mean.

After the message queue is created, begins the unending *for* loop. In it a call is made to the *msgrcv( )* function which keeps the process hanging till a message is read.

Next we have another *for* loop that takes each name from the *name* array and string compares it with the name queried for. If a match is found the statements within the *if* are executed. Here first the *mtext* member is initialized to spaces. Next the corresponding phone number of the person is assigned to the member *mtext* of the structure *send*. And the PID of the querying process is assigned to the member *mtype*. A *msgsnd( )* with this structure and the message queue identifier will now read the pid from the *mtype* member and send the message to the querying process. And that's how he will see the telephone number.

The query process will look like -

PROGRAM 251

```
#include <sys/types.h>
#include <sys/ipc.h>
#include <sys/msg.h>
#include <stdio.h>

main( )
{
    int qid,len;
    struct {
        long mtype;
        int pid;
        char mtext[100];
    } send;

    struct {
        long mtype;
        char mtext[100];
    } recv;

    qid = msgget((key_t) 10,IPC_CREAT | 0666);
    if (qid == -1)
    {
        perror("msgget Failed") ;
        exit(1);
    }
    for(;;)
    {
        init(send.mtext);
        printf("Enter name (Press <DEL> to exit) :- ");
        gets(send.mtext);
        send.mtype = 1;
        send.pid = getpid( );
        if (msgsnd(qid,&send,100,0) == -1)
```

```
        {
            perror("msgsnd failed ");
            exit(1);
        }
        init(recv.mtext);
        if(msgrcv(qid,&recv,100,getpid(),0) == -1)
        {
            perror("msgrcv failed ");
            exit(1);
        }
        printf("Telephone number is :- %s \n",recv.mtext);
    }
}

init(str)
char *str ;
{
    int i;
    for(i = 0 ; i < 100 ; i++)
        str[i] = ' ';
    str[99] = '\0';
}
```

Here too we have an unending *for* loop. In it we are first initializing the member *mtext* of the structure *send*. And then prompting for the name of the person whose phone number is required. The *gets( )* accepts this input. This input is assigned the priority of 1 so that the king program will realize it is a message meant for it. Further we are also initializing the member *pid* to the PID of this process. This is necessary so that the king process knows who to answer.

Finally the message is being sent through a call to the *msgsnd( )* function.

Now once more we are initializing *mtext* to spaces. And waiting for a reply - that's what the call to the *msgrcv( )* function accomplishes. The received phone number is then printed.

Lets just make a lateral shift here before we move on to understand the rest of the application.

In PC based networks so far we have always had the concepts of file servers. These were the controlling machines which had on them all the data files that were to be shared. A call from one of the nodes resulted in the entire data file being sent to that node. Can you imagine the time taken to do this if a file had 10,000 records ? And what if there were many such users re-queue sting data ? To overcome this problem the concept of database servers was introduced. Here instead of the entire file being transferred only the record asked for is. This considerably reduces the strain on the network and increases speed.

If you notice the client-server program we have introduced above,is what the principle of database servers is. Here we are asking for a phone number. Instead of the entire database (in this case array) being sent only the related phone number is being sent.

A Printer Spooler

Its about time we wrote an actual application with the knowledge that we have just gleaned about message queues. So here goes.

This application behaves like a print spooler. All files that we want printed are sent to the message queue. This allows us to continue with our work. This message queue can be filled with as many files as it can take. The printing is then handled by it. That's not all there is some more to this program.

Suppose we realized that among the 15 files we have sent to print one is not needed anymore, all we need to do is flush this file from the queue. Or if we don't want the queue itself to exist anymore then we just halt the process from running.

The application is made up of four programs which have further sub-functions in them -

server.c	client.c	flush.c	halt.c
proc_obj( ) serv( ) usr1( ) usr2( ) init_queue( ) warn( )	init_queue( ) enter( ) warn( )	init_queue( )	init_queue( )

DIAGRAM 4.6

Now lets see what the main programs do -

The server.c is the receiver - it waits for client processes to send it files to print.

client.c sends the files it want printed.

The flush.c is used to flush the queue of files we don't want printed.

And halt.c is to terminate the server.c program.

Now lets look at each program and its functions in more detail.

Starting with server.c.

PROGRAM 252

server.c

```
#include <stdio.h>
#include <fcntl.h>
#include <signal.h>
#include <sys/types.h>
#include <sys/ipc.h>
#include <sys/msg.h>
```

```
#include <errno.h>

#define QKEY    (key_t)0100
#define QPERM 0666
#define MAXOBN 50
#define MAXPRIOR 10

struct q_entry {
   long mtype ;
   char mtext[MAXOBN+1] ;
};

main( )
{
   int pid ;
   /* Putting server in background */
   switch ( pid = fork ( ) )
   {
      case 0: /* child */
         setpgrp( ) ;
         serv( ) ;
         break ;
      case -1:
         warn("Fork to start server failed") ;
         break ;
   }
   exit(pid != -1 ? 0 : 1);
}

static int r_qid = -1 ;
int fd;
void usr1( );
void usr2( );
serv( )
{
   long pro_type;
   struct q_entry r_entry ;
   int mlen ;
   char buff[10];
   fd = creat("ser.txt", O_WRONLY | O_CREAT | O_EXCL, 0644);
   if (fd < 0)
   {
```

```
        printf("Server already Installed\n");
        exit(0);
    }
    else
    {
        printf("Server process PID is %d\n", getpid( ));
    }
    sprintf(buf,"%d", getpid( ));
    write(fd, buf, sizeof(int));
    chmod("ser.txt", 0400);
    if (r_qid == -1 && (r_qid = init_queue ( )) == -1)
    {
        return(-1) ;
    }
    signal(SIGUSR1,usr1);
    signal(SIGUSR2,usr2);
    for(;;)
    {
        if ( (mlen = msgrcv(r_qid, &r_entry, MAXOBN, 0,
                MSG_NOERROR) ) == -1 )
     {
            perror("msgrcv Failed") ;
            return(-1) ;
        }
        else
        {
            r_entry.mtext[mlen] = '\0' ;
            proc_obj(r_entry.mtext) ;
        }
    }
}

proc_obj(msg)
char *msg ;
{
    printf("%s\n", msg);
    system(msg);
}


void usr1( )
{
    pause( );
```

```
}

void usr2( )
{
   signal(SIGUSR1,usr1);
   signal(SIGUSR2,usr2);
}

init_queue ( )
{
   int queue _id ;
   /* Attempting to Creaste Message Queue */
   if ( (queue _id = msgget(QKEY, IPC_CREAT I QPERM)) == -1 )
   {
      perror("msgget Failed") ;
      return(queue _id) ;
   }
}

warn(s)
char *s ;
{
   fprintf(stderr, "warning : %s\n", s) ;
}
```

After initializing a number of hash defines and one global structure we enter the main body of the program. In this main body a child process is forked. The parent process terminates and the time slice is given to the child. That is of course if there was no error on forking, in which case the process would have terminated after calling the *warn( )* function with a parameter. The *warn( )* function would have displayed this parameter on screen.

The child process would be detached from the terminal it was run on by the call to the *setpgrp( )* function and become a group leader. A call is then made to *serv( )* function.

serv( ) - in this function after all the global and local declarations and definitions we are creating a file called ser.txt in read write mode for us and a read only mode for everybody else. The file descriptor is assigned to the variable *fd*. If the file is successfully created the processes PID is printed. This file is opened in exclusive mode to ensure that the program can't be run again. If it was we would get an error and the process would terminate.

A call is then made to the *sprintf( )* function with three parameters - the address of array *buf*, a %d and the PID of the current process. As a result the PID of the process is stored into the array *buf*. And then the contents of this array are written to the file ser.txt using the *write( )* function.

A call to the *chmod( )* function, which is passed the filename ser.txt and the permissions it should now have, is made. The initial permissions of read/write for us and read only for everybody are changed to read only for everybody to ensure that the contents of the file remain unchanged.

A check is made to see what the value of the static variable *r_qid* is -1 as well as whether the call made to the *init_queue( )* function has returned a -1 or not. This is done because we want to call the *init_queue( )* function only once. The first time this function is called the value of variable *r_qid* is -1 as a result the first part of the *if* statement -

```
if (r_qid == -1 && (r_qid = init_queue ( )) == -1)
```

will evaluate to a true. Now when this true is ANDed with the second half of the *if* the *init_queue( )* will get called and return the queue ID which is assigned to *r_qid*.

The next time however the *r_qid* will have a different value. This is possible because this variable is of static type. As a result the first part of the *if* condition will evaluate to a false and *init_queue( )* will not be called.

The *init_queue( )* is basically creating a message queue and returning its identifier. If this value is -1, it means the message queue was not successfully created, in which case the process terminates. That's what the *return(1)* in the *serv( )* function ensures.

We are defining two signals to be handled, SIGUSR1 and SIGUSR2. When these signals are sent, the second parameter which defines a function is executed. These signals will be sent when the flush.c program is executed. (We will explain them when we come to this program).

Now starts the unending *for* loop. In it we are waiting to receive the message sent by some client process. The *msgrcv( )* function is passed the following parameters - *r_qid* which is the variable that holds the value of the message queue identifier we have created, the starting address of the structure *r_entry* which receives the message that is sent. MAXOBN is the length of the message. 0 stands for the priority number and in this case means any message no matter what the priority number is to be registered. And finally the MSG_NOERROR ensures that any error like a message too long does not result in the program backfiring on us. If a message is received successfully the statements within the *else* are executed.

The first statement terminates the message which is stored in the member *mtext* with a '\0'. And then this member is passed to the function *proc_obj( )*. This function takes this message as a pointer to character and then prints it. But then since this message is in actuality a system call we are passing it to the *system( )* function which executes it but on the server. Remember this program is spooling files to the printer. So the message passed to it would be one that resulted in the file being spooled to the printer.

Now for the client.c program that is used whenever a user wants to send a file to the printer. This is actually a generalized program and can take care of any UNIX command sent to it. However if you want to actually send a file to the printer be sure to add the UNIX print command.

PROGRAM 253

```
#include <stdio.h>
#include <sys/types.h>
#include <sys/ipc.h>
#include <sys/msg.h>
```

```
#include <errno.h>

extern int errno;
#define QKEY (key_t)0100
#define QPERM 0666
#define MAXOBN 50
#define MAXPRIOR 10
struct q_entry {
    long mtype ;
    char mtext[MAXOBN+1] ;
};

main(argc, argv)
int argc ;
char *argv[ ] ;
{
    int priority ;
    if (argc != 3)
    {
    fprintf(stderr, "USAGE : %s objname priority\n", argv[0]) ;
        exit(1) ;
    }

    if ( (priority = atoi(argv[2])) <= 0 | | priority > MAXPRIOR )
    {
        warn("Invalid proirity") ;
        exit(2) ;
    }

    if ( enter(argv[1], priority) < 0)
    {
        warn("Enter Failure");
        exit(3);
    }
    exit(0) ;
}

static int s_qid = -1;
enter(objname, priority)
char *objname ;
int priority ;
{
    int len;
```

```
    char *strncpy( ) ;
    struct q_entry s_entry;
    if ( (len=strlen(objname)) > MAXOBN)
    {
       warn("Name too Long") ;
       return(-1) ;
    }

    if ( priority > MAXPRIOR | | priority < 0 )
    {
       warn("Invalid Priority Level") ;
       return(-1) ;
    }

    if ( s_qid == -1 && (s_qid = init_queue ( )) == -1 )
       return(-1) ; /* Initilizing array to be sent. */

    s_entry.mtype = (long)priority ;
    strncpy(s_entry.mtext, objname, MAXOBN) ;

    if ( msgsnd(s_qid, &s_entry, len, 0) == -1)
    {
       perror("Msgsnd Failed") ;
       return(-1) ;

    }
    else
       return(0);
}


init_queue ( )
{
   int queue _id ;
   /* Attempting to Creaste Message Queue */
   if ( (queue _id = msgget(QKEY, IPC_CREAT | QPERM)) == -1 )
   {
      perror("msgget Failed") ;
      return(queue _id) ;
   }
}

warn(s)
```

```
char *s ;
{
   fprintf(stderr, "warning : %s\n", s) ;
}
```

This program has to be passed two parameters at the command line - the system call and the priority number. If the parameters passed as well as the priority number is valid the third *if* is executed. It calls the *enter( )* function with two parameters - the system call and the priority number.

In the *enter( )* function after all the declarations have been made a check is made to see if the length of the message (system call) passed to it is longer than the maximum length. If it is an error message is flashed and we are returned to the main program from which an exit occurs. If the length is fine a check is made to see if the priority number is valid. If it isn't we are taken back to the main program and exited from there.

The *init_queue( )* function as we have seen earlier creates a message queue and returns its identifier. If the queue is already created the rest of the function is executed.

Here first of all the priority number is assigned to the member *mtype* of the structure *s_entry*. Next the message is assigned to the member *mtext* of the same structure. And finally the message is sent to the server.c process. The command as usual is *msgsnd( )*. It is passed the queue identifier, The starting address of the structure that holds the message and the priority of the message, the length of the message and a 0 for waiting. If the *msgsnd( )* is not successful an error is flashed. Else of course the message is received by the server.c process which proceeds to *system( )* it.

Now assume many files have been sent to the message queue for spooling to the printer using the client.c process. And we suddenly realize that one of those many files was a mistake. Fixed huh? Not at all just run the flush.c program.

PROGRAM 254

flush.C

```
#include <stdio.h>
#include <signal.h>
#include <fcntl.h>
#include <setjmp.h>
#include <sys/types.h>
#include <sys/ipc.h>
#include <sys/msg.h>
#include <errno.h>

#define QKEY    (key_t)0100
#define QPERM 0666
#define MAXOBN 50
#define MAXPRIOR 10

struct q_entry {
   long mtype ;
   char mtext[MAXOBN+1] ;
};

static int f_qid = -1;
static int s_pid = -1;

main(argc, argv)
int argc;
char *argv[ ];
{
   int no_server = 0,fd;
   long pro_type;
   struct q_entry r_entry ;
   int mlen ;
   char buff[10];

   if (argc == 1)
   {
      printf("USAGE : flush <priority>\n");
      printf("where priority = 0 -> flush all messages \n");
      printf("where priority > 0 -> flush a particular priority\n");
      printf("where priority < 0 -> flush all messages below
            absolute value of priority\n");
      exit(0);
```

```
    }

    if (f_qid == -1 && (f_qid = init_queue ()) == -1)
       return(-1) ;

    pro_type = atoi(argv[1]);
    fd = open("ser.txt", O_RDONLY);

    if (fd < 0)
       no_server = 1;
    if (no_server != 1)
    {
       read(fd, buf, sizeof(int));
       s_pid = atoi(buf);
       kill(s_pid,SIGUSR1);
    }
    for(;;)
    {
       if ( (mlen = msgrcv(f_qid, &r_entry, MAXOBN, pro_type ,
              MSG_NOERROR I IPC_NOWAIT) ) == -1 )
       {
          break;
       }
       else
       {
          r_entry.mtext[strlen(r_entry.mtext)] = '\0' ;
          printf(" Command flushed -> %s\n",r_entry.mtext);
       }
    }
    if (no_server != 1)
       kill(s_pid,SIGUSR2);
}

init_queue ( )
{
    int queue _id ;
    /* Attempting to Creaste Message Queue */
    if ( (queue _id = msgget(QKEY, IPC_CREAT I QPERM)) == -1 )
    {
       perror("msgget Failed") ;
       return(queue _id) ;
    }
}
```

This program too has to be passed a parameter at the command line. This parameter is the priority number. A 0 will result in all messages being flushed, a number greater than 0 will result in messages with only that priority being flushed and a number less than 0 will result in all messages below that priority number being flushed.

A check is now made to see if the value of the static variable *f_qid* is -1 and the value returned by the *init_queue( )* function is -1. If both these conditions are satisfied it means an error and the process terminates. Next the file ser.txt is opened in read only mode. If no error is returned by the file open function the process identifier of the server.c process which is stored in the file is assigned to the array. This value is then converted to an integer value and assigned to variable *s_pid*. Now a call is made to the *kill( )* function (we have seen this earlier under signals). It is passed two parameters the process identifier and the SIGUSR1 signal. The moment this signal is sent the *user1( )* function in the server.c program is activated.

In this function a *pause( )* results in the server.c process being kept in abeyance till another signal is sent. This *pause( )* is necessary as we are trying to commit a flush operation on a message queue that is constantly being used by the server.c process. Two processes accessing the same queue for different reasons will result in an error. To prevent this we are putting server.c to sleep till the *flush( )* process finishes flushing the messages from the queue .

To flush as many messages as have the priority number specified an unending *for* loop is activated. This executes till the relevant messages are flushed. In this *for* loop we are receiving only those messages which have the specified priority number using the *msgrcv( )* function. By putting a *'\0'* at the end of the message we are terminating it so that it can be printed on screen correctly. The statements within the *else* run as long as there are messages with the specified priority number. After which a break is made from the *if* statements. This receiving of messages results in the messages being flushed from the queue .

Now that all the messages have been flushed we need to wake the server.c process again. That's what the second call to *kill( )* accomplishes. This results in the SIGUSR2 signal being sent. As a result first the *pause( )* which has been set by the *usr1( )* function is removed. And the *usr2( )* function is called. This results in both the signals being reinitialized. This is necessary as once the signals have been sent they become done with.

The server.c restarts from the point where it was stopped. But there is one drawback here. While the server.c process should start from the message it was processing it does not. This message is eaten up and instead the process starts executing the next message. So how do we get rid of this problem ? That's where SEMAPHORES come in. Patience my friend, one thing at a time.

Now for the last program in this application. I bet most of you all must be breathing a sigh of relief, that is if you have stayed with us this long.

This last program halts the server.c program thus getting rid of the message queue entirely. There are some variation in it. For example if we were to run it without any parameter it would just terminate the server.c process. But if we were to pass a parameter 1 it would terminate the process as well as the queue .

PROGRAM 255

Halt.C

```
#include <sys/types.h>
#include <sys/ipc.h>
#include <sys/msg.h>
#include <stdio.h>
#include <fcntl.h>
#include <signal.h>

#define QKEY    (key_t)0100
#define QPERM 0666
#define MAXOBN 50
#define MAXPRIOR 10
```

```
static int s_pid = -1 ;
int fd;
main(argc,argv)
int argc;
char *argv[ ];
{
    int msq_id;
    struct msqid_ds msq_status;
    char buf[10];
    fd = open("ser.txt", O_RDONLY);
    if (fd < 0)
    {
        printf("Server does not exists\n");
        exit(1);
    }
    read(fd, buf, sizeof(int));
    s_pid = atol(buf);
    if( (kill(s_pid,SIGTERM)) == -1)
    {
        perror("Halt Server");
        exit(2);
    }
    else
    {
        unlink("ser.txt");
        printf("Server Halted\n");
    }
    if (atoi(argv[1]) == 1)
    {
        /* Get message queue identifier */
        if ( (msq_id = init_queue ( )) == -1)
        {
            perror("msgget failed");
            exit(2);
        }
        /* Remove queue */

        if(msgctl(msq_id, IPC_RMID, &msq_status) < 0 )
        {
            perror("msgctl failed");
            exit(3);
        }
        printf("Queue deleted \n");
```

```
    }
}

init_queue ( )
{
    int queue _id ;
    /* Attempting to Creaste Message Queue */
    if ( (queue _id = msgget(QKEY, IPC_CREAT I QPERM)) == -1 )
    {
        perror("msgget Failed") ;
        return(queue _id) ;
    }
}
```

Lets see how this program works.

After all the initial declarations we are opening the file Ser.txt in the read only mode. This as we know contains the PID of the server process. This value is then read into the array *buf*. From here the converted integer value is assigned to the variable *s_pid*.

Now a call to the SIGTERM signal with this PID results in the process terminating. If this is successful the file ser.txt is deleted using the *unlink( )* function.

Now that both the process and the file have been removed a check is made to see if a parameter of 1 was passed. If so the statements within the *if* are executed. In it a call is made to the *init_queue( )* function which returns the queue identifier. Next a call is made to the *msgctl( )* function that is passed three parameters - the queue identifier, IPC_RMID which means remove the queue and the starting address of the structure *msq_status*. And the queue is removed from memory.

Conclusion: Message Queues

Standing in this queue has been a rather wearing experience. From what seemed a simple topic when we started, we have moved on to something really complex. But the last application has been well worth the effort. This we believe is what should be derived from reading this book - the ability to create genuine real life applications with consummate ease.

You can't rest on your laurels yet for there are more efficient ways of communicating still to be explored. And that is our purpose - to find better and more interesting ways to communicate. After all most of us have a lot to say in this world of information explosion.

But if all of us were to say whatever we had to say together, nothing will really be said. All will be lost in a cacophony of noise that even the Gods won't be able to decipher. And if courtesy does not prevent someone interrupting us - shut him up with a SEMAPHORE.

Semaphores

Most networks in the U.S maintain an electronic bulletin board. A user can access this bulletin board download the messages to his computer, reply to them and send them back to the bulletin board. To simulate this entire procedure as an interactive process most users have code written that downloads a message allows them to add their bit to it, send it back and then only download the next message.

Why is this blocking of the next message till the reply to the previous one is sent necessary ?

Suppose the block didn't occur lets see what would happen. The first message would be written to our screen. And we would proceed to reply to it. In the meantime the second message would be written on screen. Can you imagine the confusion ? Everything on screen would be all jumbled.

That is probably one very esoteric example for most of us in India who have barely worked even on a city wide network. So here is another one that will be easier to relate to.

Assume that two processes were accessing the same file. The one that got the time slice first would initialize a variable before working on the file. When the other process is given the time slice it would first check the value of this variable realize it has been initialized by some other process and refrain from accessing the file. When the first process finished it would reinitialize this variable. As a result the second process which has been waiting for just this to happen will get access to the file.

This variable in UNIX terms is known as a semaphore and is basically an integer which acts as a counter. Its value depends on the number of resources there are to share. For example if we had one file which is to be shared then the semaphore can have a value 0 or 1. A 0 initialized semaphore signifies that the resource in this case the file is in use and therefore all other processes would have to wait. The moment the process that has access to the file finishes it sets this semaphore value to 1. Thereby allowing one other process access.

Considering that a semaphore has to be shared by various processes, it (the semaphore) has to be a global variable. And it is precisely for this reason that its value is stored in the kernel. So that it can now be accessed by all processes.

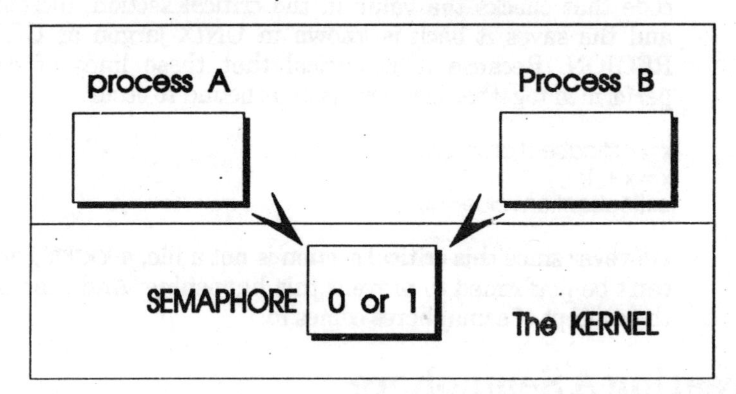

DIAGRAM 4.7

So we have seen two aspects of semaphores - one is that they can be used to restrict two processes from accessing the same file simultaneously and two they help in resource synchronization.

No doubt you must be wondering why would we need to use a semaphore on a file when we have such powerful file locking functions. True, but where we could and should use this concept is when we are dealing with certain other resources like memory.

If you recall that example in the file locking section where we had a file that had only one value the next ticket number that could be issued. We saw how if we did not lock the file the ticket numbering could go haywire. Now if there were many processes using this file there would be a lot of time spent in reading it from disk every time an access was required. To counter this we could read the value just once and then permanently store it in some area in memory. This area is called the CRITICAL SECTION.

Now all the processes could access this area for the latest value, read it, increment it and then save it back to the critical section. But there is one problem here. What if after a process read a value its time slice got over. As a result another process which accessed this value would see the same value. And this of course would lead to a lot of confusion with values being repeated every time a break like this occurs in time slices. These three lines of code that checks the value in the critical section, increments it and the saves it back is known in UNIX jargon as CRITICAL REGION. Because it is critical that these lines of code are performed together else confusion is bound to occur.

```
x = criticalsectionvalue;
x = x + 1;
criticalsectionvalue = x;
```

However since this critical section is not a file, a *lockf( )* or *fcntl( )* can't be performed to prevent this happening. And that is where the concept of semaphores comes in.

Creating A Semaphore

Now that we have a basic idea of semaphores and why they are used lets get to the hows, i.e. how to create and implement them.

To start with do a ipcs -s at the prompt. This will tell us if there are any semaphores existing. Details about any semaphore will be under the following column headings - ID, KEY, MODE, OWNER and GROUP.

```
IPC status from /dev/kmem as of Wed Apr 3 12:21:13 1991
T          ID      KEY      MODE      OWNER      GROUP
Semaphores:
```

Notice how the creators of UNIX have kept consisting sounding functions for creating semaphores and message queues - *semget( )* and *msgget( )*.

Now run the following program that creates a semaphore.

PROGRAM 256

```
#include <sys/types.h>
#include <sys/ipc.h>

main( )
{
   int semid,key,nsem;
   key = (key_t) 0x20;
   nsem = 0;
   semid = semget(key,nsem,IPC_CREAT | 0666);
   printf("Created Semaphore with ID : %d\n",semid);
}
```

There are 3 integer variables being defined. To the variable *key* we assign a hexadecimal value 0x20, this is the name that we create the semaphore with. We casting the value to be of data type *key_t* which has been defined in the sys/ipc.h header file.

To the variable *nsem* we are assigning a value of 0. A call is made to the function *semget( )* which is passed three parameters- the *key, nsem* (explained in a moment)and a value that will create the semaphore in read and alter mode (there is no write mode in semaphores).

semget( ) returns an value which is the identifier of the semaphore. If this value is a -1 it means an error.

And that's what this program returned. So where's the problem ? Why because we haven't specified how many semaphores we want.

UNIX doesn't just create one semaphore , what it allows us instead is the ability to create a set of semaphores. And in this set there should be a minimum of at least 1 sub-semaphore. The second parameter we pass the *semget( )* function defines how many sub-semaphores there will be in this set of semaphores. Unfortunately we have assigned a 0 to this variable *nsem* which is below the minimum required. As a result an error is returned.

Do a ipcs -s to verify that this semaphore has not been created.

The next one we guarantee will actually create a semaphore.

PROGRAM 257

```
#include <sys/types.h>
#include <sys/ipc.h>

main( )
{
   int semid,key,flag,nsem;
   key = (key_t) 0x20;
   flag = IPC_CREAT | 0666;
   nsem = 1;
   semid = semget(key,nsem,flag);
   printf("Created Semaphore with ID : %d\n",semid);
}
```

Variable *nsem* is now being assigned a value 1. Therefore since the minimum requirement is fulfilled the semaphore will get created.

Do a ipcs -s at the prompt to see a listing of the semaphores and an entry for the semaphore will be displayed. Our computer screen showed this when we ran the command -

```
IPC status from /dev/kmem as of Wed Apr 3 12:22:36 1991
T               ID    KEY          MODE         OWNER      GROUP
Semaphores:
s               40  0x00000020  --ra-ra-ra-   vmci        other
```

Under mode we have -ra-ra-ra- where the r stands for 'read' and the a stands for 'alter'.

Just as with queues even with semaphores there is a maximum limit. We are allowed to create only 10 set of semaphores. Check it out-

PROGRAM 258

```
/* to find maximum no of semaphore sets available in our UNIX
system */

#include <sys/types.h>
#include <sys/ipc.h>

main( )
{
   int semid,nsemset,nsem,flag,key;
   nsem = 1;
   flag = 0666 | IPC_CREAT;
   for(nsemset = 0;;nsemset++)
   {
      key = (key_t) nsemset;
      semid = semget(nsemset,nsem,flag);
      if (semid > 0 )
         printf("\nCreated Semaphore with ID : %d\n",semid);
      else
      {
         printf("Maximum number of semaphore set are %d\n",
               nsemset);
         exit(0);
      }
   }
}
```

We have an infinite *for* loop. In this loop we make a call to the *semget( )* function, passing it the three parameters it requires. If function this call is successful a valid ID will be returned else it will execute the *printf( )* statement within the *else* before exiting. This signifies that the limit has been reached.

When we did a ipcs -s we saw that 10 semaphores had been created with the following ID's.

```
IPC status from /dev/kmem as of Wed Apr 3 12:39:33 1991
T           ID     KEY         MODE        OWNER  GROUP
Semaphores:
s           0      0x00000000 --ra-ra-ra-  vmci   other
s           1      0x00000001 --ra-ra-ra-  vmci   other
s           2      0x00000002 --ra-ra-ra-  vmci   other
s           3      0x00000003 --ra-ra-ra-  vmci   other
s           4      0x00000004 --ra-ra-ra-  vmci   other
s           5      0x00000005 --ra-ra-ra-  vmci   other
s           6      0x00000006 --ra-ra-ra-  vmci   other
s           7      0x00000007 --ra-ra-ra-  vmci   other
s           8      0x00000008 --ra-ra-ra-  vmci   other
s           9      0x00000009 --ra-ra-ra-  vmci   other
```

But each of these set of semaphores can in turn have a maximum of 25 semaphores. That's what the next program shows -

PROGRAM 259

```
#include <sys/types.h>
#include <sys/ipc.h>

main( )
{
    int semid,key,flag,nsem,i;
    key = (key_t) 0x30;
    flag = IPC_CREAT | 0666;
    for(i = 0;;i++)
    {
        nsem = i + 1;
        semid = semget(key,nsem,flag);
        if (semid > 0)
            printf("Created Semaphore with ID : %d\n",semid);
        else
        {
            printf("Maximum no of semaphores in one set are %d\n",i);
```

```
        exit(0);
    }
    semctl(semid,0,IPC_RMID,0);
  }
}
```

In the *for* loop we first increment the value of variable

nsem, the first time it becomes 1. Now a call is made to the *semget( )* function with the three parameters *key* which is the name, *nsem* which signifies how many semaphores to create this set of semaphores with and *flag* which has been assigned IPC_CREAT | 0666. As a result a semaphore is created with 1 sub- semaphore. Since it is successfully created the *printf( )* within the *if* is executed. This prints the ID returned by the *semget( )* function.

Now we delete this semaphore using the *semctl( )* function. This function is passed 4 parameters - the ID of the semaphore, a 0 (ignore for now, IPC_RMID which is the value *semctl( )* understands as a call to get rid of the semaphore and a 0 once again, which we want you to ignore for now.

After this function deletes the semaphore control is handed to the beginning of the loop. Variable *nsem* is incremented to 2. A call to the *semget( )* now creates a new semaphore with the same name but with two sub-semaphores. And once again the *printf( )* in the *if* executes printing the ID of the new semaphore. This semaphore is deleted and the loop starts again from the beginning. This goes on till the limit is reached, which is 25 in which case the *printf( )* within the *else* is executed before the process terminates.

Did you notice the ID numbers that were printed on screen with every loop ? They kept increasing by 10 each time. Why ? Since we can have a maximum of 10 sets of semaphores they will if created one after another have a numbering sequence of ID's 0 - 9. Now if we were to delete say the first set of semaphores and create a new one with the same KEY, the ID returned will not be

0, nor can it be any number between 1 - 9 since they are already in use. The next ID number therefore has to be 10.

Suppose we were to now delete the semaphore with a KEY of 1 and create another in its place with the same KEY, it would get an ID of 11. Semaphore with KEY 2 would get an ID of 12 and so on so forth.

Now if semaphore with KEY 0 were to be deleted once again and a new one created with the same KEY, i.e. 0, it would have an ID 20. The same procedure if enacted on semaphore with KEY 1 would get us a semaphore with ID 21 and so on so forth.

A table should make this clearer -

Semaphore Identifiers

KEY	I	II	III	IV	V
1	0	10	20		
2	1	11	21		
3	2	12	22		
4	3	13	:		
:	:	:			
9	9	:			

DIAGRAM 4.8

Although a maximum of 10 sets of semaphores with each containing 25 sub-semaphores are allowed this is not really so. UNIX stops creating semaphores long before this limit is reached. At least this is what we found in our version of UNIX - System V Release 3.

```
PROGRAM 260
/* maximum no of semaphores in UNIX system */
#include <sys/types.h>
#include <sys/ipc.h>
main( )
{
   int semid,key,flag,nsem,j,i;
   flag = IPC_CREAT | 0666;
   nsem = 25;
   for (j = 0; j < 10; j++)
   {
      key = (key_t) (j + 1);
      semid = semget(key,nsem,flag);
      if (semid > 0)
         printf("Created Semaphore with ID : %d\n",semid);
      else
      {
         for(i = 0;;i++)
         {
            nsem = i + 1;
            semid = semget(key,nsem,flag);
            if (semid > 0)
               printf("Created Semaphore with ID : %d\n",semid);
            else
            {
               printf("Max no of semaphores in UNIX system are %d\n",
                     (i + j * 25));
               exit(0);
            }
            semctl(semid,0,IPC_RMID,0);
         }
      }
   }
}
```

Variables *flag* and *nsem* are initialized. And a *for* loop executed 10 times. In this loop we create a semaphore with the *semget( )* function. This function returns the ID if its successful else it returns a -1. If it was successful the main loop executes once more creating another semaphore (we are incrementing variable *key* which is the name of the semaphore) but with the same number of sub-semaphores namely 25.

If this is successful the ID is displayed and once more the same process takes place. In our machine this main loop executed twice only creating a set of two semaphores with a mere 50 sub-semaphores. Since the third time round the ID was not returned the *if* condition evaluated to a false, as a result the statements within the *else* were executed.

This started another loop in which variable *nsem* is first initialized to a 1. A call is now made to the *semget( )* function which is commanded to create a set of semaphores with only 1 sub- semaphore because that's the value of *nsem.* If it is successful it returns the ID, deletes the semaphore and starts the loop again. Else if the *semget( )* is unsuccessful a value which signifies the maximum number of semaphores (with sub-semaphores) we can create at one time is printed.

In our case it was 60. 50 by the first loop. And 10 through the inner loop which created sub-semaphores one at a time.

Here is another example that shows this -

```
PROGRAM 261
#include <sys/types.h>
#include <sys/ipc.h>

main( )
{
   int semid;
   semid = semget(0x20,25,0666 | IPC_CREAT);
   if (semid > 0)
      printf("1st semget succeeded\n");
   else
   {
      perror("1st semget");
      exit(0);
   }
   semid = semget(0x30,25,0666 | IPC_CREAT);
   if (semid > 0)
```

```
        printf("2nd semget succeeded\n");
    else
    {
        perror("2nd semget");
        exit(0);
    }
    semid = semget(0x40,10,0666 | IPC_CREAT);
    if (semid > 0)
        printf("3rd semget succeeded\n");
    else
    {
        perror("3rd semget");
        exit(0);
    }
    semid = semget(0x50,1,0666 | IPC_CREAT);
    if (semid > 0)
        printf("4th semget succeeded\n");
    else
    {
        perror("4th semget");
        exit(0);
    }
}
```

We create 1 semaphore with **25 sub-semaphores**. If *semget( )* does not return a -1 the statement within the *if* is executed. Else the process terminates.

Next an attempt is made to create another semaphore with 25 sub- semaphores. This too is successful.

The third attempt to create yet another semaphore with 10 sub-semaphores is also successful. So now we have 60 semaphores in all.

The last *semget( )* which attempted to create another semaphore with 1 sub-semaphore evaluated to a false, however.

QED !

Semaphore Exclusivity

It may be that one user will create a semaphore with a certain KEY say 1 and another user may attempt to do the same with the same KEY. Unless we specify that this semaphore is to be created in the exclusive mode the second user will not get an error message. All he will be returned is the same ID. If you run the second (above) program of this topic twice, one after the other you will know what we mean.

However if we do want an error returned we can always create the semaphore in the exclusive mode as shown below.

PROGRAM 262

```
#include <sys/types.h>
#include <sys/ipc.h>

main()
{
   int semid,key,flag,nsem,i;
   for(i = 0; i < 2;i++)
   {
      key = (key_t) 0x30;
      flag = IPC_CREAT | 0666 | IPC_EXCL;
      nsem = 1;
      semid = semget(key,nsem,flag);
      if (semid > 0)
         printf("Created Semaphore with ID : %d\n",semid);
      else
         perror("semget ");
   }
}
```

Note : delete the semaphore with KEY 30 before running this program.

What are we doing here ? First we assign a value of hex 30 to the variable *key*. Next in the *for* loop which executes twice we initialize variable *flag* with IPC_CREAT | 0666 | IPC_EXCL. This last parameter results in the semaphore being opened in exclusive mode.

The first time the loop is executed *semget( )* returns the ID of the semaphore. And the check to see if this value is greater than 0 results in a true thereby executing the *printf( )* that prints the ID.

The next time round however the value returned by *semget( )* is less than 0 signifying that the semaphore already exists. As a result the *perror( )* function within the *else* gets executed.

We know that if this semaphore is not created in exclusive mode and another user does try to create it he will just be returned the ID. The IPC_CREAT in his program will be ignored. But there is one hitch in this. And that deals with the mode the semaphore is created and then "recreated" in.

Intricacy Of Semaphore Permissions

Suppose the first process that created it did so in read-alter-read-alter-read-alter mode that is with a value of 0666. Now any attempt by the next user would have to have a mode which is the same or is a subset - for example 0644.

PROGRAM 263

```
#include <sys/types.h>
#include <sys/ipc.h>

main( )
{
    int semid,key,flag,nsem;
    key = (key_t) 0x40;
    flag = IPC_CREAT | 0666;
    nsem = 1;
    semid = semget(key,nsem,flag);
    if (semid > 0)
        printf("Created Semaphore with ID : %d\n",semid);
    else
        perror("1st semget ");
    flag = IPC_CREAT | 0644;
    semid = semget(key,nsem,flag);
    if (semid > 0)
        printf("Created Semaphore with ID : %d\n",semid);
```

```
    else
        perror("2nd semget ");
}
```

Here in the same program we attempt to create the same semaphore twice (by doing this through one program we hope to aid understanding).

The first time the semaphore is created with the mode read-alter-read-alter-read-alter. The *if* condition evaluates to a true and therefore the ID of the semaphore is printed.

Now the value in variable *flag* is changed to reflect a read-alter-read-alter mode - 0644. The call to *semget( )* is successful once again. As a result the *if* evaluates to a true and the *printf( )* that prints the ID is executed.

So far so good. But if it had been the other way round with the semaphore first being created in 0644 mode and then an attempt being made to change it to 0666 mode, an error would have occurred.

PROGRAM 264

```
#include <sys/types.h>
#include <sys/ipc.h>

main( )
{
    int semid,key,flag,nsem;
    key = (key_t) 0x30;
    flag = IPC_CREAT | 0644;
    nsem = 1;
    semid = semget(key,nsem,flag);
    if (semid > 0)
        printf("Created Semaphore with ID : %d\n",semid);
    else
        perror("1st semget ");

    flag = IPC_CREAT | 0666;
    semid = semget(key,nsem,flag);
    if (semid > 0)
```

```
        printf("Created Semaphore with ID : %d\n",semid);
    else
        perror("3rd semget ");
}
```

We first create the semaphore in the 0644 mode and then attempt to create it once more but in the 0666 mode. This is unsuccessful, however and an error is flashed.

The moral of the story - if the new mode is a subset of the old one as it was in the previous program, no error. But if it is a superset as shown above then an error is our lot.

Something similar happens if we first create a set of semaphores with a certain number of sub-semaphores and then try to create it once more with another number of sub-semaphores.

PROGRAM 265

```
#include <sys/types.h>
#include <sys/ipc.h>

main( )
{
    int semid,key,flag,nsem;
    key = (key_t) 0x30;
    flag = IPC_CREAT | 0600;

    nsem = 2;
    semid = semget(key,nsem,flag);
    if (semid > 0)
        printf("Created Semaphore with ID : %d\n",semid);
    else
        perror("1st semget ");

    nsem = 1;
    semid = semget(key,nsem,flag);
    if (semid > 0)
        printf("Created Semaphore with ID : %d\n",semid);
    else
        perror("2nd semget ");

    nsem = 4;
```

```
    semid = semget(key,nsem,flag);
    if (semid > 0)
        printf("Created Semaphore with ID : %d\n",semid);
    else
        perror("3rd semget ");
}
```

Initially we create the set of semaphores with 2 sub-semaphores. The first *if* evaluates to a true and the ID of the semaphore is printed.

The value of variable *nsem* is now changed to 1 and a call made to the *semget( )* function again with this new value. This time too the semaphore is created but with a sub-semaphore of one. As a result the ID is printed once more.

Now for the last time we are changing the value of variable *nsem*, to 4. The call to *semget( )* however fails this time. From this it is clear that another call to the *semget( )* will be successful only if the number of sub-semaphores are less.

Getting And Setting Semaphore Values

So far we have seen how *semget( )* creates a set of semaphores with as many sub-semaphores as specified by us. All the programs, we dealt with above, worked with the set of semaphores and not the sub-semaphores. But it is the value of these sub-semaphores that a process uses to determine whether it has access to a resource or not.

The function to find out what the value of a semaphore is *semctl( )*. This function we have seen was used to remove a semaphore (remember we passed a IPC_RMID to it as the 3rd parameter). To get the value of the sub-semaphore we specify GETVAL instead.

PROGRAM 266

```
#include <sys/types.h>
#include <sys/ipc.h>
#include <sys/sem.h>
```

```
#include <errno.h>

main()
{
    int semid,retval;
    semid = semget(0x20,1,0666 | IPC_CREAT);
    retval = semctl(semid, 0 , GETVAL ,0);
    printf("Value returned is %d\n",retval);
}
```

We create a semaphore, with a KEY (name) of 20 and 1 sub-semaphore, in the read-alter for all users.

A call is now made to the *semctl( )* function. It is passed 4 parameters - the ID of the semaphore, a 0 which signifies the sub-semaphore that we are enquiring about (in this case it is the first), the GETVAL which forces *semctl( )* to return the value of the sub-semaphore and the last is a 0 (ignore it for now).

Function *semctl( )* now returns the value of the sub-semaphore to the variable *retval.* This value is 0 and will always be so when we first create the semaphore.

Although semaphores are always initialized to a 0 they can be assigned different values. After all they are just like ordinary variables. However we cant assign values to these semaphores in the normal way. For this we need to pass the SETVAL value as the third parameter and the last parameter has to be the value we want to assign the semaphore.

PROGRAM 267

```
#include <sys/types.h>
#include <sys/ipc.h>
#include <sys/sem.h>
#include <errno.h>

main()
{
    int semid,retval;
    semid = semget(0x20,1,0666 | IPC_CREAT);
    semctl(semid, 0 , SETVAL ,1);
```

```
    retval = semctl(semid, 0 , GETVAL ,0);
    printf("Value of the semaphore after setting is %d\n",retval);
    semctl(semid, 0 , SETVAL ,2);
    retval = semctl(semid, 0 , GETVAL ,0);
    printf("Value of the semaphore after setting is %d\n",retval);
}
```

We create a semaphore with one sub-semaphore. And then call the

semctl( ) to assign a value of 1 to the sub-semaphore. For now just note that this 1 is an integer. Function *semctl( )* is passed 4 parameters - the ID of the semaphore, the sub-semaphore we want to assign a value to - in this case it is sub-semaphore 0, the SETVAL - as a result of which *semctl( )* assigns a values and a 1, which is the value to be assigned to the sub-semaphore. The second call to the *semctl( )* now returns this value - i.e. 1 to the variable *retval.*

Now once more we assign a value ,2, to the sub-semaphore. This is just to demonstrate how a semaphore is like any other variable and can be assigned values again and again.

Who Is Using The Resource ?

A semaphore is basically used by different processes to synchronize access to a resource. Of course what value the semaphore should have to determine access or not has to be specified by us. For example maybe we have designed our system in such a way that when a semaphore is deciphered as having a value of 1 it means that a certain resource is in use by another process. And a value of 2 means that the resource is free and that our process can now access to it.

Using the *semctl( )* function we can find out which process has set the value of a semaphore. A value of GETPID passed to the *semctl( )* will result in it passing the PID of the process that has set the value of the semaphore.

PROGRAM 268

```
#include <sys/types.h>
#include <sys/ipc.h>
#include <sys/sem.h>
#include <errno.h>

main( )
{
   int semid,retval;
   semid = semget(0x20,1,0666 | IPC_CREAT);
   retval = semctl(semid, 0 , GETPID , 0);
   printf("PID returned by semctl is %d and actual PID is
%d\n",retval,getpid( ));
}
```

Note : kill this semaphore first and then run this program twice.

The *semget( )* creates a semaphore with 1 sub-semaphore. Function *semctl( )* is called - with the ID of the semaphore, a 0 signifying the sub-semaphore we are interested in, GETPID which results in the PID of the process being returned to the variable *retval* and a 0 since we don't want to set the value.

Hey what happened ? Both times the program was run the value of *retval* was 0. That's because while we created a semaphore with a sub-semaphore we haven't yet assigned a value to it using the SETVAL parameter.

So why don't we do that and then check the result. Once again remove this semaphore before running the next program.

PROGRAM 269

```
#include <sys/types.h>
#include <sys/ipc.h>
#include <sys/sem.h>
#include <errno.h>

main( )
{
   int semid,retval;
   semid = semget(0x20,1,0666 | IPC_CREAT);
```

```
    retval = semctl(semid, 0 , GETPID , 0);
    printf("PID returned by semctl is %d and actual PID is %d\n",
         retval,getpid( ));
    retval = semctl(semid, 0 , SETVAL , 1);
}
```

We create a semaphore. And call *semctl( )* with the GETPID parameter. But as we saw before this will return a 0 since the semaphore is being created for the first time.

After the *printf( )* which prints a 0 (the value of *retval*) and the PID of the current process a call is made to the *semctl( )* function to set the value of the sub-semaphore to 1. And the process terminates.

At this point we have a semaphore with the name 20 in memory. Its sub-semaphore 1 has the value 1.

Now if were to run this program once more, the IPC_CREAT would be ignored since the semaphore already exists. The call to the *semctl( )* will now return the PID of the process that set the value of the sub-semaphore (which in our case is also the process that created the semaphore). This value (the PID)which is assigned to the variable *retval* and the PID of the current process are printed. Function *semctl( )* is called again. And a 1 reassigned to the sub-semaphore before the program terminates.

When we ran this program the first time round *retval* was 0 and *getpid( )* returned 576. The second time round *retval* was 576 that is the PID of the previous process while *getpid( )* now returned 577.

If we have a number of sub-semaphores in a set of semaphores and we wanted to get their values a far more efficient way then passing GETVAL as the parameter would be to pass GETALL. Because a GETVAL means that each sub-semaphore would have to be accessed individually. Whereas with a GETALL a single statement would do the needful. A GETALL requires an array to be passed too to the *semctl( )* function.

PROGRAM 270

```
#include <sys/types.h>
#include <sys/ipc.h>
#include <sys/sem.h>
#include <errno.h>

main( )
{
   int semid;
   ushort val[5];
   semid = semget(0x20,5,0666 | IPC_CREAT);
   semctl(semid,0,SETVAL,1);
   semctl(semid,1,SETVAL,2);
   semctl(semid,2,SETVAL,3);
   semctl(semid,3,SETVAL,4);
   semctl(semid,4,SETVAL,5);
   semctl(semid,0,GETALL,val);
   printf("val 1 : %d val2 : %d val3 : %d val4 %d : val5 :%d\n",
         val[0], val[1],val[2],val[3],val[4]);
}
```

We declare an array called *val* with 5 elements. And then create a semaphore with 5 sub-semaphores.

Now each of these sub-semaphores are assigned a value from 1-5. Once more *semctl( )* is called with 4 parameters - the ID of the semaphore, a 0 signifying sub-semaphores, GETALL which results in the values of all the semaphores being returned and passed to the array *val* which is specified as the last parameter.

The *printf( )* finally prints these different values.

And if UNIX is intelligent enough to give us method by which we can get the values of all the sub-semaphores in one go, then surely it will also provide a way to assign values to these sub-semaphores in the same manner. All at one time.

PROGRAM 271

```
#include <sys/types.h>
#include <sys/ipc.h>
#include <sys/sem.h>
```

```
#include <errno.h>

main( )
{
    int semid;
    static ushort val[5] = {1,2,3,4,5}, val1[5];
    semid = semget(0x20,5,0666 | IPC_CREAT);
    semctl(semid,0,SETALL,val);
    semctl(semid,0,GETALL,val1);
    printf("val1[0] : %d val1[1] : %d val1[2] : %d val1[3] %d : val1[4] : %d\n",
            val1[0],val1[1],val1[2],val1[3],val1[4]);
}
```

A call to *semget( )* creates a semaphore with 5 sub-semaphores. After which *semctl( )* is called to assign the values from the array *val* to the sub-semaphores. *semctl( )* is passed 4 parameters - the ID of the semaphore, a 0 signifying the sub- semaphores (here it means all) , SETALL means that we want to assign to these sub-semaphores the values from the last parameter which is the array *val*.

Once this is done we get all the values of these sub-semaphores and assign them to the various elements of the second array *val1* using GETALL. These values are then printed.

Atomicity Through Structures

So what next? We've seen how to create semaphores, and to some extent how to assign them values. These values will be interpreted by the different processes to ascertain whether they have access to a particular resource or not.

But there's one problem in using the SETVAL and GETVAL to initialize values and synchronize between processes. Assume there are three processes all interacting with the same semaphore and that this semaphore has 1 sub-semaphore.

The first time round the process A initializes the semaphore and proceeds to work with the resource. Its time slice gets over and process B gets activated. In this process an attempt is made to work with the resource, but since it's in use (the process checks the semaphore) the process waits till the resource is freed.

Now the time slice is given back to Process A. It finishes with the resource and initializes the semaphore to indicate that the resource is now free. As a result process B wakes up to begin work with the resource. But suppose that just before it set the semaphore to a value (to indicate that the resource is in use) its time slice was snatched and given to process C -- which checks the semaphore, sees that it is open to access and sets its value to begin work with the resource.

Now when process B gets the time slice it will be at the point where it is about to see the value and will, in fact, do just that. So we will have two processes with access to the same resource at the same time.

Hey, but wasn't this one of the problems we believed the semaphore would take care of? It does, but for that we need to work with the semaphore a little differently. Since GETVAL and SETVAL don't really give us "atomic" code we need to use structures so that the kind of situation shown above does not occur.

Let's look at what these 3 processes would look like because from this bird's eyeview we'd get an idea of what CRITICAL REGION means.

Process A would have lines that would:

* create a semaphore

* set the value of a semaphore

* work with the resource

.

.

* reset the value of the semaphore

Process B would have lines -

* initialize a variable with some value

* check the value of the semaphore

* if the value of the semaphore doesn't match the variable value then wait at this point

* else

* set the value of the semaphore

* work with the resource

.

.

.

* reset value when finished

Process C would have similar lines as Process B.

So when process A is working with the resource Process B will be waiting at the *if* check point. The moment process A finishes it will reset the semaphore. When the time slice is now given to process B the *if* will prove false and the else part will be entered. But assume that just before it sets the value of the semaphore, process C gets activated. In it, too, the *if* will evaluate to a false. As a result it will set the value of the semaphore. But when process B gets the time slice it will directly start executing the statements within the *else* which set the value of the semaphore.

Thus we have two processes that have set the value of the semaphore and "confusion shall flourish over our heads". OK, guys, guess what the CRITICAL REGION is: the *if* and the statements within it, of course. Therefore we should have a way of making sure that if the *else* is entered a snatching away of the time slice should not have the results shown above.

And it is to overcome this problem that instead of GETVAL and SETVAL we use structures and the *semop( )* function. Because they give us the atomicity we desire. That is, if one of the operations can't be done, none will be. "One for all and all for one".

The structure we need to use is in the sys/sem.h header file and is called *sembuf*. It looks like:

```
struct sembuf {
   ushort  sem_num; /* semaphore # */
   short sem_op;       /* semaphore operation */
   short sem_flg;    /* operation flags */
};
```

sem_num is the number that is associated with a sub-semaphore. 0 indicates thé first sub-semaphore. *sem_op* is a value that defines the operation we want performed on the semaphore. Through this value we can define whether we want to capture the resource or release it.

If the resource is not available then the process will normally sleep till the resource becomes available. But what if we don't want to wait for this resource and do something else in the mean time? This can be achieved by assigning IPC_NOWAIT to the *sem_op* member.

sem_flg defines the step to take if the semaphore is already in use by another process. An IPC_NOWAIT allows the process to carry on with some other task.

To all these members of the structure *sop* we assign a value of 0. We then create a semaphore. And then a call is made to the *semop( )* function. This function is passed 3 parameters: the ID of the semaphore, the address of the structure, and the number of operations -- in this case only 1.

This last parameter is related to the structure in the same way as the *argc* and **argv[ ]* are related to each other. We know that the *argc* will tell us how many parameters are passed at the command line and these parameters are stored in the *argv[ ]*. Similarly, the last parameter here tells the *semop( )* function how many structures it has to go through to perform its operations.

What is it that the *semop( )* basically does? In message queues we had functions that created and killed message queues as well as a function that received and sent messages. As far as semaphores are concerned we have only one function that sets and resets the value of the semaphore, and this is done by the *semop( )* function. It returns a value which indicates success or failure. The *sem_op* member can be passed three kinds of values. And based on these values the *semop( )* proceeds to do some task.

If the value is a negative number, eg. -2, and if the absolute value of the semaphore is the same or greater (i.e. 2 or greater than 2) then the process won't wait at the *semop( )* but will perform the operation successfully. If, however, the value of the semaphore is, say 1, then the *semop( )* will wait till the value becomes 2 or greater.

Suppose the value of the member *sem_op* was positive, say 5, then this value would have been added to the value of the semaphore. For example, assume that the value of the semaphore was 1, the call to the *semop( )* would make it 6.

The last instance is the value of the member *sem_op* being 0 (this is a special case). Now if the value of the semaphore is also 0, the *semop( )* will perform. But if it is any other value the *process( )* will wait at the *semop( )* till the value becomes 0.

Now let's go a step further and this step will further demonstrate the essence of semaphores.

Run the program shown below with a parameter of 0.

PROGRAM 272

X.C

```
#include <sys/types.h>
#include <sys/ipc.h>
#include <sys/sem.h>

main(argc,argv)
int argc;
char *argv[ ];
{
   int semid,val = 0;
   val = atoi(argv[1]);
   semid = semget((key_t) 0x20,1,IPC_CREAT);
   semctl(semid,0,SETVAL,val);
}
```

A semaphore with 1 sub-semaphore is created using the *semget( )* function. The *semctl( )* then sets the value of this sub-semaphore to the parameter we have passed at the command line. In this case the parameter is 0.

At this point we now have one semaphore in memory.

If we were to run the following program now what would happen ?

PROGRAM 273

Y.C

```
#include <sys/types.h>
#include <sys/ipc.h>
#include <sys/sem.h>

main( )
{
   int semid,retval;
   struct sembuf sop;
   sop.sem_num = 0;
   sop.sem_op = 0;
   sop.sem_flg = 0;
```

```
    semid = semget(0x20,1,0600 | IPC_CREAT);
    printf("Before semop\n");
    retval = semop(semid,&sop,1);
    printf("semop returned %d\n",retval);
}
```

Since the semaphore has already been created by the previous (X.C) program, here we will just be returned the ID.

When the *semop( )* function is called the value of the member *sem_op* is a 0, which is also the value of the sub-semaphore. As a result the operation will perform successfully and the program will terminate.

However, what if we ran the X.C program with the parameter 1 and then re-ran the Y.C program once more? Program Y.C would get caught in a wait state.

Hey, what happened?

The first time we ran the program with 0 as a parameter and then ran the previous program -- which also had the value 0 assigned to the member *sem_op*. As a result, when the *semop( )* function was called it compared the status of the semaphore and the value of the *sem_op* member, found that they were identical and terminated immediately.

But the second time round we ran the program with a 1 as parameter, and this value was not the value of the member *sem_op* (which is 0). These values not matching means the resource is in use by another process which has set the value of the semaphore. As a result, the process begins to wait till the resource is freed.

But in our case, in the process that had set the value there were no further statements that would release the resource, i.e. no statements that were resetting the value of the semaphore. And as a result the second process keeps waiting. The same would happen if any value other than a 0 had been passed to the program.

Since this program is going to wait till infinity, what we can do is run the X.C program from another terminal, with a 0 as command line parameter. This will terminate the program.

OK, guys, let's get the show on the road. We've seen and read enough about semaphores and how they behave and can be used. Now it's time to see semaphores in action. Starting with using them through two processes: parent and child.

But before you run the next program just make sure that the semaphore we're creating, i.e. with key 20, does not exist. If it does, remove it.

PROGRAM 274

```
#include <sys/types.h>
#include <sys/ipc.h>
#include <sys/sem.h>

main( )
{
   int semid,pid;
   struct sembuf sop;
   semid = semget(0x20,1,IPC_CREAT | 0666);
   pid = fork( );
   if (pid == 0)
   {
      sleep(2);
      printf("child before semop\n");
      sop.sem_num = 0;
      sop.sem_op = 0;
      sop.sem_flg = 0;
      semop(semid,&sop,1);
      printf("Child over\n");
   }
   else
   {
      printf("parent before 1st semctl\n");
      semctl(semid,0,SETVAL,1);
      printf("Parent sleeping\n");
      sleep(5);
      printf("parent before 2nd semctl\n");
      semctl(semid,0,SETVAL,0);
```

```
        printf("Parent over\n");
    }
}
```

After declaring the structure we create a semaphore with one sub- semaphore. A *fork( )* now creates a child process, which is immediately put to sleep. As a result the time slice is handed to the parent process. In it we set the value of the semaphore to 1. And put the parent process to *sleep( )*.

The child now gets activated first. In it (the child process) we initialize all the members of the structure to zeros. And make a call to the *semop( )* function. The *semop( )* checks to see if the value of the member *sem_op* matches that of the semaphore. It doesn't since the parent process has initialized it to 1 whereas the value of the member *sem_op* is 0. As a result, the child process begins its wait.

In time the parent process wakes, resets the value of the semaphore to 0 and terminates. The child process, which has been waiting at the *semop( )*, once again checks to see if the values match, finds that they do, and terminates.

Semaphore Arithmetic

But there are more numbers than just 0's and 1's that can be assigned to a sub-semaphore. Now why would we do that? No doubt if it is a simple straight forward application like the one shown above there is no need to. But what if there were a chain of processes in a tree like structure:

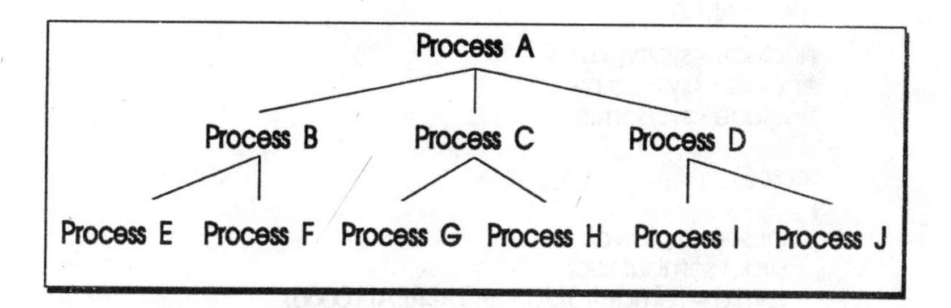

DIAGRAM 4.9

Assume that Process A created the semaphore with one sub-semaphore and set its value to 1 (that is, locked it from any other process accessing it). It then proceeded to carry out some task. Based on the result of the task it reset the value of the semaphore to 2, 3 or 4. Now based on this value one of the processes, that is B, C or D got activated. Assume the value was set to 2. And this is the value Process B understood to mean that the semaphore now belongs to it.

Process B carries out some task. The results of which determine the value it is going to reset the semaphore to. This value could be 3, 10 or 11. If it is 3 then process C will understand it to mean that the semaphore is free for it, 11 will mean that process E has access and 12 will mean that process F will have access. And whatever process gets access will, after finishing its work, in turn set the value of the semaphore. And this entire process will carry on till the entire program terminates.

Hey, that's semaphore arithmetic. And don't say we've told you about this before? Remember, when we were explaining the *semop( )* function and the *sem_op* member of the structure, we said that depending on the value of the semaphore and that of the *sem_op* member the *semop( )* does a plusing or minusing.

Well, now let's try out some programs that confirm this. The one below does a plus with both the semaphore values being set to 2, and that of *sem_op* being set to 3.

PROGRAM 275

```
#include <sys/types.h>
#include <sys/ipc.h>
#include <sys/sem.h>

main( )
{
   int semid,pid,val;
   struct sembuf sop;
   semid = semget(0x20,1,IPC_CREAT | 0666);
   pid = fork( );
   if (pid == 0)
   {
      sleep(2);
      printf("child before semop\n");
      sop.sem_num = 0;
      sop.sem_op = 3;
      sop.sem_flg = 0;
      semop(semid,&sop,1);
      printf("Child over\n");
   }
   else
   {
      printf("parent before 1st semctl\n");
      semctl(semid,0,SETVAL,2);
      printf("Parent sleeping\n");
      sleep(5);
      printf("parent before 2nd semctl\n");
      val = semctl(semid,0,GETVAL,0);
      printf("Semaphore value is %d\n",val);
      printf("Parent over\n");
   }
}
```

We create a semaphore with one sub-semaphore and then fork a child process which is immediately put to *sleep( )*. As a result, the parent process gets activated.

In the parent process the *semctl( )* sets the value of the sub-semaphore to 2. After which the parent process promptly goes to *sleep( )*.

In time the child process wakes. In it we initialize the members

of the structure *sop*. Here the member *sem_op* is assigned a 3. Now when the *semop( )* function is called it will check the value of the semaphore and the member *sem_op*, find that they are both positive and add them. This process has no more statements except the *printf( )* which it executes before terminating.

After the stipulated 5 seconds, the parent process wakes gets the value of the semaphore, which is now 5, prints it and terminates.

Now suppose the value assigned to the member *sem_op* was negative. A negative number means a wait till the absolute value of the semaphore matches or becomes greater.

PROGRAM 276

```
#include <sys/types.h>
#include <sys/ipc.h>
#include <sys/sem.h>

main( )
{
   int semid,pid,ctr,val;
   struct sembuf sop;
   semid = semget(0x20,1,IPC_CREAT);
   semctl(semid,0,SETVAL,0);
   pid = fork( );
   if (pid == 0)
   {
      printf("child before semop\n");
      sop.sem_num = 0;
      sop.sem_op = -3;
      sop.sem_flg = 0;
      semop(semid,&sop,1);
      printf("Child over\n");
   }
   else
   {
      for (ctr = 1; ; ctr++)
```

```
            {
                printf("ctr is %d\n",ctr);
                semctl(semid,0,SETVAL,ctr);
                printf("Parent sleeping\n");
                sleep(5);
                val = semctl(semid,0,GETVAL,0);
                printf("Val is %d\n",val);
                if (val == 0)
                    break;
            }
            printf("Parent process over\n");
        }
    }
```

We create a semaphore with one sub-semaphore, set its value to 0 and then fork a child process.

In the child process we assign various values to the members of the structure *sop*. A -3 is assigned to the member *sem_op*. The *semop( )* is called. But since it sees that the value of the semaphore is 0 and that of the member *sem_op* is -3, it temporarily halts the child process from executing further.

The parent process gets the time slice. In it a *for* loop is executed as many times as it takes for the value of the semaphore to match the absolute value of the member *sem_op*. That is, the loop will execute thrice. So let's see what happens.

The loop starts the first time round with the value of variable *ctr* as 1. This value is printed and the semaphore set to it. Now the parent process goes to sleep. The time slice goes to the child. But the value of member *sem_op* and the semaphore's value yet don't match. As a result the child does not wake.

After 5 seconds the parent wakes, *semctl( )* returns the value of the semaphore -- which is 1 -- and the *printf( )* prints it. A check is made to see if the value is 0. Since it is not the loop executes once more. The value of *ctr* is now 2. This is the new value the semaphore is set to before the parent is put to sleep.

Once again a check is made to see if the value defined in the child process matches. Since it does not, the time slice is handed to the parent, which executes once the 5 seconds are over. Once again we print the value of the semaphore before starting the loop all over again.

This time the value of *ctr* is set to 3. Ad the parent is put to sleep. Now since this value matches the absolute value of the *sem_op* member the child wakes. *semop( )* goes to the semaphore with a -3, which is balanced by the +3 of the semaphore. The result is 0. And the child process terminates.

In the parent process the value returned by the *semctl( )* will be 0. And the parent process will also terminate.

Here's a simple way to view the above concept. The point to remember is that the absolute value should be the same or greater.

PROGRAM 277

```
#include <sys/types.h>
#include <sys/ipc.h>
#include <sys/sem.h>

main( )
{
   int semid,pid,val;
   struct sembuf sop;
   semid = semget(0x20,1,IPC_CREAT);
   semctl(semid,0,SETVAL,5);
   printf("The value of semaphore is 5\n");
   printf("before semop going with -3\n");
   sop.sem_num = 0;
   sop.sem_op = -3;
   sop.sem_flg = 0;
   semop(semid,&sop,1);
   val = semctl(semid,0,GETVAL,0);
   printf("Semaphore value is %d\n",val);
}
```

We create a semaphore with one sub-semaphore and assign it a value of 5. Then the members of the structure are assigned some values. A -3 like before is assigned to *sem_op*. When *semop( )* is called it will see a -3 and a 5 and realize that a 5 is greater than the absolute value of the *sem_op* member. And the program terminates.

But before it terminates it prints the value of the semaphore, which is 2 because a 5 and -3 equal a 2.

If you are the type of guy who is impatient and does not like to wait around, setting the member *sem_flg* to some value will be a real godsent.

Don't Let An Unsuccessful 'semop( )' Stop Us

We have seen how, unless the value of the semaphore and that of *sem_op* match, the process does not terminate. But if we want it to carry on despite this we need to set the *sem_flg* member.

PROGRAM 278

```
#include <sys/types.h>
#include <sys/ipc.h>
#include <sys/sem.h>

main( )
{
   int semid,pid;
   struct sembuf sop;
   semid = semget(0x20,1,IPC_CREAT);
   semctl(semid,0,SETVAL,0);
   printf("The value of semaphore is 0\n");
   printf("child before semop going with -3\n");
   sop.sem_num = 0;
   sop.sem_op = -3;
   sop.sem_flg = IPC_NOWAIT;
   semop(semid,&sop,1);
   printf("Process exiting\n");
}
```

We create a semaphore with 1 sub-semaphore setting its value to 0. A -3 is assigned to the member *sem_op* and a IPC_NOWAIT to *sem_flg*. A call is then made to the *semop( )* function. Under normal circumstances since the values don't match, the process would halt right here. But this time because of the IPC_NOWAIT the process terminates.

The Importance Of Resetting

It is important that a process that sets the value of a resource resets it to indicate that the resource has been released. Else the next process will never get access. Check out the next program:

PROGRAM 279

```
#include <sys/types.h>
#include <sys/ipc.h>
#include <sys/sem.h>

main( )
{
  int semid,pid;
  struct sembuf sop;
  semid = semget(0x20,1,IPC_CREAT | 0666);
  semctl(semid,0,SETVAL,1);
  pid = fork( );
  if (pid == 0)
  {
    printf("child before semop\n");
    sop.sem_num = 0;
    sop.sem_op = -1;
    sop.sem_flg = 0;
    semop(semid,&sop,1);
    printf("Child in critical section\n");
    sleep(2);
    printf("Child coming out of critical section\n");
  }
  else
  {
    printf("parent before semop\n");
    sop.sem_num = 0;
    sop.sem_op = -1;
```

```
        sop.sem_flg = 0;
        semop(semid,&sop,1);
        printf("parent in critical section\n");
        sleep(2);
        printf("Parent coming out of critical section\n");
    }
}
```

The sub-semaphore is created and set with a value of 1. A *fork( )* then creates a child process.

Assume the time slice is given to the child process. Notice the -1 assigned to *sem_op*. The operation that the *semop( )* performs succeeds and the new value of the semaphore is now 0 because a 1 and -1 even out. The child process is put to *sleep( )* (think of this *sleep( )* as many statements which the child is executing). As a result, the time slice is handed to the parent. Here, too, we call *semop( )*. But the operation it performs fails as the values don't match.

Now when the child process wakes it terminates. But the parent process will keep waiting as the child process has not reset the value of the semaphore.

Which means that we always have to do what the next program shows: reset the value of the semaphore once we're done with it, indicating that the resource has been released.

PROGRAM 280

```
#include <sys/types.h>
#include <sys/ipc.h>
#include <sys/sem.h>

main( )
{
    int semid,pid;
    struct sembuf sop;
    semid = semget(0x20,1,IPC_CREAT | 0666);
    semctl(semid,0,SETVAL,1);
    pid = fork( );
    if (pid == 0)
```

```
    {
        printf("child before semop\n");
        sop.sem_num = 0;
        sop.sem_op = -1;
        sop.sem_flg = 0;
        semop(semid,&sop,1);
        printf("Child in critical section\n");
        sleep(2);
        printf("Child coming out of critical section\n");
        sop.sem_num = 0;
        sop.sem_op = 1;
        sop.sem_flg = 0;
        semop(semid,&sop,1);
    }
    else
    {
        printf("parent before semop\n");
        sop.sem_num = 0;
        sop.sem_op = -1;
        sop.sem_flg = 0;
        semop(semid,&sop,1);
        printf("parent in critical section\n");
        sleep(2);
        printf("parent coming out of critical section\n");
        sop.sem_num = 0;
        sop.sem_op = 1;
        sop.sem_flg = 0;
        semop(semid,&sop,1);
    }
}
```

Here we create a semaphore with one sub-semaphore and set its value to 1. A *fork( )* now creates a child process.

In the child process the *semop( )* function performs successfully. The child then goes to sleep. In the parent process, which is now given the time slice, the *semop( )* will not perform successfully since the values don't match. The value of the semaphore is now 0. So the parent is kept in a wait state.

Now when the child process is activated again it resets the value of the semaphore to 1. This is done by calling the *semop( )*

function with the value of the member *sem_op* as 1. This is a positive number and is therefore added to the already existing value of the semaphore. The child now terminates.

When the parent is given the time slice the *semop( )* performs successfully as the values now match (a 1 and -1). The parent is put to *sleep( )*. If there was another process trying to access the semaphore at this point it would be unsuccessful.

When the process wakes after 2 seconds, it resets the value of the semaphore to a 1 so that any other process can now access it.

But instead of having to code a reset every time, it would be better to use the SEM_UNDO flag.

PROGRAM 281

```
#include <sys/types.h>
#include <sys/ipc.h>
#include <sys/sem.h>

main( )
{
    int semid,pid;
    struct sembuf sop;
    semid = semget(0x20,1,IPC_CREAT | 0666);
    semctl(semid,0,SETVAL,1);
    sop.sem_num = 0;
    sop.sem_op = -1;
    sop.sem_flg = SEM_UNDO;
    pid = fork( );
    if (pid == 0)
    {
        printf("child before semop\n");
        semop(semid,&sop,1);
        printf("Child in critical section\n");
        sleep(2);
        printf("Child coming out of critical section\n");
    }
    else
    {
        printf("parent before semop\n");
        semop(semid,&sop,1);
```

```
        printf("parent in critical section\n");
        sleep(2);
        printf("parent coming out of critical section\n");
    }
}
```

We create a semaphore, assigning it a value of 1. And then initialize the members of the structure: *sem_op* with a -1 and *sem_flg* with SEM_UNDO. A *fork( )* creates a child process.

In the child process we call the *semop( )* function which performs successfully since the value of the semaphore is 1 and we are going to it with a -1. Immediately after the child is being put to *sleep( )*.

The parent gets the time slice but the *semop( )* in it is not successful since the values don't match. After 2 seconds the child wakes and terminates.

The next time slice round, when the parent is activated the *semop( )* in it will perform successfully. Since when the child terminated it reset the value of the semaphore to the original, i.e. 1. This was done because we specified SEM_UNDO as the flag.

The parent goes to *sleep( )*. And when it wakes, it too resets the semaphore to 1 before terminating. This SEM_UNDO resets the value only when a process terminates. This is demonstrated by the next program.

PROGRAM 282

```
#include <sys/types.h>
#include <sys/ipc.h>
#include <sys/sem.h>

main( )
{
    int semid,pid,val;
    struct sembuf sop;
    semid = semget(0x20,1,IPC_CREAT | 0666);
    semctl(semid,0,SETVAL,3);
    val = semctl(semid,0,GETVAL,0);
```

```
printf("Value of semaphore 1st time is %d\n",val);
pid = fork( );
if (pid == 0)
{
    printf("child doing semop with -2 \n");
    sop.sem_num = 0;
    sop.sem_op = -2;
    sop.sem_flg = SEM_UNDO;
    semop(semid,&sop,1);
    printf("Child in critical section\n");
    sleep(5);
    printf("Child coming out of critical section\n");
}
else
{
    sleep(1);
    val = semctl(semid,0,GETVAL,0);
    printf("Value of semaphore 2nd time is %d\n",val);
    sleep(5);
    val = semctl(semid,0,GETVAL,0);
    printf("Value of semaphore 3rd time is %d\n",val);
}
}
```

We create a semaphore with the value of 3 and fork a child process. The parent process is put to *sleep( )* so that the time slice is given to the child. In the child the members are initialized. The *semop( )* performs successfully since the value of the semaphore, when added to the value of the member *sem_op*, yields a positive number. Now since the child is put to sleep the parent is given the time slice.

In the parent process the value of the semaphore is printed. It evaluates to +3-2 = 1. Since the parent is put to sleep the time slice is once more handed to the child, which terminates.

The next time the parent gets activated it once more prints the value of the semaphore, which turns out to be 3 once again.

In this program since the child did a *semop( )* with a -2 and the value of the semaphore was 3 the end result positive. The *semop( )* performed successfully. But what if the value of the member *sem_op* was a positive number.

Below is the same program, but with one difference: the value assigned to the *sem_op* is a positive one.

PROGRAM 283

```
#include <sys/types.h>
#include <sys/ipc.h>
#include <sys/sem.h>

main( )
{
   int semid,pid,val;
   struct sembuf sop;
   semid = semget(0x20,1,IPC_CREAT | 0666);
   semctl(semid,0,SETVAL,3);
   val = semctl(semid,0,GETVAL,0);
   printf("Value of semaphore 1st time is %d\n",val);
   pid = fork( );
   if (pid == 0)
   {
      printf("child doing semop with 2\n");
      sop.sem_num = 0;
      sop.sem_op = 2;
      sop.sem_flg = SEM_UNDO;
      semop(semid,&sop,1);
      printf("Child in critical section\n");
      sleep(5);
      printf("Child coming out of critical section\n");
   }
   else
   {
      sleep(2);
      val = semctl(semid,0,GETVAL,0);
      printf("Value of semaphore 2nd time is %d\n",val);
      sleep(5);
      val = semctl(semid,0,GETVAL,0);
      printf("Value of semaphore 3rd time is %d\n",val);
   }
}
```

The program performs in the same manner. Creates a semaphore with a value of 3. And then forks a child process.

In the child process *semop( )* performs successfully, but goes to *sleep( )* immediately. The parent process prints the semaphore value which is now 5 before going to *sleep( )*.

The child process gets active once more and terminates. The parent process wakes and prints the value of the semaphore, which is now 3 once again.

How does UNIX undo or reset the value of the semaphore to its original irrespective of whether the number is negative or positive?

By making use of another temporary variable called *semadj* (semaphore adjustment value). Each process has one version of *semadj*. Whenever a *semop( )* operation is applied and a SEM_UNDO is set, the following sequence of events takes place:

1. Before the process starts the value of the *semadj* is set to 0.

2. Then the value of *sem_op* is subtracted from that of *semadj*. The sign of *sem_op* plays an important role here.

3. And, finally, the value of *semadj* is added to the value of the sub-semaphore. This happens when the process terminates-- abnormally or normally.

Let's take an example to understand this better:

Assume that the value of the sub-semaphore is 3 to start with and that of *semadj* is of course 0. A *semop( )* is done with -2. *semadj* will therefore be *semadj* = *semadj* - (-2), the result of which is 2. And the sub-semaphore will become 1.

Now assume that another *semop( )* is done with a +3. Now *semadj* = *semadj* - (+3) computes to +1. The value of the sub-semaphore will be 4.

The process finally terminates. At this point UNIX will subtract the value of the semadj from that of the sub-semaphore and assign the result back to the sub-semaphore. In this case it will be 4 - 1, which is 3. And isn't this the value of the sub-semaphore with which we started.

So what's the significance of the *semadj* variable?

The idea behind resetting the value of the sub-semaphore is so that it can become accessible to other processes that may be waiting for it.

Now suppose a process changed the initial value of the sub-semaphore, which was 1, to 2, indicating in the process that it had control over the resource. And it also proceeded to exercise this control. But before it finished whatever it was doing it got terminated abnormally, maybe because some other process tried to kill it by sending some signal. As a result the value of the sub-semaphore would not get changed to its original which was 1. This would keep holding up all the other processes that were trying to access the said resource.

One way out of a situation like this is to have our program capture the signals. That is, when the KILL signal is received, instead of the related UNIX function executing we have our function execute. In this function we reset the value of the sub-semaphore to 1.

But there is one problem here: if the signal is one that can't be captured like SIGKILL then we are in trouble. Of course we can always have the other processes that are waiting for this sub-semaphore to become 1 query -- using *semctl( )* -- to see what was the last time the value of the sub-semaphore was changed. If this was too far back in history then the process can take the necessary steps.

But basically this kind of method is a rather painful. And it is for this very reason that the *semadj* is used.

Limit The Same Software Program In Memory

Besides for synchronization between processes semaphores can also be used to ensure that no more than a defined number of copies of some software can be loaded into memory. For example, suppose we had written an application and we wanted to make sure that at one time no more than 3 users could work on it. Then the way to implement this would be through semaphores. Let's see how:

PROGRAM 284

```
#include <sys/types.h>
#include <sys/ipc.h>
#include <sys/sem.h>

main( )
{
    int semid,val;
    struct sembuf sop;
    semid = semget((key_t) 0x20,1,IPC_CREAT | 0666);
    sop.sem_num = 0;
    sop.sem_op = 1;
    sop.sem_flg = SEM_UNDO;
    val = semctl(semid,0,GETVAL,0);
    if (val > 2)
    {
        printf("Sorry only three copies simultaneously\n");
        exit(0);
    }
    semop(semid,&sop,1);
    printf("Application program starts\n");
    sleep(10);
    printf("Application program finishes\n");
}
```

We create a semaphore with one sub-semaphore. Next we assign members of the structure some values. The *semctl( )* returns the current value of the semaphore which, if run for the first time, will be 0. The *if* condition is evaluated. If it is true the process terminates, else a *semop( )* operation takes place. This will increase the value of the sub- semaphore. And the process will go to *sleep( )*. After 10 seconds it will terminate.

OK, now that we've seen what the process is doing let's see how it works for what we want to do.

The first time that the process is run the value of the sub-semaphore will be 0. *semctl( )* will return this 0 to variable *val*. The *if* will evaluate to a false. The *semop( )* operation will increase the value of the sub-semaphore by 1, which in this case will result in the semaphore becoming 1. And the process will be put to *sleep( )*.

Now assume that this program is run from another terminal. Since the semaphore is already created it won't be recreated, but its ID will be returned. The members of the structure will be initialized. And *semctl( )* will return the current value of the semaphore which is 1. The *if* will evaluate to a false. The *semop( )* operation will increase the value of the semaphore to 2. And the second process will now be put to *sleep( )*.

From another terminal the process is run once more. The value returned by *semctl( )* will be 2. The *if* will once more evaluate to a false. The *semop( )* will increase the value to 3. And the process is put to *sleep( )*.

If someone else now tried to run this program the *if* will evaluate to a false. And as a result the 4th process would terminate.

Now as each of the three processes begins to terminate as the 10 seconds get over they will reset the value of the semaphore to what it was before.

While on the face of it this works fine, there is one problem. Suppose just before the *semop( )* the time slice is taken away and given to the second program that is run. Assume at this point the value of the sub-semaphore was 2.

The next process that is accessing the semaphore will also see the value 2 and will proceed to increment it. Now when the time slice is given back to the first process the *semop( )* will be performed (as far as this process is concerned the value of the semaphore is yet 2). So when the *semop( )* performs it will increase this value to 3. Hey, two processes just incremented the semaphore to the same value. And that means confusion.

To counter this problem we need to initialize two different semaphores. One would act as a "controller" of the CRITICAL REGION and the other would act as the "counter" for the number of copies.

PROGRAM 285

```
#include <sys/types.h>
#include <sys/ipc.h>
#include <sys/sem.h>

main( )
{
   int semcpy,semcon,pid,val,i;
   struct sembuf sop[2];
   semcpy = semget((key_t) 0x20,1,IPC_CREAT | 0666); /* counter */
   semcon = semget((key_t) 0x30,1,IPC_CREAT | 0666); /* controller*/

   sop[0].sem_num = 0;
   sop[0].sem_op = 0;
   sop[0].sem_flg = SEM_UNDO;

   sop[1].sem_num = 0;
   sop[1].sem_op = 1;
   sop[1].sem_flg = SEM_UNDO;
   semop(semcon,&sop[0],2);

   val = semctl(semcpy,0,GETVAL,0);
   printf("val is %d\n",val);
   if (val > 2)
   {
      printf("Sorry only three copies simultaneously\n");
      exit(0);
   }
   sop[0].sem_num = 0;
```

```
    sop[0].sem_op = 1;
    sop[0].sem_flg = SEM_UNDO;
    semop(semcpy,&sop[0],1);

    sop[0].sem_num = 0;
    sop[0].sem_op = -1;
    sop[0].sem_flg = SEM_UNDO;
    semop(semcon,&sop[0],1);

    printf("Application program starts\n");
    sleep(10);
    printf("Application program finishes\n");
}
```

Here we declare a structure as before, but this time we declare it as an array of structures (with 2 elements).

The first time the process starts it creates two semaphores with their IDs assigned to *semcon* and *semcpy*, both with the value 0. The members of the structures are initialized and a call is made to the *semop( )* function. Since the structure passed to it is array element 0, the value of the member *sem_op* of this structure is added to the value of the sub-semaphore *semcon*. This value is 0. So the value of the sub-semaphore which was also 0 remains the same.

But this *semop( )* performs twice because we have specified the last parameter as 2. And it performs on both the array elements of *semop*. As a result the value of the semaphore with the ID *semcon* becomes 1. UNIX guarantees that these two operations will be atomic.

Now the value of the sub-semaphore with the ID *semcpy* , which is 0, is returned to *val*.

The *if* evaluates to a false. The members of the first array element (structure 1) are reinitialized. The *semop( )* is now performed once again, but this time taking the second semaphore with ID *semcpy* as parameter. The value of this sub-semaphore is incremented and becomes 1. At this point both the semaphores have the value 1. Which means that there is one copy of the program in memory. But since we want to allow three copies at one time we need to reinitialize the value of *semcon* to its original, because that is the control semaphore. And to do this we re-initialize the members of the first array element and call the *semop( )* to perform. Since we are calling the *semop( )* with a -1 it evens out the value of the *semcon* semaphore which is +1. The value of this semaphore now becomes 0.

Now assume this program was run on some other terminal. The *semop( )* would be called to perform twice since 2 is the last parameter passed to it. As a result the value of the semaphore *semcon* would once more become 1. The value of the *semcpy* semaphore is 1 at this point. Consequently, the *if* evaluates to a false.

A call to the *semop( )* now increments the value of the *semcpy* semaphore to 2. And once more semaphore *semcon* is initialized to 0. So at this point we have two copies of the program in memory.

Now another user runs this program. And the process repeats. This is the third copy. But the fourth time round the *if* will evaluate to a true and the program won't be allowed to run.

The critical region in this program is between the first *semop( )* and the second *semop( )*. But even if the process terminates just before the second *semop( )* can increment the value of *semcpy* the next process won't be able to run the program. It will be blocked right at the beginning, that is at the first *semop( )*. Because the value of the *sem_op* members and that of the *semcon* semaphore won't match. While the member is 0 the semaphore is 1. As a result the program will be put in a wait state till the value of the semaphore becomes 0.

Semaphore Structures

For every set of semaphores in the system, the kernel maintains a structure of information. The structure name is *semid_ds*, and is defined in the sys/ipc.h header file.

```
struct semid_ds
{
   struct ipc_perm sem_perm; /*operation permission structure*/
   struct sem *sem_base; /*ptr to first sema in set*/
   ushort sem_nsems; /*no. of sema in set*/
   time_t sem_otime; /*time of last semop()*/
   time_t sem_ctime; /*time of last change*/
};
```

The *ipc_perm* structure we have already seen before. It contains the access permissions for a semaphore.

Notice the differences between the above structure and the structure shown below, which is used when working with message queues.

```
struct msqid_ds {
struct ipc_perm msg_perm; /* operation permission struct */
struct msg *msg_first; /* ptr to first message on q */
struct msg *msg_last; /* ptr to last message on q */
ushort msg_cbytes; /* current # bytes on q */
ushort msg_qnum; /* # of messages on q */
ushort msg_qbytes; /* max # of bytes on q */
ushort msg_lspid; /* pid of last msgsnd */
ushort msg_lrpid; /* pid of last msgrcv */
time_t msg_stime; /* last msgsnd time */
time_t msg_rtime; /* last msgrcv time */
time_t msg_ctime; /* last change time */
};
```

In semaphores the structure has two basic components, a pointer to the structure *sem_base* and the number of semaphores. In message queues we have a pointer to the first message and a pointer to the last message. Why this difference? Because in semaphores we use arrays since the storage for the kernel data structures is fixed. Check out the figure drawn below. Assuming that we have created a semaphore with two sub-semaphores, this is what it would look like diagrammatically:

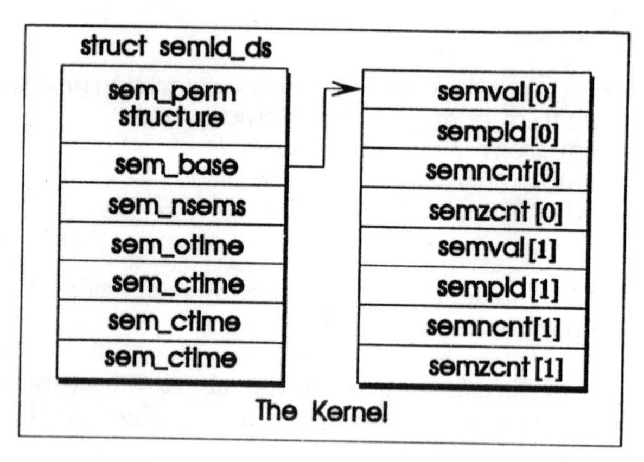

DIAGRAM 4.10

For a message queue, however, we don't use arrays but a linked list. Why? Because a message can be of varying lengths and an array has to have a predefined number of elements. Therefore, if the message is longer than the array can hold, snip, snip will go our message. Diagrammatically this looks like:

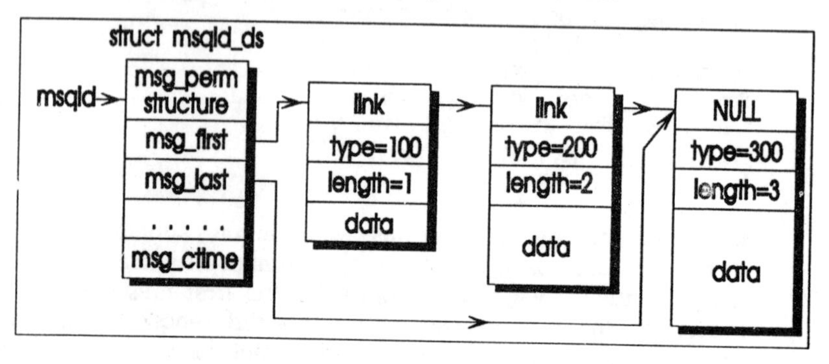

DIAGRAM 4.11

Watch how the size of the data area varies and how the linked list is maintained.

The *sem* structure is the internal data structure used by the kernel to maintain the set of values for a given semaphore. Every member of a semaphore is described by the following structure:

```
struct sem
{
   short semval;    /* semaphore text map address */
   short sempid;       /* pid of last operation */
   ushort   semncnt;  /* # awaiting semval > cval */
   ushort   semzcnt;  /* # awaiting semval = 0 */
};
```

Here is a program that prints the values of a semaphore using the structures we have just seen.

PROGRAM 286

```
#include <sys/types.h>
#include <sys/ipc.h>
#include <sys/sem.h>

main( )
{
   int semid;
   struct semid_ds status;
   semid = semget((key_t)0x20,10,IPC_CREAT | 0666);
   semctl(semid,0,IPC_STAT,&status);
   printf("No of semaphores in set are %d\n",status.sem_nsems);
   printf("My user id is %d\n",getuid( ));
   printf("Owners user id is %u\n",status.sem_perm.uid);
   printf("My group id is %d\n",getgid( ));
   printf("Owners group id is %u\n",status.sem_perm.gid);
   printf("Creator user id is %u\n",status.sem_perm.cuid);
   printf("Creator group id is %u\n",status.sem_perm.cgid);
   printf("Access mode is %o \n",status.sem_perm.mode);
   printf("Queue key is %d\n",status.sem_perm.key);
}
```

After creating a structure we use the *semctl( )* function to get the details of the semaphore. This function is passed IPC_STAT and the pointer to a structure *status*. Because of the IPC_STAT, members of the structure *status* are assigned values. Note that the fourth parameter passed is a pointer to a structure, whereas earlier it was an integer. The type of the fourth parameter keeps changing depending on the third parameter. Since this fourth parameter keeps changing, a more simple method would be to make it a union. With the following members:

```
union semun
{
   int val; /* used for SETVAL command only */
   struct semid_ds *status; /* used for IPC_STAT& IPC_SET */
   ushort *array; /* used for IPC_GETALL &IPC_SETALL */
}
```

The values are printed through the *printf( )* statements. There are certain members we can change. And that's what the next program shows.

PROGRAM 287

```
#include <sys/types.h>
#include <sys/ipc.h>
#include <sys/sem.h>

main( )
{
   int semid;
   struct semid_ds status;
   semid = semget((key_t)0x20,10,IPC_CREAT | 0666);
   semctl(semid,0,IPC_STAT,&status);
   printf("No of semaphores in set are %d\n",status.sem_nsems);
   printf("My user id is %d\n",getuid( ));
   printf("Owners user id is %u\n",status.sem_perm.uid);
   printf("My group id is %d\n",getgid( ));
   printf("Owners group id is %u\n",status.sem_perm.gid);
   printf("Creator user id is %u\n",status.sem_perm.cuid);
   printf("Creator group id is %u\n",status.sem_perm.cgid);
   printf("Access mode is %o \n",status.sem_perm.mode);
   printf("Queue key is %d\n",status.sem_perm.key);
   status.sem_perm.gid = 102 ;
   status.sem_perm.uid = 102 ;
   status.sem_perm.mode = 0444 ;
   semctl(semid,0,IPC_SET,&status);
   printf("Owners group id is %u\n",status.sem_perm.gid);
   printf("Creator user id is %u\n",status.sem_perm.cuid);
```

```
    printf("Access mode is %o \n",status.sem_perm.mode);
}
```

We change the members *gid* (group id), uid (user id) and mode (permissions). And then reprint these members to confirm that the change has taken place.

We can use this structure to figure out how many people are waiting for the semaphore to become greater than 0 so that it can be accessed. For this we have to pass GETNCNT as parameter.

PROGRAM 288

```
#include <sys/types.h>
#include <sys/ipc.h>
#include <sys/sem.h>

main( )
{
    int semid,pid,retval;
    semid = semget((key_t) 0x20,1,IPC_CREAT | 0666);
    if (semid < 0)
    {
        perror( " ");
        exit(1);
    }
    semctl(semid,0,SETVAL,0);
    pid = fork( );
    if (pid == 0)
    {
        struct sembuf sop;
        sop.sem_num = 0;
        sop.sem_op = -2;
        sop.sem_flg = 0;
        semop(semid,&sop,1);
        printf("Child process Terminates\n");
    }
    else
    {
        retval = semctl(semid,0,GETNCNT,0);
        printf("1st semctl returned %d\n",retval);
        semctl(semid,0,SETVAL,2);
        retval = semctl(semid,0,GETNCNT,0);
```

```
        printf("2nd semctl returned %d\n",retval);
    }
}
```

We create a semaphore, set its value to 0 and then fork a child process. In the child we do a *semop( )* with a value of -2. As a result the child is put in a wait state.

In the parent process we call *semctl( )* with GETNCNT. This returns a value of 1 since there is one process that is waiting for the semaphore to become greater than 0.

Next we set the semaphore's value to 2. This results in the child process, which has been waiting, now terminating. In the parent process the value returned by the second *semctl( )* will return a 0 since there are no more processes waiting for the semaphore.

This value that signifies how many processes are waiting for a semaphore is stored in the member *semncnt* in the *sem* structure.

Similarly, we can find out which processes are waiting for the semaphore to become 0. The member that stores this value is once again in the *sem* structure with the name *semzcnt*.

PROGRAM 289

```
#include <sys/types.h>
#include <sys/ipc.h>
#include <sys/sem.h>

main( )
{
    int semid,pid,retval;
    semid = semget((key_t) 0x20,1,IPC_CREAT | 0666);
    if (semid < 0)
    {
        perror(" ");
        exit(1);
    }
    semctl(semid,0,SETVAL,1);
    pid = fork( );
```

```
    if (pid == 0)
    {
        struct sembuf sop;
        sop.sem_num = 0;
        sop.sem_op = 0;
        sop.sem_flg = 0;
        semop(semid,&sop,1);
        printf("Child process terminates\n");
    }
    else
    {
        retval = semctl(semid,0,GETZCNT,0);
        printf("1st semctl returned %d\n",retval);
        semctl(semid,0,SETVAL,0);
        retval = semctl(semid,0,GETZCNT,0);
        printf("2nd semctl returned %d\n",retval);
    }
}
```

The procedure we follow is the same as that in the above program. The child process will wait since the *semop( )* will perform unsuccessfully. When the time slice is handed to the parent process the *semctl( )* will return a value of 1 the first time round. After the value of the semaphore is reset to 0 the child process will terminate and the next *semctl( )* will return a value 0, indicating no processes waiting.

Down Memory Lane

Now let's go back a little in the past to those programs on message queues, and in particular to the one that simulated a print spooler. (Feel free to refer to that page if your memory has not been jogged yet.) If you remember, in that entire application we had one program that flushed the message queue. But there was one problem: we always ended up losing one extra message. And even at that time we had indicated that using semaphores was the way out.

And that solution is the best way to terminate this rather overdrawn topic, don't you think. The application is made up of four programs which have further sub-functions in them:

server.c	client.c	flush.c	halt.c
proc_obj( ) serv( ) init_queue( ) warn( ) pv( )	init_queue( ) enter( ) warn( )	init_queue( ) pv( )	init_queue( )

DIAGRAM 4.12

Now let's see what the main programs do:

The server.c is the receiver. It waits for client processes to send it files to print.

client.c sends the files it want printed.

The flush.c is used to flush the queue of files we don't want printed.

And halt.c is to terminate the server.c program.

Let's just reiterate the idea behind this process before we go into the code. A word of advice here: just drink some coffee or tea because the journey is going to be rather long and tedious.

We create a message queue that is going to be used as a print spooler. All messages which are actually going to be commands to print some file or files are going to be sent to this queue. If we feel that some file has been wrongly sent we use the flush program to delete it from the queue. And, of course, if we want the server to be terminated the halt program is what we resort to.

The idea of having semaphores is to make sure that when a signal is sent to flush a message, the message that is being performed at that point in time is not lost. Normally that's what happens. By using a semaphore we ensure that only after the message being processed finishes will the file (message) be flushed from the queue.

PROGRAM 290

```
#include <stdio.h>
#include <fcntl.h>
#include <sys/types.h>
#include <sys/ipc.h>
#include <sys/msg.h>
#include <sys/sem.h>
#include <errno.h>

#define QKEY    (key_t)0100
#define SEMKEY (key_t)0x20
#define QPERM 0666
#define MAXOBN 50
#define MAXPRIOR 10

struct q_entry {
      long mtype ;
      char mtext[MAXOBN+1] ;
      };

main( )
{
   int pid ;
   /* Putting server in background */
   switch ( pid = fork ( ) )
   {
      case 0: /* child */
         setpgrp( ) ;
         serv( ) ;
         break ;
      case -1:
         warn("Fork to start server failed") ;
         break ;
   }
   exit(pid != -1 ? 0 : 1);
```

```
}

proc_obj(msg)
char *msg ;
{
    printf("%s\n", msg);
    system(msg);
}

static int r_qid = -1 ;
int fd;
serv( )
{
    long pro_type,semid,retval;
    struct q_entry r_entry ;
    struct sembuf sop;
    int mlen ;
    char buf[10];
    fd = creat("ser.txt", O_WRONLY | O_CREAT | O_EXCL, 0644);
    if (fd < 0)
    {
        printf("Server already Installed\n");
        exit(0);
    }
    else
    {
        printf("Server process PID is %d\n", getpid( ));
    }
    sprintf(buf,"%d", getpid( ));
    write(fd, buf, sizeof(int));
    chmod("ser.txt", 0400);
    if (r_qid == -1 && (r_qid = init_queue( )) == -1)
    {
        return(-1) ;
    }
    semid = semget(SEMKEY,1,IPC_CREAT | QPERM);
    if (semid > 0)
        semctl(semid,0,SETVAL,1);
    else
    {
        perror("server's semget failed ");
        exit(1);
    }
```

```
    for(;;)
    {
       pv(semid,-1);
       if ( (mlen = msgrcv(r_qid, &r_entry, MAXOBN, 0 ,
              MSG_NOERROR) ) == -1 )
       {
          perror("msgrcv Failed") ;
          return(-1) ;
       }
       else
       {
          printf("Ser val is %d\n",semctl(semid,0,GETVAL,0));
          r_entry.mtext[mlen] = '\0' ;
          proc_obj(r_entry.mtext) ;
          printf("a.out over\n");
       }
       pv(semid,1);
    }
}

init_queue( )
{
   int queue_id ;
   /* Attempting to Create Message Queue */
   if ( (queue_id = msgget(QKEY, IPC_CREAT | QPERM)) == -1 )
   {
      perror("msgget Failed") ;
      return(queue_id) ;
   }
}

warn(s)
char *s ;
{
   fprintf(stderr, "warning : %s\n", s) ;
}

pv(semid,val)
int semid,val;
{
   int retval;
   struct sembuf sop;
   sop.sem_num = 0;
```

```
    sop.sem_op = val;
    sop.sem_flg = SEM_UNDO;
    retval = semop(semid,&sop,1);
    if (retval < 0)
    {
        perror("semop failed");
        exit(1);
    }
    return 0;
}
```

main() forks a child process. The parent process is killed. And the *case* conditions checks to see if the *fork()* has been successful or not. If it has been the program terminates, else the statements within the *case 0:* are activated.

The first call is to the *setpgrp()* system call which disassociates the child process from the terminal it was run on. Plus making it its own group leader.

Next the *serv()* function is called. In it the file ser.txt is created in read-write-read-read mode. Since this file is being opened in exclusive mode another call to execute this program will fail and the program will terminate.

The PID of the process is printed and assigned to the array variable *buf* in integer format. This value is then written to the file ser.txt. This value in the file is used when we want to halt the server since at that point we will require the PID of the process that initiated the server in the first place. The mode of this file is changed to all-read mode so that no one else can write to this file now.

Now we come to the creating of the semaphore. That's what the *semget()* does. And its value is set to 1. Now starts the unending *for* loop.

In this loop a call is made to the *pv()* function which is passed two parameters, the ID of the semaphore and a -1. The *pv()* function does a *semop()* with these values. As a result the value of the semaphore becomes 0 (a -1 and +1 cancel out). We'll explain why we do this when we come to the flush program because that's where this step is really utilized.

The rest of the code is waiting to receive a message: the function is *msgrcv( )*. If the message is successfully received the statements within the *else* are executed. The value of the semaphore is printed. It will be 0. A *\0* is attached to the end of the message sent and the message is passed to the function *proc_obj( )*. The *proc_obj( )* performs a *system( )* on this message, which in our case is sending a file to the printer.

A call to *pv( )* with the ID of the semaphore and a +1 re-initializes the value of the semaphore to 1.

Now let's see what kind of a reaction the flush program would cause to the program. Assume that there were a number of messages for printing files already in the queue. Say we wanted to kill message number 5. And at this point message number 2 was being carried out. The original flush program which we saw in message queues would temporarily halt the program from running by sending a signal. But the signal is a very unintelligent being. It does not bother to find out what the status of the process it is interrupting is. In our case if the signal is sent bang in the middle of the second message being processed, there will be an immediate halt. And after the 5th message is flushed it will unfortunately not resume where it stopped.

Let's take an example. Suppose the second message was a program with two statements:

```
sleep(10);
printf("Sleep Over");
```

Assume that when the signal was sent the *sleep( )* was halfway through, that is 5 seconds were over. The signal would thus halt this process at this point. After flushing the 5th message one would think that it should execute the remaining 5 seconds of sleep. But this does not happen. Those 5 seconds are lost and the next line, that is the *printf( )* is executed instead.

It is to counter this haphazard signal processing that we use semaphores. A semaphore will ensure that only when there is no message being processed that the flush takes place.

Note: run the program below as a background process.

PROGRAM 291

FLUSH.C

```
#include <stdio.h>
#include <fcntl.h>
#include <sys/types.h>
#include <sys/ipc.h>
#include <sys/msg.h>
#include <sys/sem.h>
#include <errno.h>

#define QKEY    (key_t)0100
#define SEMKEY    (key_t)0x20
#define QPERM 0666
#define MAXOBN 50
#define MAXPRIOR 10

struct q_entry {
        long mtype ;
        char mtext[MAXOBN+1] ;
        };

static int f_qid = -1;
static int s_pid = -1;

main(argc, argv)
int argc;
char *argv[ ];
{
   int no_server = 0,fd,semid;
   long pro_type;
   struct q_entry r_entry ;
   int mlen ;
   char buf[10];
   if (argc == 1)
   {
      printf("USAGE : flush <priority>\n");
```

```
        printf("where priority = 0 -> flush all messages \n");
        printf("where priority > 0 -> flush a particular priority\n");
        printf("where priority < 0 -> flush all messages below
            absolute value of priority\n");
        exit(0);
    }

    if (f_qid == -1 && (f_qid = init_queue( )) == -1)
        return(-1) ;

    pro_type = atoi(argv[1]);
    fd = open("ser.txt", O_RDONLY);
    if (fd < 0)
        no_server = 1;
    if (no_server != 1)
    {
        semid = semget(SEMKEY,1,0);
        pv(semid,-1);
    }
    for(;;)
    {
        if ( (mlen = msgrcv(f_qid, &r_entry, MAXOBN, pro_type ,
                MSG_NOERROR | IPC_NOWAIT) ) == -1 )
        {
            break;
        }
        else
        {
            r_entry.mtext[strlen(r_entry.mtext)] = '\0' ;
            printf(" Command flushed --> %s\n",r_entry.mtext);
        }
    }
}

init_queue( )
{
    int queue_id ;
    /* Attempting to Create Message Queue */
    if ( (queue_id = msgget(QKEY, IPC_CREAT | QPERM)) == -1 )
    {
        perror("msgget Failed") ;
        return(queue_id) ;
    }
```

```
}

pv(semid,val)
int semid,val;
{
    int retval;
    struct sembuf sop;
    sop.sem_num = 0;
    sop.sem_op = val;
    sop.sem_flg = SEM_UNDO;
    retval = semop(semid,&sop,1);
    if (retval < 0)
    {
        perror("semop failed");
        exit(1);
    }
    return 0;
}
```

Flush is run with some parameter. If this value is a 0 all the messages are flushed. If the value is greater than 0 that particular message is flushed. And if the value is less than 0 all messages below that absolute value are deleted from the queue.

The parameter is passed in string form and therefore converted to an integer, *atoi( )*. The file ser.txt is opened in read only mode. This file contains the PID of the process that initialized the server. A check is made to see if the *open( )* has been successful. If the server is not running then file ser.txt will not be there and open will fail. Therefore there is no need for us to synchronize these two processes. We can simply flush the message.

If the *open( )* is successful a call to the *semget( )* returns the ID of the semaphore that has been created already. And the function *pv( )* is called with this ID and a -1. Now this is the crucial part.

Suppose a message was already being processed. The value of the semaphore at this point would be 0. Now when the *pv( )* is called at this point by the flush program, the *semop( )* in it will not perform successfully since the value it is being performed with is less than the value of the semaphore.

As a result this program will be waiting at the *semop( )* operation. So the rest of the program will not execute. Now when the message that is being processed finishes, the second call to the *pv( )* in the server program will add a 1 to the value of the semaphore. The value of the semaphore, which was 0, will now become 1. The waiting *semop( )* will get activated as a 1 and -1 will cancel out. And we will be returned to the flush program.

In the flush program the unending *for* loop will get executed. In it a *msgrcv( )* is performed and if it returns a -1 as the length of the message it means there are no more messages to flush. The flush program terminates. Else a *\0* is attached to the end of the message and the message is printed. This results in it being terminated.

Have you noticed that we haven't reset the value of the semaphore in the flush program. It isn't necessary at all because we specify a SEM_UNDO to the member *sem_flg*. So when flush terminates, the value of the semaphore is automatically reset.

So far we have already been trying to find ways of overcoming the consequence of having the time slice snatched away right when we are in the middle of some processing . But sometimes even the opposite is true. Like in the last program for example.

If you look at the *serv( )* function, we call the *pv( )* with a -1 at the beginning of the loop and then call the same *pv( )* with a 1 at the end. The two lines, pv(semid,1) and pv(semid,-1), are consecutive. As a result a flush which has set the *semop( )* to a waiting state for the message to get processed may never get the time slice at the right moment.

It is to counter this problem that, instead of having one semaphore, we have two. The only change occurs in the *serv( )* function. The rest of the program and functions remain the same.

The *serv( )* function:

```
static int r_qid = -1 ;
int fd;
```

```
serv( )
{
    long pro_type,semid1,retval,semid2;
    struct q_entry r_entry ;
    struct sembuf sop;
    int mlen ;
    char buf[10];
    fd = creat("ser.txt", O_WRONLY | O_CREAT | O_EXCL, 0644);
    if (fd < 0)
    {
        printf("Server already Installed\n");
        exit(0);
    }
    else
    {
        printf("Server process PID is %d\n", getpid( ));
    }
    sprintf(buf,"%d", getpid( ));
    write(fd, buf, sizeof(int));
    chmod("ser.txt", 0400);
    if (r_qid == -1 && (r_qid = init_queue( )) == -1)
    {
        return(-1) ;
    }
    semid1 = semget((key_t) 0x20,1,IPC_CREAT | IPC_EXCL | 0666);
    if (semid1 > 0)
        semctl(semid1,0,SETVAL,1);
    else
    {
        perror("Server's 1st semget failed ");
        exit(1);
    }
    semid2 = semget((key_t) 0x30,1,IPC_CREAT | IPC_EXCL | 0666);
    if (semid2 > 0)
        semctl(semid2,0,SETVAL,0);
    else
    {
        perror("Server's 2nd semget failed ");
        exit(1);
    }
    for(;;)
    {
        pv(semid2,0);
```

```
        pv(semid1,-1);
        if ( (mlen = msgrcv(r_qid, &r_entry, MAXOBN, 0 ,
            MSG_NOERROR) ) == -1 )
        {
            perror("msgrcv Failed") ;
            return(-1) ;
        }
        else
        {
            r_entry.mtext[mlen] = '\0' ;
            proc_obj(r_entry.mtext) ;
        }
        pv(semid1,1);
    }
}
```

We create a file ser.txt, assign the PID of this process to the

array *buf* and then from the array transfer this value to the file.

A call to *semget( )* now creates the first semaphore whose ID is returned to the variable *semid1*. Its value is then set to 1 using the *semctl( )* function. Another call to the *semget( )* creates another semaphore whose ID is assigned to the variable *semid2*. The value of this semaphore is set to 0.

In the *for* loop the *pv( )* is first called with the *semid2* semaphore and a value of 0. Since the value of the semaphore is also 0 at this point the *semop( )* in this function operates successfully. The *pv( )* is now called again but with the *semid1* semaphore and a value of -1. The value of this semaphore has been previously set to 1. As a result the *semop( )* will perform successfully once again. Control is once more returned to the main program, i.e. *serv( )*.

Now if the message is successfully received its processing begins. At the end, *pv( )* is called once more with the *semid1* semaphore and a 1. The value of this semaphore at this point is 0. The 1 is added to it, incrementing its value to 1. And the *for* loop starts once more from the beginning.

Now assume that when the message was being processed the flush program was called. But this time it has to handle two semaphores. So what it will have to do is set the value of *semid2* and *semid1* so that when the *for* loop of the above program starts again with a call to the *pv( )* with *semid2* and 0 as parameters, the *semop( )* will not perform successfully.

And that's exactly what happens. Assume we had 10 messages in queue. And the 2nd was being processed. If we wanted to flush the 5th message we would call the flush program listed below with a 5 as parameter.

PROGRAM 292

Flush.C

```
#include <stdio.h>
#include <fcntl.h>
#include <sys/types.h>
#include <sys/ipc.h>
#include <sys/msg.h>
#include <sys/sem.h>
#include <errno.h>

#define QKEY   (key_t)0100
#define QPERM 0666
#define MAXOBN 50
#define MAXPRIOR 10

struct q_entry {
      long mtype ;
      char mtext[MAXOBN+1] ;
      };

static int f_qid = -1;
static int s_pid = -1;

main(argc, argv)
int argc;
char *argv[ ];
{
   int no_server = 0,fd,semid1,semid2;
   long pro_type;
```

```
struct q_entry r_entry ;
int mlen ;
char buf[10];
if (argc == 1)
{
    printf("USAGE : flush <priority>\n");
    printf("where priority = 0 -> flush all messages \n");
    printf("where priority > 0 -> flush a particular priority\n");
    printf("where priority < 0 -> flush all messages below
            absolute value of priority\n");
    exit(0);
}

if (f_qid == -1 && (f_qid = init_queue( )) == -1)
    return(-1) ;

pro_type = atoi(argv[1]);
fd = open("ser.txt", O_RDONLY);
if (fd < 0)
    no_server = 1;
if (no_server != 1)
{
    semid1 = semget((key_t) 0x20,1,IPC_CREAT);
    semid2 = semget((key_t) 0x30,1,IPC_CREAT);
    pv(semid2,1);
    pv(semid1,-1);
}
for(;;)
{
    if ( (mlen = msgrcv(f_qid, &r_entry, MAXOBN, pro_type ,
            MSG_NOERROR | IPC_NOWAIT) ) == -1 )
    {
        break;
    }
    else
    {
        r_entry.mtext[strlen(r_entry.mtext)] = '\0' ;
        printf(" Command flushed --> %s\n",r_entry.mtext);
    }
}
}
```

In this program the file ser.txt is opened in read only mode. And if this is successful the *semget( )* is called twice. Both times it will return the IDs of the two semaphores created by the *serv( )* function above.

The *pv( )* function is called twice. Once with *semid2* and a 1. This results in the value of this semaphore being set to 1. The second time *pv( )* is called with *semid1* and a -1. This results in the value of this semaphore being set to 0. If the *semop( )* performs successfully both times we are returned to this program which starts an unending *for* loop to flush all the messages before terminating. On this process' terminating the value of both the semaphores are reset to their originals.

Let's see how the flush actually works:

Assume that the 2nd message was being processed and the flush program is run with a value of 5, meaning flush the 5th message. The first call to the *pv( )* with *semid2* and 1 will result in the *semop( )* performing successfully. This value will be added to the already existing value of the semaphore which is 0. Control is returned back to the flush program and the second *pv( )* is called. Since it is called with a -1 and the value of this semaphore (semid1) is 0 the *semop( )* does not perform successfully and the wait begins for the semaphore value to become 1. So the flush keeps waiting at the *semop( )* in the *pv( )* function.

Now when the processing of the message is done by the *serv( )* function it calls the *pv( )* function, as we have seen, with the *semid1* and a 1. As a result the semaphore's value becomes 1. Consequently, the call to the *pv( )* with *semid2* and 0 in the *serv( )* function does not perform successfully because the flush process has indicated its presence by making the value of this sub-semaphore 1. The *semop( )* now waits for this semaphore's value to become 0.

This causes the *semop( )*, which was performed by the flush program which called the *pv( )*, to activate. And now the flush program begins to flush the message.

It is only when the flush finishes that the value of the semaphore is reset and the *serv( )* moves ahead.

But there is a more sophisticated way of implementing the above program. And that is by using two sub-semaphores in one set instead of two separate semaphores.

The sub-semaphore evolved from the fact that many processes may be wanting to work with a number of semaphores at the same time. This would invariably lead to clashes. To avoid this the creators of UNIX decided upon having a set of semaphores with each being allowed to have a number of sub-semaphores.

Check out the next example. This time the changes are in the *serv( )* function and in the *pv( )* function.

The *serv( )* function :

```
static int r_qid = -1 ;
int fd;
serv( )
{
   long pro_type,semid,retval,semid2;
   struct q_entry r_entry ;
   struct sembuf sop;
   int mlen ;
   char buff[10];
   fd = creat("ser.txt", O_WRONLY | O_CREAT | O_EXCL, 0644);
   if (fd < 0)
   {
      printf("Server already Installed\n");
      exit(0);
   }
   else
   {
      printf("Server process PID is %d\n", getpid( ));
   }
```

```
    sprintf(buf,"%d", getpid( ));
    write(fd, buf, sizeof(int));
    chmod("ser.txt", 0400);
    if (r_qid == -1 && (r_qid = init_queue( )) == -1)
    {
        return(-1) ;
    }
    semid = semget((key_t) 0x20,2,IPC_CREAT | IPC_EXCL | 0666);
    if (semid > 0)
    semctl(semid,1,SETVAL,1); /* server's semaphore */
    else
    {
        perror("server's semget failed ");
        exit(1);
    }
    for(;;)
    {
        pv(semid,0,-1);
        if ( (mlen = msgrcv(r_qid, &r_entry, MAXOBN, 0 , MSG_NOERROR) ) ==
-1 )
        {
            perror("msgrcv Failed") ;
            return(-1) ;
        }
        else
        {
            r_entry.mtext[mlen] = '\0' ;
            proc_obj(r_entry.mtext) ;
        }
        pv(semid,100,1);
    }
}

pv(semid,val1,val2)
int semid,val1,val2;
{
    int retval;
    struct sembuf sop[2];
    sop[0].sem_num = 1;
    sop[0].sem_op = val2;
    sop[0].sem_flg = SEM_UNDO;
    if (val1 != 100)
    {
```

```
        sop[1].sem_num = 0;
        sop[1].sem_op = val1;
        sop[1].sem_flg = SEM_UNDO;
        retval = semop(semid,sop,2);
    }
    else
        retval = semop(semid,sop,1);
        if (retval < 0)
        {
            perror("semop failed");
            exit(1);
        }
    return 0;
}
```

The start of *serv( )* is the same as before but for one change. We create only one semaphore but this time with two sub-semaphores. If the creation is successful we set the value of the second sub-semaphore to 1 and the first sub-semaphore gets a value of 0 by default.

Now, in the unending *for* loop we call the *pv( )* function with two parameters - the ID of the semaphore. And the second parameter on which depends whether the *semop( )* function will perform successfully or not. If it is 100 the *semop( )* will be successful else not.

Since in this it is called with a 0 the *semop( )* will be performed. The last parameter, which is -1, is the value we want the *semop( )* to be performed with. If the *semop( )* in this function performs successfully we are returned to the *serv( )* function and the *msgrcv( )* function is activated. If there are any messages a call is made to the *proc_obj( )* with them. When the message is processed *pv( )* is called once again with the ID of the process a 100 (this indicates that the *semop( )* is to be performed only on one sub-semaphore) and a 1.

In the *pv( )* function, after the members of the structure are initialized, we check to see if the second parameter is equal to 100 or not. If it is not equal to hundred we perform the *semop( )* on both the sub-semaphores. If it is equal to 100, on only one.

Now the first operation performs with a 0 in *sem_op*. Since the first sub-semaphore's value is also 0, this operation is successful. Similarly the next operation is performed on the second sub-semaphore with the value of *sem_op* as -1. And since the value of the second sub-semaphore is 1, this operation also succeeds. And we receive the message and process it. At the end of the *for* loop we once again call *pv( )* with 100,1. This time the operation is performed only on the second sub-semaphore, setting it back to 1.

Suppose while processing the second message the flush is called? The flush which consists of the following lines of code:

PROGRAM 293

```
#include <stdio.h>
#include <fcntl.h>
#include <sys/types.h>
#include <sys/ipc.h>
#include <sys/msg.h>
#include <sys/sem.h>
#include <errno.h>

#define QKEY   (key_t)0100
#define QPERM 0666
#define MAXOBN 50
#define MAXPRIOR 10

struct q_entry {
   long mtype ;
   char mtext[MAXOBN+1] ;
   };

static int f_qid = -1;
static int s_pid = -1;

main(argc, argv)
int argc;
char *argv[ ];
{
   int no_server = 0,fd,semid;
   long pro_type;
   struct q_entry r_entry ;
```

```
        int mlen ;
        char buf[10];
        if (argc == 1)
        {
            printf("USAGE : flush <priority>\n");
            printf("where priority = 0 -> flush all messages \n");
            printf("where priority > 0 -> flush a particular priority\n");
            printf("where priority < 0 -> flush all messages below
                    absolute value of priority\n");
            exit(0);
        }

        if (f_qid == -1 && (f_qid = init_queue( )) == -1)
            return(-1) ;

        pro_type = atoi(argv[1]);
        fd = open("ser.txt", O_RDONLY);
        if (fd < 0)
            no_server = 1;
        if (no_server != 1)
        {
            semid = semget((key_t) 0x20,2,IPC_CREAT);
            pv(semid,1,-1);
        }
        for(;;)
        {
            if ( (mlen = msgrcv(f_qid, &r_entry, MAXOBN, pro_type ,
                    MSG_NOERROR | IPC_NOWAIT) ) == -1 )
            {
                break;
            }
            else
            {
                r_entry.mtext[strlen(r_entry.mtext)] = '\0' ;
                printf(" Command flushed --> %s\n",r_entry.mtext);
            }
        }
}

pv(semid,val1,val2)
int semid,val1,val2;
{
    int retval;
```

```
    struct sembuf sop[2];
    sop[0].sem_num = 0;
    sop[0].sem_op = val1;
    sop[0].sem_flg = SEM_UNDO;
    sop[1].sem_num = 1;
    sop[1].sem_op = val2;
    sop[1].sem_flg = SEM_UNDO;
    retval = semop(semid,&sop[0],2);
    if (retval < 0)
    {
        perror("semop failed");
        exit(1);
    }
    return 0;
}
```

Flush calls *pv( )* with 1 and -1. We add **the value** 1 to the first sub-semaphore. And to the next sub-semaphore, whose value is 0 at present, we go with a -1. Therefore this second operation fails. And the *semop( )* sleeps.

At this time the *serv( )* gets the time slice. The *serv( )* finishes the process and sets the value of the second sub- semaphore to 1 and the *for* loop starts once again. This time the *pv( )* is called with 0 and -1. So we now go to the first sub-semaphore with a value of 0. But since its value is 1 the *semop( ) sleep( )*s. Now flush gets the time slice and flushes all the messages. When it finishes, due to SEM_UNDO the value of the first sub-semaphore becomes 0 and that of the second sub-semaphore becomes 1 and *serv( )* continues.

Now finally for the Halt program. This will have one extra step to it. It will remove the semaphore besides removing the ser.txt file, killing the server program and deleting the message queue.

PROGRAM 294

```
#include <sys/types.h>
#include <sys/ipc.h>
#include <sys/msg.h>
#include <stdio.h>
#include <fcntl.h>
```

```
#include <signal.h>


#define SEMKEY    (key_t)0x20
#define QKEY   (key_t)0100
#define QPERM 0666
#define MAXOBN 50
#define MAXPRIOR 10

static int s_pid = -1 ;
int fd;
main( )
{
   int msq_id,semid;
   struct msqid_ds msq_status;
   char buf[10];
   fd = open("ser.txt", O_RDONLY);
   if (fd < 0)
   {
      printf("Server does not exists\n");
      exit(1);
   }
   read(fd, buf, sizeof(int));
   s_pid = atoi(buf);
   if( (kill(s_pid,SIGTERM)) == -1)
   {
      perror("Halt Server");
      exit(2);
   }
   else
   {
      unlink("ser.txt");
      printf("Server Halted\n");
   }
   /* Get message queue identifier */
   if ( (msq_id = init_queue( )) == -1)
   {
      perror("msgget failed");
      exit(2);
   }
   /* Remove queue */
   if(msgctl(msq_id, IPC_RMID, &msq_status) < 0 )
   {
```

```
        perror("msgctl failed");
        exit(3);
    }
    printf("Queue deleted \n");
    /* Remove semaphore */
    /* Attempting to Create Semaphore */
    if ( (semid = semget(SEMKEY,1, IPC_CREAT | QPERM)) == -1 )
    {
        perror("semget Failed") ;
        exit(0);
    }
    if(semctl(semid,0, IPC_RMID, 0) < 0 )
    {
        perror("semctl failed");
        exit(3);
    }
    printf("Semaphore deleted \n");
}

init_queue( )
    {
    int queue_id ;
    /* Attempting to Create Message Queue */
    if ( (queue_id = msgget(QKEY, IPC_CREAT | QPERM)) == -1 )
    {
        perror("msgget Failed") ;
        return(queue_id) ;
    }
}
```

The moment this program is run a signal is sent which halts the server program. Next the ser.txt file is unlinked. The ID of the message queue is obtained and a call to the *msgctl( )* with it deletes the queue.

And with this semaphores comes to a halt.

Conclusion: Semaphores

O Semaphore ! O Semaphore ! Grant me access to the device you hold in the palm of your hands.

That's what the semaphore is all about. The arbiter of social equality, the conductor of the symphony of processes and their access time. Without semaphores the chances of traffic jams and bottlenecks are rife.

After having looked at semaphores in such great detail, it's time to move on to another resource that harnesses the power of semaphores - Shared Memory.

Shared Memory

A client-server relationship as we have seen implemented through message queues is long winding . A lot of time is taken to share data through this method. And CPU time we know is of prime importance in a multi-tasking, multi-user OS.

Typically we have the server reading from the input file, which means the kernel reads the data into its internal buffers and then copies it to the servers buffers.

The server in turn writes this data to the message queue.

It's now the client's turn. It reads the data from the channel, which again brings the kernel into the picture. The kernel reads the data into its buffers and then the transfer is done to the client's buffer.

And finally the data is copied from the client's buffer into the output file.

A "cleaner" way out is to use shared memory. Basically shared memory is a way of allowing two or more processes to work on the same area in memory. Any data sent by the sender becomes instantly available to the receiver. Its like having global variables. Any program anywhere in the system can access the value in these variables.

Hey, isn't this what Dynamic Data Exchange is all about ? Here we have two processes dynamically exchanging data with each other. For example we could have one process writing details like Basic, HRA etc., of all employees from a file into the shared memory and another process performing some salary calculations and printing the salary slip. Or better still imagine one window where we are changing some data and another window where these modifications are reflected in graphical form. As the changes in data takes place the graph changes accordingly.

However, the processes have to coordinate the use of the memory among themselves. For example if one process is reading into shared memory another process must wait for the read to finish. And for this synchronization we need to use semaphores.

A client-server relationship through shared memory has the following steps -

The server accesses a shared memory segment using a semaphore.

The server reads the data from the input file into the shared memory segment.

After the read finishes the server signals the client using a semaphore.

And finally the client transfers the data from the segment into the output file.

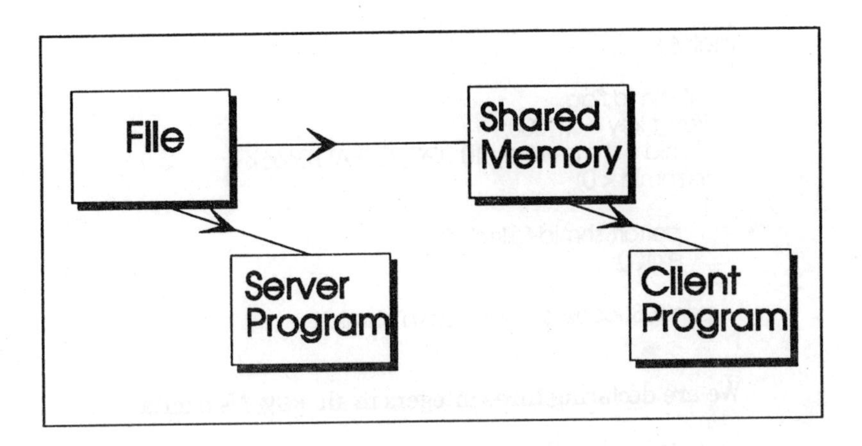

DIAGRAM 4.13

Initially when this segment is created it is outside the address space of the process but a system call subsequently maps it. As a result a segment memory is a lot like a variable and therefore access to it is just as quick.

This whole process of creating and then mapping it is analogous to an amoeba. Think of an amoeba spotting food and moving towards it. Once it reaches the food it proceeds to engulf it and bring it within its body space.

Creating A Shared Memory Segment

A shared memory segment is created using the *shmget( )* function. It returns an identifier to the segment.

But before you run a program to create a shared memory segment run the ipcs -m to see whether there is any shared memory created.

PROGRAM 295

```
#include <sys/types.h>
#include <sys/ipc.h>
#include <sys/shm.h>
```

```
main()
{
    int shmid,flag;
    key_t key = 0x1000;
    shmid = shmget(key,10 , IPC_CREAT | 0666);
    if (shmid < 0)
    {
        perror("shmid failed : ");
        exit(1);
    }
    printf("Success shmid is %d\n",shmid);
}
```

We are declaring three integers in all. *key_t* is a data

type defined in the sys/ipc.h header file. And basically stands for an integer or long because on a 386 processor even an integer is stored as four bytes.

shmget() is passed three parameters - the *key* which is the name we are giving the segment, a 10 signifying the number of bytes we want to reserve for the block and a create with read-write-read-write-read-write permissions.

Do a ipcs -m and you will see an entry for the segment just created. This is what we saw on our screens.

```
IPC status from /dev/kmem as of Tue Apr 9 10:56:13 1991
T        ID    KEY            MODE           OWNER     GROUP
Shared Memory:
m        0     0x00000100  -Crw-rw-rw-    vmci      other
```

Another call to a segment once created would just return the identifier. But there are a couple of hitches. For one the next call to the *shmget()* has to be with the same number of bytes or less as the first, not more. That's what the next program demonstrates.

PROGRAM 296

```
#include <sys/types.h>
```

```
#include <sys/ipc.h>
#include <sys/shm.h>

main( )
{
   int shmid,flag;
   key_t key = 0x10;
   shmid = shmget(key,100 , IPC_CREAT | 0666);
   if (shmid < 0)
      perror(" 1st shmid failed ");
   else
      printf("Success shmid is %d\n",shmid);
   shmid = shmget(key,110 , IPC_CREAT | 0666);
   if (shmid < 0)
      perror("2nd shmid failed ");
   else
      printf("Success shmid is %d\n",shmid);
   shmid = shmget(key,90 , IPC_CREAT | 0666);
   if (shmid < 0)
      perror("3rd shmid failed ");
   else
      printf("Success shmid is %d\n",shmid);
}
```

To start with we create a shared memory segment of a 100 bytes. Then another call is made to the *shmget( )* but this time with the segment size as 110. The result - an error. The third and last call to the *shmget( )* however is successful because - yes, you guessed it, the number of bytes defined are less. And the *printf( )* prints the identifier of the segment.

In our machine we were able to create a maximum of a 100 shared segments. Run the next program on your machine to find out what your maximum is.

PROGRAM 297

```
#include <sys/types.h>
#include <sys/ipc.h>
#include <sys/shm.h>

main( )
{
```

```
    int shmid ;
    key_t i ;
    for (i = 1 ; ; i++)
    {
        if((shmid = shmget(i , 1 , IPC_CREAT | 0666)) < 0 )
        {
            printf("Maximum number of SM segments %d\n",i);
            break ;
        }
    }
}
```

The *for* loop performs as long as the *shmget( )* does not fail.

The changing variable *i* is passed to shmget every time the *for* loop executes. The moment *shmget( )* returns a value less than 0 signifying that no more segments can be created the program terminates.

Further the maximum size of each segment is 512 KB. Check out the next program which is demonstrating how much maximum memory is allocatable.

PROGRAM 298

```
#include <sys/types.h>
#include <sys/ipc.h>
#include <sys/shm.h>

main( )
{
    int shmid ;
    long i ;
    for (i = 1024 ; ; i+=1024)
    {
        shmid = shmget(1 , i , IPC_CREAT | 0666);
        if (shmid < 0)
        {
            i = i - 1024;
            i = i / 1024;
            printf("Maximum shared memory size is in Kb is %ld \n",i);
            exit(0);
```

```
            printf("shmid is : %d\n",shmid);
            shmctl(shmid , IPC_RMID , 0) ;
        }
    }
}
```

The loop increments by 1024 each time. In the loop we are creating a segment with the size as whatever the value of variable *i* is. If the system call is successful the ID is printed and a call to *shmctl( )* made. *shmctl( )* deletes the segment. That's what the IPC_RMID indicates.

The moment a segment cant be created, it means the size limit has been reached. The *if* statement is entered. In it we are first subtracting 1024 since we don't need the last increment of variable *i*. Further by dividing it by 1024 we get the size in Kilobytes. And that's what is printed.

Does this mean we can create 100 segments of 512 KB each ? That's a total of 524288 bytes reserved for shared segments.

PROGRAM 299

```
#include <sys/types.h>
#include <sys/ipc.h>
#include <sys/shm.h>

main( )
{
    int i , shmid ;
    for(i = 0 ; ; i++)
    {
        shmid = shmget((key_t) i + 1 , 524288 , IPC_CREAT | 0666);
        if (shmid < 0)
        {
            printf("Maximum no of blocks : %d\n",i);
            exit(0);
        }
    }
}
```

The *for* loop as is obvious executes till the *shmget()* is successful. In our case for a 100 rounds.

The Amoeba Devours

A *shmget( )* merely creates a shared memory segment. At this point it is yet outside the purview (the address space)of any process. And therefore inaccessible. To map it to the address space of our process we need to use yet another system call - *shmat( )*. This system call returns a pointer to the shared memory segment created.

PROGRAM 300

```
#include <sys/types.h>
#include <sys/ipc.h>
#include <sys/shm.h>

main()
{
   int shmid ;
   char *msg ;
   shmid = shmget((key_t)1 , 10 , IPC_CREAT | 0666);
   msg = shmat(shmid ,0,0);
   printf("%u\n",msg);
}
```

The *shmget( )* creates a shared memory segment. Next a call to the *shmat( )* with three parameters - the ID of the shared memory and two 0's (we will see what these two parameters indicate later) returns a pointer to the shared memory segment. And a *printf( )* displays this value on screen.

Above we have seen that we can create a 100 segments of 524288 bytes each. But when the chips are done, that is when the *shmat( )* is used to map the segments to processes all we get are 6 segments in memory. After that the address returned is the same. And that's what the next program shows.

```
PROGRAM 301
#include <sys/types.h>
#include <sys/ipc.h>
#include <sys/shm.h>

main( )
{
   int i , shmid ;
   char *ptr;
   for(i = 0 ; ; i++)
   {
      shmid = shmget((key_t) i + 1 , 524288 , IPC_CREAT | 0666);
      if (shmid < 0)
      {
         printf("Maximum no of blocks : %d\n",i);
         exit(0);
      }
      ptr = (char *)shmat(shmid,0,0);
      printf("Ptr is %u\n",ptr);
   }
}
```

The loop will execute a 100 times (that's the maximum remember). The pointer variable *ptr* will be returned the address of the segment.

In our case we got -

```
ptr is 2151677952
ptr is 2155872256
ptr is 2160066560
ptr is 2164260864
prs is 2168455168
ptr is 2172649472
ptr is 4294967295
ptr is 4294967295
ptr is 4294967295
ptr is 4294967295
.
.
.
ptr is 4294967295
```

The first 6 *ptr* were pointing to different address that indicated the different shared memory segments. But as soon as the pre-allocated memory for shared memory as defined by our system was exhausted, UNIX started mapping the remainder segments onto the hard disk.

While we could write to the first 6 segments we found the seventh segment onwards were not writable to. But then again remember we did not have any virtual memory, so maybe that was the reason.

PROGRAM 302

```
#include <sys/types.h>
#include <sys/ipc.h>
#include <sys/shm.h>

main()
{
   char *ptr1,*ptr2,*ptr3,*ptr4,*ptr5,*ptr6,*ptr7 ;
   int shmid1,shmid2,shmid3,shmid4,shmid5,shmid6,shmid7 , pid, i;
   shmid1 = shmget((key_t)1 ,524288,IPC_CREAT | 0666);
   shmid2 = shmget((key_t)2 ,524288,IPC_CREAT | 0666);
   shmid3 = shmget((key_t)3 ,524288,IPC_CREAT | 0666);
   shmid4 = shmget((key_t)4 ,524288,IPC_CREAT | 0666);
   shmid5 = shmget((key_t)5 ,524288,IPC_CREAT | 0666);
   shmid6 = shmget((key_t)6 ,524288,IPC_CREAT | 0666);
   shmid7 = shmget((key_t)7 ,524288,IPC_CREAT | 0666);
   ptr1 = (char *) shmat(shmid1 ,0,0);
   ptr2 = (char *) shmat(shmid2 ,0,0);
   ptr3 = (char *) shmat(shmid3 ,0,0);
   ptr4 = (char *) shmat(shmid4 ,0,0);
   ptr5 = (char *) shmat(shmid5 ,0,0);
   ptr6 = (char *) shmat(shmid6 ,0,0);
   ptr7 = (char *) shmat(shmid7 ,0,0);

   printf("shmid1 : %d ptr1 : %u\n",shmid1,ptr1);
   for(i = 0; i < 10 ; i++)
   {
      ptr1[i] = 'A';
   }
   printf("Read from ptr1 %s\n",ptr1);
```

```
    printf("shmid2 : %d ptr2: %u\n",shmid2,ptr2);
    for(i = 0; i < 10 ; i++)
    {
        ptr2[i] = 'B';
    }
    printf("Read from ptr2 %s\n",ptr2);

    printf("shmid3 : %d ptr3 : %u\n",shmid3,ptr3);
    for(i = 0; i < 10 ; i++)
    {
        ptr3[i] = 'C';
    }
    printf("Read from ptr3 %s\n",ptr3);

    printf("shmid4 : %d ptr4: %u\n",shmid4,ptr4);
    for(i = 0; i < 10 ; i++)
    {
        ptr4[i] = 'D';
    }
    printf("Read from ptr4 %s\n",ptr4);

    printf("shmid5 : %d ptr5 : %u\n",shmid5,ptr5);
    for(i = 0; i < 10 ; i++)
    {
        ptr5[i] = 'E';
    }
    printf("Read from ptr5 %s\n",ptr5);

    printf("shmid6 : %d ptr6: %u\n",shmid6,ptr6);
    for(i = 0; i < 10 ; i++)
    {
        ptr6[i] = 'F';
    }
    printf("Read from ptr6 %s\n",ptr6);

    printf("shmid7 : %d ptr7: %u\n",shmid7,ptr7);
    for(i = 0; i < 10 ; i++)
    {
        ptr7[i] = 'G';
    }
    printf("Read from ptr7 %s\n",ptr7);
}
```

We create seven shared memory segments. And then map them into

our process. The addresses returned are assigned to the various *ptr*s. The ID of the shared memory as well as the address returned by the *shmat()* call is printed.

For each of the segments we are initiating a loop that executes 10 times. And in the process assigns an alphabet to the segment.

The output :

```
shmid1 : 77000 ptr1 : 2151677952
Read from ptr1 AAAAAAAAAA
shmid2 : 1201 ptr2: 2155872256
Read from ptr2 BBBBBBBBBB
shmid3 : 1202 ptr3 : 2160066560
Read from ptr3 CCCCCCCCCC
shmid4 : 10803 ptr4: 2164260864
Read from ptr4 DDDDDDDDDD
shmid5 : 804 ptr5 : 2168455168
Read from ptr5 EEEEEEEEEE
shmid6 : 805 ptr6: 2172649472
Read from ptr6 FFFFFFFFFF
shmid7 : 806 ptr7: 4294967295
Memory fault - core dumped
```

The first 6 segments got assigned the alphabets but on the seventh an error occured.

Writing To And Reading From Shared Memory Segments

Writing and reading to and from shared memory is as easy as saying "C". Its basically just like working with any other variable. Here is an example of two processes sharing a segment of memory.

PROGRAM 303

```
#include <sys/types.h>
#include <sys/ipc.h>
#include <sys/shm.h>

main( )
{
    char *ptr ;
    int shmid , pid;
    shmid = shmget((key_t)1 , 20 , IPC_CREAT | 0666) ;
    ptr = (char *)shmat(shmid , (char *)0 ,0) ;
    pid = fork( );
    if(pid == 0)
        strcpy(ptr,"hello world ");
    else
    {
        wait(0);
        printf("Parent reads -- %s \n",ptr);
    }
}
```

After creating a shared memory segment and assigning its address to the variable *ptr* we are forking a child process.

In the child we are string copying *hello world* to the segment. And in the parent process we are printing whatever is in stored in this address.

So here we have data being shared across two processes.

Once a value is assigned to a global variable unless it is explicitly overwritten the value always remains. It is the same with shared memory. If some data is read into it a write does not clear the segment like it happened with message queues. The data remains there unless explicitly cleared.

PROGRAM 304

```
#include <sys/types.h>
#include <sys/ipc.h>
#include <sys/shm.h>
#define SIZE 5 * 1024
```

```
main()
{
   char *ptr ;
   int shmid , pid;
   shmid = shmget((key_t)1 , SIZE, IPC_CREAT I 0666) ;
   ptr = (char *)shmat(shmid , (char *)0 ,0) ;
   pid = fork( );
   if(pid == 0)
      read(0 , ptr , SIZE ) ;
   else
   {
      wait(0) ;
      printf("Parent starts reading from shared memory
            and out putting to screen\n");
      write(1 , ptr , SIZE) ;
   }
}
```

Note : run this program like - a.out < <program filename>. Where the program filename is whatever you name the above program.

A segment, a pointer to it and a *fork( )* gets us started. In the child a call to *read( )* with three parameters - the standard input which is the keyboard, the address of the segment and the number of bytes to be read (that is write into shared memory). The segment now contains our little program listed above.

In the parent process a *write( )* which takes 3 parameters - the standard output which is the screen, the address of the shared memory segment and the number of bytes to read. The result - the file is listed on screen. Much like the cat command.

Now run this program once more but this time don't pass any parameters. That is just specify the name a.out. And the program will wait for you to input some data. Write Hello World and press enter.

Hey ! What happened ? The Hello World was displayed but so was the output of the last run. Well didn't we tell you that data in a shared memory segment is never cleared. But if you notice carefully you will realize that the Hello World did overwrite the first few characters of the last output.

There are two solutions to this. The first one is listed below.

PROGRAM 305

```
/* this program is solution of previous program */
#include <sys/types.h>
#include <sys/ipc.h>
#include <sys/shm.h>
#define SIZE 5 * 1024

main( )
{
    char *ptr ;
    int shmid , pid,nread;
    shmid = shmget((key_t)1 , SIZE, IPC_CREAT | 0666) ;
    ptr = (char *)shmat(shmid , (char *)0 ,0) ;
    pid = fork( );
    if(pid == 0)
    {
        nread = read(0 , ptr , SIZE ) ;
        ptr[nread] = '\0';
    }
    else
    {
        wait(0) ;
        write(1 , ptr , strlen(ptr)) ;
    }
}
```

After the *read( )* is over we are immediately assigning a *\0* after the last character. The *read( )* returns how many characters have been read and this tells us what the last character is. This value is stored in the variable *nread*.

In the parent process a *write( )* is done with *strlen( )*. This results in only as many characters being read till a *\0* is reached.

There is a more sophisticated way to do this, however.

PROGRAM 306

```
#include <sys/types.h>
#include <sys/ipc.h>
#include <sys/shm.h>
#define SIZE 5 * 1024

main( )
{
    struct databuf {
          int nread ;
          char buf[SIZE] ;
          };
    struct databuf *ptr ;
    int shmid , pid;
    shmid = shmget((key_t)1 , 5 * 1024, IPC_CREAT | 0666) ;
    ptr = (struct databuf *)shmat(shmid , (char *)0 ,0) ;
    pid = fork( );
    if(pid == 0)
    {
       ptr->nread = read(0 , ptr->buf , SIZE ) ;
    }
    else
    {
       wait(0) ;
       write(1 , ptr -> buf , ptr -> nread) ;
    }
}
```

We are defining a structure and a pointer to it. To the pointer *ptr* we are assigning the address returned by the *shmat( )* call.

In the child process the member *nread* is being assigned the number of characters read. The read reads the whatever is inputted at the standard input into the member *buf*.

Now in the parent process we are reading from the member *buf*. The number of bytes that are read are as defined in the member *nread*. And the output is sent to the screen.

Essentially what we have done here is made the shared memory segment and the structure synonymous.

Hardware And Shared Memory

Shared memory depends a lot on the hardware. The hardware not only limits the number of shared memory segments that can be simultaneously accessed by a process but also limits the size of a segment. Further, on the hardware also depends whether a shared memory segment can be given permissions other than that specified. For example suppose we were to give a shared memory segment only write permissions and if the hardware insisted on all permission then the hardware default would be considered.

In our case however we have the hardware following the software. Whatever we specify as the permissions are taken as valid by the hardware and not overwritten by it.

PROGRAM 307

```
#include <sys/types.h>
#include <sys/ipc.h>
#include <sys/shm.h>
#define SIZE 5 * 1024

main( )
{
   struct databuf {
          int nread ;
          char buf[SIZE] ;
          } ;
   struct databuf *ptr ;
   int shmid , pid;
   shmid = shmget((key_t)1 , SIZE, IPC_CREAT | 0222);
   ptr = (struct databuf *)shmat(shmid , (char *)0 ,0) ;
   pid = fork( );
   if(pid == 0)
      ptr -> nread = read(0 , ptr ->buf , SIZE ) ;
   else
   {
      wait(0) ;
```

```
        write(1 , ptr -> buf , ptr -> nread) ;
    }
}
```

So here since we are specifying the segment with only write (into the shared memory) permissions, in the parent process the *write( )* (which outputs the contents of the SM to the standard output) fails.

The *0222* which we are specifying at the time of shared memory creation stands for all write permissions.

The hardware also decides how much minimum memory to allocate to the shared memory segment. In our case the program below showed us how much this was. We passed it various values and finally landed up with 4096 as the minimum.

PROGRAM 308

```
#include <sys/types.h>
#include <sys/ipc.h>
#include <sys/shm.h>

main(argc,argv)
int argc;
char *argv[ ];
{
    char *ptr ;
    int shmid , pid, i;
    shmid = shmget((key_t)1 , 1, IPC_CREAT | 0666);
    ptr = (char *)shmat(shmid , 0 ,0) ;
    pid = fork( );
    if(pid == 0)
    {
        for(i = 0; i < atoi(argv[1]) ; i++)
            ptr[i] = 'A';
    }
    else
    {
        wait(0) ;
        i = write(1 , ptr , atoi(argv[1]));
        printf("Write ret %d\n",i) ;
    }
```

```
}
```

Note : run this program like this - a.out <number> where number is the number of times *A* is going to be read into the shared memory.

We are specifying that shared memory be created with only 1 byte. Now this should mean that we can only save a characters worth of data. But this does not happen.

In the child process we are reading into the shared memory segment as many *A*'s as the number we are passing as parameter.

And then in the parent process a *write( )* is taking place. The *write( )* returns the number of characters written. The *write( )* returned us a -1 (for error) when we passed 4097 as parameter. Till then the *write( )* returned the number of bytes written.

Getting Rid Of The Segment

After the amoeba finishes with the food it has a way of getting rid of it. It spews it out of its system. In a similar manner after we have finished with the shared memory segment we can disassociate it from our process. The system call is *shmdt( )*.

PROGRAM 309

```
#include <sys/types.h>
#include <sys/ipc.h>
#include <sys/shm.h>

main( )
{
    int shmid,i;
    char *msg;
    shmid = shmget((key_t)1 , 1 , IPC_CREAT | 0666) ;
    msg = (char *)shmat(shmid , (char *)0 ,0) ;
    printf("%u\n",msg);
    i = shmdt((char *)msg);
    printf("%d\n",i);
}
```

After creating and mapping the shared memory segment into our process we are immediately calling the *shmdt()* with the address of the segment. It will return a 0 if successful in detaching the segment from our process. And that's what we are displaying through the *printf()*.

However a detachment like the one shown above does not rid the main memory of this segment. Run the ipcs -m to verify this. But no further read or write to this segment can now take place. Check out the next program -

PROGRAM 310

```
#include <sys/types.h>
#include <sys/ipc.h>
#include <sys/shm.h>

main()
{
   char *ptr;
   int shmid ;
   shmid = shmget((key_t)1 , 1 , IPC_CREAT|0666) ;
   ptr = (char *)shmat(shmid ,0 ,0) ;
   read(0,ptr,10);
   write (1,ptr,10) ;
   shmdt(ptr);
   write (1,ptr,10);
   perror(" ");
}
```

Note : Run the program with a parameters - a.out < <filename>.

After reading and writing from the standard input and output, the segment is disassociated with the process. The second *write()* now gives an error.

Structures Of Information Associated With A Shared Memory Segment

For every shared memory segment the kernel keeps the following structure of information. This structure is defined in the sys/shm.h header file.

```
struct shmid_ds {
     struct ipc_perm shm_perm;/* operation permission struct */
     int    shm_segsz;   /* size of segment in bytes */
     struct region *shm_reg; /* ptr to region structure */
     char    pad[4];     /* for swap compatibility */
     ushort       shm_lpid;  /* pid of last shmop */
     ushort       shm_cpid; /* pid of creator */
     ushort       shm_nattch; /* used only for shminfo*/
     ushort       shm_cnattch;   /* used only for shminfo */
     time_t       shm_atime;  /* last shmat time */
     time_t       shm_dtime;  /* last shmdt time */
     time_t       shm_ctime;  /* last change time */
  };
```

Since shared memory is hardware dependent we cant describe the actual data structures used by the kernel to point to the shared memory segment.

Below is a program that uses *printf( )*s to display the values assigned to the members of the structure when a segment is created.

PROGRAM 311

```
#include <sys/types.h>
#include <sys/ipc.h>
#include <sys/shm.h>

main( )
{
   struct shmid_ds set ;
   int shmid ;

   shmid = shmget((key_t)1 , 1 , IPC_CREAT | 0666) ;
   shmctl(shmid , IPC_STAT , &set) ;
```

```
        printf("owner's userid is %d\n " , set.shm_perm.uid);
        printf("owner's groupid is %d\n " , set.shm_perm.gid);
        printf("creator's userid is %d\n " , set.shm_perm.cuid);
        printf("creator's groupid is %d\n " , set.shm_perm.cgid);
        printf("permission modes are is %o\n " , set.shm_perm.mode);
        printf("slot sequence number is %d\n " , set.shm_perm.seq);
        printf("queue name is %d\n " , set.shm_perm.key);
        printf("size of segment is %d\n " , set.shm_segsz);
        printf("pid of process last operated is %d\n " , set.shm_lpid);
        printf("pid of creator is %d\n " , set.shm_cpid);
        printf("current number of shared memory attached %d \n",
                set.shm_nattch);
        printf("in-core number of shared memory attached %d\n",
                set.shm_cnattch);
        printf("last attached time is %s\n",ctime(&set.shm_atime));
        printf("last detached time is %s\n",ctime(&set.shm_dtime));
        printf("last changed time is %s\n",ctime(&set.shm_ctime));
}
```

The system call to fill the structure with details is *shmctl( )*. It is passed three parameters - the ID of the shared memory segment, IPC_STAT which signifies a number that tells *shmctl( )* that the third parameter which is the structure address has to be filled with the details regarding the segment.

Changing User ID And Group ID Of Segment

By default the creator's user ID as well as his group ID are set to the shared memory segment. But by using the *shmctl( )* and passing it IPC_SET as a parameter we can reset these values thereby making the segment belong to some other user.

PROGRAM 312

```
/* IPC_SET sets the various permissions */
#include <sys/types.h>
#include <sys/ipc.h>
#include <sys/shm.h>

main( )
{
```

```
    struct shmid_ds set ;
    int shmid ;
    shmid = shmget((key_t)1 , 1 , IPC_CREAT | 0666);
    set.shm_perm.uid = 1 ;
    set.shm_perm.gid = 1 ;
    set.shm_perm.mode = 0444;
    shmctl(shmid , IPC_SET , &set) ;
    printf("userid is %d\n " , set.shm_perm.uid);
    printf("groupid is %d\n " , set.shm_perm.gid);
    printf("permission modes are is %o\n " , set.shm_perm.mode);
}
```

In this program over and above the ID's we are also changing the permissions.

To the members related to the ID we are assigning the new values. And then calling *shmctl( )* with the ID of the shared memory, IPC_SET which will take the values defined in the structure and assign them to the segment.

The *printf( )*s will now print these new values.

Another way to verify this change is through the next program.

PROGRAM 313

```
#include <sys/types.h>
#include <sys/ipc.h>
#include <sys/shm.h>

main( )
{
    struct shmid_ds set ;
    int shmid ;
    shmid = shmget((key_t)1 , 1 , IPC_CREAT | 0666) ;
    shmctl(shmid , IPC_STAT , &set) ;
    printf("userid is %d\n " , set.shm_perm.uid);
    printf("groupid is %d\n " , set.shm_perm.gid);
    printf("permission modes are is %o\n " , set.shm_perm.mode);
    set.shm_perm.uid = 1 ;
    set.shm_perm.gid = 1 ;
    set.shm_perm.mode = 0444;
    shmctl(shmid , IPC_SET , &set) ;
```

```
    printf("userid is %d\n " , set.shm_perm.uid);
    printf("groupid is %d\n " , set.shm_perm.gid);
    printf("permission modes are is %o\n " , set.shm_perm.mode);
}
```

After creating the shared memory segment we are calling the *shmctl( )* with IPC_STAT and the address of the structure. The members of this structure are filled with the details of the segment.

A reinitializing of some of the members is done next. Another call is made to the *shmctl( )* but this time with IPC_SET. So that whatever values the member of the structure have are assigned to the shared memory segment. And that's exactly what happens. The *printf( )*s verify this.

Without deleting the segment created by the above program we ran a program that tried to create a segment with the same key. But to our surprise we got an error. Typically, this shouldn't have happened, since we normally get the ID returned if the segment has already been created. But here their was a difference.

We had just changed the ID's and the permission modes. And the result was an error.

The program below demonstrates.

PROGRAM 314

```
#include <sys/types.h>
#include <sys/ipc.h>
#include <sys/shm.h>

main( )
{
    struct shmid_ds set ;
    int shmid ;

    if((shmid = shmget((key_t)1 , 1 , IPC_CREAT | 0666)) < 0)
```

```
        printf("failed for first time\n") ;
    else
        printf("succeeded for first time\n") ;

    set.shm_perm.uid = 1 ;
    set.shm_perm.gid = 1 ;
    set.shm_perm.mode = 0444;

    shmctl(shmid , IPC_SET , &set) ;

    printf("userid is %d\n " , set.shm_perm.uid);
    printf("groupid is %d\n " , set.shm_perm.gid);
    printf("permission modes are is %o\n " , set.shm_perm.mode);

    if((shmid = shmget((key_t)1 , 1 , IPC_CREAT | 0666)) < 0)
        printf("failed for second time\n") ;
    else
        printf("succeeded for second time\n") ;
}
```

We are changing the ID's and the permission modes of the segment. And then another call to *shmget( )* is made with the same key. The permission is the same defined at initial creation time.

But since there has been a change the call fails. Basically what has happened is that we are trying to access a shared memory segment to which we have no rights. Its like going to a party where we have not been invited. We are bound to be thrown out.

Just A Shared Memory Segment Away

A shared memory is another way of having processes send mail to each other. Or better still think of it as a telecommunication link up.

That's what the application below shows. There are two processes shown below that work in conjunction.

The modus operandi is something like this - either one of the processes initializes the shared memory segment, depending on which is run first. The second process is just returned the ID of the segment from which it gets the location.

Now assume process A sends a message. The message will be prefixed with a $. It will then enter and remain in a loop, waiting for an answer.

In the meantime in process B a constant check is being made to see if the character assigned to the first memory location of the segment is a $. If it is and the second location does not have a @ the message sent is written on screen.

A *gets( )* now allows a reply to be sent. This reply is prefixed with a *. In the *while* loop that the process A has been stuck in, waiting for the first location to be * a break occurs. The reply is displayed on screen and the process starts all over again.

If ever any of the users wrote a @ in the second location the communication would terminate.

Just one more point about the signs * and $ which we are using to synchronize the two processes. If you notice they are being assigned to the location after the string has been written. Why ? Because had they been assigned first the opposite process would immediately take over and there will be no communication ever taking place.

PROGRAM 315

```
#include <sys/types.h>
#include <sys/ipc.h>
#include <sys/shm.h>
#include <stdio.h>

main( )
{
   char c , *ptr;
   int shmid,i;
   shmid = shmget((key_t)1 , 500, IPC_CREAT I 0666) ;
   ptr = (char *)shmat(shmid ,0,0);
   while(1)
   {
```

```
        gets(&ptr[1]);
        ptr[0] = '$';
        if (ptr[1] == '@')
           break;
        while(1)
        {
           if (ptr[0] == '*')
           break;
        }
        puts(&ptr[1]);
    }
    shmctl(shmid,IPC_RMID,0);
}
```

When this program is run a segment is created of 500 bytes. Its address returned and to the variable *ptr*.

In the first *while* loop a *gets( )* waits for a string (message) to be inputted. This string is stored from the second location of the segment onwards. That is if the segment starts at address 10, the message will be stored from the 11th address onwards. The first location is assigned the character $.

The *if* checks to see if the second location of the segment has a @ assigned to it. If it has the program terminates. From this it is clear that a @ indicates end of conversation.

In the inner *while* loop a check is made to see if the first address byte holds a $. If it does this loop is exited from else this program keeps moving in this loop.

If the inner loop is exited from the contents of the segment are displayed on screen. And execution once more starts from the top of the outer loop.

PROGRAM 316

```
#include <sys/types.h>
#include <sys/ipc.h>
#include <sys/shm.h>
#include <stdio.h>
```

```
main()
{
   char c , *ptr;
   int shmid,i;
   shmid = shmget((key_t)1 , 500, IPC_CREAT | 0666) ;
   ptr = (char *)shmat(shmid ,0,0);
   while(1)
   {
      while(1)
      {
         if (ptr[0] == '$')
            break;
      }
      if(ptr[1] == '@')
         break ;
      puts(&ptr[1]);
      gets(&ptr[1]);
      ptr[0] = '*';
   }
}
```

In this program we enter the inner *while* loop. If the check for a $ in the first location evaluates to a true, the inner loop is broken from.

A check is now made to see if the message was signifying an end of conversation. If so the program terminates. Else the message sent is displayed on screen and a *gets( )* waits for input. The input is prefixed by a *, which is understood by process A to mean message sent.

A shared memory segment can be used to copy files. That's what the next program shows. Its a little tricky so lets take it a step at a time.

The basic flow is like this -

There are two processes parent and child. The parent reads data from a file into a shared memory segment and the child process takes the data from this segment and writes it to the output file.

But if this was all the program was doing it would have been relatively simple. We would just need one segment . However this would also mean a wait state for either one of the processes. Because while the parent is reading into the segment the child will be forced to twiddle its thumbs and vice-versa. Another problem with the above method is that the file size is predefined.

To overcome the time gap we introduced two segments. And two semaphores. Now the process changes slightly. The first time round while the parent is reading into segment A, the child cannot access the segment (ensured by using a semaphore). Once it finishes writing the number of bytes specified the child gets access and proceeds to write the data from the segment into an output file. At this point the parent is not waiting idly. The moment it gets the time slice it starts reading the rest of the file into the second segment. The assumption is that the child has not finished transferring data from the first segment yet.

When the child finishes with the first segment it goes to the second if the parent has finished reading data into it. And starts transferring data from there. The parent now starts reading data into the first segment. And this process carries on till the file has been complete.

Further the restriction on file size is also solved by the program below.

PROGRAM 317

```
#include <stdio.h>
#include <signal.h>
#include <sys/types.h>
#include <sys/ipc.h>
#include <sys/shm.h>
#include <sys/sem.h>
#define SIZ 5 * 1024
#define SHMKEY1 (key_t)0x10
#define SHMKEY2 (key_t)0x15
#define SEMKEY (key_t)0x20

struct databuf {
```

```
        int nread ;
        char buf[SIZ] ;
      } ;
static int semid , shmid1 , shmid2 ;
struct sembuf p1, p2, v1 , v2 ;

main( )
{
   struct databuf *buf1 , *buf2;
   int semid , pid ;

   semid = semget(SEMKEY ,2 ,IPC_CREAT | 0600 ) ;
   semctl(semid , 0 , SETVAL , 0 ) ;
   semctl(semid , 1 , SETVAL , 0 ) ;

   shmid1 =shmget(SHMKEY1,sizeof(structdatabuf),0600 | IPC_CREAT) ;
   shmid2 =shmget(SHMKEY2, sizeof(structdatabuf),0600 | IPC_CREAT) ;

   buf1 = (struct databuf *)shmat(shmid1,0 ,0) ;
   buf2 = (struct databuf *)shmat(shmid2,0 ,0) ;
   pid = fork( ) ;
   if (pid == 0)
   {
      writer(semid , buf1 , buf2) ;
      remove( ) ;
      exit(1) ;
   }
   else
   {
      reader (semid , buf1 , buf2) ;
      exit(1) ;
   }
   exit(0) ;
}

reader ( semid , buf1 , buf2 )
int semid ;
struct databuf *buf1 , *buf2 ;
{
   p2.sem_num = 1 ;
   p2.sem_op = -1 ;
   p2.sem_flg = 0 ;
```

```
    v1.sem_num = 0 ;
    v1.sem_op = 1 ;
    v1.sem_flg = 0 ;
    for(;;)
    {
        buf1 -> nread = read(0 , buf1 -> buf , SIZ) ;

        semop(semid , &v1 , 1) ;
        semop(semid , &p2 , 1) ;

        if(buf1 -> nread <= 0 )
            return ;

        buf2 -> nread = read(0 , buf2 -> buf , SIZ) ;

        semop(semid , &v1 , 1) ;
        semop(semid , &p2 , 1) ;

        if(buf2 -> nread <= 0 )
            return ;
    }
}

writer(semid , buf1 , buf2 )
int semid ;
struct databuf *buf1 , *buf2 ;
{
    p1.sem_num = 0 ;
    p1.sem_op = -1 ;
    p1.sem_flg = 0 ;

    v2.sem_num = 1 ;
    v2.sem_op = 1 ;
    v2.sem_flg = 0 ;
    for(;;)
    {
        semop(semid , &p1 , 1) ;
        semop(semid , &v2 , 1) ;

        if(buf1 -> nread <= 0 )
            return ;
        write(1 , buf1 -> buf , buf1 -> nread) ;
```

```
        semop(semid , &p1 , 1) ;
        semop(semid , &v2 , 1) ;

        if(buf2 -> nread <= 0 )
            return ;
        write(1 , buf2 -> buf , buf2 -> nread) ;
    }
}

remove( )
{
    shmctl(shmid1 , IPC_RMID , 0 ) ;
    shmctl(shmid2 , IPC_RMID , 0 ) ;
    semctl(semid , IPC_RMID , 0 ) ;
}
```

Note : run this program in the following manner -

a.out < <input filename> > <output filename>
Just lets see a diagram to understand this -

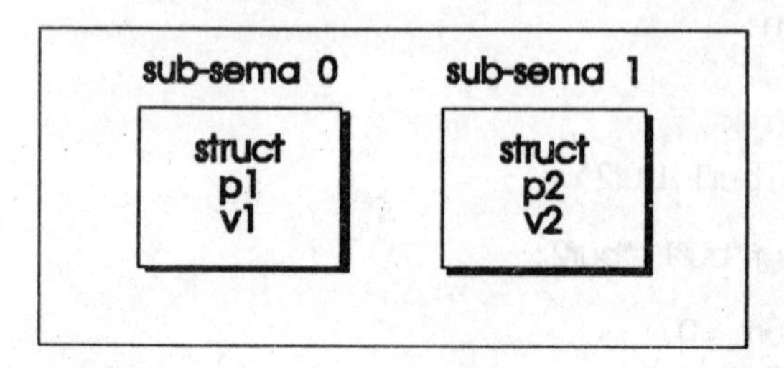

DIAGRAM 4.14

The diagram shows that there are two structures *p1* and *v1* that have values related to the sub-semaphore 0. And structures *p2* and *v2* have values related to sub-semaphore 1. These structures are passed to the *semop( )* function. And based on the value of the member *sem_op* the process either halts or carries on at that point.

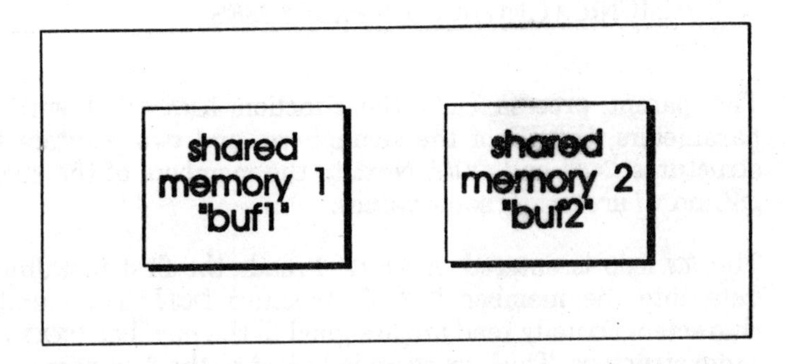

DIAGRAM 4.15

The pointers *buf1* and *buf2* are related to the segments *shmid1* and *shmid2*. Whatever we assign to the members of the structures these pointers are pointing to is reflected in the segments themselves.

When the program is run two semaphores and two shared memory segments are created. The values of both the sub-semaphores is set to 0. *fork( )* now creates a child process which is normally handed the time slice first.

In the child process a call is made to the *writer( )* function. The *writer( )* function is passed three parameters - the ID of the semaphore and the two pointers point to the structure the two shared memory segments have been related to.

The first thing that occurs in the *writer( )* function is that the members of the structures *p1* and *v2* are assigned values. In the *for* loop two *semop( )*s are done. The first *semop( )* is going to the first sub-semaphore,i.e. the 0th sub-semaphore, with a -1. At this moment the value of this sub-semaphore is 0. As a result the process halts here. This indicates that this segment is out of bounds at the moment. There could be two reasons for this - either some data is being read into it or there is no data at present. In this case it is the latter. The time slice is handed to the parent process.

The parent process calls the function *reader( )* with three parameters, the ID of the semaphore, and two pointers to the structures *buf1* and *buf2.* Next to the members of the structure *p2* and *v1* are assign some values.

The *for* loop is entered. A *read( )* reads the first installment of data into the member *buf* of structure *buf1.* The number of characters actually read are assigned to the member *nread* of the same structure. This structure is linked to the first segment that is *shmid1.* Which means whatever is stored in the structure members is actually stored in the segment. Now that the first segment is full it is time for the child process to transfer this data to an output file. But for it to do this the segment which it had been restricted from reading from has to be made accessible and in the process the parent process has to be locked from reading into this segment. And that's where the two calls to the *semop( )* do.

The first call is made with structure *v1.* Structure *v1* is working with sub-semaphore 0. At this point the value of this sub-semaphore is 0. So when *semop( )* goes to it with 1 it gets incremented and the second *semop( )* goes to the second sub-semaphore with a value of -1. Thereby locking it. The *reader( )* process halts at this stage.

The time slice is handed to the child process. Now since the value of the sub-semaphore 0 has become 1 the first *semop( )* operation overcomes the wait and in the process nullifies the value of the sub-semaphore. The second *semop( )* now goes with a 1 thereby incrementing the value of the sub-semaphore 1.

The *write( )* now reads the data from the first segment *shmid1* and writes it to the output file. After the write finishes a *semop( )* takes place with structure *p1.* The value of the *sem_op* member of this structure is -1. The value of the sub- semaphore at this point is 0. As a result the process halts at this point.

The parent process which was waiting at the second *semop( )* gets the time slice. Its halt now terminates as the value of the sub-semaphore 1 (which is 1) and that of the member *sem_op* gets nullified. And the next specified number of bytes are read into the second segment.

Once the *read( )* finishes, the *semop( )* is done with structure *v1*. The result is that the value of the sub-semaphore 0 is incremented. The second *semop( )* goes with structure *p2* which has a value of -1 to the sub-semaphore 1. Since the values don't nullify each other the process halts at this point.

The child which has been waiting for the value of sub-semaphore 0 to become 1 gets the time slice wakes and proceeds. It first nullifies the value of the sub-semaphore 0 and then calls *semop( )* again, incrementing the value of sub-semaphore 1. The child now proceeds to write data from the second memory segment into the output file.

This process carries on till there is no more data to be written. Once the data to be written is over the *remove( )* function executes. This function removes the two shared memory segments and the semaphore with three calls to the *shmctl( )* function.

King Arthur And The Knights Of The Round Table

Now for the grand finale. An application that took us a lot of time and brain-storming. But what fun it was. Exploring semaphores, shared memory, message queues, not to mention other UNIX functions.

The end result a working ROUND TABLE CONFERENCE. Yes, in the footsteps of ProComm or any other such communication package. We genuinely hope you enjoy it. And of course learn from it.

So here's how it goes. To start with we have the main program initializing variable, shared memory segments, semaphores and a message queue.

After this it proceeds to figure out who all have logged in and subsequently sends them a message saying COMMENCING COMMUNICATION :RESPOND—.

Actually in real life this would be a lousy way to intimate everyone that communication is possible, since whatever work they were indulging in would be cleared from screen. A better way would be to beep maybe 10 times at regular intervals. Like a telephone huh ?

The logged in users who have been temporarily halted when this message was displayed can now after pressing the enter key resume. If they are interested in responding they now need to run the client program. One by one each of the users who responds is given the ID's of the shared memory segments,message queue etc. Of course at one time only one user is allowed to send a message and the message sent is received by all the others.

Finally each user can log off by saying bye. And when the last user says bye, that is the end.

Now that we have a conceptual overview lets proceed to look at the actual code.

We will start with the server program - that is the one that initially sets the process working.

PROGRAM 318

SERVER.C

```
#include <sys/types.h>
#include <stdio.h>
#include <utmp.h>
#include <pwd.h>
#include <fcntl.h>
#include <sys/ipc.h>
#include <sys/sem.h>
#include <sys/msg.h>
#include <errno.h>
#define UTMP "/etc/utmp" /* passwd file for user names */
#define NAMELEN 8
```

```
#define QKEY    (key_t)0100 /* the message queue for SERVER */
#define SHMKEY1  (key_t)0100 /* SHM for the PID array */
#define SHMKEY2  (key_t)0101 /* SHM for the message */
#define SEMKEY    (key_t)0100 /* SEM for clients */
#define QPERM 0666

struct {
        long mtype ;
        char mtext[500] ;
    }send; /* the SEND buffer for SERVER */

main(argc,argv)
int argc ;
char *argv[ ] ;
{
   int pid;
   pid = fork( );
   if (pid == 0)
       child(argc,argv);
}

child(argc,argv)
int argc ;
char *argv[ ] ;
{
   int i , *ptr1 ; /* for PID array */
   FILE *fp;
   struct utmp u;
   struct passwd *p;
   char temp[NAMELEN + 1],name[20],buf[10],msgbuf[100];
   char *ptr2 ; /* for SHM for storing a message */
   int msgid ,fd,shmid1,shmid2,semid;
   struct sembuf sop[2] ;/* for semid */
   int pid ;
   char num[5] ;

   fd = open("ser.txt", O_WRONLY | O_CREAT | O_EXCL, 0666);
   if (fd < 0)
   {
      printf("Server already Installed\n");
      exit(0);
   }
   else
```

```
printf("Server process PID is %d\n", getpid( ));
sprintf(buf,"%d", getpid( ));
write(fd, buf, sizeof(int));

msgid = msgget(QKEY, IPC_CREAT | QPERM);

shmid1 = shmget(SHMKEY1,100,IPC_CREAT | QPERM) ;
shmid2 = shmget(SHMKEY2,5000,IPC_CREAT | QPERM) ;
ptr1 = (int *) shmat(shmid1,0,0);
ptr2 = (char *) shmat(shmid2,0,0);
*ptr1 = 0 ; /* initialize PID array */

semid = semget(SEMKEY,2,IPC_CREAT | QPERM) ;

fp = fopen(UTMP,"r");

while(!feof(fp)) /* inform all users that server is ON */
{
   fread(&u,sizeof(u),1,fp);
   if (u.ut_name == NULL)
      continue;
   strncpy(temp,u.ut_name,NAMELEN);
   p = getpwnam(temp);
   if (p == NULL)
      continue;

   for(i = 1 ; i < argc ; i++)
   {
      if(strcmp(u.ut_name , argv[i])==0)
      {
         sprintf(name,"r>/dev/%s",u.ut_line);
         system(name);
      }
   }
}
fclose(fp);

for(;;)
{
   sop[0].sem_num = 1;
   sop[0].sem_op = -2;
   sop[0].sem_flg = 0;
   sop[1].sem_num = 1;
```

```
        sop[1].sem_op = 1;
        sop[1].sem_flg = 0;
        semop(semid,sop,2);
        if (ptr2[0] == '*')
        {
           msgctl(msgid , IPC_RMID , 0);
           semctl(semid , 0 ,IPC_RMID , 0);
           shmctl(shmid1 , IPC_RMID , 0) ;
           shmctl(shmid2 , IPC_RMID , 0) ;
           unlink("ser.txt");
           exit(0);
        }
        memset(send.mtext,'\0',500); /* receive message */
        memcpy(send.mtext , ptr2 , strlen(ptr2) );
        memset(ptr2 , '\0' , 5000 );
        /* send to all those in PID array */
        strncpy(num , send.mtext , 4);
        pid = atoi(num) ;
        for(i = 0 ;*(ptr1 + i) ; i++)
        {
           if (pid != *(ptr1 + i))
           {
              send.mtype = *(ptr1 + i); /* priority = PID in array */
              if (msgsnd(msgid,&send,500,0) == -1)
              {
                 perror("msgsnd failed ");
                 exit(0);
              }
           }
        }
        sop[0].sem_num = 1;
        sop[0].sem_op = -1;
        sop[0].sem_flg = 0;
        semop(semid,sop,1);
    }
}
```

PROGRAM 319

R.C

```
main( )
{
    system("clear");
```

```
    printf("\n\nCommencing Communication :RESPOND---\n");
}
```

This program has one user-defined function ,*child( )*, in it. The *main( )* body of the program just *fork( )*s a child in which the user-defined function *child( )* is called.

The *main( )* program accepts parameters at the command line. These parameters are the users we want to notify that communication is now possible. These arguments are passed to the *child( )* function.

In the *child( )* we first start by initializing variables. And then opening the file ser.txt in read-write mode. After which the PID of this process is assigned as a decimal number to the array *buf*. From where it is transferred into the file ser.txt.

Now a message queue is created with the name 100 which is the value assigned to the symbol QKEY. The ID of the message queue returned by the *msgget( )* function that creates the queue is assigned to the variable *msgid*.

Next two shared memory segments are created using the *shmget( )* functions. One is for saving all the PID's of the process that are willing to communicate and one is for the actual messages. This second shared memory segment is important because if we were to just use message queues, the moment a message is read the queue empties out. But in this case we can't have that happening since there will be others we need to send the message to. So instead of sending the message to the queue we store it in the shared memory segment.

These shared memory segments are incorporated into our memory space by the *shmat( )* function. Into the first shared memory segment we are putting a 0, that what **ptr1 = 0* is doing. This 0 actually acts as a *\0* - string terminator. Why we are doing this you will realize a little later.

And lastly a semaphore with two sub-semaphores is created, both of which are initialized to 0.

The file *utmp* in the etc sub-directory is opened in read mode. And now starts the *while* loop that is going to look into the passwd file for all the users we have specified at the command line. These are the users we want to hold a conference with. If these users have logged on they are notified.

Now that we know what the loop is doing lets see it line by line. First of all the loop executes till end of the *utmp* file is reached. On this file an *fread( )* is performed. And the details are saved to the structure *u*. A check is done on the *ut_name* member. Its being empty signifies there is no entry. If the user has logged in an entry will be there in this file and the users name is string copied from the member to the array *temp*. This array is then passed to the *getpwnam( )* function which looks for the name that is in the array in the passwd file and returns the address where it starts. This last step is necessary as utmp contains besides a list of users some other details also. By checking for the entry read from the utmp file in the passwd file we can find out if it is a user or some other detail.

The *for* loop that starts goes through the entire list of arguments, each time matching the name in the member *ut_name* with the arguments. The moment it finds a match the *if* is executed. In this *if* the *sprintf( )* function is executed. It takes three parameters - an array *name*, the call to a program *r* which outputs on screen the device name which is got from the last parameter member *ut_line*. This ensures that Communication .... message is outputted on each user screen.

This entire process , i.e. the *while* loop carries on till all users, who we have specified, have been told that the conference is open. At the end the *utmp* file is closed.

Now that the basic envirnoment has been set, the actual communication can start. That where the supposedly unending *for* loop comes in.

In this loop the first thing we are doing is initializing both the members of the array of structures *sop*. Here we are initializing semaphore number 1, i.e. the second semaphore first with a -2 and then in the second array structure with a 1. When the *semop( )* operation is performed (it is to be perfomed twice since the last parameter is 2) it will halt at the first *semop( )* since we are going with a -2.

This halt is for the other users who have been notified that conference can start to get in. For that they need to execute the client.c program which is listed below. (We will go back to the server.c program later).

client.c basically consists of two - user defined functions - *receive( )* and *sendmsg( )* A *fork( )* results in a child process in which we are executing *receive( )*. By having two asynchronous processes one for receiving messages and one for writing them we are ensuring a duplex form of communication. There are two points here - one is that it is not necessary that a process can only write or receive at a point in time. It can, while a string is being written listen for a message which will be stored in some buffer. Only when we finish writing and send our message is the one in the buffer displayed on screen.

Another point here is that it is not that the buck stops with you even if you dont have a message to send. The "message bowl" keeps moving around. Anybody who has anything to send will use it. If you dont it does not matter.

PROGRAM 320

Client.C

```
#include <sys/types.h>
#include <stdio.h>
#include <fcntl.h>
#include <sys/ipc.h>
#include <sys/msg.h>
#include <sys/sem.h>

#define QKEY    (key_t)0100 /* same as SERVER */
#define SHMKEY1 (key_t)0100
#define SHMKEY2 (key_t)0101
#define SEMKEY  (key_t)0100
```

```
struct {
      long mtype;
      char mtext[500];
   } recv;

int i,fd,msgid,shmid1,shmid2,semid,*ptr1,retval,pid,len;
char name[20],buf[10],temp[500],*ptr2;
struct sembuf sop[2] ;

main( )
{
   fd = open("ser.txt", O_RDONLY);
   if (fd < 0)
   {
      printf("Server does not exists\n");
      exit(1);
   }
   msgid = msgget(QKEY, 0);
   shmid1 = shmget(SHMKEY1,100,0) ;
   shmid2 = shmget(SHMKEY2,5000,0) ;
   ptr1 = (int *) shmat(shmid1,0,0);
   ptr2 = (char *) shmat(shmid2,0,0);
   semid = semget(SEMKEY,2,0) ;
   pid = fork( );
   if (pid == 0)
      receive( );
   else
      enter( );
}

receive( )
{
   sop[0].sem_num = 0 ;
   sop[0].sem_op = 0 ;
   sop[0].sem_flg = 0 ;
   sop[1].sem_num = 0 ;
   sop[1].sem_op = 1 ;
   sop[1].sem_flg = 0 ;
   semop(semid , sop , 2) ;

   for(i = 0 ; *(ptr1 + i) ; i++)
      ;
```

```
    *(ptr1 + i) = getppid( ) ;
    i++;
    *(ptr1 + i) = 0 ;
    sop[0].sem_num = 0 ;
    sop[0].sem_op = -1 ;
    sop[0].sem_flg = 0 ;
    semop(semid , sop , 1) ;
    for(;;)
    {
        memset(recv.mtext,'\0',500);
        retval = msgrcv(msgid,&recv,500,getppid( ),0);
        if (retval == -1)
            exit(0);
        printf("\nMESSAGE:[ %s ]\n" , recv.mtext ) ;
    }
}

enter( )
{
    int pids[100],j;
    for(; ;)
    {
        printf("Please wait ...\n ");
        sop[0].sem_num = 1 ;
        sop[0].sem_op = 0 ;
        sop[0].sem_flg = 0 ;
        sop[1].sem_num = 1 ;
        sop[1].sem_op = 1 ;
        sop[1].sem_flg = 0 ;
        retval = semop(semid , sop , 2) ;
        if (retval == -1)
            exit(0);
        else
        {
            memset(temp,'\0',500);
            sprintf(temp , "%4d : " , getpid( ));
            strcpy(&temp[7],getlogin( )) ;
            strcat(temp ," : ");
            printf("MESG : > ") ;
            len = strlen(temp);
        }
        for(; ;)
```

```
{
    fflush(stdin);
    gets(&temp[strlen(temp)]);
    if(temp[len] == '\0')
        continue ;
    break ;
}
memset(ptr2 , '\0', 5000 ) ;

if (strcmp(&temp[len],"bye"))
    memcpy( ptr2 , temp , strlen(temp));
else
{
    memcpy( ptr2 , temp , strlen(temp));
    sop[0].sem_num = 0 ;
    sop[0].sem_op = 0 ;
    sop[0].sem_flg = 0 ;
    sop[1].sem_num = 0 ;
    sop[1].sem_op = 1 ;
    sop[1].sem_flg = 0 ;
    semop(semid , sop , 2) ;
    for(i = 0 ,j = 0; *(ptr1 + i) ; i++ )
    {
        if ( *(ptr1 + i) == getpid( ))
            continue;
        pids[j] = ptr1[i];
        j++;
    }
    if (j == 0)
        ptr2[0] = '*';
    else
    {
        pids[j] = 0;
        memset(ptr1,'\0',100);
        for(i = 0; pids[i] ; i++)
            ptr1[i] = pids[i];
        *(ptr1 + i) = 0;
    }
    sop[0].sem_num = 0 ;
    sop[0].sem_op = -1 ;
    sop[0].sem_flg = 0 ;
    semop(semid , sop , 1) ;
    sop[0].sem_num = 1 ;
```

```
            sop[0].sem_op = 1 ;
            sop[0].sem_flg = 0 ;
            semop(semid , sop , 1) ;
            exit(0);
        }
        sop[0].sem_num = 1 ;
        sop[0].sem_op = 1 ;
        sop[0].sem_flg = 0 ;
        semop(semid , sop , 1) ;
        sleep(1);
    }
}
```

The main part of the program forks a child after attempting to

initialize the message queue, shared memory segments and semaphores but since they have already been created only the ID is returned.

Since it is normally the child that gets the time - slice the *receive()* function is executed.

In this function after the initializations take place the members of the array of structures semop is initialized. If you notice we are defining semaphore 0 to be initialized to 0 and then 1. A *semop()* when performed on these two structures will sail through after initializing the value of this sub-semaphore to 1. Can you guess why we are doing this ? Because if its the first user responding the *semop()* will be performed successful and the value of this sub-semaphore will become 1, but the second user trying to log in will not have his *semop()* succeed since he will be going with a 0 and the value will be 1. In this way we can ensure that no other user can get logged in till the current user has put his PID in the first shared memory segment.

And that is what is happening after the *semop()* is successful. The *for* loop that executes will do so till a *\0* is found. The first time round it will be once. (Remember we had initialized a 0 in this segment in the server.c program). The moment the loop stops the PID of the current process is assigned to the segment and the next location in the segment is initialized to a 0.

Once more the *semop( )* is called on the first semaphore, this time with a -1. As a result the value of this sub-semaphore becomes 0. If any other user had been halted at his *semop( )*, he can now login. He too will follow the same procedure and add his PID to segment 1.

Once all this is over the *for* loop starts. In it the first function that is performed is a *memset( )*. This initializes the array member *mtext* to *\0*s. Next a *msgrcv( )* is performed but since as yet there are no messages in the queue, the program will wait here. In fact all the users who are logging in into the conference will wait here.

The time-slice will now go to the parent process which will result in the *sendmsg( )* function being executed. Lets see what this function is upto.

We are right away starting a *for* loop in this function. In this *for* loop we are initializing the members of the two array of structures. That is we are assigning a 0 and then a 1 to the sub-semaphore 1. When the *semop( )* is called by the first users parent process this *semop( )* will perform successfully. But if another users parent process runs this function he will be halted here since he will be going with a 0 to the sub-semaphore whereas its value is now 1. Thus we are stopping any other user from being able to send a message at the same time.

In the *else* part which would get activated if the *semop( )* performed without an error we are first initializing the array *temp* with a *\0*. Then assigning the PID of the current process to it, string copying the name the user has logged in with from the 7th member onwards. After which a colon is concatenated to the end of this array and the message MESG : > is printed on screen. This is where the user can key in the message he wants to send.

Now in the *for* loop we are first flushing the stdin, i.e. the keyboard. A *gets( )* which is now passed the array *temp* into which whatever is keyed is saved. So that its is saved from the last empty location onwards we are doing a *strlen( )* on *temp*.

The *If* here is to ensure that if no message is passed the *for* lop continues. If a message is keyed in a break takes us out of the loop.

All the bytes in the second shared memory segment are initialized to *\0*. And the message keyed in is string compared for a *bye*. If it is not a *bye* the message is copied into the memory segment *ptr2* using the *memcpy( )* function. And a *semop( )* performed on sub-semaphore 1 with a value of 1. Since its value was a 1 it now becomes 2. A *sleep( )* makes a beauty of this process.

So we have a sub-semaphore with a value of 2 and a message in the shared memory segment. This message has now to be sent to all the users logged in, into the conference.

And that's where the waiting server.c program wakes. Remember it was waiting at the *semop( )* with a -2. The *semop( )* now performs successfully and the second call to it on the same sub-semaphore makes the value of this sub-semaphore 1.

A check is done to see if the first character in this segment is a *. If it is all the shared memory segments, semaphores and message queues are removed, that's what the statements within the *If* are doing. But if this first character is not a * a *memset( )* first initializes the member *mtext* to a *\0*, then through a *memcpy( )* copies the message from the shared memory segment to this member and once more initializes the segment to *\0*.

The first four characters of the array *temp*, which are the PID (remember we inserted it in the *enter( )* function), are then string copied to the array *num* from where they are converted to their integer equivalent.

Starts the *for* loop. In it we are checking the PID we have isolated with those PID's of the various users who have logged and which we have stored in the memory segment *ptr1*. If the PID is not the same (this is to ensure that the sender himself does not receive the message), the statements within the *If* are executed. The first thing that is done is that the PID we are pointing to in the segment *ptr1* is assigned to the member *mtype*. This *mtype* if you remember we have used before to send the message to the user with the same priority number. This time we are using the PID as the priority number. The *msgsnd( )* now sends this message to the user. This loop carries on till all the users who have been waiting at the *msgrcv( )* (where we too had stopped) have each got their message.

Once we exit from the loop the *semop( )* is performed on sub-semaphore 1 with a -1, as a result its value becomes 0. And the time-slice is handed to the next user in queue, that is the client.c program, for him to send a message.

That is how the entire application is working. Now there is just one point left out and that is what happens if in the client.c program the message had been a bye. Then as we have seen the statements within the *else* would have got executed. In them the message stored in the array *temp* would have been transferred to the segment *ptr2*. And a *semop( )* done on sub-semaphore 0 with a 0 and 1. The value of this sub-semaphore was 0 and therefore the *semop( )* would have performed successfully, incrementing its value to 1.

In the *for* loop that followed we would have to reset the segment *ptr1* to get rid of the PID of the user who wants out. That's what we are doing. If the PID is the same as that of the current process it is not being assigned to the array *pid*. If you notice we are incrementing *j*.

The *If* checks the value of this *j* to make sure that at least one user remains. If not we know its time to shutdown. That's what the * is doing. Else if there is at least one user we can't shutdown totally and that's where the statements within the *else* are executed. In them we are first initializing *ptr1* to *\0* using *memset( )* and then transferring the PID's from array *pid* to the segment *ptr1*.

A *semop( )* is performed on sub-semaphore 0 with a -1. Its initial value being a 1 , it performs successfully. A *semop( )* is then done on sub-semaphore 1 with a 1. Since its initial value is 1, it now becomes 2. And the server.c program wakes up from where it had gone to *sleep( )*.

One last point here - you must be wondering why we have the statements -

```
if (retval == -1)
    exit(0);
```

in the our functions, where *retval* is the variable that the result of the preceding function (eg. *semop( ), msgrcv( )* etc.) call is returned to.

Suppose all the people using this communication program have finished by saying bye and the last guy is waiting at the *semop( )* or *msgrcv( )*. This would result in all the shared memory segments and message queues having been destroyed by the server.c program. As a result the value returned by the waiting function will be a -1. And the program will terminate.

Conclusion: Shared Memory

Share my chocolate, not a chance. But as far as shared memory goes - be my guest.

Shared Memory is but one more method adopted by UNIX to allow processes to communicate between themselves.

Right from the creation of shared memory segments through to its use and finally topping it off with an application that merged the use of shared memory and semaphores we have covered this topic in great detail.

The Leftovers

There are a lot of other functions and system calls besides the ones we have already seen that are a part of UNIX. These are very useful and any discussion on UNIX needs to perforce examine them.

The 'mknod( )'

This system call is used to create a new file. It is passed three parameters: the filename; the mode which defines the set of permissions plus the kind of file it is to be; and the device type (disk, for example).

The header file <sys/stat.h> contains the symbolic constants that define the various modes.

A thing to remember about this system call is that it can only be used under su status. That is, by someone with super-user status.

PROGRAM 321

```
#include <sys/types.h>
#include <sys/stat.h>

extern errno;
main( )
{
    int i;
    i=mknod("try",S_IFDIR | 0777,0);
    printf("Mknod Returns : -> %d\n",i);
    if ( i == -1 )
        perror("errno");
}
```

The *S_IFDIR | 0777* that is passed as a parameter to *mknod( )* signifies that try is a directory file with read-write-execute permissions for everyone. The read for a directory means a ls works, the write allows us to create a file in it. And the execute enables us to go into that directory.

By just changing the second parameter to S_IFCHR we can create a character special file. A character special file includes devices such as the modem and printer devices. Data transfer is done in streams of bytes and not in blocks.

PROGRAM 322

```
#include <sys/types.h>
#include <sys/stat.h>

extern errno;
main()
{
    int i;
    i=mknod("try1",S_IFCHR | 0777,0);
    printf("Mknod Returns : -> %d\n",i);
    if ( i == -1 )
        perror("errno");
}
```

After running this program do a `ls -l try1` and you'll see an entry for `try1` as a character special file.

A block file includes devices like disks and magnetic tapes where transfer is done in blocks of 1024 bytes. These files can be created as shown below.

PROGRAM 323

```
#include <sys/types.h>
#include <sys/stat.h>

extern errno;
main()
{
    int i;
    i=mknod("try2",S_IFBLK | 0777,0);
    printf("Mknod Returns : -> %d\n",i);
    if ( i == -1 )
        perror("errno");
```

```
}
```

The parameter specified is S_IFBLK .

If you remember, in the file locking section we showed how a mandatory file lock can be implemented when a file is created. A easier way to do this is by using the *mknod( )* call with S_ENFMT as parameter.

PROGRAM 324

```
#include <sys/types.h>
#include <sys/stat.h>

extern errno;
main( )
{
    int i;
    i=mknod("try3",S_ENFMT | 0777,0);
    printf("Mknod Returns : -> %d\n",i);
    if ( i == -1 )
        perror("errno");
}
```

Do a ls -l try3 and you will see an l in the permissions.

The 'nice( )'

In a multi-tasking system processes are given priorities which define the number of time-slices they get. By default the system itself assigns the priority number but we can change it (the priority number) by using the *nice( )* system call. The new priority number is added to the already existing value. Normally this value is a non-negative number and the closer it is to 0 the less the priority.

PROGRAM 325

```
#include <stdio.h>

main( )
{
    int pid,retnice;
```

```
        printf("Press DEL to stop process\n");
        pid=fork( );
        for(;;)
        {
            if ( pid == 0 )
            {
                retnice = nice(-5);
                printf("Child gets higher CPU priority %d\n",retnice);
                sleep(1);
            }
            else
            {
                retnice = nice(4);
                printf("Parent gets lower CPU priority %d\n",retnice);
                sleep(1);
            }
        }
}
```

A call to *nice( )* in the child process with a -5 results in this

process getting a higher priority. Whereas the parent process which is called with a priority of 4 gets a lower rating.

The 'clock( )'

We can find out how much of CPU time a certain process or a loop is taking. But there is one problem here: *clock( )*, the function that shows this has to be called twice since the time taken is only between two calls to *clock( )*.

```
PROGRAM 326
#include <stdio.h>

main( )
{
    int i;
    long timetaken;
    printf("Started executing code...\n");
    for ( i=0 ; i<=50 ; i++ )
        printf("%d\t",i);
    timetaken = clock( );
```

```
    printf("CPU time used was : %ld\n",timetaken);

    for ( i=0 ; i<=50 ; i++ )
        printf("%d\t",i);
    timetaken = clock( );
    printf("CPU time now used was : %ld\n",timetaken);

}
```

Which is why we first start a loop and then call *clock( )*. This first call will output a 0. After the second loop, the *clock( )* function now returns the actual time taken.

The 'ulimit( )'

Any process usually has some limits as defined by the supervisor. For example, the limit for a certain process may be on the basis of how much data in terms of block sizes it can write to a file. This limit can be changed only by the supervisor or anyone logged in as a super-user.

```
PROGRAM 327
main()
{
    long retval,ulimit( );
    retval = ulimit(2,1024);
    printf("retval is %ld \n",retval);
}
```

Remember to be a super-user before you run this.

The 'fcntl( )'

The *fcntl( )* call allows us control over files. Although we have used this call before there are a lot of functions left to be looked into.

fcntl( ) takes three parameters: file descriptor obtained from an *open( )*, *create( )* etc; the second parameter is a constant as defined in the fcntl.h header file; and the third parameter depends on the second parameter.

PROGRAM 328

```
#include <fcntl.h>
#include <stdio.h>

main()
{
    int fd,retval;
    retval = fcntl(0,F_DUPFD,0);
    printf("\nNext handle is %d\n",retval);
}
```

F_DUPFD returns a new file descriptor. The new file descriptor is the next available file descriptor. Or it could be the value representing the last parameter passed, if that value is not already defined as a file descriptor.

In the above program we call *fcntl( )* with 0 which stands for standard input, F_DUPFD which returns a new descriptor and a 0 saying what the value of the new descriptor should be. But since standard input already has the value 0 as its file descriptor the next available value is returned. The next available value is 3.

Another call to *fcntl( )* in the same program will now return a 4 as the file descriptor. That's what the next program shows.

PROGRAM 329

```
#include <fcntl.h>
#include <stdio.h>

main()
{
    int fd,retval;
    retval = fcntl(0,F_DUPFD,0);
    printf("\nNext handle is %d\n",retval);
    retval = fcntl(0,F_DUPFD,0);
    printf("\nNext handle is %d\n",retval);
}
```

Below is another example that shows how a duplicate handle can be used to output to the same file.

PROGRAM 330

```
#include <fcntl.h>
#include <stdio.h>
main( )
{
    int fd,retval,retval1;
    retval = fcntl(1,F_DUPFD,0);
    printf("\nHandle number is %d\n",retval);
    retval1 = fcntl(1,F_DUPFD,0);
    printf("\nHandle number is %d\n",retval);
    write(1,"Hello World 1\n",15);
    write(retval,"Hello World 1\n",15);
    write(retval1,"Hello World 1\n",15);
}
```

This program shows that there are three handles that we can use to write to standard output, that is, our screen.

The output need not only be directed to standard output, it can also be directed to a file created by us. Check out the next program:

PROGRAM 331

```
#include <fcntl.h>
#include <stdio.h>

main( )
{
   int old ,new ;
   old = open("test",O_WRONLY | O_CREAT,0666);
   write(old,"Hello world 1\n",15);
   printf("value of old = %d \n",old);
   new = fcntl(old,F_DUPFD,0);
   printf("value of new %d\n",new);
   write(new,"Hello world 2\n",15);
   write(old,"Hello world 3\n ",15);
}
```

The file we open is test. Assume it returns a file handle with the value 3. A *write( )* is committed with this file handle. Now another file handle is created using *fcntl( )*. Thus, for this file we have two file handles. Two more *write( )*s use these two file handles to write to the file.

We have seen that when we specify the last parameter as 0 we get the next available handle. However, if we specify a value there, the new handle will reflect that value. The maximum value we can specify is 99.

PROGRAM 332

```
#include <fcntl.h>
#include <stdio.h>

main( )
{
    int fd,fd2;
    fd = open("test",O_WRONLY | O_CREAT,0666);
    write(fd,"Hello world 1 ",15);
    fd2 = fcntl(fd,F_DUPFD,99);
    printf("fcntl returned %d\n",fd2);
    write(fd2,"Hello world 2",14);
}
```

The value returned by *fcntl( )* is 99. And the second *write( )* prints to the same file, i.e. test.

When an *exec( )* is performed in a process the file descriptor of whatever file is open is also passed to the *exec( )*ed process. For example, if we had process A which had opened a file test before performing an *exec( )*, then the file descriptor of this file would have been passed to the *exec( )*ed process B.

If we don't want this file descriptor passed we need to use *fcntl( )* on the close-on-exec-flag associated with a file. To start with we first need to find out whether the close-on-exec- flag is ON or OFF. By default it is always ON. If the F_GETFD is passed to the *fcntl( )* system call it will return a value indicating this. Below are two programs that demonstrate this.

PROGRAM 333

```
#include <fcntl.h>

main( )
{
   int fd,retval;
   fd = open("test",O_WRONLY | O_CREAT,0666);
   write(fd,"Hello world",15);
   retval = fcntl(fd,F_GETFD,0);
   printf("fcntl returned %d\n",retval);
   execlp("hello","hello",(char *)0);
}
```

PROGRAM 334

Hello.C

```
main( )
{
   printf("Hello Program is running\n");
   write(3,"Written from Hello.C\n",22);
   printf("Hello program is over\n");
}
```

The file opened is test. On the file descriptor associated with this file (we're assuming it is 3) we do an *fcntl( )*. The second parameter passed to *fcntl( )*, F_GETFD , ensures that a close-on-exec-flag is returned. If the return value is 0 this flag has been set, i.e. close-on-exec is ON.

When hello.c is *execl( )*ed the *write( )* works, proving that the close-on-exec-flag is ON. However, we can use the F_SETFD parameter to set this close-on-exec-flag OFF.

PROGRAM 335

```
#include <fcntl.h>

main( )
{
   int fd,retval;
   fd = open("test",O_WRONLY | O_CREAT,0666);
   write(fd,"Hello world",12);
   fcntl(fd,F_SETFD,1);
```

```
    retval = fcntl(fd,F_GETFD,0);
    printf("fcntl returned %d\n",retval);
    execlp("hello","hello",(char *)0);
}
```

fcntl( ) has been passed F_SETFD as the second parameter. As a result, the next call to it to find out the value of the close-on-exec-flag will show a value 1, signifying that the flag is OFF.

This time the *write( )* in program hello.c will not write to the file.

Another use of the *fcntl( )* system call is to find out the mode a file has been opened in. A parameter of F_GETFL returns a value that has to be ANDed with a file open permission. See the next example:

PROGRAM 336

```
#include <fcntl.h>

main( )
{
    int fd,retval,dum;
    fd = open("test",O_WRONLY,0666);
    write(fd,"Hello world",12);
    if((retval = fcntl(fd,F_GETFL,0)) == -1)
    {
        printf("Filestate failed\n");
        return(-1);
    }
    printf("fcntl returned %d\n",retval);
    if(retval & O_WRONLY)
        printf("Write only\n");
    if(retval & O_RDWR)
        printf("Read-Write only\n");
    if(retval & O_RDONLY)
        printf("Read only\n");
    if(retval & O_APPEND)
        printf("Append only\n");
}
```

We open a file in write only mode. The call to *fcntl( )* returns a value 1. Next, it is anded with the symbolic constants and whichever *if* evaluates to a true that's the mode the file has been opened in. In our case, as is obvious, the write only condition will be satisfied.

We can use *fcntl( )* to change the mode of a file. That's what the next program demonstrates.

PROGRAM 337

```
#include <fcntl.h>

main( )
{
   int fd,retval,dum;
   fd = open("test",O_WRONLY,0666);
   write(fd,"Hello world",12);
   if((retval = fcntl(fd,F_GETFL,0)) == -1)
   {
      printf("Filestate failed\n");
      return(-1);
   }
   printf("Before change\n");
   if(retval & O_APPEND)
      printf("Append only\n");
   if(retval & O_WRONLY)
      printf("Write only\n");
   if(retval & O_RDWR)
      printf("Read-Write only\n");
   if(retval & O_RDONLY)
      printf("Read only\n");

   if((retval = fcntl(fd,F_SETFL,O_APPEND)) == -1)
   {
      printf("Fcntl error\n");
      return(-1);
   }

   if((retval = fcntl(fd,F_GETFL,0)) == -1)
   {
      printf("Filestate failed\n");
      return(-1);
```

```
	}
	printf("After change\n");
	if(retval & O_APPEND)
		printf("Append only\n");
	if(retval & O_WRONLY)
		printf("Write only\n");
	if(retval & O_RDWR)
		printf("Read-Write only\n");
	if(retval & O_RDONLY)
		printf("Read only\n");
}
```

We open a file in write only mode. The first call to *fcntl( )* verifies this. The second call to *fcntl( )* with the parameters *fd*, F_SETFL and O_APPEND changes the mode of the file. And the next call to *fcntl( )* with F_GETFL proves this.

The 'ftw( )'

ftw( ) is a recursive function that goes down the path passed as parameter, listing all files and sub-directories. It is passed three parameters: the pathname, the user defined function to call and an integer value that signifies the depth. This last parameter controls the number of different file descriptors opened by *ftw( )*. The larger this value is, the lesser are the reopenings of directories that have to be performed and therefore faster the speed. The safest value is 1, though.

PROGRAM 338

```
#include <sys/types.h>
#include <sys/stat.h>
#include <ftw.h>

long fno=1 , dno=1 ;
main(argc , argv)
int argc ;
char *argv[ ] ;
{
	int fun( );
	if (argc <= 1)
		ftw(".",fun,1);
```

```
        else
            ftw(argv[1],fun,1);
        printf(" Number of files = %ld \n",fno);
        printf(" Number of Directory = %ld \n",dno);
        exit(0);
    }

    fun(fname , statbuf, flag)
    char *fname ;
    struct stat *statbuf ;
    int flag;
    {
        if( flag == FTW_NS)
            return(0);
        if(flag == FTW_F)
        {
            printf("File %s status %o\n",fname,statbuf->st_mode&0777);
            fno++ ;
        }
        else
        {
            printf("Directory %s status %o\n",fname,statbuf->st_mode&0777);
            dno++ ;
        }
        return(0);
    }
```

If no pathname is specified the current directory is assumed and the *ftw( )* within the *if* is executed. This *ftw( )* makes a call to the function *fun( )* which has been specified as its second parameter.

Function *fun( )* is always called with three parameters: a null-terminated string holding the object name (this could be a file or directory), a pointer to a stat structure containing data about the object name and an integer value that can also be passed as a symbolic constant (declared in the ftw.h header file).

In the *fun( )* function, if the last parameter evaluates to a FTW_NS it means that an error has occurred. If it evaluates to a FTW_F it means that all files are to be listed. Else all files and directories are to be listed. After all the files or directories are listed we are returned to the calling program, where the number of listings are displayed.

The 'access( )'

The *access( )* system call can be used to determine whether a process has access to a file or not, according to the real-user ID of the process and not its effective-user ID.

It can be used to figure out what permissions are associated with a file.

Run the program below by passing it a filename at the command line. And the permission the process has over it will be returned.

PROGRAM 339

```
# include <stdio.h>

main(argc,argv)
int argc ;
char *argv[ ] ;
{
   FILE *fp ;
   int ch ;
   if(access( argv[1], 0) == -1)
   {
      printf(" File %s does not exist.\n",argv[1]);
      exit(1) ;
   }
   printf("File %s is --- ",argv[1]);
   if((access( argv[1], 1)) == 0)
   {
      printf(" Executable.") ;
   }
   if((access( argv[1], 2)) == 0)
   {
      printf(" Write.") ;
   }
   if((access( argv[1], 4)) == 0)
   {
      printf(" Read.") ;
```

```
    }
    printf("\n");
}
```

access( ) is called with 2 parameters: the argument passed at the command line and an integer value that determines the permission. Based on the integer value the file permission is compared. If the return value is a 0, that's what the permission is.

The 'clearerr( )'

This essentially clears any error that may take place, or it can be used to overlook an end-of-file also. For example, suppose we were listing a file which may have a lot of end-of-file marker errors, we may not want the listing to stop.

In the next example we'll use *clearerr( )* to do something similar.

PROGRAM 340

```
#include <stdio.h>

main( )
{
    FILE *fp ;
    int i = 0 ;
    fp = fopen("test.c","r");
    while(!feof(fp))
    {
        i++ ;
        printf("%c ... %d ",fgetc(fp),i );
        clearerr(fp);
    }
    printf("%d \n",i);
}
```

The file test.c is being opened in read mode. The *while* loop executes till an end-of-file is reached. In the loop variable *i* is incremented. And a character from the file is printed.

Now, whenever an end-of-file is reached it will be overlooked and the loop will continue. Till the DEL is pressed.

'ctermid( )', 'ttyname( )', 'cuserid( )' And 'getlogin( )'

There are a number of functions that can tell us some essential details like how we have logged in or the pathname of the terminal. Check out the next program.

PROGRAM 341

```
#include <stdio.h>
main()
{
    printf("Pathname of the terminal %s \n",ctermid( ));
    printf("Terminal %s \n",ttyname(1));
    printf("Loged In as %s \n",cuserid( ));
    printf("Loged In as %s \n",getlogin( ));
}
```

Four function calls do the needful.

The 'memccpy( )'

This function enables a copy to be done between arrays. It copies a character string from a source array to a destination array. Copying stops when a character defined as a parameter is found in the string or when a specified number of characters are copied.

PROGRAM 342

```
#include <string.h>
#include <stdio.h>

main()
{
    char dest[50] ,dest1[50];
    char *scr = "this is the source string" ;
    char *scr1 = "this is the second source string" ;
    char *ptr ,*ptr1 ;
```

```
    ptr = memccpy(dest , scr , 'y' , strlen(scr) ) ;
    ptr1 = memccpy(dest1 , scr1 , 'e' , strlen(scr1) ) ;
    printf("dest = %s ..dest1 = %s \n",dest,dest1);
}
```

We declare two arrays and four pointers. Two of them point to a string of characters.

A call to *memccpy( )* is passed 4 parameters: the destination array *dest*, the pointer *scr*, a *y* which signifies that if a *y* is reached the copying should stop, and a parameter that specifies the number of characters to copy if the third parameter is not specified.

In this (first call to *memccpy( )*) case the entire string will be copied since a *y* is not found and the number of characters has been specified as the length of the string.

The second call to the *memccpy( )* copies only till the *e* of *second* is reached. The *printf( )* verifies both the results.

The 'memset( )'

This is a variation of the above function. It copies the occurrence of a character to an array.

PROGRAM 343

```
#include <memory.h>

main( )
{
    char ptr[17] ;
    memset(ptr,'A',strlen(ptr));
    printf(" ptr = %s \n",ptr);
}
```

memset( ) is passed three parameters: an array, the character to be copied and the number of times it is to be copied. The *printf( )* will print the As on screen.

The 'mktemp( )'

Using this system call we can generate a unique filename for a temporary file. The last 6 characters of the filename have to be defined as XXXXXX. They will be replaced by a randomly chosen letter and a 5-digit number for the current process ID.

```
PROGRAM 344
#include <stdio.h>

main()
{
    char *fname = "TXXXXXX", *ptr ;
    ptr = (char *)mktemp(fname) ;
    printf("%s \n", ptr) ;
}
```

mktemp( ) is passed a pointer that points to a filename. The return value is the new name. The output in our case is Ta00305.

The 'getpass( )'

This system call can be used to prompt for a password.

```
PROGRAM 345
main()
{
    char *password ;
    password = (char *)getpass("Input A Password\n") ;
    printf("the password is %s \n" ,password) ;
}
```

The *getpass( )* returns a pointer to a character string. When the program is run input will be accepted at the screen. However, whatever is keyed in will not be reflected on screen.

About 'setjmp( )' And 'longjmp( )'

A number of times in an application we may want to return to a program at a specific place. For example, assume that Process A called Process B. A return from Process B will take us back to the line after the call to Process B. But suppose we did not want to return to that point but some other point above? That's where the two system calls come in.

setjmp( ) and *longjmp( )* can be used to transfer control to the required point. The following program shows how.

```
PROGRAM 346
#include <setjmp.h>
jmp_buf jumper;

main( )
{
   int value ;
   value = setjmp(jumper) ;
   if (value !=0 )
   {
      printf("longjmp with value %d \n" , value) ;
   }

   printf("About to call subroutine ...\n") ;
   subroutine( ) ;
   }

   subroutine( )
   {
      longjmp(jumper, 1) ;
   }
```

When the main body of the program is executed, to the variable *value* is assigned the current position of the instruction pointer. If *setjmp( )* does not return a 0, function *subroutine( )* is called.

In it a call is made to the *longjmp( )* system call. It is passed the place we want to return to and a 1 to distinguish this return from a *setjmp( )* return. Hence control is handed to the *if* after the call to *setjmp( )* in the main program.

The *if* prints the value in variable *value* and once more calls function subfunction. And the process carries on till a DEL is pressed.

The 'ioctl( )'

ioctl( ) is used to perform device specific functions for character-special devices. There is one problem with programs using this function: they are not portable across versions of UNIX.

Do a stty at the terminal. You will see output that looks like this:

```
speed 9600 baud; -parity
erase = ^h; kill = ^u; swtch = ^`;
```

The second line shows some key combinations that have been defined.

We can also list the contents of the stty file using a program. The structure used to contain the contents is termio.h. Given below is what it looks like:

```
struct termio {
    unsigned short  c_iflag; /* input modes */
    unsigned short  c_oflag;    /* output modes */
    unsigned short  c_cflag;    /* control modes */
    unsigned short  c_lflag; /* line discipline modes */
    char c_line;        /* line discipline */
    unsigned char  c_cc[NCC];  /* control chars */
};
```

Here's a program that takes this structure, fills it and then prints those details.

PROGRAM 347

```
#include <termio.h>

main( )
{
    struct termio test ;
```

```
    ioctl(0,TCGETA,&test);
    printf("Input modes %o \n",test.c_iflag);
    printf("Output modes %o \n",test.c_oflag);
    printf("Control modes %o \n",test.c_cflag);
    printf("Line disc. modes %o \n",test.c_lflag);
    printf("Line disciplines %c \n",test.c_line);
    printf("Interrupt key ^%c \n",(test.c_cc[0] + 96));
    printf("Quit key ^%c \n",(test.c_cc[1] + 96));
    printf("Erase character ^%c \n",(test.c_cc[2] + 96 ));
    printf("Kill character ^%c \n",(test.c_cc[3] + 96));
    printf("End of file character ^%c \n",(test.c_cc[4] + 96));
    printf("Optional end of line marker ^%c\n",test.c_cc[5]+96);
}
```

The address of the defined structure is passed to the *ioctl( )* function. Besides this the other two parameters are a 0 which stands for the terminal referenced, i.e. the current terminal, and TCGETA, which is a symbolic constant signifying that the termio structure is to be filled with the information about the terminal. Now that the filling is done "its printing time folks".

The first *printf( )* prints the first member which is the input flag. This flag is for controlling terminal input. The bits of this integer can be put ON or OFF signifying the various modes the flag can depict. Below are the modes:

```
#define   IGNBRK   0000001
#define   BRKINT   0000002
#define   IGNPAR   0000004
#define   PARMRK   0000010
#define   INPCK    0000020
#define   ISTRIP   0000040
#define   INLCR    0000100
#define   IGNCR    0000200
#define   ICRNL    0000400
#define   IUCLC    0001000
#define   IXON     0002000
#define   IXANY    0004000
#define   IXOFF    0010000
```

Let's take some of the more important modes:

Three of the flags, INLCR, IGNCR and ICRNL identify a carriage return. This is the sequence sent when we press an enter to mark end of line. When we try to convert DOS files to UNIX this information is what will come in handy.

INLCR - translate a new line sequence to carriage return.

IGNCR - ignore carriage return.

ICRNL - map carriage return to newline

The three flags, IXON, IXANY and IXOFF are concerned with flow control.

IXON - Allows control over output. A start and stop. If this flag is set we can stop output with CTRL S. A CTRL Q will restart output.

IXANY - Allows any character to restart output.

IXOFF - Allows start stop control over input. For example, the system itself will generate a CTRL S character when its buffers are full.

The second *printf()* prints the output flags. This flag can have the following mode:

```
#define    OPOST    0000001
#define    OLCUC    0000002
#define    ONLCR    0000004
#define    OCRNL    0000010
#define    ONOCR    0000020
#define    ONLRET   0000040
#define    OFILL    0000100
#define    OFDEL    0000200
#define    NLDLY    0000400
#define    NL0      0
#define    NL1      0000400
#define    CRDLY    0003000
#define    CR0      0
#define    CR1      0001000
```

```
#define   CR2     0002000
#define   CR3     0003000
#define   TABDLY  0014000
#define   TAB0    0
#define   TAB1    0004000
#define   TAB2    0010000
#define   TAB3    0014000
#define   BSDLY   0020000
#define   BS0     0
#define   BS1     0020000
#define   VTDLY   0040000
#define   VT0     0
#define   VT1     0040000
#define   FFDLY   0100000
#define   FF0     0
#define   FF1     0100000
```

The most important flag here is OPOST . Its being set or not determines whether the character is outputted as is or interpreted before being outputted. It is like opening a file in DOS in binary, in which case a carriage return would not be interpreted but sent as the character it is, i.e. a 0x13.

The ONLCR maps newline to carriage-return-newline. If it is set, each line begins on the left-hand side of the screen. Contrarily, if the OCRNL is set the carriage-returns become newlines. And if ONOCR is set then no carriage-return is sent if a line of 0 length is outputted.

The next *printf( )* prints the control flag. It is used to control terminal functions. The following are the modes it can have. It defines the hardware control of the terminal. It is useful in applications like communications packages. No need to go into them, but remember one of the modes can be used to set the baud rate.

```
#define   CBAUD   0000017
#define   B0      0
#define   B50     0000001
#define   B75     0000002
#define   B110    0000003
```

```
#define   B134      0000004
#define   B150      0000005
#define   B200      0000006
#define   B300      0000007
#define   B600      0000010
#define   B1200     0000011
#define   B1800     0000012
#define   B2400     0000013
#define   B4800     0000014
#define   B9600     0000015
#define   B19200    0000016
#define   EXTA      0000016
#define   B38400    0000017
#define   EXTB      0000017
#define   CSIZE     0000060
#define   CS5       0
#define   CS6       0000020
#define   CS7       0000040
#define   CS8       0000060
#define   CSTOPB    0000100
#define   CREAD     0000200
#define   PARENB    0000400
#define   PARODD    0001000
#define   HUPCL     0002000
#define   CLOCAL    0004000
#define   RCV1EN    0010000
#define   XMT1EN    0020000
#define   LOBLK     0040000
```

After that we come to the *c_lflags* member. It is used to control terminal functions. Let's see what the various modes do before we examine some of them in detail:

```
#define   ICANON    0000002
#define   XCASE     0000004
#define   ECHO      0000010
#define   ECHOE     0000020
#define   ECHOK     0000040
#define   ECHONL    0000100
#define   NOFLSH    0000200
```

If ICANNON is set we get input in line form before it is read. And if this mode is not set the terminal is said to be in "raw" mode, usually associated with communications packages.

If the ISIG flag is set it enables us to abort a running program. If it is not set no checking for a quit keypress is done.

If the ECHO bit is ON all output will be displayed. If it is put OFF the output won't appear on screen. This last is what is used at the password entry level.

Now let's move on to the next member, *c_line*. This flag is what the previous member -- in which all the modes are assigned -- works with.

And lastly, we have the array member *c_cc*, the members of which contain the various control sequences for jobs like erasing a character, etc. You must be wondering why we add a 96 to the array members. Because the value of these members needs to be changed to a character value. A 96 when added to the value gives us the respective character.

Suppose we keyed in something wrongly at the command line, we would need to erase it. A CTRL H or the backspace would serve the purpose. We would be able to erase one character at a time backwards.

Similarly, assume that we keyed in a command which we realized was syntactically wrong. Without pressing an ENTER we could terminate this command. We just need to press CTRL U.

All these key combinations which have been defined already can be redefined at the command line as well as through a program.

Suppose we wanted to change the erase character at the command line. All we need to do is say `stty erase "^p`, where `p` is the new character we want the erase to be. You won't see the ^p coming on screen. But if you've done it correctly, rest assured it will be recognized. `cat` the `stty` file on the screen to verify the change. If you want to change it back to its original value do so using the same command. The only difference is that a CTRL H is specified.

That was how it would be done at the command line. Through a program this change would be done as shown below:

PROGRAM 348

```
#include <termio.h>

main()
{
    struct termio test ;
    ioctl(0,TCGETA,&test);
    test.c_cc[2] = 020;
    ioctl(0,TCSETA,&test);
}
```

We first get the current values and storing it to the structure. Next we assign the ascii value of CTRL P to the array member. And call *ioctl( )* again with this change. The second parameter is a command to set the erase with this new value.

The *ioctl( )* is being performed twice so that the other values do not get changed or deleted entirely.

Now run stty at the command line and you will see that the erase has a CTRL P attached to it. Further write something and then use the CTRL P to delete it character by character.

The TCSETA parameter can be used to set the other members too. The next program shows how we use it to not display the characters inputted, on the screen. Much like in the password.

PROGRAM 349

```
#include <stdio.h>
#include <termio.h>

main()
{
    char buff[15];
```

```
    struct termio test ;
    printf("Password : ");
    ioctl(0,TCGETA,&test);
    test.c_lflag &= ~ECHO;
    ioctl(0,TCSETA,&test);
    gets(buff);
    test.c_lflag |= ECHO;
    ioctl(0,TCSETA,&test);
    printf("\nThankyou\n");
}
```

After defining the array and structure we call the *ioctl( )* function to fill the structure. Next, in the member *c_flag* we AND the symbolic constant ECHO and then set it via a call to the *ioctl( )* function.

The *gets( )* now waits for us to key in something. After which the ECHO flag is once more set OFF. The *ioctl( )* now resets the structure and the Thankyou is displayed on screen.

To end this rather contorted topic let's reassign the program abort key DEL, to a CTRL C, like in DOS.

PROGRAM 350

```
#include <termio.h>

main( )
{
    struct termio test ;
    ioctl(0,TCGETA,&test);
    test.c_cc[0] = 03;
    ioctl(0,TCSETA,&test);
}
```

As usual, we first get the values into the structure *test*. After which we assign the octal value of 3 to the first member of the array *c_cc*. This represents a CTRL Y. And once more the *ioctl( )* is being called to set this new value.

Hey, Presto! a program is now terminated only if the CTRL Y keys combo is pressed.

Conclusion

While we have not examined any serious applications in this chapter, what we have tried to do is list and demonstrate some of the more used functions in UNIX.

Stock these functions in your attic and use them on a rainy day.

On Curses

Hi! Welcome to curses. CURSES?? Yes, curses. No, it's not a misprint. And no, it's not what you're thinking of either! We all know what curses in everyday lingo means and oftentimes even employ it as a rather rude means of releasing pent up emotions. Picture the scene. You've been sitting at the computer a good one hour or more and your programs are turning out great and in all the excitement, you've forgotten to save them and then suddenly the screen goes blank.....there's a cut in the current! A split second later you realize everything is lost and all hell breaks loose. You curse nobody in particular and everybody at the State Electricity Board, you curse yourself for not pressing one key; just one key and you forgot!! When you gasp for breath, you realize the fan is still working. Checking all the cables and plugs you suddenly espy the culprit. Your dog Fido is sitting there all dewy eyed, wagging his tail with such enthusiasm he has managed to unplug the wires. What do you do? Pat him lovingly and forgive him immediately or ......@#$%^&*<#$$^%$%#!!!!! Ooooops! That really hurt my ears but, point proven. Curses is great for communicating.

Yes, that's right! You will be learning how to communicate with your terminal through curses. Just one important note - in the world of C, curses has an absolutely different connotation from the one we all know so well. curses is simply the name of a library of routines. These routines are used to write screen management programs. The name curses stems from the cursor optimization that these routines provide.

About Curses

Screen management means handling input and output like, movement of the cursor, printing of display, division of the screen into windows, or changing color definitions. Cursor optimization handles screen updation in a manner applicable for the terminal on which a curses program is run. In other words, curses library has the facility to update many different terminal types. Hopefully, it can update your terminal too!

The curses routines are usually located in /usr/lib/libcurses.a . To compile a program using these routines you must use the cc command to summon the C compiler. To instruct the link library to search and load them, the -l option is used with the cc command. The usual procedure for compiling a program in curses is :

```
cc <file.c> -lcurses [-o file.out]
```

where file.c is the source program and file.out is the executable object module. If -o option is denied, then the executable object module is a.out.

All programs must include the file curses.h. This is done with the following statement :

```
#include <curses.h>
```

The statement *#include* recalls the header file curses from the directory /usr/include. (All files with extension h are by default stored in this directory). This header file contains window structures, definitions, macros, function definitions and prototypes, keyboard definitions, screen attributes........ The list is long and it certainly will not do to have you dozing off at the introductory page so, to put it in a nutshell, this file contains all explanations of the functions needed in curses application. This file is as important in a curses application as books are in a library! However, the inclusion of this file name in a program does not indicate that it is a function itself. It is only a pre-compiler directive used at the time of compilation.

Switching To ETI

The Unix terminal by default, understands only one line at a time. It is therefore, necessary to change the default mode to an 'in curses mode', where you are allowed control of the whole screen. Let's call this the Extended Terminal Interface or simply, the ETI mode. Switching to the ETI mode is as easy as typing the function :

initscr( )

Now, before you do just that, use proper language for effective results! Your program should therefore read :

PROGRAM 351

```
#include <curses.h>

main()
{
   initscr();
}
```

To describe this function more precisely, curses.h defines several variables, structures and function prototypes. Two of these variables are *LINES* and *COLS*. When the routine *initscr( )* is called, it assigns the vertical and horizontal dimensions of your monitor to the two variables. The value of *LINES* would therefore be the number of rows and the value of *COLS* the number of columns. This routine is called only once and it is done at the beginning of the program. Note that the values of *LINES* and *COLS* are not accessible at this stage as the mode to retrieve it will be discussed much later.

Making the switch to the ETI mode has been easy. What if you want to go back to the default mode? Let's talk about that later and try typing something whilst in this mode. Try typing in your name. What do you see on the screen? Nothing? Never mind, try again. What, nothing? Are you sure you're using the keyboard correctly? Try a last time. ....nothing?! Before you panic and resign yourself to forever being hung in the ETI mode, here's some help! You can either :

- logout and relogin

or

- simply use this function in your program :

endwin()

This function helps you make your exit from the ETI mode into the default mode. The previous routine simply switched the modes one way. A program using *endwin()* like the following one will make the mode-switch from the default mode to the ETI mode and back again to the default mode. The variables *LINES* and *COLS* will then hold no values.

PROGRAM 352

```
#include <curses.h>

main()
{
   initscr();
   endwin();
}
```

Enter, A Character

Now that you are more comfortable with switching modes whenever you need to, lets try printing something in the ETI mode calling the right function :

addch();

addch( ) simply lets you write one character at a time. The character you want printed should be within single quotes and can be any ASCII printable character between value 32 and 126. Let's print the letter *u* as an example. The function is thus written :

addch('u');

and the program using this routine :

PROGRAM 353

```
#include <curses.h>
```

```
main( )
{
    initscr( );
    addch('u');
    endwin( );
}
```

Run the program to check this function. What do you see? Nothing, ...again?! It's not a trick, believe me. No, don't logout ! Relax, while I explain something about 'screens'.

Curses provides a default screen called the Standard Screen or *stdscr*. *stdscr* exists within the memory. In other words it is a virtual screen and is of the same size as the terminal screen. For easier reference, let's call the terminal screen the 'physical' screen. *addch( )* only writes a character on to the *stdscr*. So, if you remember that all printing is first done on the *stdscr* and then on the physical screen, you will understand that though it wasn't apparent some work was done when the previous program was run. This brings us to the function :

refresh( )

This is the function that will actually plot characters and strings on the physical screen. So, what it does is, it updates your physical screen and therefore recurs often in a program.

Here is an example of how the two functions, *addch( )* and *refresh( )*, are used :

PROGRAM 354

```
#include <curses.h>

main( )
{
    initscr( );
    addch('u');
    refresh( );
    endwin( );
}
```

If you have 'run' the previous program, you are probably still puzzled. If you haven't, 'run' it. Right. Explanation time. Always keep in mind that the computer executes one function immediately after the other till the program comes to an end. It is a fast worker and there are no time lapses between these executions.

You can well imagine then what happened when the previous program was 'run'. As soon as the character *u* was plotted, processing continued. *endwin( )* switched the present mode back to the default one and the cursor was positioned on the first column of the last line. All you saw was the character *u*. What you need to do here is to try and stall the processing long enough for you to see the display. The for statement can thus, be called for this purpose. This statement delays the processing of the routine after it, allowing the function before it to be interpreted for a definite period of time.

```
int i;
for (i=0;i<1000;i++);
```

In the for statement, the value of *I* which is initialized at 0, is constantly checked and then incremented by 1 if it meets with the equation *I<1000*. After each increment, the statement is re-read till the value of *I=1000* at which stage the condition *I<1000* is 'not true'. It is only then, that the computer processes the next function.

The for statement therefore, acts as a delay loop while the character *u* is being displayed on the screen. Note that while the value of *I* is being constantly incremented till it is not less than *1000*, the program is stalled at *refresh( )*. Run the following program as a check :

PROGRAM 355

```
#include <curses.h>

main( )
{
  int i;
```

```
    initscr( );
    addch('u');
    refresh( );
    for(i=0;i<1000;i++);
    endwin( );
}
```

So, you finally see something on the screen! For a more precise, neat program, there is a function that can replace *addch( )* and *refresh( )*, doing the work of both :

echochar( )

echochar( ) writes a single character to the virtual screen as well as to the physical one. The program below will have the same output as the previous one.

PROGRAM 356

```
#include <curses.h>

main( )
{
    int i;
    initscr( );
    echochar('u');
    for (i=0;i<1000;i++);
        endwin( );
}
```

Run the following program to confirm the action of *echochar( )*. You will find that this function also updates the monitor with all other information stored on *stdscr*. It is definitely more sensible to use *refresh( )* but, the more you know about all the curses routines, the better!

PROGRAM 357

```
#include <curses.h>

main( )
{
    int i;
```

```
    initscr( );
    addch('i');
    echochar('u');
    for (i=0;i<1000;i++);
        endwin( );
}
```

In case you feel that these functions are really no big deal, hold on! There is more to it than just printing single characters. Let's take it one step at a time, starting with printing strings.

From Characters To Strings

```
char * mess = "Hello World";
```

In this statement, the variable *mess* is a pointer to a char. *mess* is pointing to the string value hello world. To print this message, a function similar to the *addch( )* is used :

addstr( )

This function, as with the *addch( )*, writes strings (in this case Hello World), on the logical screen. The *refresh( )* function updates the monitor with the information from the virtual screen. Here's an example of a program using these two functions :

PROGRAM 358

```
#include <curses.h>

main( )
{
    int i;
    char *mess="Hello World";
    initscr( );
    addstr(mess);
    refresh( );
    for(i=0;i<1000;i++);
        endwin( );
}
```

In the previous programs, the for statement was used as a delay loop. A definite count had to be expressed and you had no control over decreasing or increasing this count once the program was 'run'. The only way you could control the count would be to keep changing the equation or the increment step in the statement after each 'run'. A tedious process indeed!

getch( )

This routine also stalls program processing but, waits for a keystroke from you after which, processing resumes. It therefore gives you a choice in determining the length of time that your message is displayed for. Check out with this program :

PROGRAM 359

```
#include <curses.h>

main( )
{
    initscr( );
    addstr("Hello World");
    refresh( );
    getch( );
    endwin( );
}
```

Remember that you are working with curses routines and bugs should be aplenty! *getch( )* demonstrates by calling *refresh( )* when it has no business to. However, this happens on some terminals only.

From determining time lapses between the execution of functions, we go on to determining the position of your message display on the screen. Do you feel more in control now? Good. That's how you should feel! Previously, all characters and messages were being plotted in the last position of the cursor. With the following two functions, you can plot your message anywhere on the screen. Keeping in mind, of course, the dimension of your monitor!

clear( )

This function clears the logical screen. *refresh( )* should be called for clearing your monitor or the physical screen.

move( )

This function simply means, position cursor at specified row and specified column. Run this program to plot Hello World at row 5, column 35 :

```
PROGRAM 360
#include <curses.h>

main( )
{
   initscr( );
   clear( );
   move(5,35);
   addstr("Hello World");
   refresh( );
   getch( );
   endwin( );
}
```

As you are aware, this method *(char *mess)* is limited in that only a definite message can be assigned and printed per program. What if you want to use the same program for display printing various messages?

char buff(31)

This statement creates an array of 31 bytes. In the program the computer waits for you to input a message of your choice. Your message will be then accepted in *buff* and hence note that your message in this case should be 30 bytes long, allowing for the necessary null in an array.

flushinp( )

As the name hints at, this function 'flushes' all unwanted characters existing in the keyboard buffer! In simpler terms, it clears the keyboard buffer.

getstr( )

With a call to this function, your response from the keyboard is accepted and assigned in the array when you press the enter key. To go over these functions briefly,

- an array is created

- the keyboard buffer is cleared

- your response from the keyboard is accepted

PROGRAM 361

```
#include <curses.h>

main( )
{
   char buff [31];
   initscr( );
   flushinp( );
   refresh( );
   getstr(buff);
   endwin( );
}
```

Using the functions already discussed, you can display a string of a defined length at a particular position on the monitor. Example :

PROGRAM 362

```
#include <curses.h>

main( )
{
   char buff [31];
   initscr( );
   flushinp( );
```

```
    addstr("Enter Your String : ");
    refresh( );
    getstr(buff);
    clear( );
    move(5,30);
    addstr(buff);
    refresh( );
    getch( );
    endwin( );
}
```

In this program

- an array of 31 bytes is created

- the keyboard buffer is cleared

- a message is displayed

- your input is accepted

- the cursor is positioned at row 5, column 30

- your response is displayed

- the program is stalled till you press a key and then finally terminated.

Manipulate the routines introduced and get creative!

You've come quite a way from switching modes to controlling cursor positions. Here's a function that goes further and returns to you the current position of the cursor i.e. its position after your message has been displayed.

getyx(stdscr,y,x)

The row and column positions of the cursor (in *stdscr*) is assigned to variables *y* and *x* respectively.

sprintf( )

The function *sprintf( )* takes a minimum of two parameters

- an array

- a string

Its job is to build up the first parameter by assigning to it the format string defined as the second parameter. The second parameter could accept variable values by indicating the format specifiers for the rest of the parameters. Therefore, the number of parameters is determined by the number of format specifiers in the second parameter.

For example if you want a formatted message along with the position of the cursor, this function could be used as in this program :

PROGRAM 363

```
#include <curses.h>

main( )
{
   char buff [41];
   int x,y;
   initscr( );
   move(5,28);
   addstr("Hello World");
   refresh( );
   getyx(stdscr,y,x);
   sprintf(buff,"The String Ends at ROW %d & COL %d",y,x);
   move(22,20);
   addstr(buff);
   refresh( );
   getch( );
   endwin( );
}
```

The display will be the formatted message, giving you the row and column coordinates at which the string ends. As seen, *sprintf( )* here has 4 parameters -

- an array

- a string

- 2 variables whose values are assigned to *%d*

Upto now, all the functions that we have discussed carried out one task only. O.K., you might point out that *echochar( )* functions both as *addch( )* and *refresh( )* but, that is irrelevant at this stage when you have left the world of single characters far behind. We're now talking compound functions! One of such, is:

mvprintw( )

As you might guess, *mvprintw( )* is a combination of *move( )* and a write function. This routine performs two things :

- positioning the cursor at a particular row and column (on the *stdscr*) as called by you

- writing a formatted message.

All printing by this function is done only on the logical screen and your program will therefore need *refresh( )*.

PROGRAM 364

```
#include <curses.h>

main( )
{
    char buff [31];
    initscr( );
    mvprintw(5,20,"Enter Your String : ");
    refresh( );
    getstr(buff);
    clear( );
    mvprintw(10,20,"The String Entered Was : %s",buff);
    refresh( );
    getch( );
    endwin( );
}
```

If you enjoy a puzzle now and then, 'run' this program!

PROGRAM 365

```
#include <curses.h>

main( )
{
   char buff [31];
   initscr( );
   mvprintw(5,15,"Enter Your String Here : ");
   refresh( );
   noecho( );
   getstr(buff);
   endwin( );
}
```

When you ran this program you must have wondered what happened to your input. It wasn't displayed. However, no fears! It's simply the action of :

noecho( )

Your input was definitely written and retained in the variable. The function of this routine is simply not to *echo* or move the cursor position at the time of accepting an input. If you are wondering where this function could come into use, dry- run the next program carefully.

PROGRAM 366

```
#include <curses.h>

main( )
{
   char buff [21];
   initscr( );
   noecho( );
   mvprintw(5,23,"Enter Your Password : ");
   refresh( );
   getstr(buff);
   clear( );
   if (! (strcmp (buff,"Great007")))
```

```
        mvprintw (22,30,"Correct Password");
    else
        mvprintw (22,30,"Incorrect Password");
    refresh( );
    getch( );
    endwin( );
}
```

This program allows you to enter a secret password which if correct returns a positive message else a definitely negative one. The function *noecho( )* thus blanks out all inputs giving you privacy while typing in responses. All responses are checked for true or false by the *If..else* statement. Here is a line by line explanation of this program :

- an array of 21 bytes is created

- the current default mode is switched to the ETI mode

- the *noecho( )* function is called

- the cursor is positioned

- a formatted message is displayed

- your input is accepted and assigned to buff

- your response is checked

Let's take a break at this point and view the *If..else..*

```
If(!(strcmp(buff,"Great007")))
```

In this part of the statement, there is a comparison between two strings as defined with the *strcmp( )*. The two strings are :

- *buff*, which holds your input

- Great007

It is an important point to note that *strcmp( )* is a normal 'C' function which deals with strings (collection of characters). It has no relation to curses but, by using it in a combination we are able to get effective use of it in our programs.

The *!* here, is a 'not' operator. The return value from *strcmp( )* is the number of mismatched bytes and hence, when both strings are equal, the return value from the *strcmp( )* function is a 0, which as you know means 'false'. This operator negates the result and makes the condition 'not false' or 'true'. The same applies when the strings are not equal. The return value in this case is 1 which means 'true'. The condition is made 'not true' or 'false' by *!*.

When the condition is proved 'true', the routine following immediately is executed. If proved otherwise, the function following the else statement is executed as in the second part :

```
   mvprintw(22,30,"ENTER");
else
   mvprintw(22,30,"GET LOST");
```

Resuming the explanation :

- the appropriate formatted message is displayed

- the program is stalled till a key press

- the program is terminated

Moving on to another compound function, here is :

mvscanw( )

This is a combination of *move( )* and *scanw( )* which is an improvisation of *scanf( )*. This routine takes on a minimum of 4 parameters -

- the row

- the column

- the format specifiers

- the address of the variable whose value is to be accepted

This routine sets the cursor at a specified row and column (on the *stdscr*) and waits for you to key in the value asked for which is then assigned to the array *buff* (4th parameter).

PROGRAM 367

```
#include <curses.h>

main( )
{
   char buff [21];
   initscr( );
   mvprintw(5,25,"Enter String Here : ");
   refresh( );
   mvscanw(7,25,"%s",buff);
   endwin( );
}
```

The same routine is again applied in the following, more elaborate program, along with the other functions discussed earlier.

PROGRAM 368

```
#include <curses.h>

main( )
{
   char buff[21];
   int x,y;
   initscr( );
   mvprintw(5,20,"Enter Row  : ");
   mvprintw(6,20,"Enter Column : ");
   mvprintw(7,20,"Enter String : ");
   refresh( );
   mvscanw (5,35,"%d",&y);
   mvscanw (6,35,"%d",&x);
   mvscanw (7,35,"%s",buff);
   clear( );
   mvprintw(y,x,buff);
```

```
    refresh( );
    getch( );
    endwin( );
}
```

mvscanw( ) called the first and second time helps you to positions the cursor at the specified rows and columns and with the calls for the third and last time it accepts the string which is stored in the array buff and later displayed at the specified co-ordinates.

The functions are of course not read simultaneously, so don't key in the values together!.

You must have noted the special character *&* in the first two calls to *mvscanw( )*. This is used to retrieve the address of the variable after it. This character is absent in the third call to *mvscanw( )* as the name of the array gives its address.

BEEP...'beep( )'

All this while you have been running programs and simply reading the results on the screen. There has been no verbal reply from the computer. So, communication has been more or less 'silent'. Let's of course, not ignore the possibility of some expletives exhaled till so far into programming! The terminal, does not possess colorful expressions but can whistle, beep and sound its chimes. These may usually be used to get the user's attention. An example of such 'sound-designed' routines is :

beep( )

PROGRAM 369

```
#include <curses.h>

main( )
{
    initscr( );
    beep( );
    endwin( );
```

```
}
```

The call to *beep( )* in this program will sound a beep. If the terminal cannot beep for some reason or the other, it will flash the screen. Note that in this case the call to *beep( )* still holds for the screen flash.

Earlier, we dealt with the function *clear( )* which merely blanked the whole screen. We will now deal with two routines which blank out specified portions of the screen. Let's start with clearing to the End of Lines or *eol* in short.

clrtoeol( )

This routine erases the remainder of a line. Its action begins at the current cursor position inclusive. Except for *clrtoeol( )*, the other routines have been dealt with earlier. Dry-run this program (without having to read up on the routines again) to study the procedure and also check your retentiveness!

PROGRAM 370

```
#include <curses.h>

main( )
{
   int i;
   initscr( );
   for(i=2000;i--;addch('a'));
   move(22,10);
   addstr(" Press any key to Clear Right Half of The First 10 Lines....");
   refresh( );
   getch( );
   for (i=0;i<10;i++)
   {
      move(i,40);
      clrtoeol( );
   }
   refresh( );
   getch( );
   endwin( );
}
```

The output from this program is

- a screen-full of *a*

- a message at row 22, column 10

- subsequent deletion of last 40 characters on the first 10 lines.

The second routine for blanking is :

clrtobot( )

This function changes the remainder of the screen to blanks. Just as with *clrtoeol( )*, this routine too, clears from the current position of the cursor inclusive. The same procedure applies in this program, as in the preceding one. Run this program for some amusement !

PROGRAM 371

```
#include <curses.h>

main( )
{
   int i;
   initscr( );
   for (i=2000;i--;addch('a'));
   move(10,25);
   addstr(" Press any key to Clear Below ... ");
   move(11,0);
   refresh( );
   getch( );
   clrtobot( );
   refresh( );
   getch( );
   endwin( );
}
```

Do Not Disturb!

If you have been running your programs with no interruptions whatsoever, beware! There are several keys that, when punched, could really mess up your mood. These keys literally 'kill' your program no matter what routine is being processed. To avoid such drastic interruptions you could use :

cbreak( )

The terminal interprets all characters typed in by you but, the inclusion of this routine in the program will invalidate the action of the erase, kill line and CTRL D characters.

PROGRAM 372

```
#include <curses.h>

main( )
{
   initscr( );
   cbreak( );

   /*do something */

   nocbreak( );
   endwin( );
}
```

In the above program you will notice that there is a *nocbreak( )* included. This routine 'turns off' *cbreak( )*. It allows normal interpretations of characters and permits the program to interpret the 'killer' characters thus allowing program termination or interruption.

If you haven't already experienced an interruption in program processing, run this program. Press CTRL D or the Del key and watch your program get killed!

PROGRAM 373

```
#include <curses.h>

main( )
{
   char *mess=" I am Running in a never Ending Loop ";
   char *mess1=" Press ^d or Del key to kill me... ";
```

```
    initscr( );
    while(1)
    {
        printw("%s\n",mess);
        printw("%s\n",mess1);
        refresh( );
        getch( );
    }
    endwin( );
}
```

Not a very pleasant thing to experience. Run this program and type in a tame character like *K*. A formatted message will tell you that the character typed in was *K*. This is done by

- defining a *chtype* variable *ch*

- assigning to it the character input by you

- calling the *printw( )*.

What is *chtype*?? When you define *ch* as *chtype*, you are defining it as a *char* with additional attributes. Thus, *chtype* has two parts to it. One has information on the character and the other sets attributes to the character. Attributes will be discussed in detail at a later stage.

PROGRAM 374

```
#include <curses.h>

main( )
{
    chtype ch;
    initscr( );
    cbreak( );
    mvprintw(5,25," Enter a Character : ");
    refresh( );
    ch=getch( );
    move(22,25);
    printw("The Character Entered Was %c\n",ch);
    refresh( );
    getch( );
```

```
    endwin( );
}
```

Here is an interesting program. All the routines applied have been dealt with but, notice how they have been combined.

PROGRAM 375

```
#include <curses.h>

main( )
{
    chtype ch;
    initscr( );
    noecho( );
    cbreak( );
    mvprintw (3,30,"Enter a Character :");
    mvprintw (22,30,"Last Character Was : ");
    move(3,52);
    refresh( );
    while(1)
    {
        ch=getch( );
        if(ch==27)
            break;
        else
        {
            move(22,50);
            echochar(ch);
            move(3,52);
        }
    }
    endwin( );
}
```

If you are unaware of just which key is represented by the code 27, you are in a lot of trouble! There is a loop called, which will not allow *endwin( )* to be read unless a condition is met. *noecho( )* has also been called concealing the character typed in. Try and discover the magic key!

P.S. For all you people with lazy dispositions, it was the *Esc* key!

There probably have been times when you wanted to be in total control of situations, barking out orders to underlings, expressing your opinions to all and sundry and, in short, being THE BOSS! As such, you would be controlling and manipulating circumstances to get things done your way, all the time. Wow! I can almost see your eyes shining at the prospect of being in such a position. Coming down to earth and viewing the present situation, maybe you could exercise some control over.......this terminal? Right, let's start with the blinking dummy of a cursor. This should be some fun!

Fooling Around With The Cursor

Using the curses routines, you can write a free format editor program which will allow you to type in text as well as maneuver the cursor up, down, left and right anytime you choose to do so. That's some start. If you look closely at the following program you will notice that most of the routines are familiar.

PROGRAM 376

```
/* free format editor */

#include <curses.h>

main( )
{
   chtype ch;
   int y,x;
   y=x=0;
   initscr( );
   noecho( );
   cbreak( );
   move(y,x);
   refresh( );
   while(1)
   {
      ch=getch( );
      switch(ch)
      {
         case 'U' : y--; break; /* Up    */
         case 'D' : y++; break; /* Down  */
```

```
                case 'L' : x--; break; /* Left      */
                case 'R' : x++; break; /* Right     */
                case 8 : x--; break; /* Back Space */
                case 10 : y++; break; /* Enter Key */
                case 27 : out( );  /* Escape Key */
                default :   /* All Other Keys */
                addch(ch);
                refresh( );
                x++;
            }
            if (y<0) { beep( ); y= 0; }
            if (y>23) { beep( ); y=23; }
            if (x<0) { beep( ); x= 0; }
            if (x>79) { beep( ); x=79; }
            move(y,x);
            refresh( );
        }
    }

out( )
{
    endwin( );
    exit(0);
}
```

Let us consider what this program achieves by going through it routine by routine.

- *chtype* variable *ch* defined

- *y,x* defined and initialized at 0

- call to *initscr( )*

- call to *noecho( )*

- call to *cbreak( )*

- cursor positioned at row *y*, column *x*

- call to *refresh( )*

- call to *while*

Let's pause here to discuss this routine. *while......break* forms a loop within which certain operations are carried out. In this program it is used whilst your input, which is assigned to *ch* as in :

ch=getch( )

is being checked against *U, D, L, R, 8, 10, 27* as in :-

```
switch(ch)
{
    case 'U' : y--; break;
    case 'D' : y++; break;
    case 'L' : x--; break;
    case 'R' : x++; break;
    case 8 : x--; break;
    case 10 : y++; break;
    case 27 : out( );
    default :
    addch(ch);
    refresh( );
    x++;
}
```

These statements simply mean :

- if ch = 'U' , decrement *y* by 1

- if ch = 'D' , increment *y* by 1

- if ch = 'L' , decrement *x* by 1

- if ch = 'R' , increment *x* by 1

- if ch = 8 , decrement *x* by 1

- if ch = 10 , increment *y* by 1

- if ch = 27 then reach out to *endwin( )* with the help of *out( )*

- if any other character then display the character

After these comparisons, the program also provides a check for the values of *y* and *x*. As you know, the screen has a definite dimension available to you. For example, if the value of say, *y* is greater than 23, the cursor will not show on the screen at all because there are only 23 rows available to you. The same condition holds for the value of *x* which cannot exceed 79 for the similar reason that there are only 79 columns available to you. Thus, the statements :

```
if (y<0) { beep( ); y=0; }
if (y>23) { beep( ); y=23; }
if (x<0) { beep( ); x=0; }
if (x>79) { beep( ); x=79; }
move (y,x);
refresh( );
```

After the values of *y* and *x* are checked / modified then *move( )* and *refresh( )* are called.

out( ) here is another user defined function which indicates a direction that the program should take. In this case, the program is directed to *endwin( )* whereby *exit( )* terminates the program.

Write out variations of the above program to really get the hang of moving the cursor here, there and everywhere, always keeping in mind the number of rows and columns available to you. However, making the cursor disappear occasionally should make your programs interesting!

Let's go one more step further and try something new. Previously, all print displays were 'dead', in the sense that the messages were displayed in a boring manner. Let's try putting some life into the text we print by adding attributes to them and thereby using *chtype* variable to its extent.

Cosmetic Changes

An attribute is any feature whose value can be set or read by an appropriate function. The first of such functions is :

A_BLINK

As is obvious, this routine turns on blinking texts. A call to this routine will cause all following texts that you type in to assume the blink attribute. This program uses this function to print a blinking letter at row 10, column 10 with a message preceding it. Note that the symbol / is used here. / stands for bit-wise or. It is this symbol that turns on the attribute to the character. A_BLINK on its own cannot set the attribute to the character.

```
#include <curses.h>

main( )
{
   initscr( );
   move (5,10);
   addstr("This is BLINK -> ");
   addch('H' | A_BLINK);
   refresh( );
   getch( );
   endwin( );
}
```

Setting attributes is as easy as demonstrated above and needs no detailed explanation. The following is a list of the rest of the attributes and what they mean :

A_BOLD - extra bright or bold

A_DIM - half bright

A_REVERSE - reverse video

A_UNDERLINE - underlining

A_STANDOUT - highlighting

It is important to note here that your terminal should support the attribute specified else the specified description holds no value.

This program demonstrates the use of all the **attributes** listed, as well as A_BLINK.

PROGRAM 377

```
#include <curses.h>

main()
{
    int i;
    chtype ch;
    i=1;
    ch='A';

    initscr();

    move(i+=2,20);
    addstr("This is a Blink   :-> ");
    addch(ch | A_BLINK);

    move(i+=2,20);
    addstr("This is a Bold    :-> ");
    addch(ch | A_BOLD);

    move(i+=2,20);
    addstr("This is a Dim     :-> ");
    addch(ch | A_DIM);

    move(i+=2,20);
    addstr("This is a Reverse  :-> ");
    addch (ch | A_REVERSE);

    move(i+=2,20);
    addstr("This is a Underline :-> ");
    addch (ch | A_UNDERLINE);

    move(i+=2,20);
    addstr("This is a Standout :-> ");
    addch (ch | A_STANDOUT);
    refresh();
```

```
    getch( );
    endwin( );
}
```

Attributes can be turned on singly or in combination. For example you may want your text in bold and underlined. There are several functions for manipulating attributes. Given is a list of these functions and what they mean :

attrset( ) - turns off previously defined attribute and sets requested one

attrset( ) - turns off all attributes

attron( ) - adds attributes to the existing ones in a string

attroff( ) - turns off the requested attribute

standend( ) - switches off all attributes

The following program uses these functions at various stages to manipulate attributes.

PROGRAM 378

```
#include <curses.h>

main( )
{
    int i;
    i=1;

    initscr( );

    move(i+=2,10);
    attrset(A_BLINK);
    addstr("This is Blink ");

    attron(A_BOLD);
    move(i+=2,10);
    addstr("This is Bold ");
```

```
    attroff(A_BOLD);
    attron(A_DIM);
    move(i+=2,10);
    addstr("This is Dim");

    standend( );

    attrset(A_BLINK | A_REVERSE | A_UNDERLINE);
    move(i+=2,10);
    addstr("This is Blink Reverse Underline ");

    attrset(0);
    move(i+=2,10);
    addstr("This is Normal : All Attributes Off ");
    refresh( );
    getch( );
    endwin( );
}
```

Now that you have gained control over the movements of the cursor as well as over text, you can now attempt to take over total management of this terminal!

It has been mentioned and demonstrated earlier, that your terminal will not be updated till *refresh( )* is called. There is an internal representation of the screen called *stdscr* which is of the window type, where output is first written. A call to *refresh( )* sends all information from this window to the screen.

Enter, The Window

Here is an important bit of information. All the routines that you have dealt with earlier were actually macros. Surprised?? But, all too true. They were merely translated into functions which acted on the default window *stdscr*. However, you are not restricted to merely using this window as you can create a number of your own.

You can create windows on the physical screen and use them instead of the default screen. You can, in a way, say that a window is that part of the screen considered to be active at a time and hence cannot be greater than the *stdscr*.

Windows are useful in maintaining several different screen images. For example, you could use one window to control input and output and one to print error messages. This will distinguish one print display from the other and make programming 'mess free'. There are several routines that you can use to manipulate and create windows. If for example, if you want to create a window called *win*, you must first declare this window in the following code :

```
WINDOW * win
```

Here, **win* is a pointer to the structure WINDOW which is defined in the header file, and *win* is the name of the window. After declaring a new window, you must give specifications as to its size. For this, use the routine :

newwin( )

As is in the sample program below, the parameters specified with *newwin( )* are assigned to the name of the new window. The parameters are :

- number of rows
- number of columns
- beginning of row
- beginning of column

PROGRAM 379

```
#include <curses.h>

main( )
{
    WINDOW *win;
    initscr( );
    win=newwin(5,15, 8,30);
```

```
    wrefresh(win);
    wgetch(win);
    endwin( );
}
```

Thus, the new window will be 5 rows long, 15 columns wide, will begin at the 8th row and 30th column.

All routines used for input to and output from this new window remains the same except that *w* precedes each routine and includes the window name as the first parameter. For example, in this program, the routines *addstr( )*, *getch( )* and *refresh( )* are called as *waddstr( )*, *wgetch( )* and *wrefresh( )* . *waddstr( )* has *win* as the first parameter. The name of the window must also be defined in *wrefresh( )*.

PROGRAM 380

```
#include <curses.h>

main( )
{
    WINDOW *win;
    initscr( );
    win=newwin(5,15, 8,30);
    waddstr(win,"Hello World");
    wrefresh(win);
    wgetch(win);
    endwin( );
}
```

Not satisfied with creating one window? Fortunately, you can declare more than one window at a time. Let's attempt two windows now. The same routines and rules apply. Make sure you declare both windows at the beginning of your program.

PROGRAM 381

```
#include <curses.h>

main( )
{
    WINDOW *w1, *w2;
```

```
    initscr( );
    w1=newwin( 5,20, 1,10);
    w2=newwin(10,40, 3,25);
    waddstr(w1,"Your Window");
    waddstr(w2,"My Window");
    wrefresh(w1);
    wrefresh(w2);
    wgetch(w2);
    endwin( );
}
```

The above program will display Your Window first and then My Window. This is because of the two separate calls to *wrefresh( )*. You cannot define more than one window name with *wrefresh( )*. In other words, only one *wrefresh( )* can be called for one window display.

However, there is an alternate routine for *wrefresh( )* which allows you two window displays at the same time. Run this program to verify.

PROGRAM 382

```
#include <curses.h>

main( )
{
    WINDOW *w1, *w2;
    initscr( );
    w1=newwin( 5,20, 1,10);
    w2=newwin(10,40, 3,25);
    waddstr(w1,"His");
    wnoutrefresh(w1);
    waddstr(w2,"Hers");
    wnoutrefresh(w2);
    sleep(10);
    doupdate( );
    wgetch(w2);
    endwin( );
}
```

The routine,

wnoutrefresh( )

simply means - don't refresh. Note that the name of the window has to be indicated. This routine keeps track of the information to be updated.

The output is displayed simultaneously on both windows with a call to :

doupdate( )

This function simply transfers all information from the logical screen (retained for display on the monitor by *wnoutrefresh( )*), to the specified window.

sleep( ) has been included in the program as a stall to prove that updation of the monitor is done with the call to *doupdate( )*. It is not a curses function; it is from the UNIX library. You could name it as a system call. Its job is to sleep for the number of seconds specified as its parameter.

The windows that you have created so far have not been apparent till a print display has indicated that they are there. You can identify a window on the screen by putting a border around it. This framing can be done with the routine :

box( )

You can choose any character to frame the window by just enclosing the character within single quotes and defining it with *box( )*. You must specify three parameters :

- the name of the window

- the vertical border

- the horizontal border

PROGRAM 383

```
#include <curses.h>
```

```
main( )
{
    WINDOW *win;
    initscr( );
    win=newwin(5,15, 8,30);
    box(win,' | ','-');
    wrefresh(win);
    wgetch(win);
    endwin( );
}
```

The following sample program uses the same routines to :

- project two windows

- frame them simultaneously

- display messages on them simultaneously

PROGRAM 384

```
#include <curses.h>

main( )
{
    WINDOW *w1, *w2;
    initscr( );

    w1=newwin( 5,20, 1,10);
    w2=newwin(10,40, 3,25);

    box(w1,' | ','-');
    box(w2,' | ','-');

    waddstr(w1,"WINDOW-1");
    waddstr(w2,"WINDOW-2");

    wnoutrefresh(w1);
    wnoutrefresh(w2);

    doupdate( );
    wgetch(w2);
```

```
    endwin();
}
```

Now that you know the basic routines for printing a character right upto creating a window, most of the following programs are examples of manipulating the same routines to get different outputs. In short, you will be 'playing around' with the functions. There will be no detailed explanation on the program except when necessary. So, off we start with exercises!

Windows Within Windows Within Windows Within...

The first is creating windows with reference to another window. This is done using the routine :

subwin()

This routine has the same characteristics as *newwin( )* but can only be used in context with another window. You can have a number of subwindows for a particular window. The following are its parameters.

- the referenced window.

- the no of rows required

- the no of cols required

- the starting row number(always with reference to the stdscr or the actual screen)

- the starting col number(same as above).

As an example, the following program uses this function to create a window with reference to *stdscr*. The same syntaxes and rules apply.

PROGRAM 385

```
#include <curses.h>

main()
{
   WINDOW *win;
   initscr();
   win=subwin(stdscr, 5,20, 1,10);
   box(win,'|','-');
   wrefresh(win);
   wgetch(win);
   endwin();
}
```

You can create multiple subwindows for a particular window for example :

PROGRAM 386

```
#include <curses.h>

main()
{
   WINDOW *win, *w1, *w2;
   initscr();
   win=newwin(15,40, 3,20);
   w1=subwin(win, 5,10, 4,21);
   w2=subwin(win, 5,10, 4,32);
   box(win,'|','-');
   box(w1,'|','-');
   box(w2,'|','-');
   wrefresh(win);
   wrefresh(w1);
   wrefresh(w2);
   wgetch(w2);
   endwin();
}
```

Remember that as with *addstr( )* and *refresh( )*, the other routines like *mvaddstr( )* and *mvaddch( )* also have *w* in them. This program is an example of simply using the same routines to manipulate output on the screen.

PROGRAM 387

```
#include <curses.h>

main( )
{
    WINDOW *win;
    initscr( );
    box(stdscr,'|','-');
    mvwaddstr(stdscr,7,30,"------ this is 10,30");
    mvwaddch(stdscr,8,30,'|');
    mvwaddch(stdscr,9,30,'V');
    wrefresh(stdscr);
    win=subwin(stdscr, 9,20,10,30);
    box(win,'|','-');
    wgetch(win);
    endwin( );
}
```

On running this program, the display will be :

- a border around the *stdscr* with an arrow and message pointing to the position row 10, column 30.

- a window within *stdscr* of the dimension 9, 20 with a border framing it.

To innovate on setting up windows, we advance to creating arrays as in :

```
WINDOW * win [13]
```

This will create an array of 13 pointers allowing you to define several pointers to the structure of WINDOW type. The routines used in this program have all been dealt with and need no further explanations. Observe that the *clear( )* function is called as *wclear( )* and that you must identify the name of the window which you want to cleared. The output from this program is stimulating and should inspire you to write variations of the same.

PROGRAM 388

```
#include <curses.h>

main( )
{
   WINDOW *win[13];
   int i=0, l=15, c=30, y=0, x=0;
   initscr( );
   for (i=0;i<12;i++)
   {
      win[i]=newwin(l,c,y,x);
      box(win[i],'|','-');
      wrefresh(win[i]);
      y++;
      x++;
      l--;
      c--;
   }
   win[12]=newwin(l,c,y,x);
   box(win[12],'|','-');
   beep( );
   mvwprintw(win[12],1,5,"Ouch !!!");
   wrefresh(win[12]);
   beep( );
   wgetch(win[12]);
   for (i=12;i>=0;i--)
   {
      wclear(win[i]);
      wrefresh(win[i]);
   }
   endwin( );
}
```

A Simple Variation of the above program would be like :

PROGRAM 389

```
#include <curses.h>

main( )
{
   WINDOW * win[5];
   int i,l,c,y,x;
```

```
    l=0; l=15; c=40; y=5; x=20;
    initscr( );
    for (i=0;i<5;i++)
    {
       win[i]=newwin(l,c, y,x);
       box(win[i],'|','-');
       wrefresh(win[i]);
       y++; x+=2;
       l-=2; c-=4;
    }
    mvwprintw(win[4],3,5,"Hello World...");
    wrefresh(win);
    wgetch(win[4]);
    for(i=4;i>=0;i--)
    {
       wclear(win[i]);
       wrefresh(win[i]);
    }
    endwin( );
}
```

Windows On The Move

The following program is an example of how the function *move( )* can be applied. It is, of course, called as *wmove( )*. In this case it is used in a combination.

mvwin( )

is used to shift the existing position of a window inclusive of all data associated with it. The original window is not erased but simply duplicated at a different position. Another bug! As with most of the routines, the name of the window has to be defined along with the row and column position.

PROGRAM 390

```
#include <curses.h>

main( )
{
   WINDOW *win;
```

```
    chtype ch;
    initscr( );
    win=newwin(5,10,0,0);
    box(win,'|','-');
    mvwprintw(win,2,1,"Hello ~~");
    wrefresh(win);
    wgetch(win);
    mvwin(win,0,69);
    wrefresh(win);
    wgetch(win);
    endwin( );
}
```

To shift the window several times in a program, all you need to insert is a ....yes, you've got it; a *while* loop within which the cursor position can be changed any number of times. This program is only a variation of the previous one. Nevertheless, there is a catch in the program. By now, you should be smart enough to detect it!

PROGRAM 391

```
#include <curses.h>

main( )
{
    WINDOW *win;
    int x,y;
    chtype ch;
    x=y=0;
    initscr( );
    noecho( );
    cbreak( );
    win=newwin(5,10,0,0);
    box(win,'|','-');
    beep( );
    mvwaddstr(win,2,2,"Hello~~");
    wrefresh(win);
    while(1)
    {
        if (x<18)
        {
            ch=wgetch(win);
```

```
            if(ch==27)
               break;
         }
         else
            break;

         x+=2;
         y+=7;
         mvwin(win,x,y);
         beep( );
         wrefresh(win);
   }
   endwin( );
}
```

Let's now tackle another routine :

overwrite( )

As its name suggests, this function is used to overwrite the contents of a window with that of another. The names of the windows defined with this routine specify :

- the source window

- the designated window

This function is used to destroy the contents of a window and fill it with that of another. For example, if *w2* already contains information etc., a call to *overwrite(w1,w2)* will delete the substance of *w2* automatically as it overwrites it.

PROGRAM 392

```
#include <curses.h>

main( )
{
   Int i;
   WINDOW *w1,*w2;
   initscr( );
   w1=newwin(10,20, 5,10);
   w2=newwin(10,20, 5,50);
```

```
    box(w1,'|','-');
    box(w2,'|','-');
    mvwaddstr(w1,4,5,"Window - 1.");
    mvwaddstr(w2,4,5,"Window - 2.");
    wmove(w1,0,0);
    wmove(w2,0,0);
    wrefresh(w1);
    wrefresh(w2);
    wgetch(w2);
    for(i=0;i<200;i++)
        waddch(w1,'#');
    mvwaddstr(w1,1,4,"Window – 1.");
    wrefresh(w1);
    wrefresh(w2);
    wgetch(w2);
    overwrite(w1,w2);
    wrefresh(w2);
    wgetch(w2);
    endwin( );
}
```

This next routine has a very simple task to perform. It deletes characters plotted on the cursor position indiscriminately. It is called *wdelch( )*

Note again that the name of the window on which you want a character deleted, has to be specified with it.

PROGRAM 393

```
#include <curses.h>

main( )
{
    WINDOW *win;
    initscr( );
    win=newwin(5,15, 7,25);
    mvwaddstr(win,2,2,"Hello !!");
    wrefresh(win);
    wmove(win,2,6);
    wgetch(win);
    wmove(win,2,6);
    wdelch(win);
```

```
    wrefresh(win);
    wgetch(win);
    endwin( );
}
```

After refreshing the string Hello !!, *wgetch(win)* is called for a keystroke. When you respond, the cursor is again positioned at row 2, column 6 and the letter *o* is deleted with a call to *wdelch(win)*.

The above program can again be modified to obtain a different output. With the inclusion of the *for* and loop statements, the contents of a window can be deleted character by character, using the same delete routine.

PROGRAM 394

```
#include <curses.h>

main( )
{
    int x,y,i;
    WINDOW *win;
    initscr( );
    win=newwin( 5,10,10,35);
    waddstr(win,"0123456789");
    waddstr(win,"0123456789");
    waddstr(win,"0123456789");
    waddstr(win,"0123456789");
    waddstr(win,"012345678X");
    x=3;
    y=0;
    while(1)
    {
        wrefresh(win);
        wmove(win,4,9);
        wgetch(win);
        wmove(win,x,0);
        wdelch(win);
        wrefresh(win);
        x--;
        if(x<0)
        {
```

```
            x=4;
            y++;
            if(y>=10)
               break;
        }
    }
    endwin( );
}
```

Here we first fill the entire window with numbers after which we move to the end of the window to accept a character. Everytime a character is accepted characters from the beginning of every line are deleted. This shifts the second character to the beginning of the line whereby it is also deleted in the next round. This process continues till all characters which were displayed, are deleted. You must have noted two important points at the time of execution.

- The last character of the Window i.e.*X* is never deleted as it is always overwritten by the character you type in. This is so because the position of *X* is on the character acceptance place.

- When you delete from the last line all characters automatically move by one space to the left. If you press any key other than the space-bar or the Enter key, you will actually see these characters moving to the left.

You can again achieve the same thing by using another routine :

wdeleteln( )

This routine deletes the line on which the cursor is positioned. A scroll is effected as the line below the deleted one shifts one row up.

The name of the window, on which you want the line to be deleted, must be specified. In this sample program, this function is applied for deleting all the contents of win, row by row.

```
PROGRAM 395
#include <curses.h>

main( )
{
    int i;
    WINDOW *win;
    initscr( );
    win=newwin(5,10, 8,35);
    waddstr(win,"1234567890");
    waddstr(win,"abcdefghij");
    waddstr(win,"ABCDEFGHIJ");
    waddstr(win,"abcdefghij");
    waddstr(win,"1234567890");
    wmove(win,0,0);
    wrefresh(win);
    for(i=0;i<5;i++)
    {
        wmove(win,0,0);
        wgetch(win);
        wdeleteln(win);
        wrefresh(win);
    }
    endwin( );
}
```

Enough with deletion. Let's move along to the insert mode now. The routine :

winsch( )

permits you to insert characters without deleting the existing character on the cursor position. To be more precise, this routine allows you to type in anything - characters and even spaces. It does not erase any existing text but, incorporates the new.

Eating 'em RAW

raw( )

sets your terminal to the raw mode, causing each character entered at the keyboard to be sent immediately, as direct input. This function disables the attributes of editing and signal keys as all characters are treated at par.

This sample program with a call to *winsch( )* allows you to key in any character which is constantly being inserted till an Esc character is interpreted.

PROGRAM 396

```
#include <curses.h>

WINDOW *win;

main( )
{
   chtype ch;
   initscr( );
   noecho( );
   raw( );
   win=newwin(20,60, 2,5);
   waddstr(win,"You are in the INSERT mode.. Press [Esc] to exit");
   mvwaddstr(win,1,0,"Try Catching >> >>");
   wmove(win,1,15);
   wrefresh(win);
   ch=wgetch(win);
   while(ch!=27)
   {
      winsch(win,ch);
      getpos( );
      wrefresh(win);
      ch=wgetch(win);
   }
   endwin( );
}

getpos( )
{
   int x,y,x1,y1;
   getmaxyx(win,y1,x1);
   getyx(win,y,x);
   x++;
```

```
    if(x==x1)
    {
        x=0;
        y++;
        mvwaddstr(win,y,x,">>");
        if(y==y1)
        {
            y=y1;
            x=x1;
        }
    }
    wmove(win,y,x);
}
```

In the above program, characters are accepted till you press the Esc. key. This is achieved with the help of *wgetch(win)* and *winch(win,ch)*. However, remember that after a character has been inserted, you have to move the cursor position one place to the right if you wish to insert more characters. The cursor remains at the same position after each insertion causing every new character to be incorporated to the left of the previous inserted character. Do you smell a bug?!

Before you start tearing your hair out here's how you can avoid confusion during insertion - simply use :

getpos( )

This routine helps by :

- figuring out the current cursor position

- the size of the window

and if possible, shifts the cursor from its current position one place to the right else to the next line. It also stations the cursor at its position if it happens to be at the end of the window.

There is another insertion routine :

winsertln( )

This function allows you to insert a line. Insertion in this case, will be expressed in blank lines. As with deletion, here too, a scroll will be effected after every insertion. In this example, this routine inserts a blank line at the beginning of the window with every keystroke till the Esc key is interpreted.

```
PROGRAM 397
#include <curses.h>

main( )
{
   chtype ch;
   int i;
   WINDOW *win;
   i=0;
   initscr( );
   noecho( );
   raw( );
   win=newwin(20,60, 2,5);
   mvwprintw(win,0,0,"%4d INSERT Line Mode.. Press [Esc] To Exit",i);
   wrefresh(win);
   ch=wgetch(win);
   while(ch!=27)
   {
      winsertln(win);
      mvwprintw(win,0,0,"%4d Current Line Inserted [Esc] To Exit....",++i);
      wrefresh(win);
      wmove(win,0,0);
      ch=wgetch(win);
   }
   endwin( );
}
```

Having Fun With Attributes

Routines for creating windows and setting attributes have been used together in the following program.

On running this program, you will notice that the text will assume an attribute, corresponding to particular keystrokes from you. Certain characters that you key in, if preceded by punching the Esc key first, will emulate the features of routines which are used for setting attributes to text. For example, if you press the Esc key and then punch in *u*, you will find that the rest of the text that you type in will be underlined. If you punch the esc key and the character *r*, the text typed in will be in reverse video. This is achieved by calling a certain routine, after the character that you have typed in is checked in a *while* loop. The default mode is left as normal. This, again, is a demonstration of how you can deploy the same routines for absolutely varying outputs.

PROGRAM 398

```
#include <curses.h>

WINDOW *win;
chtype ch;
int x,y;

main( )
{
   x=y=0;
   initscr( );
   disptext( );
   win=newwin(10,25, 8,50);
   while(1)
   {
      ch=wgetch(win);
      if(ch==27)
         escaperoute( );
      wrefresh(win);
      getyx(win,y,x);
   }
}

disptext( )
{
   mvwaddstr(stdscr,6,50,"Fun with Screen Attributes....");
   mvwaddstr(stdscr,6,5,"Press [Esc] to Activate Triggers..");
   attrset(A_BLINK);
   mvwaddstr(stdscr,9,5,"[ b ] for Blink.");
   attrset(A_REVERSE);
   mvwaddstr(stdscr,10,5,"[ r ] for Reverse.");
   attrset(A_UNDERLINE);
```

```
    mvwaddstr(stdscr,11,5,"[ u ] for Underline. ");
    attrset(A_NORMAL);
    mvwaddstr(stdscr,12,5,"[ n ] for Normal Disp.");
    mvwaddstr(stdscr,13,5,"[ q ] to Quit.");
    mvwaddstr(stdscr,16,5,"[ * ] Current Status : Edit Mode.");
    wrefresh(stdscr);
}
escaperoute( )
{
    mvwaddstr(stdscr,16,5,"[  ] Current Status : Esc Mode.");
    wrefresh(stdscr);
    ch=wgetch(win);
    wmove(win,y,x);
    if(ch=='r')
    {
        wattrset(win,A_REVERSE);
        wattrset(stdscr,A_REVERSE);
    }
    if(ch=='u')
    {
        wattrset(win,A_UNDERLINE);
        wattrset(stdscr,A_UNDERLINE);
    }
    if(ch=='b')
    {
        wattrset(win,A_BLINK);
        wattrset(stdscr,A_BLINK);
    }
    if(ch=='n')
    {
        wattrset(win,0);
        wattrset(stdscr,0);
    }
    if(ch=='q')
    {
        wattrset(win,0);
        endwin( );
        exit(0);
    }
    mvwaddstr(stdscr,16,5,"[ * ] Current Status : Edit Mode.");
    wrefresh(stdscr);
    return;
```

}

Let's go over some of the functions and their actions in the above program, starting with the first call to *while*. Within this loop a character is accepted and a check is made for the Esc. key.

disptext( ) is used only once at the beginning to specify various options available to you and to display the default mode on the *stdscr*.

Immediately after the Esc. key is encountered, the *escaperoute( )* is activated whereby when the next character is accepted, a default attribute is set to the specified value. On encountering a *q*, you exit from this function.

There are endless possibilities for 'playing around' with the routines you have learnt so far. All you need is imagination! Another such example is the following where all capital letters in a line are changed to the lower case. This program

- creates a window and frames it

- calls *getch( )* and checks input

- follows a certain direction according to your response

- performs a routine to check end of line or window

While in the process of inputting, you press the esc key, the program is deviated to another part where you will notice the routine

getmaxyz(w,x,y);

This routine gives the maximum cursor coordinates of the window. In this instance, the value of *x* will be 20 and that of *y* will be 70 as these are the maximum rows and columns expressed while creating the window.

The *if* statement

```
if( (w->_y[j][i] >= 'A') && (w->_y[j][i] <= 'Z') )
  w->_y[j][i]+=' ';
```

checks for any upper case character from *A* inclusive to *Z* inclusive that is, at row *j* and column *i*. Once such a character is encountered, the machine code of ' ' which as you know is 32, is instantly added to the value of that character. For example, if *A* is located at position *j,i*, 32 will be added to its ASCII value 65, getting the new value 97. This is the value of *a*. Thus, with a call to *wrefresh( ) A* will be replaced by *a* on the screen. Once this is done, the values of *j* and *i* are incremented and checked and characters at the new positions checked and replaced. This procedure continues till all capitals in the line within the window are replaced by small letters.

PROGRAM 399

```
#include <curses.h>

WINDOW *win;

main( )
{
   int x,y;
   initscr( );
   mvwaddstr(stdscr, 21,10,
   "Press [Esc Twice] to Decapitalise the Line/[Ent] to Quit");
   wrefresh(win);
   win=newwin(20,70, 0,10);
   box(win, '|','-');
   wmove(win,1,1);
   wrefresh(win);
   while( (ch=wgetch (win) ) != 10)
   {
      if(ch==27)
         decap( );
      position( );
      wrefresh(win);
   }
   endwin( );
}

decap( )
```

```
{
   int a,b,i,j,x,y;
   getyx(win,a,b);
   getmaxyx(win,y,x);
   for(i=0,j=a;i<=x;i++)
      if( (win->_y[j][i] >= 'A') && (win->_y[j][i] <= 'Z') )
         win->_y[j][i]+=32;
   wrefresh(win);
   wgetch(win);
   y--; a++;
   if(a>=y)
      a=1;
   wmove(win,a,1);
}

position( )
{
   int x,y;
   getyx(win,y,x);
   if(x==65)
      beep( );
   if(x>=69)
   {
      x=1; y++;
      if(y>=19)
         y=1;
      wmove(win, y,x);
   }
}
```

This program is a modification of the previous one. Here, instead of replacing upper case letters with lower case ones, the reverse is done and all letters are given an attribute. If you read through this program carefully, you will note that all letters are deleted and then displayed with the A_REVERSE feature. All the other routines remain the same.

```
PROGRAM 400
#include <curses.h>

WINDOW *win;
chtype ch;
```

```
main( )
{
   int x,y;
   initscr( );
   mvwaddstr(stdscr,21,10,"Press [Esc] to Capitalize the Window.");
   mvwaddstr(stdscr,22,10,"Do Not Press Enter.");
   wrefresh(stdscr);
   win=newwin(20,70,0,5);
   box(win,'|','-');
   wmove(win,1,1);
   wrefresh(win);
   while(1)
   {
      ch=wgetch(win);
      if(ch==27)
         capal( );
      wrefresh(win);
      getyx(win,y,x);
      if((x==67) && (y==18))
         beep( );
      if(x>=69)
      {
         x=1;
         y++;
         if(y>=19)
            y=1;
         wmove(win,y,x);
      }
   }
}

capal( )
{
   int i,j,x,y;
   i=j=1;
   getmaxyx(win,y,x);
   x--; y-=2;
   while(1)
   {
      if((win->_y[j][i] >= 'a') && (win->_y[j][i] <= 'z'))
         ch=win->_y[j][i] -= 32;
      else
```

```
            ch=win->_y[j][i];
        wmove(win,j,i);
        wdelch(win);
        winsch(win,ch | A_REVERSE);
        i++;
        if( i==x )
        {
            i=1;
            j++;
            if(j>y)
            {
                wrefresh(win);
                wgetch(win);
                endwin( );
                exit(0);
            }
        }
    }
}
```

You may note that the only routine unfamiliar to you is *capal( )*. A little note on it - the moment you press the Esc. key, this routine is invoked. This routine does several things :

- gets a character with the help of *_y[ ]*[ ]

- deletes this character

- replaces this character in reverse video

This operation is carried out for all the characters present after which a keystroke is awaited from you.

There are some routines that are designed to work with a special type of window called pads. A pad is no more than a window whose size is not dependent on the screen or related to any part of it. For example, while creating a window, you had to make sure that its dimension was not bigger than your terminal screen i.e., not longer than 23 rows and wider than 79 columns. On the contrary, the size of a pad can be bigger than that of your screen. All window routines can be used for pads except *wrefresh( )* and *wnoutrefresh( )* which are merely substituted by *prefresh( )* and *pnoutrefresh( )*. Pads are declared by using a routine similar to that for windows. Defining the pad dimension is done with :

newpad( )

wherein *newpad( )* takes two parameters

- the number of rows

- the number of columns

PROGRAM 401

```
#include <curses.h>

main( )
{
   WINDOW *pad;
   initscr( );
   pad=newpad(100,20);
   prefresh(pad,0,0,0,20,23,40);
   endwin( );
}
```

An important point to be noted here :

- seven parameters are declared with *prefresh( )*

The seven parameters defined are in the following order :

- name of pad

- starting row within the pad

- starting column within the pad

- top left corner of the screen

- top right corner of the screen

- bottom left corner of the screen

- bottom right corner of the screen

The examples that follow are simply versions of previous programs. The only thing that you must follow carefully is the logical flow of the program.

PROGRAM 402

```
#include <curses.h>

main( )
{
   WINDOW *pad;
   chtype ch;
   int i;
   initscr( );
   pad=newpad(100,20);
   ch=' ';
   for(i=0;i<200;i++)
   {
      ch++;
      waddch(pad,ch);
      if(ch==127)
         ch=' ';
   }
   prefresh(pad,0,0,5,30,15,50);
   wgetch(pad);
   endwin( );
}
```

The output of this program will be the display of all ASCII values between 32 and 127. The display will be continuous till the entire pad is covered. After a keystroke from you the program will terminate.

This program is similar to the previous one and demonstrates the 'scrolling' effect on the pad. With every keystroke, the top line is deleted thus causing the pad to scroll.

PROGRAM 403

```
#include <curses.h>
```

```
main( )
{
   WINDOW *pad;
   chtype ch = 32;
   int i;
   initscr( );
   pad = newpad(100,20);
   for(i=0;i<199;i++)
   {
      waddch(pad,ch++);
      if(ch==127)
         ch = 32;
   }
   wmove(pad,0,0);
   prefresh(pad,0,0,5,30,20,50);
   for(i=0;i<10;i++)
   {
      ch=wgetch(pad);
      if(ch==27)
         break;
      wdeleteln(pad);
      prefresh(pad,0,0,5,30,20,50);
   }
   endwin( );
}
```

This example is for exhibiting information at different parts of the pad. It is effected by simply calling *prefresh( )* with different parameters, as many times as required.

PROGRAM 404

```
#include <curses.h>

main( )
{
   WINDOW *pad;
   int i;
   initscr( );
   pad=newpad(100,24);
   i=1000;
   while(i--)
      waddch(pad,'V');
```

```
    mvwaddstr(pad,5,3,"First Attempt. ");
    prefresh(pad,0,0,5,5,15,25);
    wgetch(pad);
    prefresh(pad,4,4,5,45,15,65);
    wgetch(pad);
    endwin( );
}
```

Following are some miscellaneous programs which should help you hone your programming skills and warm you up for more complex applications. This program uses *noecho( )* , *cbreak( )* and *raw( )* in combination. The inclusion of all three routines in one program makes your terminal as 'dumb' as possible! This renders it helpless for normal interpretation of keys. Hence, at sensitive parts of the program, you can call these three routines and release them after the task is done.

```
PROGRAM 405
#include <curses.h>

main( )
{
    chtype ch;
    int x,y;
    initscr( );
    noecho( );
    cbreak( );
    raw( );
    mvaddstr(22,30,"Press `q' to Quit.");
    move(0,0);
    refresh( );
    while(1)
    {
        ch=getch( );
        if(ch == 127)
            addstr("Delete key was pressed and the program did not
                interrupt");
        if(ch==4)
            addstr("Control d [^d] was pressed and the program did not
                interrupt");
        if(ch==27)
            break;
```

```
        getyx(stdscr,y,x);
        move(y+1,0);
        refresh( );
    }
    endwin( );
}
```

This program demonstrates the use of two routines :

keypad( )

keypad( ) **enables the terminal to interpret the ASCII value of each character.**

PROGRAM 406

```
#include <curses.h>

main( )
{
    chtype ch;
    char *arr[4];
    arr[0]="UP  ARROW";
    arr[1]="DOWN ARROW";
    arr[2]="RIGHT ARROW";
    arr[3]="LEFT ARROW";
    initscr( );
    keypad(stdscr,TRUE);
    noecho( );
    cbreak( );
    raw( );
    mvaddstr(22,20,"Press [Esc] key to Exit.");
    move(10,21);
    refresh( );
    ch=' ';
    while(ch!=27)
    {
        ch=getch( );
        if(ch==KEY_UP)
            disp(arr[0],KEY_UP);
        if(ch==KEY_DOWN)
            disp(arr[1],KEY_DOWN);
        if(ch==KEY_RIGHT)
```

```
        disp(arr[2],KEY_RIGHT);
      if(ch==KEY_LEFT)
        disp(arr[3],KEY_LEFT);
      if(ch==27)
        break;
   }
   endwin( );
}

disp(st,no)
char *st;
int no;
{
   mvprintw(10,10,"Key Pressed : %s and its Octal Value is 0%o.",st,no);
   refresh( );
}
```

If you remember, the first step you took in trying to control this terminal was to master the movements of the cursor. Then, all you had to be content with was using the letters *U,D,L,R* for cursor movement. With the use of some macros, you can actually use the arrow keys instead. This makes your program user friendly especially if you find memorizing the meaning of each letter too troublesome! You could produce a really neat program by merging this with the previous one. Go on, do it!

PROGRAM 407

```
#include <curses.h>

main( )
{
   int y=35;
   int x=10;
   chtype ch;
   initscr( );
   keypad(stdscr,TRUE);
   noecho( );
   cbreak( );
   raw( );
   ch=' ';
   while(ch!=27)
   {
```

```
move(x,y);
refresh( );
switch(ch=getch ( ))
{
  case KEY_LEFT :
  y--;
  if(y<=0)
  {
    beep( );
    y=0;
  }
  break;

  case KEY_RIGHT :
  y++;
  if(y>=79)
  {
    beep( );
    y=79;
  }
  break;

  case KEY_UP:
  x--;
  if(x<=0)
  {
    beep( );
    x=0;
  }
  break;

  case KEY_DOWN  :
  x++;
  if(x>23)
  {
    beep( );
    x=23;
  }
  break;

  default    :
  beep( );
}
```

```
    }
    endwin( );
}
```

About Ourselves And How Fast We Are

The following program demonstrates the use of the routine

baudrate( )

which simply returns to you the speed at which information is processed. The speed is calculated in bits per second or BPS.

PROGRAM 408

```
#include <curses.h>

main( )
{
    int baud;
    initscr( );
    baud=baudrate( );
    mvprintw(5,10,"Terminal is operating under %d BPS ",baud);
    refresh( );
    getch( );
    endwin( );
}
```

Another demonstration program, this one uses

longname( )

which gives the terminal description.

PROGRAM 409

```
#include <curses.h>

main( )
{
    char *lname;
    initscr( );
    lname=longname( );
```

```
    mvprintw(5,10,"Terminal INFORMATION : %s ",lname);
    refresh( );
    getch( );
    endwin( );
}
```

Controlling The Cursor

This program illustrates the use of

slk_init( )

which gives finer control of the cursor. It is usually called for subwindows. The quality of the cursor is set, using

cur_set( )

With 0 as a parameter, it makes the cursor invisible, with 1 it makes it visible and with 2 it makes it brighter or more visible. But, this depends on the fact that your terminal should support it.

PROGRAM 410

```
#include <curses.h>

main( )
{
    initscr( );
    slk_init(1);
    addstr("cursor settings ... ");
    refresh( );
    getch( );

    cur_set(0);
    addstr("cursor set to invisible");
    refresh( );
    getch( );

    cur_set(1);
    addstr("cursor set to visible");
    refresh( );
```

```
    getch();

    cur_set(2);
    addstr("cursor set to very visible");
    refresh( );
    getch( );

    endwin( );
}
```

The Screen

This program demonstrates the uses of

scr_dump()

scr_restore()

As their names suggest, these routines have something to do with screens. *scr_dump()* allows you to save the contents of the screen in a file and *scr_restore()* recalls it. The file name is declared in both cases. This file screen.scr, is just a temporary storage facility but, is not deleted automatically at the end of a program. Yes, you're catching on! Another bug to get rid of.

PROGRAM 411

```
#include <curses.h>

main( )
{
   int i;
   initscr( );
   mvaddstr(10,15,"This is to Demonstrate the Screen Saving &
Restoring");
   mvaddstr(20,15,"Strike Any key .. the Screen will be Saved");
   refresh( );
   getch( );
   scr_dump("screen.scr");
   clear( );
   for(i=' ';i<='z';i++)
      printw("%c---X---",i);
```

```
    for(i=' ';i<='z';i++)
        printw("%c---X---",i);
    printw("\n\t\tPress any key to Restore The Saved Screen....");
    refresh( );
    getch( );
    scr_restore("screen.scr");
    refresh( );
    endwin( );
}
```

This demonstration program displays several windows at different co-ordinates in the screen. Each window has a different border. This is done by first setting the terminal to accept and draw boxes by designating A_ALTRCHARSET as a parameter of *attrset( )*. *box( )* is called with several names specified with it. These are already defined in curses.h and contain characters which frame the window.

PROGRAM 412

```
#include <curses.h>

main( )
{
    WINDOW *w1,*w2,*w3,*w4,*w5,*w6;
    initscr( );

    w1=newwin(18,70, 3, 5);
    w2=newwin(16,60, 4, 9);
    w3=newwin(14,50, 5,13);
    w4=newwin(12,40, 6,17);
    w5=newwin(10,30, 7,21);
    w6=newwin( 8,20, 8,25);

    wattrset(w1,A_ALTCHARSET);
    box(w1,ACS_VLINE,ACS_HLINE);

    wattrset(w2,A_ALTCHARSET);
    box(w2,ACS_VLINE,ACS_TTEE);

    wattrset(w3,A_ALTCHARSET);
    box(w3,ACS_VLINE,ACS_BOARD);
```

```
    wattrset(w4,A_ALTCHARSET);
    box(w4,ACS_BULLET,ACS_HLINE);

    wattrset(w5,A_ALTCHARSET);
    box(w5,ACS_UARROW,ACS_S9);

    wattrset(w6,A_ALTCHARSET);
    box(w6,ACS_LTEE,ACS_BTEE);

    wrefresh(w1);
    wgetch(w1);

    wrefresh(w2);
    wgetch(w2);

    wrefresh(w3);
    wgetch(w3);

    wrefresh(w4);
    wgetch(w4);

    wrefresh(w5);
    wgetch(w5);

    wrefresh(w6);
    wgetch(w6);

    endwin( );
}
```

With the above program, we wrap up the section on curses. No tearful parting words nor boring counseling. Just a friendly handshake and a big Welcome! to the end of this section.

This may not make much sense but, here it is again - welcome to the end of this section! It's not going to be turn the page and goodbye, yet. Oh no. It is just the beginning in fact. Pardon the philosophical tone but, is there an end to all things?? The quest for the answer is what makes the world go round. Hopefully, you too will feel zestful enough to go beyond mere teachings and seek answers. The end of this section merely opens yet another door to you and now that the introductions are done with, may your relationship with curses be long and fruitful. Fruitful?? Yes, even if you may have to spend precious programming time smelling out the bugs! But, therein lies the fun and eventually, sweet satisfaction.

A little nugget of information as a parting word - you can combine the routines of the normal 'C' library with the curses library to achieve greater efficiency. You can definitely do a lot with curses as a media and now that you have the power to open a new door - what are you waiting for ?? - open sesame!!

Remember the treasures Alladin found? Goodluck.

Perspectives 1991

Sparks flew, voices were raised, tempers frayed, hair split and tantrums thrown. It had to be a UNIX discussion.

UNIX was the operating system developed at AT&T Bell Labs, and left there inconsequentially gathering dust and spluttering occasionally. It was lent out by the telephone and telegraph company to universities as a case study in their curriculum. And as students toyed with its structure, adding, deleting, molding it to fit specific needs and whims, UNIX took new and different dimensions almost everyday.

It stayed within the sacred academic portals only as long as the students remained. And as swarms of students walked out with degrees and knowledge, they took their college faithful UNIX along. UNIX slipped unwittingly into the commercial mainstream.

And an epidemic of UNIX versions rained heavily on a susceptible audience, with as many UNIX versions being developed as there were people computing. The plague spread very rapidly, across continents and cultures.

The first seeds of confusion were sown. With hapless users having to answer a barrage of questions before they could even find the UNIX for their needs and machines, the mayhem was considerable.

UNIX became the hub of bitter and protracted controversies. Was it portable? Was it the heart and soul and the sole preserve of C? Should it be standardized? Which is the right UNIX? Was it the universal language of computers - PCs, supercomputers, et al.?

Years rolled by, the sheep came home, and the debates continued.

The question of standardization became the focal issue. AT&T justifiably grabbed the first seat on the standardization bus. And sharing the berth with them was Sun Microsystems, the gnomes who built the workstations. Together they embarked on a UNIX standardization trail.

But even before they could don their overalls and put pen to paper, the war clouds rumbled on the not-so-distant horizon. Standardization was a democratic idea that fractured monopolies, regulated price indexes and maintained healthy competition marches. IBM's billions certainly did not grow on standardization trees.

So IBM allied with its bitterest enemies to counter the threat posed by the precocious twosome. IBM and DEC both of whom leaned heavily on proprietary locks, consorted with Hewlett Packard, the third giant and rival, to form the OSF - the Open Software Foundation. And the world perambulated back to Square 1. The paradox of two standards emerging parallely was agonizingly real. Both the standards were sufficiently different to be totally incompatible with each other.

UNIX had become the most controversial personality. Jostled and pushed around. Used and misused. Financially, politically and in every other conceivable way.

The standardization racket continued with new suitors jumping into the arena. The PC had become an unworthy desktop, unable to cope with developing minds and developing technologies. Suggestions and solutions poured out like cathartic confessions. Microsoft preached a logical progression from MS-DOS to Windows, IBM pointed to OS/2, and Sun Microsystems' suggestion hinged on workstations.

Politically, the Europeans, the famine-stricken in the computer world, saw UNIX as their door to the land of fame and money. And they knocked hard and persistently. Even Japan unable to swallow America's rising sun jumped into the fray. 'The UNIX malady spread world-wide.

Meanwhile, Sun veered on new ambitions. A new desktop standard was envisaged, and no one took that lying down. Least of all Microsoft or DEC or Compaq, or 20 others who pooled their cards together and played their ACE. The goal of ACE hovered around one point: If you can't convince them, confuse them. ACE called to the podium two hardware standards - one based on the Intel microchip and the other on the RISC chip. To knot an already mottled scenario, they pushed forth two operating system standards - OS/2 3.0 or OS/2 NT - New Technology, Microsoft's claim on the OS/2 they conceived with IBM, and a new version of UNIX!

UNIX was torn asunder once again. We had one more fragment of UNIX, certainly not the last.

UNIX had indeed traveled a long way from the corridors of the AT&T Bell Labs. Designed to be palatable to any kind of machine, its most endearing trait was its hardware independence. UNIX is a portable operating system? Or is it?

(This was when we had our first dogfight).

Is UNIX portable?

Viewed from the Systems angle, UNIX is. It is hardware independent and can be smeared onto different machines. Its character in that sense is flexible. A little fine tuning, a slight polish, some hammering, some gluing and UNIX will work as optimally on a VAX as on a 386. Interactive, Microport, AT&T and a myriad other bodies converse in UNIX. And each speak a different dialect. This is where it is non-portable. Non-portable from the application writer's side of the fence.

Talking about UNIX is like narrating the parable about the blind men defining the elephant. What UNIX is depends on whose side you're on.

The UNIX-C relationship, perhaps the most unambiguous part of UNIX, too draws considerable flak. Is C more powerful under UNIX or DOS?

Another dogfight....

UNIX was, in fact, the catalyst which induced the birth of C. C was written so the experiment of UNIX could be complete. To stretch the reach of UNIX over assorted machines, a universal language was necessary. A flexible, amorphous, undefined language that could arrange itself into the environment it was slapped on to. C was a moment of insight. But it shaped UNIX's intended body.

Yet, C flowered and blossomed more fragrantly under DOS and even OS/2. There are more C programmers traipsing in DOS today than in UNIX. DOS which is shoddier and clumsier than UNIX. DOS which appears unkempt and disheveled against the elegance of UNIX. DOS whose hems and back-stitches are frayed and untidy. Yet.

For one, DOS has a larger installed base. For another, UNIX is a hard nut to crack. It has its reserve and keeps its distance. An aloof and haughty sophisticate that does not descend and mingle encouragingly with the hoi polloi. Unlike DOS whose appeal is universal, UNIX caters to certain echelons only.

Another dogfight.

After euthanasia and freedom of the press, in fact, UNIX seems to be the most mouth-watering ingredient for debate. Every time UNIX sneezes, the world cacophonies, as much in sympathy as in protest.

We're in the year of the Lord, 1991. And the horizon still reeks of a bloody battle.

Index

!

A

B

C

D

E

F

G

H

I

M

N

O

P

Q

R

S

T

Other COMPUTER TITLES From BPB PUBLICATIONS

AUTOCAD

ENCYCLOPEDIA AUTOCAD (REL 11)
INSIDE AUTOCAD (REL 10)
MASTERING AUTOCAD 3RD ED. (REL 11)
ABC'S OF AUTOCAD (REL. 11)
TEACH YOURSELF AUTOCAD (RLS 11)
AUTO CAD 11 INSTANT REF

ASSEMBLY LANGUAGE

USING ASSEMBLY LANGUAGE

AUTOLISP

THE ABC'S OF AUTOLISP (VER. 10)
ILLUSTRATED AUTOLISP

BASIC

LEARNING IBM BASIC FOR THE PC
MORE THAN 32 BASIC PROG, FOR THE IBM PER/COM
THE BASIC HANDBOOK 3RD ED.
THE IBM BASIC HANDBOOK 2ND ED

C

ENCYCLOPEDIA C
TEACH YOURSELF C
DOS – THE CHARTED WATERS
ADVANCED DOS – THE UNCHARTED WATERS
UNIX – THE OPEN-BOUNDLESS C
NETWORKS AND RDBMS – NEW WORLDS TO CONQUER
C++ AND GRAPHICS – THE FUTURE OF C
WINDOWS – THE BRAVE NEW WORLD

CLIPPER

ILLUSTRATED CLIPPER 5.0
CLIPPER PROGRAMMING GUIDE 3RD ED. VERSION 5.01
THE UNOFFICIAL CLIPPER 5.0 MANUAL
UP & RUNNING WITH CLIPPER 5.01

COMPUTER VIRUS

THE COMPUTER VIRUS PROTECTION HDB (WITH DISK)

CROSSTALK XVI

MASTERING CROSSTALK XV

COREL DRAW

MASTERING COREL DRAW 2

DAC EASY

MASTERING DACEASY ACCOUNTING (VER. 3.1/4.1)
MASTERING DACEASY ACCOUNTING (VER. 4.0/3.0)
ILLUSTRATED DACEASY ACCT.

DATA BASE

SALVAGING DAMAGED DBASE FILES
THE DATABASE DICTIONARY

DBASE III PLUS

DBASE III PLUS APPLICATIONS LIBRARY
DBASE III PLUS PROGRAMMER'S REF. GUIDE
UNDERSTANDING DBASE III PLUS

DBASE IV

THE DBASE LANGUAGE HANDBOOK (INCL. DBASE IV)
UNDERSTANDING DBASE IV (VER. 1.1)
ILLUSTRATED DBASE IV (1.1)
DBASE IV (1.1) USERS' INSTANT REF.
THE ABCS' OF DBASE IV (VER 1.1)
MASTERING DBASE IV 1.1 PROGRAMMING
DBASE IV (1.1) PROGRAMMERS INSTANT REF.
DBASE IV 1.1 DESKTOP REFERENCE

COMPUTER DICTIONARY

THE COMPUTER DICTIONARY

DOS

MS DOS-PC DOS QUICK REF. (VER. 5.0)
TEACH YOURSELF DOS VER. 3.3 & 4.0
MASTERING DOS (VER. 3.3 & 4.0)
THE ABC'S OF DOS 5
MASTERING DOS 5
UP AND RUNNING WITH DOS 5
DOS 5 USER'S HANDBOOK
DOS 5 INSTANT REF

EXCEL

MASTERING EXCEL 3 FOR WINDOWS
UP & RUNNING EXCEL 3 FOR WINDOWS

FOX PRO

MASTERING FOX PRO 2

HARVARD GRAPHICS

UP & RUNNING WITH HARVARD GRAPHICS (VER. 2.3)
HARVARD GRAPHICS INSTANT REF. (VER 2.3)
MASTERING HARVARD GRAPHICS (VER. 2.3) WITH DISK
MASTERING HARVARD GRAPHICS 3 (WITH DISK)
HARVARD GRAPHICS 3 INSTANT REFERENCE

HARD DISK

HARD DISK INSTANT REFERENCE
HARD DISK MANAGEMENT 2ND ED.
MANAGING YOUR HARD DISK
UNDERSTANDING HARD DISK MANAGEMENT ON THE PC
UP & RUNNING WITH YOUR HARD DISK
HARD DISK SURVIVAL GUIDE (WITH DISK)

HARDWARE

THE ABC'S OF UPGRADING YOUR PC
TROUBLESHOOTING & REPAIRING/PERSONAL COMPUTERS
UPGRADING AND REPAIRING PCs
MICROPROCESSOR DATA HANDBOOK
FROM CHIPS TO SYSTEMS AN INTRODUCTION TO MICROPROCESSORS
THE COMPLETE PC UPGRADE & MAINTENANCE GUIDE

IBM PC/XT/AT/PS-2/386/486 & CLONES

386 COMPUTER HANDBOOK

U

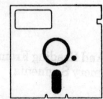